The *God's Generals* series of books are some of the most important books in my library. I consider them to be required reading for our people. This volume on The Missionaries will no doubt inspire a wave of new sold-out lovers of God to invade the nations of the world, ready to pay any price to spread this wonderful gospel of the kingdom. *God's Generals* carries such profound importance because it provides us with perspective, it creates an awareness of a God-inspired momentum, and it ignites a hunger for what might be possible again in our lifetimes. Author Roberts Liardon does an amazing job of recalibrating our need for true heroes, while, at the same time, addressing weaknesses, shortcomings, and even failures of these great missionary leaders. He does this all without slander or even downgrading the importance of their roles in history. I love this transparent approach, and I highly recommend this volume for all who consider themselves disciples of Jesus Christ.

—*Bill Johnson*
Bethel Church, Redding, California
Author, *When Heaven Invades Earth* and *Hosting the Presence*

Roberts Liardon has written an extremely well-researched book, *God's Generals: The Missionaries*. These biographies awakened many memories of the joys and hardships Rolland and I have experienced as missionaries. As a skilled storyteller, Roberts weaves factual accounts with everyday struggles, heartaches, and victories. Our great pioneers of faith had two common threads: lives bathed in much prayer, and guidance by the Holy Spirit. *God's Generals* will show you how to lay down your life and consider everything a loss compared to knowing Jesus. This is a book I will put in my library.

—*Heidi G. Baker*, Ph.D.
Cofounder and Director, Iris Global

As one of the modern-day historians in the body of Christ, Roberts Liardon has brought forth another great jewel in his *God's Generals* series. Some of my mentors over the years have been books. The lives portrayed in this classic book on pioneering missionaries will surely join my "Hall of Heroes." The shadow of these humble and sacrificial lives in Christ is being cast once again upon the lives of many people because of this amazing author. Thank you, Roberts, for being faithful to your task!

—*James W. Goll*
Founder, Encounters Network and Prayer Storm
Author, *The Seer, A Radical Faith,* and *The Coming Israel Awakening*

Roberts Liardon has done an exceptional job compiling the life and testimonies of these mighty missionaries for God, who burned with a deep desire to reach the lost and to demonstrate Christ's love. These pages are filled with the dreams, hopes, faith, struggles, and hardships that they faced on their journey to go into all the world and preach the gospel to every creature. I highly recommend *God's Generals: The Missionaries.*

—*Dr. Ché Ahn*
Apostle, Harvest Apostolic Center, Pasadena, California
Senior Pastor, HRock Church
President, Harvest International
Ministry International Chancellor, Wagner Leadership Institute

GOD'S GENERALS

THE MISSIONARIES

ROBERTS LIARDON

WHITAKER HOUSE

Unless otherwise indicated, all Scripture quotations are taken from the King James Version of the Holy Bible. Scripture quotations marked (NKJV) are taken from the *New King James Version*, © 1979, 1980, 1982, 1984 by Thomas Nelson, Inc. Used by permission. All rights reserved. Scripture quotations marked (NIV) are taken from the *Holy Bible, New International Version*®, NIV®, © 1973, 1978, 1984 by the International Bible Society. Used by permission of Zondervan. All rights reserved. Scripture quotations marked (NASB) are taken from the *New American Standard Bible*®, NASB®, © 1960, 1962, 1963, 1968, 1971, 1972, 1973, 1975, 1977, 1988 by The Lockman Foundation. Used by permission. (www.Lockman.org). Scripture quotations marked (NLT) are taken from the *Holy Bible, New Living Translation*, © 1996, 2004, 2007. Used by permission of Tyndale House Publishers, Inc., Carol Stream, Illinois 60188. All rights reserved.

Editorial Note: Original spellings are maintained in all quoted material, and, because of the numerous differences between British and American English, as well as conventions of the time, these are not noted by a "[*sic*]." Original capitalizations are also maintained, so that often "he" and "his," etc., are not capitalized when referring to God, Jesus, or the Holy Spirit. Boldface type in Scripture quotations indicates the author's emphasis.

God's Generals: The Missionaries

Roberts Liardon Ministries
P.O. Box 2989
Sarasota, FL 34230
E-mail: info1@robertsliardon.org
www.RobertsLiardon.com

ISBN: 978-1-62911-159-9
eBook ISBN: 978-1-62911-161-2
Printed in the United States of America

Whitaker House
1030 Hunt Valley Circle
New Kensington, PA 15068
www.whitakerhouse.com

Library of Congress Cataloging-in-Publication Data
Liardon, Roberts.
God's generals : the missionaries / by Roberts Liardon.
pages cm
Includes bibliographical references.
ISBN 978-1-62911-159-9 (trade hardcover : alk. paper) — ISBN 978-1-62911-161-2 (ebook)
1. Missionaries—Biography. I. Title.
BV3700.L53 2014
266.0092'2—dc23
[B]
2014031035

5 6 7 8 9 10 11 12 **W** 27 26 25

Dedication

As I was writing some final touches for this book, I stopped in the middle with an earnest question. Who is doing the work of these missionaries today? Who is serving on the mission field and is "dedicated for life," as were the men and women in this book? As I leaned back in my chair, memories came flooding back of all the godly and honorable people I have met in over thirty years of ministering in over one hundred twenty nations.

When I considered the unique qualities of the men and women included in *God's Generals: The Missionaries*, one person kept coming to mind. Her name is Deborah Strong. I want to dedicate this book in her honor.

Deborah's passionate work began over thirty years ago with a heartfelt prayer: "God, will You send me to the darkest places on earth where the needs are the greatest?"

God did just that.

Deborah Strong is an apostolic missionary. She goes into places where the gospel does not exist or is so small that the light is nearly impossible to see. At times, she has walked six days among the tallest mountains of the world to reach some of the most unreached people on earth, because that is the passion of her heart. God gives her the strength and victory to always move forward—to carry on.

Through her work in Christian Faith Ministries/Nepal Disability Relief Foundation, she has used probably every method of evangelism you know and has created some of her very own. I have known her to celebrate her birthday early with ministry friends when she is scheduled to be in a remote mountain village on that day.

I want to say, "*Thank you,* Deborah, for all you have done for Jesus and His kingdom. I salute you. I am honored to call you my friend."

Deborah's contact information:

Deborah Strong,
Christian Faith Ministries
P.O. Box 50538
Denton, Texas 76206
drdeborahstrong@gmail.com

Acknowledgments

I would like to thank Whitaker House for partnering with me in this vision to bring all of the *God's Generals* volumes to the Christian world, including *God's Generals: The Missionaries.*

I would also like to thank my editor and research assistant, Vicki Mlinar, for her invaluable assistance. Together, we walked through the miraculous history of the Holy Spirit's moving on these missionary men and women as they proclaimed the gospel throughout the world.

Contents

Foreword

Former Generations

In 1986, we had one of our Gospel Campaigns in Blantyre, Malawi, in East Africa. Blantyre is named after the town in Scotland where the great missionary David Livingstone was born. Livingstone had planted a Christian mission in the area, and had founded a city that now has more than 600,000 inhabitants, making it the largest city in Malawi. Before he died, Livingstone thought he had only one convert. Let me quote from his diary:

> We are like voices crying in the wilderness; we prepare the way for a glorious future. Future missionaries will be rewarded with conversions for every sermon. We are their pioneers and helpers. Let them not forget the watchmen of the night—us, who worked when all was gloom, and no evidence of success in the way of conversion cheered our paths. They will doubtless have more light than we, but we can serve our Master earnestly and proclaim the gospel as they will do.

Livingstone died in 1873. We were there more than one hundred years later. What about Livingstone's prophetic word? Was it merely wishful thinking? I rejoice to tell you what we saw. The seed sown so long ago is now blooming into harvest. For instance, we saw 150,000 gathered in a single meeting. The people of Malawi heard the same gospel. We were there sixteen days, and tens of thousands responded to Livingstone's message as we preached it for him, and for Jesus. It reverberated throughout the whole country. A nation was shaken. The Holy Spirit spoke to my heart and said, *You are walking on the tears of former generations.*

One Team

Suddenly, I saw it all. In God, we are linked to a single, mighty gospel movement, comprising His earlier and latter-day workers. We are all one together—we belong to their team; they belong to ours. We are reaping with joy where they sowed in tears before us. We did not have this harvest because we were superior to those precious men and women who went before, but only because the harvest season had arrived. Jesus said:

> *He that reapeth receiveth wages, and gathereth fruit unto life eternal: that both he that soweth and he that reapeth may rejoice together....I sent you to reap that whereon ye bestowed no labour: other men laboured, and ye are entered into their labours.* (John 4:36, 38)

This is harvest time—believe it! The world's multitudes have multiplied. The opportunity is vast, exciting. And we, you, all of us, are the privileged ones who have been chosen to do the reaping. Knowing that so much has already been done long before we arrived on the scene should keep us humble in the times of success. We must not fail the sowers. We have been entrusted with a great task. We owe it to them to swing the sickle, or, better still, to use a combine harvester!

The Elijahs, the Pauls, the Justin Martyrs, and the Livingstones—they all relied on us for the future. They expected us to take advantage of all their labors. We cannot be proud, only privileged!

This experience in Malawi changed my whole outlook on how much all of God's servants are interwoven and interlinked. The most humble ministries or missionaries, evangelists, teachers, and shepherds, even those who are perhaps considered failures, are part of the "big picture" and will rejoice with all of us in harvest-joy. This sums up this great book of Roberts Liardon. Let's join their ranks. The harvest goes on. Jesus is coming soon!

The Moving of the Eternal Spirit

The Holy Spirit is committed to fulfilling Christ's promise *"I will build my church"* (Matthew 16:18). That is His business. It is also our business and explains the whole vibrant scene of His work.

No one can destroy what God builds. No one can shut a door that He opens. The cross of Christ is the immoveable rock in the history of the roaring seas of mankind. Atheists and rulers have announced that God was dead or about to die. He has not died. They have! While they were busy inscribing "R.I.P." on Christ's gravestone, a hand was laid on their shoulder, and a voice said, *"I am he that liveth, and was dead; and behold, I am alive for ever more"* (Revelation 1:18)!

We are latecomers. The torch has been passed down to us from the hands of heroes, scholars, martyrs, and millions of unknown believers. They look over the cloud of glory to encourage us. Maybe it is ours to run the last lap. Well, in Jesus' name, let's do it well.

—*Reinhard Bonnke*
Founder, Christ for All Nations

INTRODUCTION

"And they overcame him by the blood of the Lamb, and by the word of their testimony; and they loved not their lives unto the death."
—Revelation 12:11

This verse from the Word of God is a clear description of the men and women in *God's Generals: The Missionaries*. Without exception, they were *overcomers*, not in their own strength but in the power of the Lamb of God, whom they loved and served wherever they were called. They had extraordinary courage to face unknown lands, persecution, family loss, and death, because they esteemed their love for Jesus Christ more highly than *their own lives*. In the midst of both triumphs and tragedies, they lived out phrases we take for granted today, such as "Fulfilling the Great Commission," "The future is as bright as the promises of God!" and "Christ is either Lord of all, or He is not Lord at all!"

The generals in this book were among the Christian pioneers who helped birth and develop modern Christian missions as we understand them today. They did not only speak about the need for preaching the gospel in "heathen" lands, but, by example, they also went and lived out their convictions on the mission field.

It is no coincidence that they shared a great many of the same personality traits and Spirit-anointed gifts. Although they ministered in three different centuries and in countries around the globe, these missionaries had a great deal in common. They had a fervent, uncompromising love for the Lord Jesus Christ. They were strong-willed, irrepressible individuals who listened to the Holy Spirit's leading and then followed it without turning back. They were men and women of bold prayer who asked for God's provision and protection, and then had the faith to see their prayers answered. For Christ's sake, they were willing to endure affliction. They sensed in their spirits that it was a "must job"; they had to do it, no matter what. *They never gave up.*

They were also independent spirits; many of them left the mission societies that originally sent them out, preferring to follow the leading of the Holy Spirit on the field rather than take direction from an organization located thousands of miles away. In God's providential choice, they were some of the most brilliant intellects of their day. In faith, they used those intellectual abilities to advance the kingdom of God in amazing ways: creating new alphabets, translating the Bible into the most difficult languages, building schools, birthing mission societies and international ministries, and leaving legacies that are still bearing fruit today!

I chose to present missionaries in this fifth volume of *God's Generals* to inspire a new generation of mission workers today. There are still places on this earth where there is little or no Christian witness—places that need the gospel of Jesus Christ.

> *But how can they call on him to save them unless they believe in him? And how can they believe in him if they have never heard about him? And how can they hear about him unless someone tells them? And how will anyone go and tell them without being sent? That is why the Scriptures say, "How beautiful are the feet of messengers who bring good news!"* (Romans 10:14–15 NLT)

Perhaps God is calling you to be a messenger of the good news to the far ends of the earth. My prayer is that this book will help you to make the decision to give your life for God and for man.

—Roberts Liardon

Chapter 1

Count Nikolaus Ludwig von Zinzendorf

A New Thought: The World Is the Field of Harvest!

The top mast of the *James* bent nearly in two; resistance against the lashing winds was in vain. The prow of the ship sank beneath the raging waves one moment and soared up toward the stormy sky the next. It was February 14, 1743, and the *James* was returning from the West Indies with missionary leader Count Ludwig von Zinzendorf aboard.

As the ship approached the coastline of southern England, the North Atlantic gale relentlessly pushed her toward the jagged rocks jutting from the shoreline. The passengers and crew of the British vessel huddled below deck in fear for their lives. The winds shrieked as the ship pitched ominously, each hour driven closer to the English coast.

Captain Nicholas Garrison resigned himself to the inevitable. Turning to the quiet passenger standing by his side, he said the foreboding words, "Within hours, Your Excellency, we will be at the bottom of this ocean. The ship will not survive a crash against that rocky shore."

Raising his eyebrows in surprise at the stark prediction, Count Zinzendorf spoke confidently above the raging storm. "Captain, within two hours, this storm will be abated, and we will be sailing in calm seas once again."

Captain Garrison shook his head in disbelief as both men fought against the lashing winds to join the crew and passengers below deck.

In two hours, the captain of the *James* climbed carefully up the wooden ladder to the deck of his vessel. In wonder, he saw that the winds had shifted, the stormy clouds had parted; there were blue skies and placid seas surrounding the ship on all sides.

"Count Zinzendorf," the captain inquired in awe, "how did you know that we would have these calm seas in exactly two hours?"

"I have had a trusting relationship with Jesus Christ for nearly forty years," the count responded. "He speaks to me in the quiet of my soul when I pray before Him. This time, He assured me that the storm would end in two hours."

Amazed at Zinzendorf's extraordinary faith, Captain Garrison accepted Christ as Lord of his life soon afterward and began a friendship with the count that lasted a lifetime. For years to come, Garrison served as the captain of the Moravian missionary ship that transported Zinzendorf's missionaries to foreign lands throughout the world.

"I Have but One Passion…"

"I have but one passion: It is He; it is He alone."
—Count Zinzendorf

Nikolaus Ludwig von Zinzendorf was a European nobleman well-known to the regal heads of eighteenth-century Europe. Destined by birth to live a life of privilege and luxury in the courts of Saxony (Germany), he chose instead to dedicate all of his expansive influence and wealth to the glory of his Savior, Jesus Christ. Rather than making his mark in his native country alone, Zinzendorf changed lives for eternity in the farthest corners of the world through his missionary vision.

Throughout Europe, the Middle East, Asia, the East and West Indies, and South America, from the southern tip of Africa to the arctic shores of Greenland, the name of Christ was extolled by the missionaries sent out under Zinzendorf's leadership. Eventually embarking on foreign journeys himself, Zinzendorf proclaimed, "The world is the field and the field is the world; and henceforth, that country shall be my home where I can be most used in winning souls for Christ."

Count Nikolaus Ludwig von Zinzendorf

Through nearly forty years of Christian ministry, Zinzendorf was revered by some people for his deep love of Christ, and reviled by others for his unorthodox ways of demonstrating that love. To Zinzendorf, the true church was an invisible body of believers hidden behind denominational barriers. Life in Christ was not what happened in the organized church; instead, it was a "Christianity of the heart."

Through nearly forty years of Christian ministry, Zinzendorf was revered by some people for his deep love of Christ, and reviled by others for his unorthodox ways of demonstrating that love.

Zinzendorf expressed that kind of Christianity in three vital ways. First, it was essential that all believers embrace a deep, personal relationship with the Lord Jesus Christ. Second, all true believers must learn to live and worship together. "There is no Christianity without community" was his personal motto. Third, every Christian was called to help spread the message of Christ's sacrificial death and redemption to the unreached world. "Missions, after all," Zinzendorf wrote, "is simply this: Every heart with Christ is a missionary, every heart without Christ is a mission field!" Whether a believer was sent to a foreign land or worked to support the one sent, to Zinzendorf, the missionary enterprise was a cooperative effort, through the power of the Holy Spirit, that could change the world for Christ. Zinzendorf did change the world, revolutionizing the worldwide Christian community with his missionary zeal, taking his place in history as one of God's greatest missionary generals.

A Prophetic Prayer

Nikolaus Ludwig von Zinzendorf was born into a family of Austrian nobility on May 26, 1700, in Dresden, Saxony. He was the only child of Count Georg Ludwig and Countess Charlotte Justine von Zinzendorf.

For generations before his birth, the Zinzendorf family had enjoyed a high rank among the Austrian nobility, serving in the court of Austria's emperors. As the Reformation spread throughout Europe, Nikolaus's grandfather, Count Maximilian von Zinzendorf, became a Lutheran, embracing *faith in Christ alone* for salvation. By the mid-1600s, in order to pursue his newfound Protestant faith, the count sold his Austrian estate, *Wachovia,* and moved his wife and five children from Catholic Austria to Lutheran Saxony.

The Zinzendorf Family: Count Georg Ludwig and Countess Charlotte Justine von Zinzendorf with Nikolaus, who is portrayed as a three-year-old boy despite the fact that Georg died a few weeks after the child's birth.
(Used by permission / Moravian Church Archives)

Maximilian pledged his allegiance to Saxony, which, in the seventeenth and eighteenth centuries, included the eastern provinces of modern-day Germany and Poland. In time, one of his sons, George Ludwig, married a Christian woman of royal birth, Charlotte Justine von Gersdorf. It was to this couple that young Nikolaus Ludwig von Zinzendorf (called "Ludwig") was born. At the time of Ludwig's birth, his father served as "counselor" to the king of Saxony. Tragically, George Ludwig contracted tuberculosis, and, on July 19, 1700, the thirty-seven-year-old father died six weeks after his son's birth.

That day, Charlotte Justine wrote a prayer for baby Ludwig in the front of her Bible: "May the Father of mercy govern the heart of this child that he may walk upright in the path of virtues....Let his ways be strengthened by the Word of God...that he will indeed experience what the Lord has promised, *'I am the Father of the fatherless.'*"[1] It was a prophetic prayer in the life of her noble little boy.

Converted at Four Years Old

As a young widow, just twenty-five years old, the grieving Charlotte took her infant son and moved to her mother's estate in Gross Hennersdorf, Saxony, where Ludwig was lovingly welcomed by a Christian grandmother, aunt, and uncle. When he was four years old, his mother remarried Field Marshall Dubislav von Natzmer, a fifty-year-old widower who lived in Berlin. She left four-year-old "Lutz," as his grandmother fondly nicknamed him, behind.

Lutz's grandmother, Countess Henrietta Katharina von Gersdorf, was a devout Christian and an active Pietist. The Pietists were a small group of Christians within the Lutheran Church who longed for a deep personal relationship with their Savior. They emphasized the priesthood of the believer and the need for a "vigorous" relationship with Jesus Christ rather than the dry worship of the formal church. Philipp Jakob Spener was considered the "father of the Pietist movement" and was a close friend of the von Gersdorf [Zinzendorf] family. Growing up in this godly environment, little Lutz learned to lean on Jesus for everything in life.

"Already in my childhood," he recorded later, "I loved the Saviour, and had abundant communion with Him. In my fourth year I began to seek God earnestly, and determined to become a true servant of Jesus Christ....I was...as certain that the Son of God was my Lord as of the existence of my five fingers!"[2]

There was no doubt that Lutz had unreservedly given his heart to Christ, as he recorded in his childhood diary, "A thousand times I heard Him speak in my heart, and saw Him with the eye of faith....If Jesus were forsaken by all the world, I still would cling to Him and love Him."[3]

Bullied at School

At the age of ten, Lutz was uprooted from his grandmother's castle by his mother and taken to the Pietist boarding school Halle Paedagogium, 120 miles from his grandmother's estate. As a nobleman of high rank, Ludwig was expected to train for service in the Saxon court. His family assumed that he would become a highly important court counselor, just like his father and grandfather before him.

Unfortunately, his years at Halle were nothing like his pleasant childhood. In spite of attending a Christian school, Lutz was bullied by the older boys because of his money, his noble rank, and his intelligence. "With a few exceptions, my schoolfellows hated me throughout,"[4] Ludwig wrote later. Even his personal tutor, Daniel Crisenius, scorned his commitment to Jesus and blackmailed him for his allowance. "I've always thought that your grandmother thought far too much of you," Crisenius sneered. "And if you tell her I said that, I shall tell her you are too lazy to study!"[5]

Because God had a plan for Ludwig's life, He used the young count's boyhood trials to build steadfastness in his "inner man," to give him the spiritual strength to endure criticism while remaining strong in his faith. Lutz became determined. "This shame shall not crush me. On the contrary, it shall raise me up!"[6] The young count grew both academically and spiritually, and found a few like-minded friends to join him in his quest to follow Christ. It was God's blessing that enabled him to excel both in knowledge and in personal character. It is an important combination that God desires us to possess.

"Order of the Grain of Mustard Seed"

At twelve years old, Lutz and his four closest school friends formed a secret Christian society dedicated to prayer, Bible study, and faithful adherence to the teachings of Jesus Christ. They were the least popular boys in school, picked on for their lack of size and strength, but they no longer cared. One of the young men, Baron Friedrich von Watteville, became Ludwig's closest friend and confidante for life.

Ludwig sensed the call to be an evangelist or minister at a very young age. His example was Jesus Himself, who was only twelve years old when He confused the great minds of His day in the temple. In the Old and New Testaments, we read about young people called into ministry—Joseph, Samuel, David, Timothy. We don't see as much of it in the church today as we should. Ludwig Zinzendorf was a great example of what a youthful evangelist might look like.

The young count named his secret society "The Order of the Mustard Seed," because he believed that their small seed of faith would become a large tree of service to the Lord. To young Lutz, it was like taking an oath of knighthood for Christ's sake. These young men would have wealth and influence, and they pledged to use both to promote the gospel of Jesus Christ. Ludwig had gold rings designed for each of them, with the Greek words translated "No man liveth unto himself" (see Romans 14:7) inscribed inside. The society also had a banner embellished with the crest of a mustard tree and a Latin inscription that read *"quod fuit ante nihil"*—"out of nothing something."

The words were prophetic. Over the next forty years, the tiny seed of faith grew from their small dormitory room to the world's political and religious stage.

Zinzendorf met Christian world leaders who accepted membership in The Order of the Mustard Seed and pledged to influence the world for Christ; these included such diverse men as James Oglethorpe, governor of colonial Georgia; Tomochichi, chief of the Yamacraw tribe in America; Christian VI, king of Denmark; John Potter, the Anglican archbishop of Canterbury; and even Louis de Noailles, the Roman Catholic cardinal of Paris.

There is an anointed unity in the Spirit among groups of Christians who bond together in Christ; Jesus and His disciples are the perfect example.

There is an anointed unity in the Spirit among groups of Christians who bond together in Christ; Jesus and His disciples are the perfect example. John and Charles Wesley formed The Holy Club, a group of believers who met at Christ Church, Oxford, and covenanted to pray and fast together, study the Bible, and take care of the needy in the Oxford area. They later became the foundation of the Methodist Church. Young men and women who were saved during the Welsh Revival of the early 1900s were committed to one another for prayer and ministry under the direction of healing evangelist George Jeffreys, and they later formed the Elim denomination. Billy Graham established his worldwide ministry with a group of young men who worked with him as a team for life, becoming old men together in Christ's service. Young Zinzendorf's secret society was one of the most influential societies among world leaders that I have ever discovered.

The Missionary Fire Is Lit

Before long, Ludwig's brilliant mind was recognized at Halle; he excelled in biblical studies, Greek, and Latin. He was no longer the brunt of student jokes and enjoyed increasing attention from the headmaster, Professor Augustus Franke. Because Ludwig was a nobleman, he was always seated near the head of the dinner table, closest to Franke and honored guests. One evening, one of those guests changed the direction of The Order of the Mustard Seed and altered Zinzendorf's life forever.

Fifteen-year-old Ludwig was seated across the table from Bartholomäus Ziegenbalg, a Halle alumnus who was home on furlough from the mission field. Ziegenbalg and fellow Halle student Heinrich Plütschau were the first two Protestant missionaries sent out by the Danish royal family. They had been sharing about Christ in the Danish colony of Tranquebar, India, for eight years.

From the early years of the Reformation, Denmark had welcomed the gospel and faith in Christ alone for salvation. The Danish Christians were among the first Europeans to produce the Bible in their national language. Although missionary work was unheard of in Protestant Europe at the time, King Frederick IV of Denmark was a Christian visionary who eventually sent Christian missionaries throughout his Danish colonies.

This is a perfect example of the power and influence for good that can be exercised by people in leadership who are not afraid to stand for God. God still uses people in government positions. I believe we will see more of that in our lifetime, even in the midst of the spiritual warfare among the nations of the world.

Unlike King Frederick, the Anglican and Lutheran churches of Europe were actually against the idea of sending missionaries to the nations of the world. At that time, they believed that Jesus' command to *"go...into all the world"* (Mark 16:15) had ceased when the apostles died, and that the first apostles had fulfilled the command by reaching the ends of the known world. The European reformers had spent the last two hundred years establishing the Protestant denominations and fighting against the religious control of Roman Catholicism in Europe. Their church vision did not include outreach into foreign nations.

The Spirit of God is always trying to breathe life into the church and the world, but religion is always trying to squelch it! In the Danish outreach, we see the first signs of the Spirit of God breathing new life into what we call the Great Commission. But the traditional church had control, and they thought that what God had said to the apostles about evangelizing the world was now irrelevant.

Ludwig's Destiny Was Sealed!

At dinner that night, Ludwig sat in rapt attention, his eyes fastened on Ziegenbalg, the first Lutheran missionary. Burning with curiosity, he asked him detailed questions about his missionary work and the language and customs of the Indian people. From the time of that momentous dinner, Ludwig's destiny was sealed.

As soon as he was excused from the dining hall, Ludwig raced down the corridor and burst into Watteville's room, eager to share every detail of his dinner conversation. What an exciting new vision for The Order of the Mustard Seed! They would consecrate their lives to sending the good news of Jesus Christ to those throughout the world who did not know Him. "It will be impossible to go ourselves," they reluctantly admitted, because of their positions of nobility. But they vowed to use their fortunes and their influence to spread the gospel message around the globe.[7]

This story is a reminder to each of us that, sometimes, our greatest sermon may be delivered to just one person. Ziegenbalg had a simple conversation with a teenage boy at dinner, and he sowed the mission seed that changed the European Protestant church! Whatever is on your heart, speak up, even if it is just to one person.

Keeping His Spirit Fed and Free

In eighteenth-century Europe, Wittenberg, Saxony, was the most famous city of the Protestant faith. There, in 1517, Martin Luther, a Catholic priest and professor at Wittenberg University, nailed his Ninety-Five Theses to the wooden door of Castle Church. Since that time, Wittenberg had served as the seat of the Lutheran Church, but when Zinzendorf arrived at the university two centuries later, there was little evidence left of Martin Luther's fiery passion for Christ. The Lutheran Church and Wittenberg University had become dry and formal in their theology.

It is a historical observation that many places of revival are dead and dull by the time the third generation comes along. For Ludwig, the church and the university seemed as dead as a doornail!

In spite of the worldliness and religious formalism that had crept into the university, Ludwig was determined to pursue Christ.

At Wittenberg, Ludwig's uncle, Count Otto von Zinzendorf, insisted that he study the law and learn how to fence and dance to prepare for service in the royal court. "My uncle was obsessed to change my [Pietist] heart and put a different head on my body," Ludwig later proclaimed.[8]

In spite of the worldliness and religious formalism that had crept into the university, Ludwig was determined to pursue Christ. "I commune with the Friend of my heart, the ever present Savior, daily...I am spending a whole hour from six to seven in the morning, as well as in the evening from eight to nine, in prayer."[9] Ludwig spent entire nights praying and full days fasting before the Lord, as well. Nothing would deter him from his passion for Jesus! This prayer time was the way he kept his spirit fresh. Likewise, our Christian walk must consist of more than a onetime prayer; we must keep our vital relationship with Christ fresh and alive, as Zinzendorf did.

The Art Gallery Visitation

After graduation from the university, each young nobleman was sent on a yearlong journey through the capital cities of Europe to complete his education. Ludwig's travels were uneventful until May 20, 1719, the day he visited the Dusseldorf art museum.

Depiction of four scenes from Zinzendorf's grand tour through the Netherlands, France, and Germany in 1719–20: (right) Zinzendorf discussing theological matters with a reformed minister in his library in Utrecht; (center bottom) a servant bringing a letter for Count Zinzendorf; (center top) Zinzendorf meeting with Cardinal de Noailles and Père la Tour in Paris; (left) Zinzendorf (seated) in Ebersdorf, with Heinrich XXIX, Count Heinrich Reuss, his mother, and Reuss's sister Erdmuthe Dorothea.

(Used by permission / Moravian Church Archives)

Walking leisurely through the gallery, Ludwig stopped at a large, somber painting of Jesus Christ with the crown of thorns on His head and blood on His cheek. The painting, by Italian artist Domenico Feti, was entitled *Ecce Homo,* Latin for "Behold the Man." This was the announcement Pontus Pilate made after Jesus was scourged. The words etched beneath the painting startled Ludwig and were burned into his heart: "This I have done for you; what are you doing for Me?"

"I stood there without an answer," Zinzendorf wrote. "I implored my Savior to draw me with force into the partnership of His suffering, even if my mind struggled against it."[10] There, in that art gallery, Ludwig von Zinzendorf dedicated the rest of his life to the service of the Son of God.

"These wounds were meant to purchase me," he declared. "These drops of blood were shed to obtain me. I am not my own today. I belong to another. I have been bought with a price. And I will live every moment of every day so that the Great Purchaser of my soul will receive the full reward of His suffering."[11]

During his six months' stay in France, Ludwig met the archbishop of Paris, Cardinal Louis Antoine de Noailles. In spite of their different beliefs regarding Catholic doctrine, the men developed a friendship based on their love for the crucified Savior. Before they parted company, the seventy-year-old cardinal accepted twenty-year-old Ludwig's invitation for membership in The Order of the Mustard Seed. For the rest of his life, Zinzendorf insisted that it was love for Christ that could end the differences among Christian believers.

Losing His Girlfriend

Before reporting to the Saxon court in Dresden, Ludwig traveled through Switzerland, first to visit his school friend Friedrich von Watteville and then to visit an aunt, the Countess of Castelle. While staying at her castle, young Zinzendorf found himself falling in love with his beautiful cousin, Theodora. Ludwig left the castle for home with his aunt's hearty approval for their engagement, but something didn't seem quite settled for Theodora.

A short time later, Ludwig discovered that a close friend, Count Heinrich Reuss, had fallen in love with Theodora, as well, and that she returned his affection. Ludwig, trusting completely in the Lord's direction for his life, stepped aside for them to marry. With a peaceful heart, he spoke to the young couple, "It is settled; God's benevolent will be done. I wish you two felicity and contentment." God had something else planned for him, of that Ludwig was certain; he would patiently wait.

Eighteen months later, on September 7, 1722, twenty-two-year-old Ludwig married Heinrich Reuss's younger sister, Countess Erdmuthe Dorothea Reuss. She was the perfect companion for him; Erdmuthe shared Ludwig's passion for following Jesus above all else. Working together, they offered their lives and their fortunes for the sake of the gospel of Christ.

Count Zinzendorf
(Used by permission / Moravian Church Archives)

Ludwig was being directed by the Lord in this decision. In Christian ministry, it is vital not to be swayed by youthful passion to marry without waiting for God's specific guidance. The right person will share the same ministry vision and embrace the same call for service. Zinzendorf was led by the Holy Spirit when he put aside the early passion of "first love" to wait for God's chosen companion.

Most people today marry according to emotion and physical passion. They don't marry according to calling; they don't consider evaluating the person to make certain that they will be spiritually compatible. When considering marriage, ask these questions: Do we believe the same things scripturally? Are we called to the same ministry or service? If I were called to go to the mission field, would you going to go with me? Most, but not all, of the missionaries in this volume made wise decisions concerning their marriage partners. Zinzendorf was certainly one of them.

Receiving a Large Inheritance

In 1722, Nikolaus Ludwig von Zinzendorf reported for duty at the court of Augustus the Strong, Elector of Saxony. He was assigned as a king's counselor, just as his mother, uncle, and grandmother had hoped. But Ludwig was discouraged; more than anything else, he longed to be a minister of the gospel. In the world of European nobility, it was not an acceptable choice. Yet Zinzendorf was certain that "winning souls for Christ and working in His spiritual kingdom was his real vocation."[12]

Each Sunday afternoon and evening in Dresden, Ludwig and Erdmuthe welcomed Christians, both nobles and commoners, into their home for fellowship, Bible study, and prayer.

That same year, Ludwig came of age and received a large inheritance from his father's estate. Since his days in Halle, he had dreamed of building a Christian community like the early church, where rich and poor could worship and work together. To make his vision a reality, he purchased the estate of Berthelsdorf from his grandmother, located just a few miles from her castle. At the time, all that existed on the estate was the small village of Berthelsdorf and a run-down Lutheran church. But Zinzendorf gazed at the empty acres with eyes of faith, envisioning the Christian community it could become. What God built on that land was greater than anything Ludwig von Zinzendorf could have imagined!

Christian Community Was His Passion

Berthelsdorf became Ludwig's passion. The more he saw of court life, the stronger his desire became to devote his life to the gospel and Christian community. Although he was required to spend his winters in Dresden, in the summer months, he was free to fulfill his dream on his new lands.

First, he appointed his Pietist friend John Andrew Rothe as the pastor of the Lutheran church on the estate. Zinzendorf commissioned him with these words: "I bought this estate because I wanted to spend my life among peasants, and win their souls for Christ. So go, Rothe, to the vineyard of the Lord. You will find me a brother and a helper rather than a patron."[13] At Rothe's induction ceremony, a Pietist preacher from the nearby village of Görlitz spoke a prophetic word, saying, "God will light a candle on this place which will illuminate the whole land!"

Ludwig decided to build a mansion on the grounds, which he named Bethel (house of God), so that he and Erdmuthe could live in the middle of the Christian community whenever they were on leave from Dresden. Once it was complete, the Zinzendorfs opened their home to everyone in the area, nobles and peasants alike, for evening Bible studies. To Ludwig's delight, his boyhood friend Friedrich von Watteville left his Switzerland estate and moved to Berthelsdorf to join Zinzendorf in fulfilling his vision.

The first settler who arrived at the Berthelsdorf estate was Christian David, a believer from Moravia (currently located in eastern Czech Republic). As a Protestant, David had been relentlessly persecuted by the ruling Catholics of Moravia and Bohemia. Although he had safely escaped the region, he wanted to return and lead other persecuted Protestants out of the country. When he heard about Ludwig's vision for a Christian community, he asked if the Moravian refugees would be welcome in Berthelsdorf. Ludwig answered with a resounding "Yes!" Unknown to either of the men, Christian David's request was the very thing that brought life to Zinzendorf's Christian vision.

Smuggling Moravian Refugees

Sneaking back into Moravia in spite of personal danger, David returned to Berthelsdorf with the first refugees—the two Niesser brothers, their wives, and four children. On a small hill on the estate, just one mile from the Berthelsdorf village, David felled a tree for the first house and declared that the Moravians had finally found their home. On that day, June 17, 1722, a new Christian community was born.

David made ten more secretive trips to Moravia to smuggle his persecuted brothers and sisters in Christ to freedom. Johann Heitz, the steward at Berthelsdorf, named the new community Herrnhut ("the Lord's Watch"). In a letter of explanation to Zinzendorf, he wrote, "God grant that Your Excellency be able to build on the hill a town which may not only itself abide under the Lord's Watch, but all the inhabitants of which may also continue on the Lord's Watch, so that no silence [of prayer] may be there by day or night."[14]

Within four years, Herrnhut had grown to three hundred members. The men of the village gathered with Zinzendorf and Watteville to lay the cornerstone for a Moravian school and medical building. They dedicated it to the glory of God, singing songs of praise for His work among them.

As Friedrich von Watteville knelt in front of the cornerstone, praying aloud for God to accept their work and worship, five newcomers were standing in the back of the crowd and listening intently. The men were Moravian refugees who had stopped at Herrnhut on their way to find religious sanctuary in Poland. When they saw the passion for Christ among the leaders and villagers, they asked for permission to remain.

Strangely, three of the five men had the same name, David Nitschmann, so they were labeled by their jobs in the village. All of the men were essential to the future growth of Herrnhut, but David "the carpenter" became a Moravian bishop in Herrnhut and one of the first missionaries sent to foreign soil.

Who Were the Moravians?

It took Zinzendorf a few years to understand the history of the Christian brothers from Moravia and Bohemia who were seeking religious sanctuary in Herrnhut. In 1412, John Hus, a Catholic Bohemian priest, spoke out against the practices of the Catholic Church, condemning the selling of indulgences for the forgiveness of sins and the immorality among the Catholic leaders. His protest occurred one hundred years before Martin Luther posted his Ninety-Five Theses. Boldly, Hus proclaimed the gospel truth: the only way to eternal salvation is through the death and resurrection of Jesus Christ.[15]

In 1415, Hus was tried for heresy by a Catholic tribunal and burned at the stake for his righteous stand, but throughout Bohemia and Moravia, his followers, "the true Christian believers," grew in number. By 1457, still sixty years before Luther made his famous protests, these Moravian believers became officially known as the Unitas Fratrum, the United Brethren; they became the earliest Protestant denomination. Members of the early Unitas Fratum were Germans; they lived as a community within what is now the Czech Republic, but they were Germans by blood, culture, and language.[16] By Luther's time, they had more than four hundred congregations and nearly 200,000 members. It was not a small, struggling denomination.[17]

The Prophecy of the Hidden Seed

In the Catholic states of Moravia and Bohemia, the United Brethren were mercilessly persecuted and martyred until, by 1547, they were driven underground to practice their faith. Their last bishop, Jan Amos Comenius, escaped the persecution in 1627 by fleeing to Holland with a remnant of the Brethren. Comenius spoke prophetically of the United Brethren who were left behind, calling them God's "hidden seed" that would someday grow to be a fruitful tree again, able to worship the Lord in freedom.

It wasn't long after the refugees began arriving at Herrnhut that Ludwig discovered that these men and women were truly the "hidden seed" that Comenius had written about, the remnant of the faithful Unitas Fratum (later called the Moravians). The count pledged to use his resources and his life to preserve and rebuild this historic denomination of faithful Christians.

"I want to be used among these people to bring a *revival*," Zinzendorf declared. "Though I may lose my property, my honor, and my life in the cause, as long as I live, and as far as I am able, this flock of the Lord shall be preserved for Him until He comes!"[18]

What Satan Meant for Evil…

Zinzendorf believed, "Everything should be done out of love. The focus of our brotherly community is the winning of souls."

As word of the Herrnhut community spread, persecuted Christians from diverse backgrounds began arriving—Moravians, Anabaptists (now the Mennonites), Calvinists, Separatists, and even Catholics. At first, denominational divisions festered under the surface, but eventually they exploded into biting verbal disagreements; before long, the vision of a loving Christian community had disintegrated before their eyes.

At first, denominational divisions festered under the surface, but eventually they exploded into biting verbal disagreements; before long, the vision of a loving Christian community had disintegrated before their eyes.

Into the turmoil, Satan sent an evil messenger, Johannes Sigismund Krüger, who preached using the Scriptures but was actually "a false brother," bringing division and hatred to Herrnhut. Krüger mocked the Lutheran Church, calling it the "whore of Babylon," with Zinzendorf the "beast of the abyss," and John Rothe the "false prophet." His messages were so persuasive that many settlers were deceived by his false accusations, including Christian David, the first Moravian settler. As a result, David, a leader in Herrnhut, and Rothe, the pastor of the Berthelsdorf church, spoke hatefully about each other.

As Krüger's messages increased in fanaticism, it became obvious that he was mentally deranged; he was arrested and eventually committed to an asylum in Berlin. But a great deal of damage had already been done.

Saddened by the reports of the spiritual dissension among the Christian believers, twenty-seven-year-old Zinzendorf took a leave of absence from the Saxony court; he and Erdmuthe, with their newborn daughter Benigna, hastened home to Herrnhut. (Their firstborn son had died two years earlier within months of his birth.)

A Forgiveness Meeting

On May 12, 1727, the youthful but determined Zinzendorf stood in front of the three hundred residents of Herrnhut. Reading from the Scriptures, he reminded them of Jesus' final prayer for His disciples:

> *That they all may be one; as thou, Father, art in me, and I in thee, that they also may be one in us: that the world may believe that thou hast sent me.*
>
> (John 17:21)

Ludwig preached passionately on the goal of Christian unity—that they might *all be one in Christ*. He reminded the Moravians of their commitment to the simple faith of the earlier United Brethren. In the end, Zinzendorf, the "lord" of the estate, made clear that every member of Herrnhut must pursue brotherly love in Christ in order to remain on his land. He asked them to sign a "Brotherly Union and Compact" to live together in Christian peace.[19] Ludwig signed the pact first, followed by Christian David, and then the other Herrnhut settlers.

The conviction of the Holy Spirit moved among the people as Zinzendorf spoke that morning. When the three-hour meeting came to a close, the Christian disciples stood and extended outstretched hands to one another in peace. Soon after, John Rothe approached Christian David and forgave him for his relationship with Johannes Krüger.

During that summer of 1727, brotherly love was restored on the Berthelsdorf estate, and twelve elders were chosen as leaders in the community. "The whole place," said Zinzendorf, "represented a visible tabernacle of God among men."[20] God was preparing Zinzendorf and the Moravian Brethren for an anointed move of the Holy Spirit.

The Holy Spirit and Fire

On Sunday, August 10, 1727, John Rothe knelt before his congregation and prayed for the Lord's Spirit to move mightily among them; together, they remained in prayer until well past midnight. Three days later, the Christian settlers of Herrnhut walked the short mile to the Berthelsdorf church, where Rothe had invited them to a Communion service to celebrate their reconciliation.

From both communities, the people entered the church quietly, sensing the sweet presence of God. As they lifted their voices in praise, the Holy Spirit swept through the congregation with His purifying fire. Humbled believers dropped to their knees, weeping in repentance before the Lord, drowning out the singing with cries to be cleansed from their sins. Swept up in the Spirit's presence, the worshipers praised Him with adoration; they prayed alone or in groups; they called on the Lord's grace and mercy until they finally sensed His release.

As their singing and weeping subsided, Ludwig prayed that the bond of peace and brotherly love would abide among them forever. No one wanted to leave God's holy presence. Zinzendorf sent for food from his kitchens, and the

Herrnhut Brethren celebrated the first of hundreds of "love feasts" breaking bread together.[21]

Zinzendorf wrote about "that blessed summer":

> We saw the hand of God and His wonders, and we were all under the cloud of our fathers, baptized with the Spirit....The Holy Spirit is the life-giving Spirit. The Holy Spirit is the source of all our comprehension of God—He uses the Scripture for this purpose. His main striving is to magnify Christ in our lives. He relentlessly pursues us to make us Christ-like.[22]

A Hundred-Year Prayer Meeting

Two weeks after the Holy Spirit fell on the Berthelsdorf gathering, twenty-four men and twenty-four women from Herrnhut pledged to "unceasing prayer" for one hour a day. This prayer time was called the "hourly intercession," and it was held around the clock, twenty-four hours a day, seven days a week!

They interceded before God for the specific needs of the people; before long, they had seventy-seven people committed to take part in twenty-four hour prayer, and they received two thousand prayer requests from Christians throughout Saxony. When the Moravians began their mission work, the prayer time focused on their missionary work. Imagine the astonishment of those prayer warriors had they known that their prayer meeting, under the anointing of the Holy Spirit, would continue among the Moravian Brethren twenty-four hours a day, every day, 365 days a year—*for the next one hundred years*!

What a marvelous, wonderful thing this was—an *unceasing commitment to prayer. "Rejoice evermore. Pray without ceasing. In every thing give thanks"* (1 Thessalonians 5:16–18). This is the closest manifestation of that Scripture that I have ever heard of!

I am blessed when I think of the nations and people who were changed forever by one hundred years of prayer for world missions. Some sources believe that it may have gone on for closer to one hundred twenty years, but in our research, we have never discovered exactly when or why this supernatural prayer time stopped. There are ministries today that are picking up some degree of that mantle. We admire them and bless them for their commitment to unceasing prayer in our day.

That same summer, Zinzendorf began to share a specific Scripture to encourage or exhort the Herrnhut congregation; he and the elders shared it from house to house among themselves. Soon after, Ludwig and the leaders gathered a collection of Bible passages that were "suited for doctrine, reproof, and instruction in righteousness" (see 2 Timothy 3:16) and placed them in a wooden box. They chose one by "the lot" each night to share with the settlers the following morning. This became known as the *Losung*, or "Watchword."

Imagine the astonishment of those prayer warriors had they known that their prayer meeting, under the anointing of the Holy Spirit, would continue among the Moravian Brethren twenty-four hours a day, every day, 365 days a year—for the next one hundred years!

Three years later, the Moravians set up a printing press in the village of Ebersdorf to publish inexpensive copies of the Bible, Christian tracts, and hymnals in the German language for the common people to read. They also published their first annual devotional book, containing the *Losung* for each day of the entire year. Today, nearly three hundred years later, that devotional, *The Moravian Daily Texts*, is still published annually in more than fifty languages by the thriving Moravian Church. (www.moravian.org)

Shortly after this, while visiting his uncle in the nearby region of Silesia, Ludwig discovered some of the earliest writings of Jan Comenius, the last bishop of the United Brethren. He found among Comenius's writings the *Ratio Disciplinae* ("Account of Discipline"), a small book of the guiding principles for the early Unitas Fratum. Zinzendorf was amazed at the similarity between Comenius's writings and his own recently written "Brotherly Union and Compact."

Without a doubt, God had placed these humble refugees, this "hidden seed," into Zinzendorf's path as a part of His plan for restoration!

Spirit-filled Life in Herrnhut

From his earliest years, Ludwig had been a writer of hymns, expressing his worship to the Lord in song. His most famous hymn, translated later by John Wesley, is "Jesus, Thy Blood and Righteousness."

The Moravian Brethren also had a heart to worship the Lord in music; they were joyous in their praise. Life in Herrnhut became a sanctuary filled with worship; each morning and evening, there was a time of praise in the village. Watchmen would walk past the homes at sunset, singing God's praises as the village slowly closed down for the night. Ludwig personally wrote more than one thousand hymns and published a number of hymnals, some of which are still in use today.

In 1728, Zinzendorf organized the members of the growing community into small groups called "bands" for the purpose of prayer and spiritual care of one another (much like cell groups in modern churches). Later, the bands were increased in size and called "choirs." The people were divided by gender or position in life, so that there were choirs for single men and single women, married couples, and even children. "The reason we have choir groups," Zinzendorf wrote, "is to disclose the conditions of our hearts. We begin to trust one another and we dare to disclose openly and honestly…from our inner being."[23]

Before long, all of the single men moved into a "single brethren's house," vowing to serve the Lord together above all else. Soon after, the single women did the same, residing together in a "single sisters' house." For these young people, marriage was secondary to discovering their call for God's service. They were hard-working people and talented craftsmen, with a passionate commitment to Christ. That Christian commitment laid the foundation for the true call of Zinzendorf and the Moravian Church—launching Protestant missionaries from Europe to the farthest corners of the world.

A Divine Appointment at the Danish Coronation

Count von Zinzendorf and Baron von Watteville were still actively involved in fulfilling the mission of The Order of the Mustard Seed. The men had not forgotten their covenant as teenage boys to bring the gospel of Jesus Christ to the world. The time had finally come for that pledge to be fulfilled.

In 1731, Zinzendorf and Watteville were invited to the Danish court to celebrate the crowning of Christian VI as king of Denmark. The Danish royal family was still sending Christian missionaries throughout its colonies. This was a time when church and state worked nicely together. The state valued the gospel but didn't force it.

At the coronation, Zinzendorf met Antonius Ulrich, a former slave from the island of St. Thomas in the West Indies. Ulrich had become a Christian while on board a ship crossing the Atlantic Ocean, but he expressed great remorse that his fellow slaves in St. Thomas had no way of hearing about Christ. "If only some missionaries would come," Ulrich mourned. "Many an evening have I sat on the shore and sighed my soul toward Christian Europe; and I have a brother and sister in bondage who long to know the living God."[24]

Zinzendorf was shocked that the Christian plantation owners in St. Thomas did not openly share the gospel of salvation with their native slaves. With the same excitement he had when meeting the first missionary fifteen years earlier, Ludwig rushed back to the Moravian leadership with a renewed passion for foreign missionary work.

That night, June 23, 1731, Leonard Dober lay in bed in the single men's house, tossing and turning until dawn. Before him loomed the African slaves of the West Indies, held captive and without hope in Christ. "Here am I; send me" was the cry of his heart. When he told his friend, Tobias Leopold, of his desire to go to St. Thomas, Leopold admitted to having the same call in his spirit. Together, they approached Zinzendorf and the elders of Herrnhut with their desire to go to the mission field.

On July 29, 1731, Ulrich arrived at Herrnhut to speak to the Brethren on the plight of the abused slaves of the West Indies. He longed to see them set free in Christ. But, Ulrich warned them, they would have to work to gain the trust of the island slaves.

Choosing by "the Lot"

Throughout his life, Zinzendorf strongly believed in "the lot" as God's way of leading His people whenever the Scriptures did not give clear direction in a matter. The lot was an ancient way of making decisions by drawing one slip of paper out of a collection of them, or by casting down stones or marbles.

Ludwig based his belief on Acts 1:24–26, when the apostles used the lot to choose a disciple to replace the betrayer, Judas Iscariot.

> *And they prayed, and said, Thou, Lord, which knowest the hearts of all men, show whether of these two thou hast chosen, that he may take part of this ministry and apostleship, from which Judas by transgression fell, that he might go to his own place. And they gave forth their lots; and the lot fell upon Matthias; and he was numbered with the eleven apostles.*

Ludwig chose to use the lot because he questioned the motives of his own heart and the hearts of others in making spiritual decisions. For each serious decision, he and the elders prayed fervently and then left it to the Lord through the lot. Calls to service were decided by the lot, as well as missionary destinations, the annual "watchwords," and even marriages. "Once the Lot had been consulted, the decision was absolute and binding."[25] The Moravians would continue the lot until it was abolished in 1818.

This is not a practice that I would recommend for today. God answered Zinzendorf and the Moravian brothers in their simple faith, but Romans 8:14 clearly tells us, *"For as many as are led by the Spirit of God, they are the sons of God."*

Today, in the body of Christ, we are guided by the eternal Word and by the Spirit of God, rather than by choosing pieces of paper from a wooden box. Even for the Moravians, what started out as a simple, honest way to hear from God became so legalistic that they couldn't even marry without it. This is why they abolished the practice in the early 1800s. But for a time, God worked with Zinzendorf in this season of spiritual learning and growth.

All citizens of Herrnhut prayed earnestly over the decision to send Dober and Leopold to St. Thomas, where uncertainty and death could await them. The large Protestant churches of Europe had not attempted such a missionary task. Was it the Lord's will for the small community of Herrnhut to do so?

After a year of prayer, Zinzendorf decided it was time to draw the lot. Christian Dober pulled a slip of paper from the wooden box and rejoiced as he read it aloud: "Let the lad go, for the Lord is with him." But for Tobias Leopold, the lot was not favorable; it was not his time to go. David Nitschmann, the carpenter, was chosen to go with Dober instead. Leopold was given the opportunity to join the mission work in the West Indies just one year later.[26]

The First Two Missionaries of the Modern Age

No one in Herrnhut, including Zinzendorf, had any idea how to launch a missionary movement! As the first missionaries to be sent out by a European Protestant church, Dober and Nitschmann were not even given enough money to travel outside of Saxony. Although Zinzendorf had the financial means to sponsor them, the Herrnhut community believed that the venture was to commence and sustain itself fully on faith.

At 3:00 AM on August 21, 1732, Ludwig escorted the young men in his carriage to a spot just twenty miles north of Herrnhut. At the crossroads, the new missionaries knelt beside the buggy, and Zinzendorf laid hands on them and prayed. His only instruction was one of faith: "In all things and in all ways, let the Spirit of Christ guide you."

On that day, the Moravian missionary movement was born! These devout Moravian disciples had no example to follow, no society to financially provide for them, and no guidelines to help them steer their course; they simply moved by the direction of the Spirit of God. Although they would never know it, at that moment, the two men became the pioneers of the great modern missionary movement of the eighteenth and nineteenth centuries.

These devout Moravian disciples had no example to follow, no society to financially provide for them, and no guidelines to help them steer their course; they simply moved by the direction of the Spirit of God.

A trip through Denmark proved to be the Lord's open door for the young pioneers. The Danish court took up their missionary cause, and the king's sister, Princess Amalie, paid their passage to the West Indies. The court's cupbearer even located a ship sailing to the Americas.[27] There was no doubt that God's hand was upon them and their mission!

Four More Missionaries Sent

"My call from the Lord is to spread the word of the blood and the cross of Jesus to the world," Zinzendorf wrote. "I am not concerned what happens to me as a result. This call was on my life before I knew the Moravian and Bohemian Brethren."

Within a year, four more missionaries were chosen to be sent out from Herrnhut. This time, Matthaus and Christian Stach, John Beck, and Friedrich Bohnisch were sent to minister to the Inuit natives of Greenland. They established a Christian village named New Herrnhut on the western shores of Greenland.

It was through the Greenland missions that the Moravians discovered the key to bringing Christ to the lost. When missionary John Beck shared lengthy explanations about the existence of God and the established Christian church, the natives were uninterested. They already believed there was a God. However, when he read the story of Christ's suffering and sacrificial death to save them for all eternity, they responded, "Tell us that again; we are ready to be saved!"

From that point, Zinzendorf counseled all of the prospective missionaries, saying, "Don't be blinded by the notion that the heathen must be taught first to believe in God, and then, afterwards, Jesus Christ....They know already that there is a God. You must preach to them that God has a Son...preach of Jesus Christ who was crucified for their sin. You must tell them that the way to salvation is belief in this Jesus, the eternal Son of God."[28]

Soon after, Zinzendorf sent missionaries to Suriname in northeastern South America and to Lapland (Finland). In 1733, Tobias Leopold left with fifteen missionaries to assist in the growing work in St. Thomas. The following year, two men were sent to the Guinea coast of Africa, and eleven more missionaries to St. Croix, some to replace those who had died of malaria.

The Herrnhut Christians' dedication and willingness to sacrifice their lives for Christ was without equal. As soon as word that one missionary had fallen to disease reached Herrnhut, two more rose to take his place. Together they consecrated their lives under the Moravian banner: "Our Lamb has conquered; let us follow Him."

Protecting the Movement

By this time, Zinzendorf had resigned from his post at the Saxon court to devote his life to the ministry of the gospel. He and his family settled into their home in Herrnhut, which now had five hundred members. The years with Erdmuthe had been full of spiritual blessings, but also painful family loss. Since the birth of their first child in 1724, Erdmuthe had given birth to five other children, but by 1733, three had already died of early childhood diseases. Tragically, Ludwig and Erdmuthe had to visit God's Acre, the cemetery in Herrnhut, to bury their children far too often. During their marriage, Erdmuthe gave birth to twelve children, six boys and six girls, but only four of them survived to adulthood.

In addition to these family sorrows, Zinzendorf was continually the subject of much suspicion by those outside the Herrnhut community. Church leaders and European nobles alike were heatedly divided in their opinions of the unorthodox count. "Some regarded him as a faithful servant of the Lord Jesus Christ, but others conceived a great mistrust of him...they were also afraid of his odd projects."[29]

Zinzendorf was concerned, not for himself, but for the Herrnhut Brethren. He realized that the Lutheran church in Saxony could force the community of Herrnhut to leave. Taking matters into his own hands, he approached the church leaders. "Test my doctrine of faith; prove that my theology is sound," he requested. In a surprise move, Ludwig also asked to be considered for ordination as a Lutheran minister. After months of interrogation and testing, Zinzendorf presented his final petition before the examining church board:

> I was but ten years old when I began to direct my companions to Jesus as their Redeemer....Now I am thirty-four, and my mind has undergone no change. My zeal has not cooled...I love and honor the established church....I will continue to win souls for my precious Savior....I shall go to distant nations, who are ignorant of Jesus and of the redemption in His blood.[30]

Zinzendorf successfully passed all phases of the examination and was ordained as a Lutheran minister in December 1735. Now he could preach in Lutheran churches throughout Europe and protect the Brethren at Herrnhut from accusations that they were "not Lutheran enough." Unfortunately, nothing Ludwig did could protect him from the false accusations of the European churchmen.

Religion always wants to make people conform to a narrow sphere. Scripture says, "*Now there are diversities of gifts, but the same Spirit. And there are differences of administrations, but the same Lord*" (1 Corinthians 12:4–5). Too often, the church gets the "*differences*" and "*the same*" turned around. Most leaders of denominations and churches want everyone around them to have the same gift and anointing that they do: "Speak like me; minister like me; walk like me." But it is the Spirit that is to be the same; there are different gifts.

When the head of a church demands conformity of gifting from his followers, the church will stay small because there is beauty and growth in the different gifts in the body of Christ under the same Lord. Christians must have a relationship with Jesus Christ and good sound doctrine, but their gifting can still be different. Sometimes, people who need the freedom to be who they are in Christ will leave a church or ministry because they are being constrained; an insecure leader will call them rebels. But they are moving in the same Spirit. The difference, as in Zinzendorf's life, is in their gifting and anointing.

Exiled—No Problem!

The Christian community at Herrnhut was thriving. Dozens of missionaries had been sent out; more were training to go. Satan was angry! How could the enemy undermine the work of Herrnhut and stop this move of God? Attack its founder.

Dozens of missionaries had been sent out; more were training to go. Satan was angry! How could the enemy undermine the work of Herrnhut and stop this move of God? Attack its founder.

Slanderous statements and half-truths about Zinzendorf began circulating through the courts of Europe. To make matters worse, the elector of Saxony, Augustus the Strong, had passed away. His son, August III, was suspicious of Ludwig and his "zealous" dedication to Christ, and listened to the lies of jealous court members.

On March 20, 1736, the new Saxon king sent forth an edict: "Count Nikolaus Ludwig von Zinzendorf is permanently exiled from the kingdom of Saxony, including the village of Herrnhut!" Ludwig, who was traveling in Holland with his family, did not hear the news until one month later. Fortunately, a special permit from the new court allowed the Moravian Brethren to remain in the community they had lovingly built, even though their leader had been banished.

As always, Zinzendorf's response reflected his belief that God was the One who established the course for his life. "I could not have come to Herrnhut, irrespective of this, for the next ten years; for it is time to gather the pilgrim church and preach the Savior to the world....That place becomes our home where I can accomplish the most for the Savior at the time."[31]

Ludwig was determined that his exile would not stop the mission work of Christ. "I am destined by the Lord to proclaim the message of the death and blood of Jesus, not with human ingenuity, but with divine power, unmindful of personal consequences to myself."[32] With his exile, Zinzendorf became a missionary and a pilgrim rather than the leader of a single Christian community.

Zinzendorf needed a new headquarters, a home base, while in exile. He chose to purchase a deserted, run-down castle in Ronneburg, northern Germany. Soon, a community called Herrnhaag ("the Lord's grove") was established on the property there. The Moravians worked quickly to repair the castle and to minister to the poor peasants in the surrounding area.

Count Nikolaus Ludwig von Zinzendorf

The Power of Sowing Seed

By now, Moravian missionaries had been sent throughout the West Indies and Suriname to minister to the natives, and to Holland to share the good news of the Messiah with the Jewish population. Revival was sweeping through Greenland, with scores of Inuit attending the Moravian services.

"We will work simply and quietly," Zinzendorf reminded his followers. "Even if we never see wonders with our own eyes or hear them with our ears, we are planting the kingdom of heaven into the nations and will look for the fruit which grows from it."

This is the best statement of a seed sower that I have ever heard from a missionary! He got it—he understood his purpose in sowing the seed. There are God-given stages in spreading the gospel message, and sowing the seed is the first stage.

The apostle Paul listed those stages clearly in 1 Corinthians 3:6: *"I have planted, Apollos watered; but God gave the increase."* We need to realize that these three stages are of equal importance. The planting is the first time that someone hears the gospel message; the watering is when they continue to hear the Word over and over as the seed is hydrated for growth; and then the third stage is the harvest. When evangelizing, most people get discouraged during the times of planting and watering. They think the only exciting part is the harvest. But we have to remember that all three parts are equally important.

For some Christians, their only job is to plant the seed—and to suffer doing so, without getting the opportunity to see the fruit of their labors during their lifetime. This was especially true of the early missionaries in many parts of the world. Many of those men and women lived a more sacrificial life in Christ than we do today, but they didn't get to see the harvests of tens of thousands of people coming to Christ. Today, most ministers get to enjoy that harvest, but many have forgotten that scores of people went before them, watering those seeds so that they could enjoy the fruit of their labor.

The message for each of us is this: Don't be discouraged if you are a "planter" or a "waterer"—and don't be arrogant if you are a "harvester." Someone planted and watered before you. Perhaps it was even a Moravian missionary!

Moravians Bring Christ's Love to South Africa

Twenty-six-year-old George Schmidt left Herrnhut for the dangerous mission field of South Africa to minister among the native Khoikhoi people. The Moravians were appalled by news that the Dutch East India Company persecuted and often killed the South African natives, whom they disparagingly called *Hottentots*, which meant "stammerers." Schmidt traveled alone to South Africa to introduce the Khoikhoi to Jesus, hoping to replace the hatred they had experienced from earlier European colonists with the love of Christ.

The Dutch government of South Africa opposed everything Schmidt did to spread the gospel. Eventually, he was forced him to leave the country, but not before he had spent five years teaching the natives to read and write and to worship the one true God. He established a Christian settlement that was later named Genadendal. It would be fifty years, in 1793, before the Dutch government permitted other Moravian missionaries to enter South Africa. When the Moravians finally returned to Genadendal, they helped to develop the small village into a hardworking, prosperous community, and a Christian sanctuary for African slaves.

Two hundred years later, on October 10, 1995, South African President Nelson Mandela visited the small village. To honor the Moravian community and their sacrificial work among the former black slaves, Mandela renamed the presidential residency in Cape Town *Genadendal*. The anointed Moravian missionary work was still blessing others from beyond the graves of those early Christian workers.

"You Are Sending Young People to Their Deaths!"

In spite of the spiritual victories of the growing Moravian community, the attacks against Zinzendorf's character never let up. "You are sending young people to their deaths, but you won't go yourself!" was the newest accusation Zinzendorf heard. Even though the overseas Moravian work was flourishing, there were also tragic deaths in the tropical climates due to malaria and yellow fever; one of the first to die was young Tobias Leopold.

Ludwig responded to this fresh accusation by humbly turning to the Lord in prayer and then through the lot. Was he to travel to the West Indies himself? God's answer through the lot was, "Go to St. Thomas." Knowing that he would not be immune to quick death in the tropical climate, Zinzendorf put his European affairs in order. To protect his estates from the suspicious Saxon government, Ludwig had already legally turned over all of his property to Erdmuthe. Now, he wrote out a detailed will concerning the rest of his personal effects and made arrangements to travel to the New World.

Erdmuthe wrote to her brother of her husband's zealous new plan. "You can easily imagine what a difficult test this is for someone like me to see my dear Ludwig begin such a long and dangerous journey. I could not bear it if I were not sure it was the Savior's will and not just some venturesome act. I believe the Savior will bring him back to me if it is His will and He will not place more on his shoulders than he can bear."[33]

Missionaries in Prison

Sailing from Europe in November 1738, Ludwig stepped onto West Indies soil at St. Thomas on January 29, 1739, officially becoming a foreign missionary for Christ.

Asking a native worker on the docks for the location of the Moravian missionaries, Ludwig was incensed to hear that they had spent the last three months in a local prison! With a smile, the slave reassured the count that the imprisonment of the missionaries had renewed the slaves' interest to hear more about Jesus. "A great revival is beginning here!" the man insisted. "You should be happy the missionaries have been in prison, for there is a great awakening among the slaves as a result! The imprisonment of the brethren is quite a sermon to them!"[34]

Ludwig preached to gatherings of six to eight hundred slaves from nearly fifty plantations every Saturday night, some meetings lasting into the following morning.

Nevertheless, knowing that his missionaries had the support of the Danish king, Ludwig stormed into the governor's office. "This is an outrage," he protested. "These missionaries have permission from the Danish authorities to preach to the people. How dare anyone throw them into prison?"[35] The governor quickly released the missionaries, fearful of the ire of the European nobleman.

Over the next six months, Ludwig preached to gatherings of six to eight hundred slaves from nearly fifty plantations every Saturday night, some meetings lasting into the following morning. The response of the natives to the gospel was exhilarating. "Saint Thomas is a greater marvel than Herrnhut!" Zinzendorf exclaimed.

By the time Ludwig returned to Europe, the Herrnhut and Herrnhaag missionaries had extended their global outreach, going out in small groups to Ceylon (Sri Lanka), Romania, Algiers (Algeria), and Constantinople (Istanbul). There were now seventy Moravian missionaries ministering the gospel around the world.

Spangenberg and the American Missions

Three years earlier, August Gottleib Spangenberg, a brilliant scholar and theologian from the University of Jena, south of Saxony, had arrived in Herrnhut. Zinzendorf's message of personal faith in the lordship of Jesus Christ and his call to send missionaries into the world had pierced Spangenberg's heart. At twenty-nine years old, he left a successful career in academia to minister with the Moravians for life.

Spangenberg wanted to take the message of Christ's salvation to North America. First, he traveled to London, meeting with James Oglethorpe, the governor of Georgia, to request a land grant for the Moravians near the town of Savannah. He was awarded one hundred acres, and, in 1736, he sailed for America aboard the British ship *Simmonds* with a small group of male and female missionaries, including Anna Nitschmann, who was Bishop Nitschmann's niece and a young Moravian leader.

Ludwig Zinzendorf was a pioneer in welcoming women into the ministry. The young women in the sisters' house who felt called to missionary work were sent out as readily as the men. Eventually, Anna became a female elder in the Moravian community.

Zinzendorf referred to Galatians 3:28 whenever he defended his elevation of women into teaching positions: "With [God], none comes up short, and he also does not prefer one person to another. He loves with an inexpressible and inimitable egality."[36] He also declared, "The sisters belong to the class of those whom the Saviour has declared to his heavenly Father as priests just as much as the men: hence there is no question that the whole band, the whole company, the whole choir of his maidens and brides, are priestesses, and not only priestesses but also priestly women."[37]

Unfortunately, the mission in Georgia never had the chance to succeed. As soon as the Moravians arrived, they were commanded by the Georgian authorities to take up arms against the Spanish soldiers who were attacking from Florida. Because they were against all military action, the new settlers refused to fight and were expelled from the settlement. In God's perfect timing, British evangelist George Whitefield was preaching in Georgia and invited the ostracized Moravians to sail north with him to Pennsylvania. Whitefield owned a section of land northeast of Philadelphia, which he sold to the Moravian Church. Deep in the forests of eastern Pennsylvania, their Christian settlements would flourish!

John Wesley and the Moravian Anointing

Another traveler aboard the *Simmonds* that year was a young, relatively unknown Anglican pastor sailing to America to be a missionary to the natives—thirty-two-year-old John Wesley. Spending months in close quarters with the Moravian missionaries, Wesley was deeply moved by the depth of their faith. He was questioning his own commitment to Christ, confessing on his return from America, that he lacked "the assurance" of his salvation. He lamented in his journal, "I who went to America to convert others was never myself converted to God." Although Wesley was likely a Christian at the time, he still struggled with believing that he was saved.

All of that changed on Wesley's return to London in 1738, thanks to the Moravian relationships he had developed. He spent that spring studying the Scriptures with a Moravian missionary named Peter Boehler. When Wesley questioned whether he still had God's call to preach, Boehler answered, with wise encouragement, "Preach faith till you have it, and then, because you have it, you will preach faith....Do not hide in the earth the talent God has given you."[38]

On May 24, 1738, Wesley went to a Moravian meeting in Aldersgate Street, where James Hutton was preaching. "About a quarter before nine," Wesley recorded in his diary, "while [Hutton] was describing the change which God works in the heart through faith in Christ, I felt my heart strangely warmed. I felt I did trust in Christ, Christ alone, for salvation; and finally an assurance was given me that he had taken away my sins, even mine, and saved me from the law of sin and death." Wesley continued to worship with the Moravians in Aldersgate Street.

On New Year's Eve, 1738, a "watch night" service was held at Aldersgate to welcome the Lord into the New Year. As they prayed during the early morning hours, the anointing fire of the Holy Spirit fell on the assembly, which included the British Moravians, John and Charles Wesley, and George Whitefield. "About three in the morning," Wesley recorded in his journal the next day, "as we were continuing instant in prayer, the power of God came mightily upon us, insomuch that many cried for exceeding joy, and many fell to the ground. As soon as we were recovered a little from that awe and amazement at the presence of His Majesty, we broke out with one voice 'We Praise Thee, O God; We Acknowledge Thee to Be the Lord!'" In the years following that anointed meeting, the evangelic preaching of John Wesley and George Whitefield exploded into the First Great Awakening!

A European Count in America

Spangenberg wrote to Zinzendorf in Europe, encouraging him to sail to Pennsylvania at once to visit the newly opened ministry field. Ludwig organized a group of missionaries, including his oldest daughter, Benigna, and set sail once again for the New World. They arrived in New York Harbor on November 29, 1741.

Once in the Lehigh Valley of Pennsylvania, Ludwig helped Spangenberg establish the Moravian towns of Bethlehem and Nazareth; the settlements were located just eight miles apart and worked together as one united Christian endeavor.

Moravian settlement in Bethlehem, Pennsylvania, in about 1800.
(Library of Congress, Washington, D.C.)

Zinzendorf had no ability to handle financial matters. So it was Spangenberg whom God spoke to about the creation of the "Economy," a voluntary system where the Christians of Bethlehem and Nazareth labored daily for the common good; a large portion of the community funds were used to support missionaries throughout North and South America. In the "Economy," the people built their own homes, made their own clothing, provided for all of their own food, and sold the surplus in the markets of nearby towns. The community vision had one major purpose—to provide for missionaries to spread the gospel of Christ in the New World.

For years, the Moravians had watched Zinzendorf unselfishly donate his wealth to establish Christian communities and to spread the gospel of Christ. It was not difficult for them to do the same. They adopted the motto "Together we pray, together we labor, together we suffer, together we rejoice."

After preaching the gospel in Pennsylvania for two years, a rejoicing Zinzendorf returned to Europe, leaving the Pennsylvania settlements in the capable hands of Spangenberg, David Nitschmann, and Anna Nitschmann. Under Spangenberg's organizational genius as the head of the American Moravian Church, the new settlements flourished.

For years, the Moravians had watched Zinzendorf unselfishly donate his wealth to establish Christian communities and to spread the gospel of Christ. It was not difficult for them to do the same.

"It is nothing," Spangenberg remarked, "but love to the Lamb and to His church." Everything they did, every task they undertook, every soul that was saved, was all for the Master's sake. Soon, they had missionary stations in Maryland, New Jersey, Rhode Island, and New York. Spangenberg divided his time between America and Europe for the next twenty years.

The Great Foolishness

After two years of successful missionary work in Pennsylvania, Zinzendorf entered a bizarre season of testing. It came to be called "the sifting time," named after Jesus' conversation with Peter in Luke 22:31–32: *"And the Lord said, Simon, Simon, behold, Satan hath desired to have you, that he may sift you as wheat: but I have prayed for thee, that thy faith fail not: and when thou art converted, strengthen thy brethren."* I prefer to call it "the time of great foolishness."

I realize that there are times when even anointed men of God are sifted as Peter was, led astray, misdirected. For nearly two decades, Zinzendorf's leadership had brought words of truth and guidance to the Moravian Brethren, but now his teaching took a fanatical turn. Ludwig began to obsess about the need to come to Jesus as a little child in order to be pleasing to Christ. He based his teachings on Matthew 18:2–4:

> *And Jesus called a little child unto him, and set him in the midst of them, and said, Verily I say unto you, Except ye be converted, and become as little children, ye shall not enter into the kingdom of heaven. Whosoever therefore shall humble himself as this little child, the same is greatest in the kingdom of heaven.*

Every Christian needs to take warning here: *Any biblical truth taken to an extreme becomes an error.* It is important to come to Christ with the faith of a child, but Zinzendorf took the concept too far.

With rousing messages, he encouraged the Herrnhaag Brethren to embrace childlike behavior in their relationship with Christ; before long, the teachings disintegrated into childish nonsense. Ludwig created a new society and called it "The Order of the Little Fools"; he sponsored childish outdoor games and festivities, turning Herrnhaag from a hardworking, economic society into a frivolous one. To make up for the loss in income, Zinzendorf used his own resources to provide for the settlers' personal needs.

Becoming ridiculous, Ludwig referred to the Lamb of God as "our little Lamby" and began to address the Holy Spirit as "our Mother," erroneously claiming that since the Spirit of God acted as the Comforter, He held the same position as the mother of the home. Zinzendorf made his only son, Christian Renatus, who was only in his late teens, one of the Herrnhaag leaders.

Both Christian David, from Herrnhut, and Spangenberg, from Pennsylvania, wrote letters warning Ludwig that he had moved dangerously beyond the biblical intent of childlike faith, but he would not listen.

Repentance and Forgiveness

The strange fanaticism continued for nearly four years and thoroughly infected Herrnhaag with unbalanced teachings. In response to the foolishness, John and Charles Wesley and George Whitefield broke fellowship with the Moravian

Brethren and condemned Zinzendorf's folly. Both Wesley and Whitefield criticized the Moravian Church in future years.

In humility, Zinzendorf came before the Lord and repented for allowing the issues to get so out of hand. He stood before the settlers at Herrnhaag and admitted, "Ah! My beloved Brethren, I am guilty! I am the cause of all these troubles!"

Finally, Carl von Peistel, a nobleman and new settler at Herrnhut, traveled to Herrnhaag and convinced Zinzendorf of the heresy in his teachings. In humility, Zinzendorf came before the Lord and repented for allowing the issues to get so out of hand. He stood before the settlers at Herrnhaag and admitted, "Ah! My beloved Brethren, I am guilty! I am the cause of all these troubles!" The Moravian communities, including Herrnhaag, that had supported the fanatical teachings, repented. (The settlers at Herrnhut had remained separated from the Sifting Time.)[39]

Unfortunately for Herrnhaag, the repentance came too late. Count Gustav Casimir, the owner of the estates surrounding their community, demanded that the settlers renounce all ties to Zinzendorf and the Moravian Church or leave his properties within three years. Refusing to break ties with their leader or with the Brethren, within one year, the six hundred Herrnhaag members had scattered to Moravian communities in Europe, America, and other parts of the world.

The situation with Zinzendorf and the "Order of the Little Fools" should not be taken lightly; even godly men can fall into heresy, especially if they do not stay within the balanced message of God's Word or accept the warning counsel of fellow brothers in Christ. Just as he had done in the case of the disciple Peter mentioned in Luke 22, Satan had won a grievous battle against Zinzendorf's Christian testimony. But the enemy would not win the war! *"I will build my church," Jesus promised, "and the gates of hell shall not prevail against it"* (Matthew 16:18).

The Exile Is Over!

Following Zinzendorf's repentance came a time of blessing. Revival was flowing in Greenland, with more than two hundred natives meeting for weekly services. Nazareth and Bethlehem, Pennsylvania, were flourishing; the Economy had founded thirty-two new businesses, and their missionary support spread throughout the Americas.

Ludwig officiated at the wedding of his daughter Benigna and John von Watteville, the adopted son of his dear childhood friend Friedrich. As a wedding present, Ludwig purchased his grandmother's Gross Hennersdorf estate for them.

The greatest blessing of all came when King Augustus II of Saxony visited Herrnhut for himself and experienced the fervent Christian spirit that governed the Moravian community. Shortly after the visit, he sent a letter to Ludwig rescinding his exile and, on October 11, 1747, after ten years of separation, the Zinzendorfs joyously returned to Herrnhut!

The Death of His Only Son

Zinzendorf continued to travel throughout Europe preaching the gospel and encouraging the Christian communities that had been built on the Herrnhut model. There were already twenty communities in Saxony and the nearby states of Prussia and Silesia. Erdmuthe stayed at home in Herrnhut, ministering to the Moravian community there and handling the work at their headquarters.

Ludwig's companion during his travels was their only surviving son, Christian Renatus, who was now in his early twenties and on fire for the Lord. To Ludwig, Christian was not only the heir to his titles, but he was also the heir to his leadership in the Moravian Church and missionary settlements. After repenting of any wrongdoing at Herrnhaag during the "Sifting Time," Christian Renatus had rededicated his life to following the Savior and His Word.

In 1749, Ludwig and Christian settled in the Chelsea section of London to set up a Moravian headquarters. Occasionally, Erdmuthe traveled from Berthelsdorf to spend a few months with them before returning to Saxony where their three married daughters lived.

In early 1752, while living in London, Christian Renatus began to experience fevers and harsh coughing spells. Within a few months, he was diagnosed with tuberculosis. Ludwig and Erdmuthe were heartbroken. In their spirited son, they had seen the hopes and dreams of their future. Neither of his parents was with him when Christian Renatus died in his apartment on May 28, 1752, at the age of twenty-four. Ludwig wept bitter tears at the loss of his precious son and heir. As he read Christian's journal of his increasing desire to serve the Lord, Ludwig grieved for the ministry they might have had together.

Erdmuthe's grief at the loss of her only son was inconsolable. She had set out for London to be with him and was traveling through Holland when she received word that he had succumbed to tuberculosis. Referring to him through her tears as her "precious Christelein," she spoke frequently of joining him in heaven and began to retire from all her ministry work. She had lost her focus in life. Two years later, Ludwig left the London headquarters permanently and rejoined Erdmuthe in Berthelsdorf.

Missionary Victories Continue

The years following Christian Renatus' death were filled with news of missionary victories. By 1753, in St. Thomas, four thousand people were attending the weekly meetings, and more than one thousand had been baptized into the body of Christ. Missionary settlements on St. Croix and St. John were growing rapidly as well. Plantation owners from the island of Jamaica sent a request for Moravian missionaries to settle there to lead the slaves to Christ. The Moravians had also expanded into Tranquebar, India; the Danish Nicobar Islands; and Tibet. There were now more than two hundred Moravian missionaries worldwide.

That same year, Lord Granville, an English aristocrat, sold 100,000 acres of his land in North Carolina to the American Moravian Church. Zinzendorf named the area Wachovia after his grandfather's original estate in Austria. A dozen male and female missionaries sailed to North Carolina and built a new Christian community modeled after Herrnhut, naming it Salem. Today, the state of North Carolina, particularly around the city of Winston-Salem, has a larger number of Moravian congregations than any other region in the United States.

"God's Princess Among Us"

Zinzendorf had spent so many of his personal resources on missionary outreach that, despite the prospering mission settlements, his wealth was nearly depleted, and several Moravian communities were in serious debt. In answer to prayer, the Lord sent a godly Christian brother with the gift of administration to handle the finances of the Moravian Church. Johann Friedrich Köber, a gifted lawyer and accountant, set up an ecumenical council and a system to repay all the debt. Zinzendorf was relieved that the matters were no longer his or his wife's responsibility.

Oftentimes, ministers with the anointing to lead or preach are not good at handling large amounts of money. Over the years, some have gotten into major financial trouble. The best plan is to allow God to call someone into the ministry who is both financially astute and spiritually alive, one who can manage all monetary aspects of the ministry. Although it was a bit late to restore Zinzendorf's personal wealth, the Moravian Church finally had financial peace and stability due to Johann Köber's leadership.

At Zinzendorf's home in Herrnhut, Erdmuthe became increasingly listless, although the doctors could not find the exact cause. After a few months confined to her bed, on June 18, 1756, Countess von Zinzendorf passed away quietly in her sleep. Ludwig entered a time of both mourning and regret for the many years that he had left his wife alone while ministering throughout Europe and the Americas during their thirty-four-year marriage. "I can say in all my life I have never endured such anguish," Zinzendorf confessed after her death.

Count Zinzendorf's second wife, Anna Nitschmann.
(Used by permission / Moravian Church Archives)

Erdmuthe had been a faithful wife, a joyful mother to the people of Herrnhut, and a vital economist in handling their family fortunes. At her funeral, Ludwig said, "The Lord, through His great power, accomplished many glorious deeds through her. She gave wise advice and had deep insights into Scripture. She was God's princess among us."[40] He had the last four words—"God's princess among us"—engraved into Erdmuthe's headstone.

The Final Years: A Hymn to God

After a year of seclusion, in which Zinzendorf wrote hymns to bring himself comfort, the Herrnhut elders suggested that he marry again. Ludwig agreed, and, on June 27, 1757, the fifty-six-year-old count and the forty-two-year-old former missionary Anna Nitschmann were married by Bishop Leonard Dober. For decades, Ludwig and Anna had worked diligently for the cause of Christ, but he was nobility, and she was a commoner. Even in the last years of his life, the count made personal decisions that rocked the noble world!

The Zinzendorfs traveled throughout Germany and Holland while Ludwig preached on his vision of missionary expansion. "A missionary seeks nothing else, day and night, but that the heathens find joy in their Savior and that the Savior might find joy in the heathens."

> *"A missionary seeks nothing else, day and night, but that the heathens find joy in their Savior and that the Savior might find joy in the heathens."*

One year later, in 1758, the couple returned to Herrnhut ready to settle down and pastor the community that they loved. It was time to leave all the traveling and missionary work in the very capable hands of the younger Moravian Brethren.

Entering the Presence of the Lord

In the spring of 1760, everything changed. For some months, Anna had been feeling ill; in April, she was diagnosed with cancer and soon after became bedridden. Ludwig continued to preach to the Herrnhut Brethren and to spend the evenings at his wife's bedside. He worked on the *Losung* for the following year, which included the final Scripture for December 31, 1761: *"We have blessed you out of the house of the LORD"* (Psalm 118:26). It would prove to be prophetic.

The first Sunday in May, during the morning worship service, Ludwig experienced pressure in his chest followed by chest pains and difficulty breathing. It was most likely a heart attack. Four days later, getting weaker, he lay in bed with a fever and a harsh cough. His dear friend, Bishop David Nitschmann, was at his bedside, along with Ludwig's three daughters, Benigna, Marie Agnes, and Elizabeth. With grateful tears, the count turned to David and asked, "Did you suppose, in the beginning, that the Savior would do as much as we now see amongst the various Moravian settlements, amongst the children of God of other denominations, and amongst the heathen? I only entreated Him for a few first fruits of the latter, but there are now thousands of them."

"I cannot say," he continued, "how much I love you all. Who would have believed that the prayer of Christ, 'That they may be one,' could have been so strikingly fulfilled among us?"[41]

That night, with his family still at his bedside, Zinzendorf whispered hoarsely to his son-in-law John, "Now, my dear friend, I am going to the Savior. I am ready. I bow to His will. He is satisfied with me. If He does not want me here anymore, I am ready to go to Him. There is nothing to hinder me now."[42]

John reached for Ludwig's hand and prayed, "Lord, now let your servant depart in peace. The Lord bless thee and keep thee; the Lord make His face to shine upon thee, and be gracious unto thee; the Lord lift up His countenance upon thee and give thee peace."

Just moments later, on the evening of Friday, May 9, 1760, Count Nikolaus Ludwig von Zinzendorf rested his head back on his pillow and quietly entered into the joy of his Lord. When John walked into Anna's bedroom with the sad tidings, she responded with a quiet smile, saying, "I have the happiest prospect of you all. I will be going to him soon."

For several days, Zinzendorf lay in state in the Berthelsdorf mansion; on May 15, the day of the funeral, peasants from the neighboring towns and dignitaries from the nearby cities walked through to see the beloved father of Herrnhut one last time. Zinzendorf was buried in God's Acre, beside Erdmuthe and eight of his twelve children.

"With tears we sow this seed in the earth," Bishop David prayed at the gravesite, "but He, in His own good time, will bring it to life and will gather in His harvest with thanks and praise! Let all who wish for this say, Amen!" And four thousand voices present that day echoed "Amen."[43]

One week later, on May 22, 1760, Anna Nitschmann Zinzendorf passed away and was buried in God's Acre as well.

The Moravian Covenant for Christian Living

The Moravian Church was forever grateful to the Lord for sending Zinzendorf to help restore the Unitas Fratum. Once his leadership was gone, the elders prayed and then called August Spangenberg home from Pennsylvania to become the official leader of the European Moravian Church. In 1777, he wrote the *Idea Fidei Fratrum*, which became the declaration of the Christian Faith of the United Brethren. Spangenberg served the Moravian Church until his death at Berthelsdorf on September 18, 1792, at the age of eighty-eight. He was buried near his friend Zinzendorf in God's Acre.

The "Brotherly Union and Compact," which was signed by the Christians of Herrnhut and Berthelsdorf in May 1727, has been revised many times over the years; today, it is known as *The Moravian Covenant for Christian Living.*[44] The motto of the Moravian Church is: "In essentials, unity; in nonessentials, liberty; in all things, love."

The Holy Spirit Lives in Herrnhut Today

Today, the small town of Herrnhut, Germany, population just under five thousand citizens, is still the international headquarters of the Moravian Church. For twenty-eight years, from 1961 to 1989, Herrnhut was located on the East German side of the Berlin Wall. Even though practicing Christianity openly was illegal during the communist repression, a group of Moravian Christians were baptized in the Holy Spirit and founded a charismatic prayer group that worshiped the Lord by meeting in homes from 1979 to 1999. In 1999, they established a Spirit-filled ministry called Christliches Zentrum Herrnhut, and they meet in a vibrant church building called *Jesus-Haus.*

Their vision today is much like Zinzendorf's nearly three hundred years ago. Here are some of their stated beliefs:

> We believe that the gospel of salvation through Jesus Christ is the Church's most precious treasure. We want to live and preach it.
>
> We treasure the Holy Spirit and His gifts. We love God's word; it teaches us what to do in every situation of our lives.[45]
>
> We want to serve the body of Christ, love our neighbours, and spread the Gospel throughout the world.[46]
>
> We identify with churches in the charismatic movement and operate in the gifts of the Holy Spirit, healing, prophecy, and praying in tongues.[47]

In addition to worshiping at Jesus-Haus in Herrnhut, visitors can see the Berthelsdorf church where God's power fell on the Moravian people in 1727. God's Acre and Count Zinzendorf's grave are still undisturbed in the village. The Zinzendorf's manor house is currently being restored to its eighteenth-century beauty and is open for guests.

The Missionary Spirit Lives On

The Moravian missionary spirit continues. By the time of Ludwig's death, the Moravians had sent out 226 missionaries and baptized more than 3,000 converts

For fifty years, the Moravians spread the gospel of Christ throughout the West Indies without help from any other denomination....They had baptized 13,000 new Christians before missionaries from any other church arrived on the islands.

around the world. From 1732 to 1782, they officially recorded the baptisms of more than 11,000 people. On the Caribbean island of Antigua alone, from 1769 to 1792, the number of converts grew from 14 to 7,400!

For fifty years, the Moravians spread the gospel of Christ throughout the West Indies without help from any other denomination. They established missions in St. Thomas, St. Croix, St. Johns, Jamaica, Antigua, Barbados, and St. Kitts. They had baptized 13,000 new Christians before missionaries from any other church arrived on the islands.[48]

Near the end of the eighteenth century, just as the earliest missionary society of Protestant Europe was sending out its first missionary, William Carey, the Moravians had one thousand missionaries already serving Christ worldwide. By the end of the nineteenth century, more than twenty-two hundred Moravian missionaries were on the mission field. Today, the Moravians still send missionaries to countries where the need is the greatest, such as Burundi, Belize, Cuba, Kenya, Peru, Uganda, and Haiti.[49]

"Zinzendorf was the instrument in the hand of God," wrote August Spangenberg years earlier, "for planting the church of the Brethren in almost every quarter of the globe. He was a man of lively disposition, quick perception, penetrating judgment, extraordinary zeal, and incomparable genius."[50]

God's Message to His People

Simply put, Count Nikolaus Ludwig von Zinzendorf was a man before his time. He was the first to challenge the Protestant church with the mission to go into all the world to reach the unsaved for Christ. He supported first century "Christian community" and the leadership of women in the church. He welcomed the presence and the power of the Holy Spirit in his personal life and in corporate worship through robust prayer and the recognition of gifts in individual lives. He lived a holy and consecrated life, submitted to the Savior in every part of his life, and encouraged the Moravians to do the same. Together, they went to the mission field, exuberantly sowing seed that would return a great harvest.

Count Nikolaus Ludwig von Zinzendorf

As a child, Zinzendorf was like the young rich ruler in the gospel of Mark who asked Jesus, "*What shall I do that I may inherit eternal life?*" (Mark 10:17). But instead of turning away in sorrow at Christ's answer to sell all that he owned, Ludwig faithfully laid down all his riches to follow his precious Lord and King. The last line on his headstone speaks of his crowning achievement: "He was destined to bring forth fruit, fruit that should remain."

Upon learning of Zinzendorf's death, Spangenberg wrote, "He was the great treasure of our time, a lovely diamond in the ring on the hand of our Lord, a servant of the Lord without an equal, a pillar in the house of the Lord, God's message to His people."[51]

I have planted, Apollos watered; but God gave the increase.

(1 Corinthians 3:6)

Will you go with God's message?

Will you plant or water the seed of God's Word to the lost, even if you are not the one who will see the harvest?

Chapter 2

David Brainerd

"I Want the Field of the Unreached"

An intent young man sat astride his horse, guiding his mount carefully through the darkening Pennsylvania forest. The journey had been long and treacherous, with no end in sight. Coughing into his coat sleeve, David Brainerd urged the mare along while searching through the trees for signs of a campsite. Nothing met his anxious gaze except more trees and overgrown trails.

It was his first meeting with the Delaware tribe. "It is important to God—I have to make it," he repeated to himself.

Was he lost? It had happened many times before.

As the sun descended behind the tree line, the young missionary's strength was nearly spent when he spied the flickering glow of scattered campfires through the dense foliage. Finally, he had reached the Delaware. *Will they be as ferocious and unwelcoming as I have been warned?* David wondered.

"Prayer is the key. Prayer is always the key. Thank You, Father," he encouraged himself, as he decided to spend the night with God in the forest beside his own campfire. Prayer would give him the strength to face the natives early the next day.

As he tied up his horse and started a fire, the weary traveler was unaware that eyes were peering at him through the forest. The Delaware chief, hidden with his warriors, gave the command, "Let us go at once and kill this man whose people have taught us to drink firewater [alcohol], and then, while we are drunk, have taken our baskets and skins and even our lands for nothing."[52]

David Brainerd

Silently, the warriors descended on the lone campsite as the solitary figure bowed, clutching something close to his heart. They heard the young man on his knees praying to God, "Let the natives embrace your salvation, Lord." Stealthily moving forward, the warriors stopped suddenly as a rattlesnake slithered up to the young man and raised its ugly head within inches of the bowed face. Then, just as suddenly, the snake uncoiled and, for no apparent reason, slithered away. Gazing at each other in surprise, the warriors did the same, leaving the praying man alone with his God.[53]

The next morning, David walked into the Delaware camp and was welcomed by the curious and awestruck villagers. "The Great Spirit is with this praying white man," the natives proclaimed.[54] And so, Brainerd's ministry to the natives at the Forks of the Delaware River in eastern Pennsylvania began.

A Flame of Fire

"Never think that you can live to God by your own power or strength;
but always look to and rely on Him for assistance,
yea, for all strength and grace."
—David Brainerd

The above story was one miraculous event in David Brainerd's life described in the book *Heroes of Faith on Pioneer Trails*. But the greatest miracle of his ministry was the supernatural power of God that *called* him, *equipped* him, and *kept* him, so that he could accomplish, in five short years, what few men accomplish in a lifetime.

An anointed disciple of Christ, Brainerd laid the foundation for mission work among Native Americans and inspired thousands of missionaries and believers to dedicate their all for Jesus. His compelling story is one of unfailing determination to love and serve God in spite of the most devastating circumstances. Rejection,

An anointed disciple of Christ, Brainerd laid the foundation for mission work among Native Americans and inspired thousands of missionaries and believers to dedicate their all for Jesus.

loneliness, sickness, hostile natives—nothing could still the cry of David Brainerd's heart: "Oh, that I could be a flame of fire to the service of my God!"

His ministry was birthed during the First Great Awakening, influenced by the preaching of George Whitefield and Jonathan Edwards. Because Brainerd and Edwards later became close friends, nearly everything we know of his missionary endeavors comes from *The Life and Diary of David Brainerd.* This work was edited and published by Jonathan Edwards in 1749, shortly after the young missionary's death.

Brainerd's powerful influence has spanned the centuries because of the intimacy of that diary. He wrote with painstaking honesty of the highs *and* lows of his life, unaware that his personal journey with Jesus would inspire thousands of believers for centuries to come. "There is a God in heaven who overrules all things for the best; and this is the comfort of my soul....How blessed it is to grow more and more like God!" As a testimony to God's anointing on this young man's life, *The Life and Diary of David Brainerd* has never gone out of print in more than 260 years of publishing history!

For David Brainerd, Jesus Christ was his *all in all—"the head over all things to the church, which is his body, the fulness of him that filleth all in all"* (Ephesians 1:22–23). "I have received my all from God," he wrote countless times. "Oh, that I could return my all to God!"

The Christian world still honors Brainerd's extraordinary commitment to Christ nearly three hundred years later. This young disciple was truly one of God's missionary generals.

An Unquenchable Stirring

David Brainerd was born in the New England village of Haddam, Connecticut, on April 20, 1718, to Hezekiah and Dorothy Brainerd. He was the sixth of nine children and the descendant of a long line of Puritan ministers. In 1633, his great-grandfather, Peter Hobart, had fled England to avoid religious persecution and settled in Massachusetts. It was just thirteen years after the Pilgrims landed at Plymouth.

David Brainerd

David had a staunch Puritan upbringing with parents who were devoted to God and spent many hours in the Congregational (Puritan) Church. His father was a representative in the Connecticut Colony government and a successful landowner. Sadly, when David was only nine years old, his father died suddenly while attending to his senatorial duties in Hartford. Five years later, another tragedy struck when his mother became ill and died as well, leaving David an orphan at just fourteen. These tragedies, as well as a personal disposition to depression, led him from his youth to be "somewhat sober, and inclined rather to melancholy than the contrary extreme."[55]

At his mother's death, David inherited a farm in Durham, Connecticut, from his family's estate. His father, Hezekiah, had been successful in business and law and owned land throughout the Connecticut River Valley. At fourteen, David was too young to manage his property, so he moved to East Haddam to live with his married sister, Jerusha Spencer. He kept up his studies in her home and attended church "religiously," trying to do everything expected of him as a Puritan believer.

Uncertain of his future, at nineteen, David took on the responsibility of running his farm. Although he worked diligently, the daily toil of farmwork was completely unfulfilling to him. In his heart, there was an unquenchable stirring from God. Day by day, he became more preoccupied with the dream of pursuing biblical studies and following his grandfather's footsteps in ministry.

"Farming will never be for me," David finally resolved. He packed up his Bible and books and moved back to Haddam to study with the Reverend Phineas Fiske while preparing to enter Yale University in the fall. He spent very little time at the farm in future years, but being a landowner provided him with the money he would need for his college education and his later missionary work.

Over the years, David worked hard to maintain a "proper religious life." He wanted to do the right thing, but he really didn't understand salvation by grace alone. Instead, he worked diligently to be "good enough," reading the Scriptures, memorizing sermons, and separating himself from "youthful foolishness."

"I proceeded on a self-righteous foundation," he admitted later, "and should have been entirely lost and undone had not the mere mercy of God prevented it!"[56]

"God Swallowed Me"

Deep in his soul, David Brainerd longed to know the power and presence of God. He poured out his heart in prayer on long walks through the Connecticut countryside. Speaking to an "unseen audience," he wrestled with the demons within his own soul, struggling to find the way to salvation. In the spring of 1739, as David approached his twenty-first birthday, the Holy Spirit began to convict him of the sin of trying to earn his way to God.

"Sometime in February 1739, I set apart a day for fasting and prayer, and spent the day in almost incessant cries to God for mercy to see...the way of life by Jesus Christ."

His struggle was with God's grace; he wanted God to accept all of his hard-earned works as a way to earn salvation. "All this time," David wrote, "the Spirit of God was powerfully at work within me; and I was inwardly pressed to relinquish all self-confidence, all hopes of ever helping myself by any means whatsoever."[57] David Brainerd was surrendering his heart and will to God.

While walking briskly through the fields near Haddam that July, the heavens appeared to open, and the Holy Spirit fell upon Brainerd with His revelatory power:

> As I was walking in a dark, thick grove, unspeakable glory seemed to open to the view and apprehension of my soul...a new view that I had of God...I stood still, wondered and admired!
>
> My soul rejoiced with joy unspeakable, to see such a God, such a glorious Divine Being; and I was inwardly pleased and satisfied that He should be God over all forever and ever. My soul was so captivated and delighted with the excellency, loveliness, greatness and other perfections of God, that I was swallowed up in Him!"[58]

God had captured his soul!

The Holy Spirit enveloped David Brainerd with both the majesty and the mercy of God, and he accepted his salvation in Christ based on grace alone. *"For by grace you have been saved through faith; and that not of yourselves, it is the gift of God; not as a result of works, that no one should boast"* (Ephesians 2:8–9 NASB). Brainerd had turned to the living God with his whole heart, and God had answered his prayer with His glorious salvation. David was exited to begin studying tor the ministry.

The Rigors of Yale University

Yale University, in New Haven, Connecticut, became Brainerd's home for the next three years. In eighteenth-century New England, it was difficult to enter

Christian ministry unless you received a degree from Harvard or Yale and were licensed to preach by the Congregational Church. So, with both excitement and anxiety, David entered his freshmen year in September 1739, just two months after his personal conversion.

At twenty-one, David was older and more serious than his frivolous classmates, who didn't seem focused on following Jesus. Because he was such an intense young man, he promptly immersed himself in his studies, gradually sliding into his bad habits of working too hard just to prove he was worthy of God's love.

After a year of rigorous study with little rest, Brainerd became physically weak and disoriented. One night, in a coughing fit, he was alarmed to find that he had coughed up blood. "It isn't serious," assured his tutor. "You just need to go home for a few weeks' rest."

Brainerd left Yale in August, and a few weeks became a few months as he slowly recovered. When he regained his strength, he walked in the meadows of his farm and surrendered his heart once again to the leading of the Holy Spirit. He wrote in October, "I again found the assistance of the Holy Spirit, both morning and night, and life and comfort in God the whole day....I enjoyed a sweet and precious communion with God wherein my soul enjoyed unspeakable comfort."[59]

During these same days, as God was renewing David's soul, the Holy Spirit was blowing revival winds across New England and through the campus of Yale University.

The Great Awakening at Yale University

David returned to Yale just as the Holy Spirit began a powerful move across the English-speaking world, throughout England, Scotland, Wales, and the American colonies. The Great Awakening swept through New England with a renewed emphasis on the conviction of sin and a "new birth" experience based on the love and grace of Jesus Christ. It was a wake-up call to the staunch Puritan church, which had begun to emphasize outward works and family connections for church membership instead of a personal relationship with Jesus.

The most famous of the Great Awakening preachers, Jonathan Edwards of Massachusetts, delivered messages on repentance and faith in Christ each week in his church services. Under the power of the Holy Spirit, people from the congregation would fall to their knees, crying out from conviction, *"What must I do to be saved?"* (Acts 16:30).

David Brainerd's faith was ignited! Students who once were indifferent to the gospel flocked to the Bible studies that Brainerd organized.

George Whitefield, a twenty-six-year-old evangelist from England, was traveling throughout Massachusetts and Connecticut, preaching a fiery message of God's justice and mercy. Over and over, he proclaimed the new birth from Jesus' words to Nicodemus in the gospel of John: *"Jesus answered and said unto him, Verily, verily, I say unto thee, Except a man be born again, he cannot see the kingdom of God"* (John 3:3).

Just one of Whitefield's open-air revivals, held in a field outside Boston, attracted thirty thousand people. Everywhere he preached, the crowds responded with overwhelming emotion—tears, cries of repentance, and renewed love for Jesus Christ. Thousands of colonists came to new birth through his messages.

On October 27, 1740, Whitefield preached to the Yale students, and the power of the Holy Spirit blazed through the chapel, drawing the students to their knees and transforming the irreverent young men into on-fire Christian disciples. The Great Awakening had arrived at Yale!

David Brainerd's faith was ignited! Students who once were indifferent to the gospel flocked to the Bible studies that Brainerd organized. They met in groups of four or five and spoke freely of this "new" power of the Holy Spirit that was moving among them and bringing repentance and new life in Christ.

Raging Opposition to the Revival

When the Spirit of God moves, Satan always responds with controversy and disruption. Evil will always oppose the power of God. Unfortunately, the opposition often comes from Christian leaders who are afraid of a fresh move of God's Spirit.

As the Great Awakening swept through New England, the revival message split people within both the Congregational and Presbyterian churches. In each denomination, there were supporters of the Awakening, called "New Lights" or "New Side," and opponents, called "Old Lights" or "Old Side."

The administrators of Yale University were in raging opposition to the revival. They disapproved of Whitefield and other revivalists' teachings. "The meetings are pure emotionalism!" they charged. "They stray too far from the Puritan doctrine." They accused the zealous Yale students of rejecting the school's biblical teachings to follow a "new gospel."

The students were outraged. Many of them accused the opposing Yale administrators of not being true believers and of rejecting the Spirit of God. The controversy came to a head when Yale's rector, Reverend Thomas Clap, pronounced an edict: "Any student who [criticizes] the professors or administration or questioned their Christian faith because of the Great Awakening [is] subject to expulsion." The students were also forbidden to attend Whitefield meetings or to join in the revival in any way!

In spite of the threat, Brainerd and many fellow students continued to meet daily for prayer and occasionally snuck out to hear the Awakening evangelists preach in the open countryside.

One night in the dormitory, while discussing the day's events, a student questioned Brainerd about Mr. Chauncey Whittelsey, a Yale tutor whose prayers were often stilted and severe. Brainerd's comment concerning Whittelsey came quick: "He has no more grace than this chair."[60]

A freshman student overheard and immediately reported Brainerd's remark. Thomas Clap declared the comment "forbidden criticism of a faculty member" and cause for immediate expulsion, unless Brainerd made an open apology to the entire student body in the College Hall.

Brainerd refused. He believed the comment was acceptable because it was made in private. In his youthful enthusiasm, or "indiscreet zeal," as he later called it, he was convinced that the rector would eventually agree with him. (His refusal to apologize became a decision that he regretted for the rest of his life.) As a result, in the winter of 1742, he was expelled from Yale.

Blazing "New Lights"

David was shocked and in a state of mourning. His appeals to be reinstated were soundly rejected. Heartbroken, he packed his belongings and left Yale, his dreams of ministry crushed. Since he couldn't preach without the Yale degree and a Congregational license, he thought all possibilities for ministry in New England had been destroyed.

Where would he go next? In deep melancholy, Brainerd traveled from New Haven to Ripton, Connecticut, just ten miles from the college.

Still longing to serve the Lord, he continued his ministry studies with Rev. Jedediah Mills, a minister who had been stirred by the Great Awakening and become a "New Lights" pastor. Several Congregational ministers had joined the revival and formed their own ministerial association as "New Lights." In fellowship with these men of God, David could continue his biblical studies and preach the gospel.

Daily, Brainerd poured his heart out in his diary, expressing overwhelming regret for his stubbornness and frustration over the college's handling of the whole situation. Some days, he sensed God's assurance that things would be well. On April 12, 1742, he wrote,

> This morning the Lord was pleased to lift up the light of His countenance upon me in secret prayer, and made the season very precious to my soul. And although I had been depressed of late, respecting my hopes of future serviceableness in the cause of God; yet now I had much encouragement respecting that matter.
>
> I felt exceedingly calm, and quite resigned to God, respecting my future employment, when and where He pleased.[61]

Other days, his heart was tortured by depression and feelings of his own worthlessness:

> I think I never felt so much of the cursed pride of my heart, as well as the stubbornness of my will before. Oh dreadful! What a vile wretch I am! O that God would humble me in the dust! I felt myself such a sinner all day that I scarce had any comfort. O when shall I be delivered from the body of this death?[62]

During these days, Brainerd was locked in the painful depression he had suffered since childhood. He was also a victim of the legalism of the time, desperately trying to fulfill other men's expectations for his life. Brainerd spent a long time trying to win back something that he should have just left to God. Once the doors of Yale had been closed, he should have rested in the direction the Lord was leading him in his

Brainerd spent a long time trying to win back something that he should have just left to God. Once the doors of Yale had been closed, he should have rested in the direction the Lord was leading him in his ministry.

ministry. Thank God that, in the body of Christ today, we realize that it is not the university or seminary degree that gives credibility to our ministry but the fruit that we bear empowered by the Spirit of God. *"Even so every good tree bringeth forth good fruit; but a corrupt tree bringeth forth evil fruit"* (Matthew 7:17).

As David sought God's comfort, his lifetime commitment to secret prayer and fasting was established. Feeling God's peace in the outdoors, he took long walks in prayer, offering his heart and soul to Christ's service. "I set apart this day for fasting and prayer to God for His grace; especially to prepare me for the work of the ministry, to give me divine aid and direction in my preparations for that great work, and, in His own time, to send me into His harvest."[63]

"Reaching the Unreached"

In spite of the persecution and suffering, God had the perfect assignment for David Brainerd's life. For some time, he felt that his call was to reach people who had never heard the gospel, those who weren't already sitting in a church pew. "I never could feel any freedom to enter into another man's labors and settle down in the ministry where the gospel was preached before," he wrote.[64]

The Society in Scotland for the Propagation of Christian Knowledge was already sending missionaries into the New England wilderness to reach the Native Americans. During the Great Awakening, the society embraced the revival teachings and was searching for Spirit-empowered men to share the love of Christ with the natives. The Rev. Ebenezer Pemberton of New York sent Brainerd a letter, offering to ordain him as a missionary to the natives of New York, New Jersey, and eastern Pennsylvania. Was he God's man for the job?

Brainerd welcomed the call! He would begin his service among the Housatonic Indians of Kaunaumeek, New York, eighteen miles outside of Albany. (Throughout Brainerd's diary, the Native Americans are referred to as "Indians," which was a common practice during the eighteenth century, so I will do the same in some places in this chapter.)

Excited about his first ministry assignment, on April 20, 1743, Brainerd's twenty-fifth birthday, he spent the day in prayer and fasting in the woods in close communion with God. That day, his diary entry ended with the cry, "O that God would enable me to live for His glory for the future!"[65]

The Testing of His Faith

Brainerd would have great success among the Native Americans during his ministry years, but not before God brought him through a deep valley of testing. The year he spent among the people of Kaunaumeek was a time when he faced the darkest spiritual challenge of his life.

Brainerd preaching to Native American tribes.[66]

When he arrived in Kaunaumeek in late April, Brainerd lived in a log cabin with a poor Scottish couple and walked through rough terrain a mile and a half each way to visit the Indian settlement. It was a struggle to find an interpreter who could communicate all that Brainerd wanted to share with the people there.

At night, his bed was merely "a little heap of straw, laid upon some boards, a little way from the ground." The only food he had was a sparse diet of hasty pudding and bread baked in ashes. While the Native Americans seemed receptive, there was no outward acceptance of Christ. Each day, he labored in prayer for God's help in his work.

Although he was convinced that he was following God's will for his life, Brainerd still suffered with extreme bouts of melancholy. Whether his depression resulted from spiritual attacks or emotional and physical illness is unknown. But again, emotional struggles were a lifetime challenge for this anointed man of God.

His writings echoed his distress. On May 18, 1743, he wrote,

> My circumstances are such, that I have no comfort, of any kind, but what I have in God. I live in the most lonesome wilderness; have but one single person to converse with, that can speak English....I have no fellow-Christian to whom I might unbosom myself...and join in...prayer....My labour is hard and extremely difficult.[67]

Yet, in the midst of Brainerd's greatest weakness, God revealed his greatest strength—his relentless commitment to loving and serving Jesus Christ. "Afterwards my soul rose so far above the deep waters that I dared to rejoice in God. I saw that there was a sufficient matter for all my consolations in the love of a blessed God."[68]

During these difficult months, the bouts of sickness he had experienced at Yale returned. Yet, even as he struggled with illness, he continually offered his heart and hands to Christ's service.

Never Giving Up

Refusing to give up his dream to become a Yale graduate, in June 1743, David traveled the sixty miles from Kaunaumeek to New Haven to apologize once again to the Yale leadership and to plead to complete his final year. This time, he was sponsored by the evangelist Jonathan Edwards and Aaron Burr Sr., both longtime Yale supporters, who gave testimony in David's defense. Once again, the prideful Thomas Clapp and the Yale administrators denied his request.

It seems obvious that religious spirits were working through these men to destroy Brainerd's passion and destiny. The "Old Lights" were the religious people who didn't want things to change. They fought the spiritual zeal of the Great Awakening because they were afraid it contained no knowledge. Instead of trying to kill the zeal of the Holy Spirit among the "New Lights," they should have added to that zeal with their biblical wisdom and knowledge. The entire body of Christ would have benefited from that choice.

What Brainerd had said about the Yale administrators' lack of spiritual life was truth; he had labeled them correctly, and it had provoked them to respond in anger. The truth is that *error cannot hide behind an institution.*

In response to the spiritual pride of the "Old Lights" and their treatment of Brainerd, Edwards and Burr withdrew their sponsorship of Yale University. Together with other "New Lights" leaders, they founded the College of New Jersey in Princeton, New Jersey, offering biblical studies to all Christian denominations. The school was later renamed Princeton University. In the following years, Yale's rector, Thomas Clapp, repented of his opposition to the Great Awakening and the teachings of God's grace, and joined the New Lights pastors in ministry![69]

It was a travesty at the time that the Yale administrators made their decisions against Brainerd. It was also a sad statement of the university's inconstancy when, years later, after the renowned success of Brainerd's ministry, Yale claimed David Brainerd as one of their own graduates. They established Brainerd Hall in the Yale School of Divinity, which is still in use today. There is a bronze plaque on the front of the building that reads: "David Brainerd, Class of 1743"—even though he was denied the honor of graduating with his class.

Although David Brainerd never lived to see these events, God was faithful to answer his prayers, to reveal the truth about his ministry, and to honor his memory.

They Are My People

Traveling back to the Kaunaumeek village after Yale's denial, Brainerd lost his way in the dense forest and was forced to lie all night in the open air. He awoke weak and disoriented, racked with pain and coughing spasms as he rode back to the village. Once again, he turned to the only source of his strength, Jesus Christ.

Determined to complete his mission, Brainerd built a small hut of his own in the Native American village and lived among the community for nearly a year.

Determined to complete his mission, Brainerd built a small hut of his own in the Native American village and lived among the community for nearly a year. As a result of prayer and God's faithfulness, the people became more responsive to the gospel, and, as their relationship grew, he referred to them in his writings as "my people."

With a thankful heart, on January 1, 1744, David recorded this prayer:

> May I always remember that all I have comes from God. Blessed be the Lord, who has carried me through all the toils, fatigues, and hardships of the year past, as well as the spiritual sorrows and conflicts that have attended it. Oh that I could begin this new year with God, and spend the whole of it to his glory, either in life or in death![70]

Brainerd depicted in his missionary travels.[71]

Three months later, Brainerd's time of testing came to an end. On Sunday, March 11, he preached his final sermon to the natives at Kaunaumeek. They had agreed to move from their isolated village to the town of Stockbridge, New York, where more than four hundred Native Americans lived in a flourishing Christian community under the ministry of John Sargeant.

Unexpectedly, Brainerd received offers from two different "New Lights" churches to serve as their pastor. He was flattered by the invitations and was especially tempted to accept the one from East Hampton, New York, where he had close Christian friends, but he was certain that his call from God was to minister to the Native Americans. He wrote, "O that God would send forth faithful labourers into His harvest. I am resolved to go on still with the Indian affair, if divine providence permit."

Menacing Natives

New orders from the Scottish Society arrived. It was time for David to move south from New York to the Forks of the Delaware, in the dense forests of Pennsylvania.

Several tribes lived along the banks of the Delaware River, including the Delaware, or Lenni-Lenapes. They had a menacing reputation because of their animosity toward the white settlers, and the Scottish Society had been reluctant to send a missionary to them any sooner. This is the tribe that had plotted to kill Brainerd before he was miraculously delivered from the rattlesnake.

Before attempting this dangerous new work, the Presbytery of New York laid hands on David to ordain him for this ministry. Humbled by God's purpose for his life, on June 12, 1744, Brainerd penned, "At this time I was affected with a sense of the important trust committed to me....O that I might always be engaged in the service of God, and duly remember the solemn charge I have received, in the presence of God, angels and men. May I be assisted of God for this purpose."[72]

Packing up his few belongings and giving the rest of them away, Brainerd set out from New York for his critical assignment.

Each day, he arose from his small campsite and set out with renewed determination; alone, he crossed the Hudson River and traveled another hundred miles "through a desolate and hideous country above New Jersey" until he reached the Delaware River. Although the tribes received him cautiously, they were willing to listen as he shared the gospel. He set up a small cabin and began his ministry, preaching messages of salvation each morning, visiting from tent to tent to explain God's sacrificial love, and sharing their meals and their lives.

One Hundred Miles of Susquehanna

Anointed to preach to all the unreached natives, Brainerd did not limit his ministry to one tribe. In October 1744, he launched deeper into the Pennsylvania wilderness in search of the hundreds of natives who lived along the Susquehanna River. His traveling companion was fellow missionary Eliab Byram, a 1740 graduate of Harvard, who worked with David as a team.

On this trip to reach the Susquehanna, Brainerd wrote, "We went way into the wilderness and found the most difficult and dangerous traveling by far that any of us had ever seen; we had scarce anything else but lofty mountains, deep valleys, and hideous rocks to make our way through."[73]

On one of those precarious paths, Brainerd's horse slipped and broke its leg. In the wilderness, with no assistance, there was nothing to do but kill the horse and continue on foot. God surely had a special plan for such an arduous journey.

Brainerd's problem of depression was magnified by the fact that he was always by himself. It is not good to spend long times in ministry alone.

Making their way one hundred miles up the Susquehanna, they shared the sacrificial love of Jesus with small groups of natives along the way. The spiritual warfare was heavy; the Native Americans were suspicious of white settlers and their white God. Their faith was settled in their *powwows*—or medicine men—who, they believed, had the power to help them—or to poison them to death.

In spite of the spiritual warfare, Brainerd experienced unusually good health on this expedition, and his spirits were lifted by having Byram ministering by his side. He wrote, "My soul loves the people of God, and especially the ministers of Jesus Christ, who feel the same trials that I do." When Brainerd ministered with other believers, he was always lifted from his melancholy spirits.

If the New England ministers had followed the biblical example, they would have known that Jesus always sent His disciples out in pairs. When two or more are sent out in Christ's name, they are blessed with the power of agreement, with spiritual encouragement, and with personal accountability. Brainerd's problem of depression was magnified by the fact that he was always by himself. It is not good to spend long times in ministry alone.

In my travels, I have noticed that this is true even of missionary couples. Biblically, the couples are not two people: they are one flesh. It is better if two couples are sent out as a ministry team so that they can pray together and help one another hear the full counsel of God as they minister in His name.

Overcoming "Medicine Man" Power

When Brainerd returned to the Forks of the Delaware in early December, he found the village preparing for a great feast in honor of their pagan gods. For two days, he camped in the woods, fervently praying and fasting for their deliverance. The Delawares spent the same two days dancing and feasting in celebration of their gods. Discouraged by the false spirituality of the Delaware Indians, Brainerd steadfastly prayed to God to deliver the natives for His kingdom.

Within days, Brainerd's prayers were rewarded! His interpreter, Moses Tattamy, approached the missionary and confessed that he wanted to know more about Jesus. Excited by the prospects of his first convert, Brainerd prayed for Moses to make a true commitment to Christ, which he did, along with his wife and daughters.

Although his primary vision was to minister among the natives, Brainerd also shared the gospel with white settlers in the area. On certain "Communion weekends," he traveled for miles to assist the church pastors in neighboring towns. As many as 3,000 Pennsylvania settlers would travel great distances to hear the gospel and to share the Lord's Supper together.

When Brainerd preached, "the Word was attended with amazing power; many scores, if not hundreds, in the great assembly were much affected." Tears would flow as settlers accepted the richness of God's love for them.

Those ministry weekends brought great encouragement to Brainerd, for, after two years of ministry in the wilderness, the Native Americans were still reluctant to turn from their powwows to faith to Christ. Discouraged by their cold hearts, he was often "exceedingly depressed with a view of the unsuccessfulness of [his] labors." But all of that was about to miraculously change!

The Power of God Falls

In the summer of 1745, David was called by the Scottish Society to move to what would become the great mission field of his ministry—Crossweeksung, New Jersey. Brainerd was prepared to move to a new area. "My heart rejoiced in my particular work as a missionary," he wrote, "rejoiced in my necessity of self-denial in many respects; and still continued to give myself up to God, and implore mercy of him; praying incessantly, every moment with sweet fervency."[74]

Brainerd arrived in the village of Crossweeksung, which was just eight miles southeast of the town of Trenton, New Jersey. On the first day, things were quiet, as most of the region's natives had been driven west by the settlers, and only four women were in the small village to listen to his message.

To his surprise, by the next evening, the women had traveled throughout the area inviting other natives to hear the white missionary speak. On the third day, thirty Native Americans had gathered in Crossweeksung. Instead of the usual opposition, Brainerd found their hearts open to the gospel message, with a hunger to know more of God.

On the third day, thirty Native Americans had gathered in Crossweeksung. Instead of the usual opposition, Brainerd found their hearts open to the gospel message, with a hunger to know more of God.

Delighted, he wrote that night, "My soul was much refreshed and quickened in my work. This was indeed a sweet afternoon to me." But it was only the beginning!

By the end of the first week in Crossweeksung, more than forty Indians were gathered to listen to his messages. They were so eager to learn more that they asked him to preach about Christ twice daily!

In great joy he recorded, "I was enabled to speak the Word with much abundance and warmth. And the power of God attended the Word; so that sundry persons were made to shed many tears, and to wish for Christ to save them....O how heart-reviving and soul-refreshing it is to me to see the fruit of my labors!"[75]

Natives Overwhelmed by the Spirit

There are times when we plant God's Word for days, weeks, or even years, and then, one day, the floodgates burst open, and the Spirit of God pours down upon us like a mighty flood. Remember those biblical steps in spreading the gospel. *"I have planted, Apollos watered; but God gave the increase"* (1 Corinthians 3:6). Brainerd had been discouraged for a time as he planted and watered, but God was about to shower him with the increase!

Brainerd Preaching to the Indians.[76]

Preparing his heart to be used to the fullest in ministry, Brainerd wrote, "I long to spend the little inch of time I have in the world more for God. I feel a spirit of seriousness, tenderness, sweetness, and devotion; and wish to spend the whole night in prayer and communion with God."

On August 6, preaching to the Crossweeksung natives, David spoke on the love of God from 1 John 3:16: *"Hereby perceive we the love of God, because he laid down his life for us."* There were more than fifty Indians in the room, and nearly all of them were in tears or lying prostrate, crying out in distress that they had not accepted Christ's love before this. They were brought to their knees by the Holy Spirit's power at work within their souls.

When he asked them, "What would you like God to do for you?" their clear answer was, "We want Christ to wipe our hearts completely clean."[77]

The Weight of God's Glory Falls

Two days later, on August 8, 1745, the Holy Spirit swept through Crossweeksung in answer to David Brainerd's fervent prayers!

Sixty-five Native Americans filed into the house where Brainerd was preaching that afternoon. He spoke from Luke 14:23: *"And the lord said unto the servant, Go out into the highways and hedges, and compel them to come in, that my house may be filled."* Brainerd preached under a mighty anointing of the Holy Spirit.

After the message, he walked around the room, praying individually for men and women who lay prostrate under conviction, when, suddenly, "the power of God seemed to descend upon the assembly *'as of a rushing mighty wind'* (Acts 2:2), and with an astonishing energy bore down all before it!"

"I stood amazed," he marveled, "and could compare it to nothing more aptly than the irresistible force of a mighty torrent or swelling deluge, when its insupportable weight and pressure bears down and sweeps before it whatever is in its way!"[78]

Throughout the house, natives were praying and crying out for mercy. The ones who had already received their salvation were rejoicing in Christ and praying for their distressed friends, sharing the good news of Jesus' sacrificial love, and inviting them to give their hearts to Him.

A Murderer Is Redeemed

An old powwow, who was a former murderer and alcoholic, fell under the convicting power of God that day. Because he had murdered a young Indian, he had stayed away from the rest of the tribe for some time, although he still continued his conjuring practices. The powwow sat transfixed while listening to the message, and, when God's convicting Spirit fell, he wept and cried out for God's mercy on his life.[79]

Within the next few months, the old powwow totally surrendered his life to Christ and became what Brainerd described as a "humble, devout, and affectionate Christian."

A young woman who did not believe she even had a soul, and who had mocked David earlier the same day, cried out continually to the Lord in her native tongue, saying, "Have mercy on me and help me to give you my heart." This became a common cry among the natives in the village.

He did not use the fear of hellfire or God's judgment to reach the people's hearts but spoke instead of the sacrificial love of God and His mercy in sending His Son to save them.

The power of God continued to fall the following day. Brainerd spent the morning praying for weeping men and women who hungered for the salvation of Christ. Later in the day, as seventy Native Americans, both old and young, gathered to hear him preach, he spoke on Matthew 11:28: "*Come unto me, all ye that labour and are heavy laden, and I will give you rest.*" Tears of repentance and acceptance of Christ continued to flow.

Their hearts were so hungry for the Word of God that Brainerd continued to preach twice daily. He did not use the fear of hellfire or God's judgment to reach the people's hearts but spoke instead of the sacrificial love of God and His mercy in sending His Son to save them. What brought the great change was their understanding of the goodness and kindness of God. "*Or despisest thou the riches of his goodness and forbearance and longsuffering; not knowing that the goodness of God leadeth thee to repentance?*" (Romans 2:4). The kindness of God does more to change a person than a thousand years of hellfire and damnation sermons. We should follow that principle in our preaching of the Word of God today.

White settlers, hearing reports of strange happenings in the Native American village, began to join the meetings, suspicious at first, but then embracing the message of salvation for themselves.

On Sunday, August 25, Brainerd shared from Revelation 3:20: "*Behold, I stand at the door, and knock.*" That afternoon, he baptized twenty-five native adults and children who had repented and given their hearts to Christ. It was a joyous answer to prayer for the young man who had traveled thousands of miles, fighting exhaustion and disease, and had cried out to God "to see the Indians embrace Christ's saving grace."

God's Power and Strength

David Brainerd's call was to travel among the lost, so he set out in September to visit the natives in both the Susquehanna and the Forks of the Delaware. Although he still fought bouts of depression and illness, he was determined to see God's kingdom expand among the tribes. He saw a little more of the Holy Spirit's stirring among them on that trip, and left them with the hope that God would still move among them.

Riding on to New York, Brainerd traveled to the church in East Hampton for some much-needed Christian fellowship. He received comfort and strength from conversations with his friends about Christ and the missionary work.

In November, he went on to Long Island to meet with the Presbytery of the Scottish Society. There, he gave a glowing report on the supernatural move of

God's Holy Spirit in Crossweeksung. He returned to New Jersey greatly encouraged in his spirit.

"My Heart Was Knit to Them"

On January 1, 1746, Brainerd wrote, "I am this day beginning a new year, and God has carried me through numerous trials and labours in the past; he has amazingly supported my feeble frame....O that I might live nearer to God this year than I did the last!"[80]

Throughout the winter, he continued to push his body as he traveled the hundreds of miles between the three Native American tribes. The Crossweeksung natives continued to grow in Christ, and he wanted the Delaware Indians to be blessed, as well. With each trip, his body became more feeble, and his coughing spasms more intense. He would spend many days back in Crossweeksung recovering from the travels, preaching to the natives in God's strength alone.

By the spring of 1746, the Native Americans were asking for more than preaching. Although he was often too sick to stand, Brainerd began to teach them more detailed doctrines of the Christian faith. They would come to his house just to be near him and to talk more about Jesus. When he was with them, he "felt a sweet union of soul. My heart was knit to them; and I cannot say I have felt such a sweet and fervent lure to the brethren for some time past."

He celebrated his twenty-eighth birthday a short time later, rejoicing at the changes that had happened in his ministry during the previous year.

After considerable prayer, the natives and Brainerd decided that the Indians in the village should move to Cranberry, New Jersey, just fifteen miles away, where they could settle into a Christian community and start some much-needed schooling. Brainerd seriously considered settling down with them to be their pastor and to rest from his weary travels. But, he became convinced once again that his call was to save the lost: "My [call] has been and still is to go forth and spend my life in preaching the gospel from place to place and gathering souls afar off to Jesus the great Redeemer....And if ever my soul presented itself to God for service, without any reserve of any kind, it did so now" (May 22, 1746).

Always praying that the Spirit of God would move through the tribes at the Forks and Susquehanna, Brainerd continued to ride hundreds of miles to revisit them.

David Brainerd

Shaken by God

In August, at the one-year anniversary of the Spirit's move in Crossweeksung, Brainerd preached on Psalm 72, and he said that "the power of God seemed to descend upon the assembly, and when I prayed from Acts 4:31, '*And when they had prayed, the place was shaken*,' there was a shaking and melting among us; and many, I doubt not, were in some measure filled with the Holy Ghost."[81]

Always praying that the Spirit of God would move through the tribes at the Forks and Susquehanna, Brainerd continued to ride hundreds of miles to revisit them. But he couldn't spend as long as he wished, because of "[his] extraordinary weakness, having been exercised with great nocturnal sweats and a coughing up of blood in almost the whole of the journey."

With each trip, while his physical condition weakened, he continued to preach, determined that the Native Americans would hear the Word of God. While he was gone, the Crossweeksung Christians prayed day and night for his spiritual success.

In subsequent diary entries, he spoke of his physical decline. "I was so weak I could not preach"; and "spent this day, as well as the whole week past, under a great deal of bodily weakness, exercised with a violent cough, and a considerable fever."

Even through this sickness, the melancholy spirit of his earlier years did not return; it had finally been lifted. His encouragement was a result of the powerful move of the Holy Spirit that had brought his beloved Crossweeksung brothers and sisters into God's kingdom.

The Doctor's Orders

Little was known about tuberculosis and its cure in the early eighteenth century. Doctors recommended that the patient travel by horseback, riding out of doors as much as possible. Even thought he was quite ill, Brainerd made a journey on horseback into New England in an attempt to receive some healing. He was gone from November through March, visiting family and friends in Connecticut, Massachusetts, and New York. Even though he was ill and in pain, Brainerd could proclaim, "There is a God in heaven who overrules all things for the best; and this is the comfort of my soul....How blessed it is to grow more and more like God!"

In March 1747, he returned to Cranberry to visit with his beloved congregation. After spending a few precious days with them, praying and sharing the Word, he left for what would be the final time. He had baptized a total of eighty-five of the natives, and more were surrendering their lives to Christ each week. There were lengthy embraces and sad tears as they parted for the last time on this earth.

Brainerd traveled to Elizabethtown, where he met with his younger brother, John, who had been assigned to take over David's ministry in Cranberry. He reminded his brother, "Never think that you can live to God by your own power and strength, but always look to and rely on Him for assistance, yea, for all strength and grace."[82] While fellowshipping with John, Brainerd celebrated his twenty-ninth—and what would be his last—birthday. He set out the next day to ride through New England, hoping that it would bring some relief to the pain in his lungs.

Meeting Jerusha Edwards

On his last trip through New England, David stopped to visit a number of influential Christian friends. In Princeton, New Jersey, he spent time with Jonathan Dickinson, the first president of the new College of New Jersey. (In future years, both Aaron Burr Sr. and Jonathan Edwards would serve as the president of Princeton.) After a trip home to Haddam, Connecticut, to visit his family, Brainerd went on to Northampton, Massachusetts, to the home of Jonathan Edwards. Although they had met briefly when Edwards had presented Brainerd's case at Yale, they had not spent much time together.

While visiting, Brainerd became extremely ill and could not immediately continue his journey. He spent hours each day talking and praying with the Edwards family. During this visit, he developed a close friendship with Edwards' seventeen-year-old daughter, Jerusha. She was a sweet girl with a desire to serve others in the love of Christ. For years, Christian biographers had assumed that David and Jerusha had developed a romantic relationship and were engaged to be married. However, there is no actual record that their relationship went beyond a close Christian friendship.

After a trip on horseback to Boston in June, once again, in the hopes of prolonging his life, and visiting with a number of supportive Christian friends there, Brainerd made his final journey back to the warmth of the Edwards home in Northampton.

David Brainerd

Surrounded by Love

In August, Brainerd became confined to his bed on the first floor of the Edwards home. He continued to share nightly prayer time with the family and to be cared for by Jerusha.

David read his passionate prayers of both despair and triumph and was reminded once again that God had faithfully been with him every step of the way!

David was delighted to receive a visit from his brother, John, with the encouraging news that his flock in Cranberry was flourishing. During their visit, John turned to his satchel and retrieved a special package to present to his brother. He had collected David's personal diaries from his log cabin in New Jersey and brought them back to their author.

As he laid the precious journals in his brother's hands, David's tears flowed. What joys and sorrows, what heartaches and rejoicings, were contained in those pages! David read his passionate prayers of both despair and triumph and was reminded once again that God had faithfully been with him every step of the way![83]

David never intended for anyone to read his private writings, but when Jonathan Edwards requested permission to publish them, Brainerd gave his consent. He realized that his heartfelt prayers and experiences might help other missionaries for Christ. Never in his wildest dreams could he have imagined that these writings would still be ministering to Christians centuries later!

"My Heaven Is to Please God"

During September 1747, David's youngest brother, Israel, also an ordained minister, visited him in Northampton. He rejoiced that David's spirits remained uplifted and that his attention remained focused on the will of God.

As friends and fellow ministers visited and spoke of God's goodness, it was easy to see that Brainerd's days of depression were far behind him now. When Satan attacked him with thoughts that he was unworthy and not fit to see God in heaven, Brainerd remembered God's grace and "instantly appeared the blessed robes of Christ's righteousness, which I could not but exalt and triumph in!"

During his final days, he prayed often for the work of the ministers he knew, including his own brothers, that they "might be filled with the Holy Spirit" for the work God had called them to do. He prayed for the spiritual prosperity of his own congregation of Native Americans in New Jersey, dissolving into tears because of the love he held for each of them.[84]

Calm and content even in his last days, Brainerd was still writing,

> My heaven is to please God, and to glorify him, and to give all to him, and to be wholly devoted to his glory; that is the heaven I long for....I do not go to heaven to be advanced, but to give honour to God. It is no matter where I shall be stationed in heaven, whether I have a high or low seat there; but to love and please and glorify God is all....Had I a thousand souls, if they were worth anything, I would give them all to God![85]

Graduation

On Brainerd's last evening, his brother, John, was with him. They reminisced late into the night about David's beloved congregation in Cranberry and planned what John could do in the future to help advance the kingdom of God among them. David was delighted that John would bring them his final words of love to let them know that they had not been forgotten by him.

At six the following morning, October 9, 1747, David Brainerd graduated to heaven to see the Lord Jesus, whom he had loved and served so fervently. His funeral three days later was officiated by Jonathan Edwards and attended by Congregational and Presbyterian ministers, professors and administrators from the local universities, and scores of Christian friends who knew and loved him.

The Edwards family had drawn him into their hearts and greatly mourned his passing. A personal tragedy struck them when Jerusha became ill just four months later and died on February 14, 1748, possibly of the tuberculosis that had taken David's life. She was buried beside David Brainerd in the Northampton churchyard.

For Christ Alone

David Brainerd was a life to be reckoned with. His desire was for Christ and Him alone—and to present the kingdom of God to all who were lost. Although he was physically frail and wrestled with depression in his lifetime, he was a spiritual giant whose relentless dedication inspired many missionaries to courageously go where no one else had gone before in Jesus' name.

David Brainerd

Knowing that God would use Brainerd's personal diaries for much good, Jonathan Edwards published his edited version of *The Life and Diary of David Brainerd* in 1749. The writings inspired many men and women of God to praise Brainerd's work and devotion to Christ:

> Let every preacher read carefully over *The Life and Diary of David Brainerd*. Let us be followers of him, as he was of Christ, in absolute self-devotion, in total deadness to the world, and in fervent love to God and man.
>
> — John Wesley

David Brainerd's diary entries have shown countless generations the undeniable proof of God's unending faithfulness. Inspired by Brainerd to serve as a missionary to India, William Carey required his mission team to read Brainerd's diary three times every year. Henry Martyn, Robert Murray M'Cheyne, and Jim Elliot were each inspired by Brainerd's intense devotion to God's call to missions.

David Brainerd's diary entries have shown countless generations the undeniable proof of God's unending faithfulness.

In the end, David Brainerd's own words clearly reveal the unquenchable passion of his heart:

> Here I am, Lord, send me; send me to the ends of the earth, send me to the rough, savage pagans of the wilderness; send me from all that is called comfort in earth, send me even to death itself, if it be but in Thy service, and to promote Thy kingdom.[86]

Then I heard the Lord asking, "Whom should I send as a messenger to this people? Who will go for us?" I said, "Here I am. Send me." (Isaiah 6:8 NLT)

Will you answer the Lord's call?

Will you declare, "Here I am, Lord! Send me to the nations!"?

Chapter 3

William Carey

Missions Revelation: A Bible and a Map

The pansi boat rocked back and forth, taking on water, as it traveled up the Hooghly River toward the shores of India. Scarcely noticing, William Carey strained forward to glimpse the approaching shoreline. He was transfixed by the colors and bustling figures along the riverbank: dark men in turbans and wide cotton pants, women in bold-colored skirts and tunics, walking briskly toward the marketplace.

Almost before the boat docked, William jumped on land, gazing in wonder at the exotic sights: large wicker baskets perched on wooden stands and overloaded with fruits and vegetables in yellows, reds, and greens. Brightly-colored tents filled with brass bowls, candlesticks, woven fabrics, and household items he had never seen before. The background murmur of a new language filled his ears. As William walked along, he smelled the fish before he saw the fishermen's tables displaying the catch of the morning.

William Carey

The murmur behind him became a clamor; he turned to see a crowd of curious townspeople gathered around his family as they cautiously climbed from the boat. Small, brown-skinned children pushed forward giggling and reaching out to touch his wife, Dolly, and their four children as they stood on the strange shore. Dolly was wide-eyed and apprehensive as her eyes met his.

The day had finally arrived! After twelve years of planning and praying, he and his family had finally reached the shores of India, arriving just south of the city of Calcutta. Tears filled William's eyes as he gazed for the first time on the land he had labored to reach.

Although he didn't know it as he walked on the sands of India's shoreline, William Carey would not leave India for the rest of his life. God had called him to the overpopulated and un-evangelized nation, and he would zealously fulfill that call until his last breath.

Missionary Trailblazer

"To know the will of God, we need an open Bible and an open map!"
—William Carey

William Carey was a missionary trailblazer. He has been called "the father of modern missions" because his zeal ignited a missionary passion in eighteenth- and nineteenth-century Europe that reshaped modern Christianity.

Before Carey obeyed God's call to foreign lands, the Protestant church in Europe had little outreach abroad; even the widespread success of Ludwig Zinzendorf and the Moravian missionaries he sent throughout the world was still being ignored by the larger established denominations.

Carey's passion to bring the gospel to the lost in foreign lands birthed a missionary revolution.

Carey's passion to bring the gospel to the lost in foreign lands birthed a missionary revolution. Along with a group of men inspired by his pioneering vision, he founded the first British missionary society to send Christian disciples around the world. "Let us give ourselves up unreservedly to this glorious cause," he wrote. "Let us never think that our time, our gifts, our strength, our families are our own. Let us sanctify them all to God and His cause."

Carey was an extremely gifted man. He had an astounding ability to read new languages, and Carey and his team were responsible for translating the Bible into Bengali and twenty-nine other languages, printing the Word of God and supplying it to hundreds of thousands of Asians.

God used William Carey to spiritually awaken a sleeping church and to set it on fire to fulfill the Great Commission of Christ. He was a giant in Christian history and one of God's generals in the missionary world.

An Unexceptional Beginning

William Carey was born on August 17, 1761, in the small village of Paulerspury in central England. This exceptional man of God had an unexceptional beginning. He was the eldest of five children born to Edmund and Elizabeth Carey. The hardworking Careys were low-class weavers, living in a two-story cottage where they set up a loom to weave the woolen cloth known as "tammy."[87]

By the time William turned six, things improved dramatically; Edmund was hired to serve as both the parish clerk and the local schoolmaster, and the Careys gratefully gave up their weaving trade to live for free in the schoolhouse. It was a special blessing for William because it meant he could attend school.

Even at a tender age, William had an insatiable desire for knowledge. With his father working as the local schoolmaster, he had access to the few books in the village. He read everything he could get his hands on: the Bible, adventure novels, books on botany, anything in print. His mother was often awakened in the middle of the night by his reading aloud. She admitted, "So intent was he from childhood in the pursuit of knowledge. Whatever he began he finished; difficulties never seemed to discourage his mind."[88]

When Carey was just eleven years old, he found a small Latin textbook in his father's study. He took up the challenge to read it! The inquisitive boy pored over his father's Latin grammar book and taught himself the classic language. William's family was astonished! From that moment, they realized that God had blessed him with a unique gift of languages. Little did they know how that gift would inspire the Christian world!

Captain Cook's Hook

From childhood, William was afflicted with a disease that caused painful blisters on his face and hands from sun exposure. The worst part was that he loved the outdoors, spending hours wandering through the forest collecting unique leaves and butterflies, examining birds eggs and insects. Carey's love of botany remained strong throughout his life and was a source of pleasure and provision for him when he arrived in India years later.

By the time he reached sixteen, with little formal schooling, William Carey was one of the most educated young men in central England!

Because of his allergic reaction to the sun, William needed an indoor trade. At fourteen years old, he was apprenticed to Clarke Nichols, a cobbler in a town only eight miles from his home. Nichols encouraged Carey to read, even while he worked, recognizing that his young apprentice was different from the other boys.

In the next two years, Carey mastered both Greek and Hebrew, spending hours studying the primers. By the time he reached sixteen, with little formal schooling, William Carey was one of the most educated young men in central England!

Carey was obviously a leader from his earliest days. In the Bible, God develops great leaders at young ages—Joshua, Joseph, Gideon, David, and Timothy, to name just a few. We see this occurring in the world today, as well, and it gives us hope for the young people of this current generation.

Carey's brilliant imagination was captivated by the book *Captain Cook's Voyages*—it was the British sailor's personal journals of his adventures in the South Seas. Envisioning each foreign port, Carey was filled with an overwhelming desire to see them for himself. He later wrote, "Reading Cook's voyages was the first thing that engaged my mind to think of foreign missions." God had used a most unlikely bait to capture the heart of His servant!

John Wesley Preaches

Although Carey had little interest in the gospel, he attended the local parish church with his family; the Church of England was the official government-established church of the English people.

Invited to hear John Wesley preach in the English countryside, William heard the gospel delivered for the first time under the anointing of the Holy Spirit. Wesley preached of the need for a personal relationship with Jesus Christ and the power of God's sanctification by grace alone and not by the outward "holiness" of man. Hearing the message, Christians were leaving the Church of England in droves, claiming that it had lost its love of Christ. These Christians were called "Nonconformists" or "Dissenters," and included Baptists, Presbyterians, and Congregationalists.

John Warr, William's fellow apprentice, was a strong Baptist "Dissenter." During their workday, they had heated debates over whether salvation in Christ could really change men's lives. William was skeptical that he needed a personal Savior. But, before long, Warr's words pricked William's heart, and on February 10, 1779, at the age of seventeen, he attended a Dissenters prayer service.[89]

What a life-changing event! William was confronted with the plan of salvation and accepted Jesus Christ as his Lord and Savior. For days, he eagerly searched the Bible to discover more of the truth! Now on the same "team," the young apprentices spent their time reading the Bible aloud to each other as they completed their shoe-repair work. William was on fire to know more about Jesus.

The Importance of Choosing the Right Wife

Unexpectedly, Nichols, the shoe master, died; William had to complete his apprenticeship with cobbler Thomas Old. Within a short time, William met Dorothy (Dolly) Plackett, Old's pretty sister-in-law. From the outset, these two young people were different from each other; Dolly was not educated and was six years older than William. Christian historians have speculated on why a man who was so committed to learning would have married an unlearned woman. But William Carey was still a teenager when he met Dolly, and his reasons for the marriage never appeared in his journal writings.

I believe that William Carey married the wrong person. Because he was just a teenager and a new Christian, he married according to youthful passion and convenience instead of waiting for God to send the right person to fulfill his life and ministry—a potential snare I mentioned in an earlier chapter. Because Dolly knew little of the Lord before their marriage, he also violated Scripture by being unequally yoked.

I respect that William remained with her and looked after her for the rest of their challenging lives together. But I would like to encourage other young people to not rush in when choosing a life partner! Marry according to your destiny and calling in Christ. Pray for the direction of the Holy Spirit and make certain that your partner shares your ministry vision.

In the summer of 1781, just before his twentieth birthday, William married twenty-five-year-old Dolly Plackett at the twelfth-century church of St. John the Baptist, in Piddington. Because Dolly couldn't read or write, she signed an X on the church's marriage register.

Two years later, on October 5, 1783, William Carey was baptized in the River Nene near Northampton by John Ryland, who would become one of his closest friends. Later, Ryland spoke with amazement of the baptism of "this poor journeyman shoemaker," never imagining that this young man would have an unparalleled impact on the entire Christian world.

Ryland wrote, "It was the purpose of the Most High, who selected for this amazing work, not the son of one of our most learned ministers, nor of one of the most opulent of our dissenting gentlemen, but the poor son of a parish clerk."[90]

Too Many Deaths

William and Dolly began their marriage happy but incredibly poor. Not only was William a cobbler, but he also preached on Sundays at the Dissenters church, yet made little money. Within a short time, they had their first child, a baby girl named Ann. Tragically, when the baby was only eighteen months old, she and William became very ill with fever, and she died within days.

Heartsick, Dolly went to her funeral and then returned home to take care of her sick husband. William's mother arrived to help the young couple and discovered that they were destitute. She cleaned the house, took care of the grieving Dolly, and nursed William back to health. Even though Carey recovered, he strangely lost all the hair on the top of his head.

Zealously, Carey uncovered all the mysteries he could about foreign lands, and then created mural-sized maps for the students, with details on every country, capital, river, and mountain.

Trying to put the tragedy behind them, William and Dolly moved to a new cottage in Moulton. Dolly was haunted by the loss of her baby girl, but William threw himself into his work. On August 10, 1786, he was ordained as a Baptist minister and became the pastor of a small church and the local schoolmaster in Moulton. Working hard to provide for his family, he taught school during the weekdays, repaired shoes at night, and preached on Sundays.[91]

During this time, William also taught himself French, Italian, and Dutch. As a teacher, his most passionate subject in the schoolroom was geography. Zealously, Carey uncovered all the mysteries he could about foreign lands, and then created mural-sized maps for the students, with details on every country, capital, river, and mountain. As the months grew into years, his longing to see these lands for himself grew.

From 1785 to 1789, Dolly gave birth to three boys: Felix, William Jr., and Peter. Their laughter filled the house and helped ease the pain in Dolly's heart over the death of little Ann. But there were still times when Carey would find her sitting alone, staring into space or crying silently. William prayed for her full emotional health to return.

Unfortunately, childhood disease was too common in the eighteenth century. Dolly and William's fifth child, born in 1791, was another baby girl, Lucy. She was a sweet, healthy baby, but, during her second year, Lucy became ill with a sudden fever and died. Once again, Dolly retreated into a state of anguished depression. And once again, William dealt with it by pushing on with his work.

God of All Peoples

When God issues a call on a man or woman's heart, it might come in the roar of a thunderstorm or in the quiet of the night, but he or she hears His voice distinctly.

William had a growing conviction that God wanted to send Christian missionaries into a hopeless world. As he walked the English countryside in prayer, God brought Isaiah 54 to his remembrance: ***"Enlarge the place of your tent,** and let them stretch out the curtains of your dwellings....Your Redeemer is the Holy One of Israel; **He is called the God of the whole earth. For the LORD has called you**"* (Isaiah 54:2, 5–6 NKJV).

The Redeemer was not just the God of England or the God of Europe! He was *"the God of the whole earth,"* and Carey was determined to proclaim this missionary truth! Because of Zinzendorf's earlier missionary success, at a meeting with a small group of Baptist pastors in Kettering, England, William Carey threw down copies of the Moravian newsletter *Periodical Accounts* before the men and declared, "See what the Moravians have done! Can't we Baptists at least attempt something in fealty to the same Lord?"

Yet, every time he broached the subject with Christian leaders, the reaction was always the same. "You are a miserable enthusiast," he was rebuked. "If God wanted the heathen of the world to be saved, He would take care of it Himself. There are enough unsaved people in our own midst."[92]

Carey responded, "Surely God means what He says. Surely He means for us who know Him to carry the message of redemption to all men everywhere!"[93]

In spite of the church's objections, William sat down to write out his missionary vision. His writings grew into a booklet that he entitled *An Enquiry into the Obligations of Christians to Use Means for the Conversion of the Heathens*. It became known simply as *The Enquiry*. In it, William asserted, "If it be the duty of all men, when the gospel comes, to believe unto salvation, then it is the duty of those who are entrusted with the gospel to endeavor to make it known among all nations for the obedience of faith!"[94]

Carey skillfully presented his argument for world missions in *five powerful sections*. It was an astounding proclamation of God's call to reach the lost.

The Mission Revelation

Section One of *The Enquiry* focused on Jesus' Great Commission: "*Therefore go and make disciples of all nations, baptizing them...*" (Matthew 28:19 NIV). Carey insisted Jesus' command to evangelize could not be restricted to the early apostles, or else baptizing believers should be restricted as well. "No!" Carey declared. As long as the majority of the world was covered in "heathen darkness," Christians had an obligation to bring them the message of Christ's salvation.

"If the English have been blessed to know and live in the grace of God's salvation for a long while," he argued, "how could they withhold such a great salvation from those in foreign lands who died without the knowledge of God's saving grace?"[95]

Section Two of *The Enquiry* retold the powerful move of the Holy Spirit in the book of Acts, as thousands of Christians were added to the church daily. (See Acts 2:47.) Carey reminded his readers that it was the missionaries of the first and second centuries who had spread Christianity to England, Germany, Spain, France, Egypt, and Libya.

Section Three, entitled "A Survey of the Present State of the World," was a comprehensive account of the populations, religious beliefs, and locations of all the people of the known world, based on Carey's eight years of study. British scholars were astounded at its detail; nothing like it had been written before!

Most importantly, Carey pointed out that most countries had "no written language and consequently no Bible, and were only led by the most childish customs and traditions." With his gift for languages, Carey's heart burned to provide written Bibles to the lost. Even the most cynical opponents of foreign missions were convicted by the fervor of Carey's call.

Sections Four and Five of *The Enquiry* were practical applications of missionary work: the transportation of missionaries to their destinations, survival in foreign lands, and financial provision. He challenged his Christian brothers, "I question whether we are justified in staying here, while so many are perishing without means of grace in other lands!"

In describing the role of the missionary, Carey actually described himself:

> The missionary must take every opportunity of doing them [the lost] good, and laboring, and travelling, night and day, they must instruct, exhort, and rebuke, with all long suffering and anxious desire for them, and above all, must be instant in prayer for the effusion of the Holy Spirit upon the people of their charge.[96]

Carey ended the booklet with a stirring challenge: "Surely it is worthwhile to lay ourselves out with all our might, in promoting the cause and kingdom of Christ!"

"Expect Great Things! Attempt Great Things!"

Thomas Potts, a successful tradesman, read *The Enquiry* and offered to publish the essay at his own expense. Immediately, Carey had invitations to speak. During one meeting, at the Kettering Baptist Church under Pastor Andrew Fuller, Carey spoke the words that became his missionary battle cry: "Expect great things [from God]! Attempt great things [for God]!"

Preaching from his favorite Bible chapter, Isaiah 54, Carey declared to the church, "Rouse up from your complacency. Find larger canvas, stouter and taller tent poles, and stronger tent pegs. Catch wider visions. Dare bolder programs. Rouse up and go forth to conquer for Christ even the uttermost parts and isles of the sea."[97]

When the congregation sat without responding, Carey turned to Fuller and cried out, "And are you, after all, going again to do nothing!" Immediately, Fuller turned to the other ministers who were there and promised, "A plan will be prepared at the next meeting at Kettering for forming a Baptist Society for Propagating the Gospel Among the Heathen." At last, Carey's plea had been heard, and the missionary vision that would change the face of European evangelism was launched!

The First European Missionary Society Is Born

On October 2, 1792, a group of fourteen Baptist men joined with Carey to form the first European missionary society, which they named the Particular Baptist Society for Propagating the Gospel (later known simply as the Baptist Missionary Society). Their initial goal was to financially give as much as they could to mission work and then appeal to other Baptist churches to give.

Just as Jesus had His three closest disciples—Peter, James, and John—Carey had a trio of men who became the cornerstone of the Baptist Missionary Society: Andrew Fuller, John Sutcliff, and John Ryland. Friends since Carey's ordination ten years earlier, they would remain his devoted supporters for life.

Of the three, Andrew Fuller was the man who would work hand in hand with William for the next twenty-five years, even though he lived half a world away. Fuller was seven years older than Carey and was a self-educated farmer. In his future role as secretary of the missionary society, Fuller would successfully reach all of England, Scotland, and America with the message of Carey's work in India for the next quarter of a century.

In the body of Christ throughout the centuries, great ministries have usually had a group of dedicated Christian men as key supporters and administrators of the ministry. Evangelists Oral Roberts, Billy Graham, and Reinhard Bonnke, for example, have all had those dedicated men who remained faithful to Christ and to the specific ministry.

In the body of Christ throughout the centuries, great ministries have usually had a group of dedicated Christian men as key supporters and administrators of the ministry.

Just as in Carey's case, these are men who share the vision of the ministry leader. They do not have an ego problem. They are secure in their role for the cause of Christ. They provide fellowship, encouragement, and teamwork for the man or woman who is called to minister to thousands.

Today in the church, we are struggling with a "celebrity culture." Many people do not want to be called "alongside" the ministry leader. They believe that to be successful, they must have the popular, out-in-front personality. Rather than desiring celebrity status, we each should be looking for our role in team ministry, finding what we are to do in the advancement not of ourselves but of the kingdom of God.

"India, Here We Come!"

As the new mission team began its search for its first missionary applicant, Carey received a letter from Dr. John Thomas, an English physician who had lived in Bengal, India, for the last four years while working for the East India Company. Thomas was a surgeon who had already made two voyages to Calcutta. As an early medical missionary, he ministered to both the physical and spiritual needs of the Indian people, but now he wanted to return to India as a missionary of the gospel.

William was thrilled at their first meeting and pummeled the doctor with questions about Indian life and languages. He was delighted to hear Thomas's account of Brahmin leaders who had requested New Testament translations in the native Bengali language.

At that moment, William Carey clearly heard the call of God—he was to serve the people of India! When Dr. Thomas requested a companion minister to double the missionary effort, William responded immediately, "I will go!"

He turned to the mission board members for confirmation. "We saw," said Andrew Fuller "there was a gold mine in India, but it was as deep as the center of the earth. Who will venture to explore it?"

"I will venture to go down," said Carey, "but remember that you [addressing Fuller, Sutcliff, and Ryland] must hold the ropes."

"We solemnly promised him to do so," Andrew responded, "nor while we live shall we desert him."[98]

And this great team of anointed men of God did not desert Carey throughout their long ministry together. The date of Carey's missionary commitment was January 10, 1793.

Miracles and Obstacles

Carey was resolved to go, but there was so much that needed to be done. The team had to set sail for India in April to complete the five-month ocean journey before the monsoon winds hit the Indian Ocean. And while Dr. Thomas's wife and daughter were excited to be returning to India, William was facing the prospect of going alone. Dolly refused to even consider going to "the ends of the earth" among foreign people and the Indian jungles.

What could William be thinking? She was pregnant with their sixth child, so they would have four children with them in the strange land of India, one a newborn infant. All of the pleading on William's part was to no avail, until Dolly finally agreed to allow their oldest son, eight-year-old Felix, to go with his father.

The challenges continued. Carey and Andrew Fuller traveled hundreds of miles throughout England trying to raise the funds through the Baptist churches. Small congregations contributed what they could. But, not a single Baptist church in London would financially support the venture. The church leaders were certain that it would be a miserable failure and that it would do nothing to advance the kingdom of God! They were advised by Dr. Samuel Stennett, a well-known pastor and hymn writer, to "stand aloof and not commit themselves."[99]

Despite the obstacles, God's hand was directing their course. While they were traveling, Carey met a young printer named William Ward. Both men were confident that someday Ward would join the venture in India and help to print Indian-language Bibles. Carey saw this chance meeting as God's hand of blessing on the trip in the midst of all the challenges.

Three Were Saying No

To William Carey, it appeared that everyone wanted to stop him from his mission: first Dolly, then the Baptist churches, and now the powerful British East India Company.

For over one hundred years, the British East India Company had a royal charter that gave them complete control over all trade between India and England. To protect their monopoly, the company convinced Parliament to ban any British missionaries from India's shores without their express permission. The company was afraid that if the people were trained in the gospel and Western ways, they would no longer agree to the open trading agreement that had made the company rich and powerful.

It was a flagrant insult to the gospel by members of a "Christian" nation! No means of persuasion would allow British missionaries Carey and Thomas entrance into India. As a result, April 1793 came and went, so that the English ship on which they had originally planned to travel, the *Oxford,* sailed with only Mrs. Thomas and her daughter aboard. Carey, Felix, and Thomas were forced to stay behind, looking for another avenue.

While they prayed for God's next step, Carey uncovered a disturbing secret concerning Dr. Thomas. In the days leading up to the departure, Thomas had begun acting suspiciously. Carey was perplexed until he discovered that Thomas was in heavy debt, owing several hundred pounds to different companies and friends in England and India. Thomas admitted his weakness in handling finances and promised Carey he would take care of the debt as soon as possible. Unfortunately, this weakness would continue to plague the ministry for years.[100]

Danish Miracle Boat

In spite of the setbacks, Carey and Thomas knew they belonged in India. Walking through the English countryside, Carey cried out to the Lord to give them a way past the East India Company restrictions and onto Indian shores.

When Carey arrived back at the house, Dr. Thomas burst through the door with a new scheme. "I have the address of a Danish seaman," he said. "He is waiting for his ship to dock in England on its way to India. If God is with us, there may be room aboard. Come let's hurry!"[101]

Thomas explained that if they traveled on a non-English ship, the captain would not require the same travel permits as the East India Company. A Danish ship, the *Kron Princess Maria,* was preparing to leave England and could take them to Serampore, India, a Danish-controlled city outside of the East India Company's jurisdiction.

Carey was exhilarated with the new plan. God was miraculously opening the doors for their journey! In faith, Carey decided to plead one more "impossible" case before Him.

"God, please change Dolly's mind!" William wanted to make the journey with his wife and all his children. Dolly had given birth to their newest child, a baby boy whom they named Jabez, and had recovered enough to make the trip. But how could he get her to change her mind?

Two important jobs occupied Thomas and Carey: persuade Dolly to make the journey and raise additional funds to take his entire family aboard the *Kron Princess Maria* before she set sail for India. The men traveled quickly to Piddington, England, where Dolly was staying with her sister, Kitty.

Miracle Money

At first, Carey's pleas went unheeded. Dolly refused to consider the dangers of a trip halfway around the world with three young boys and an infant. Then, Dr. Thomas stepped inside the cottage door and firmly reminded a sobbing Dolly Carey that her place was by her husband's side, and that it was God's will both to send William to India and to keep their family together. It seemed they had reached a complete impasse when Kitty stood to her feet and announced, "I will go with you so that Dolly has someone to help with the children." With wide eyes, Dolly acquiesced. "All right," she said resignedly, "we will go together!"[102] The house was in an uproar as they hurriedly packed their belongings for the five-month trip to India.

Now there was just the issue of the passage money to resolve. They needed an additional four hundred and fifty pounds to pay for Dolly, Kitty, and the children. William prayed, "God, You have brought me this far. You have even got Dolly and the children to come. Surely You will show us a way to get to India."[103]

Carey turned to the faithful John Ryland for help. Ryland managed to raise another two hundred pounds from Christian friends in just a day, but they were still two hundred fifty pounds short. How would they make up the difference?

Once again, the resourceful Thomas came up with an innovative solution. Servants were able to travel for free, so he and Kitty signed up for the voyage as the Careys' servants. They were still a bit short of funds, but Captain Christmas of the *Kron Princess Maria* welcomed the missionaries aboard with the money they were able to pay. God's provision was continuing to meet their needs even at the final hour.

Goodbye, Homeland; Hello, Destiny

As the *Kron Princess Maria* sailed out into the English Channel, William and Dolly turned to look at their homeland fading from view. Each would have been shocked to know that it was the last time they would ever see England.

Carey's journal entry that night was full of praise: "Thursday, June 13, 1793, on board the *Kron Princess Maria*. This has been a day of gladness to my soul. I was returned that I might take all of my family with me and enjoy all the blessings which I had surrendered to God."[104]

One more obstacle stood between Carey and India. As male British citizens, Carey and Thomas could not even set foot on India's soil without permission from the British East India Company. By an Act of Parliament ten years earlier, every subject of the king going to or from the East Indies without a license from the company was "guilty of a high crime and misdemeanor, and liable to fine and imprisonment." To circumvent this law, Captain Christmas contacted a pilot boat to take the families off the ship and up the Hooghly River to a part of the shore where there were no authorities. And so the Careys found themselves lurching toward the Indian shoreline in a fragile pansi boat, waiting to begin their great adventure in God.

On November 7, 1793, William Carey and John Thomas stepped onto the soil of Bengal, India. As soon as his family and their belongings were ashore, Thomas began to preach a Christian message in Bengali to the people at the marketplace. For three hours, they listened, and Carey rejoiced! The missionary work in India had finally begun!

A Stranger in a Strange Land

Within weeks of their arrival, trouble loomed. Dr. Thomas had grossly underestimated the amount of money they would need to become established in India. Because of his many debtors, Thomas's first priority was to set up a medical practice and to begin to earn some wages. Without consulting Carey, he used the funds meant for the mission to set up his practice in Calcutta.

Unaware of their financial condition, William heard of a piece of land that his family of three adults and four children could move onto free of rent, but he needed some start-up funds to make the move and plant fields for their food. Carey requested the necessary money from Thomas. In disbelief, he was told that all of the mission money was gone, and he and his family were destitute.

Desolate, Carey wrote in his diary that night, "I am in a strange land, alone, no Christian friend, a large family, and nothing to supply their wants. I blame Mr. T. for leading me into such expense and I blame myself for being so led."[105]

Feeling guilty over his selfishness, Thomas borrowed more money and gave it to William for the family's move into the Indian wilderness. In the next few months, the Carey family moved twice, traveling down alligator-infested rivers, trying to find a place to settle. They finally ended in the jungles of the Sundarbans, a wild and dangerous region that was plagued by tigers, swamps, and suspicious natives. Kitty and Dolly were frightened and complained daily about their surroundings.

Carey began a serious study of the Bengali language, convinced that his first job was to translate the New Testament into the native tongue.

Carey's diary entry reads, "My wife and my sister, too, who do not see the importance of the mission as I do, are continually exclaiming against me....If my family were but hearty in the work, I should find a great burden removed."[106]

Undaunted, Carey planted his crops, worked with the natives, and provided for Dolly and the children. Amazingly, as he worked in the hot Indian sun, his painful skin condition never reoccurred; he had been miraculously healed to serve in India! While in the Sundarbans, Carey began a serious study of the Bengali language, convinced that his first job was to translate the New Testament into the native tongue. Within a few months, Carey's faith and labor were rewarded with a remarkable offer.

Healed and Prosperous

Carey was a man of great faith. He never expected ongoing financial support from the missionary society. Once he was in India, he would provide for his family by his own abilities, with the Lord's leading.

While he was in the Sundarbans, Carey received a letter from Dr. Thomas with an unusual opportunity for both of them from a Christian business owner named George Udney. Udney had two indigo plants in the Mudnabatti area, and he needed a manager for each of them. Thomas and Carey would operate different plants, and, in exchange for their work, each would receive a two-story house and a yearly salary of two hundred fifty pounds. The offer was beyond Carey's wildest expectations![107]

Elated, Carey ran to tell Dolly the good news. Finally, he would be able to provide for his family and still have the funds for the continued translation of the Bible into Bengali. But Dolly was saddened by the news. It would be their third strenuous move since arriving in India the previous November. She was often sick with dysentery, and she knew the relocation would involve another arduous voyage up the Hooghly River—three long, hot weeks in a small boat with four young boys. To make matters worse, her sister, Kitty, decided to stay behind to marry Charles Short, an Englishman and the manager of the East India Company's salt factory. But, in tears, she packed for the trip.

When they finally arrived in Mudnabatti in the summer of 1794, the Careys found a lovely large house and a workforce eager to see the factory prosper. William was convinced that the Lord was directing his steps. His work in both the factory and in the Bible translation was moving quickly; he had learned the Bengali language with ease. Within a week of his arrival in India, he could preach short messages without an interpreter.

Carey wrote, "All my hope is in, and all my comfort arises from, God; without His power no European could possibly be converted, and His power can convert any Indian; and when I reflect that He has stirred me up to do this work, and wrought wonders to prepare the way, I can hope in His promises, and am encouraged and strengthened!"[108]

The Devil Attacks Dolly's Instability

In the fall of 1794, Dolly and Carey were both stricken with dysentery; Carey's fever was so high that he almost died. As he was slowly recovering, dysentery overcame his five-year-old, Peter. His small body couldn't handle the fever and constant diarrhea, and within a few hours, the lively young boy had died.

Once again, William and Dolly experienced the anguish of losing a child. But for Dolly, it was worse than in the past; this time, she slipped into a depression where William could not reach her. He prayed that she would recover once again. She did for a short while, but by March 1795, Dolly began experiencing the first of many delusions concerning her husband and their marriage.

Carey recorded in his diary, "I have had very sore trials in my own family, from a quarter which I forbear to mention. Have greater need for faith and patience than ever I had, and I bless God that I have not been altogether without supplies of these graces."[109] Carey was trying to cope with his wife's mental instability by leaning on the Lord. However, it seems to have often overwhelmed him.

Some Christian historians have questioned what happened to Dolly Carey. It was obvious that she was prone to depression, that she went to India under duress, and that she lost three precious children to disease. Although there aren't many journal entries regarding his marriage, a letter from Carey to Dolly before they left for India reveals his earnest love for his family:

> Tell my dear children I love them dearly, and pray for them constantly. Felix sends his love. Trust in God. Love to Kitty, brothers and sisters. Be assured I love you most affectionately. I am, forever, your faithful and affectionate husband, William.[110]

For a brief time in 1795, Dolly again seemed to be recovering from her mental illness, and, shortly after, she became pregnant with their seventh and final child. Another son was born to the Careys in early 1796, a healthy boy whom they named Jonathan. But almost immediately after, Dolly's mental health slipped again, followed by a complete break from reality. Dolly experienced frequent delusions, hysterically accusing her husband of having affairs with many women, including Mrs. Thomas and the mission's servants.

Dr. Thomas wrote to the Baptist Missionary Society in London on Carey's behalf: "Mrs. Carey has uttered the most blasphemous and bitter imprecations against him, when Mrs. Thomas and myself were present." He went on to describe times when she threatened Carey's life, and why she had to be confined to her bedroom. A few months after Jonathan's birth, Carey wrote in his journal, "My poor wife must be considered as insane, and is the occasion of great sorrow."

Although few details of Dolly's sickness were ever recorded, it was certainly the darkest place in Carey's life, and it has opened him up to some criticism over the years. At what point did he realize how serious her periods of melancholy were? Did he sacrifice his wife's health in his drive to translate the Bible into so many languages? These questions are not possible to answer, since there are so few diary entries concerning Dolly's illness. But no man who has served the Lord has ever been perfect in his service.

Accused as Spies

William Carey's plan to evangelize India was divided into three parts: preach the gospel of Christ, translate the Bible into as many dialects as possible, and establish schools for biblical and secular training.[111] This was an impossible task

William Carey's plan to evangelize India was divided into three parts: preach the gospel of Christ, translate the Bible into as many dialects as possible, and establish schools for biblical and secular training.

for one man, no matter how driven he was to work day and night. Andrew Fuller understood this, and so he found four men—William Ward, Joshua Marshman, William Gant, and David Brunsdon, along with their families—to send to India in an American ship, the *Criterion*, commanded by Captain Wickes. (Unfortunately, Gant and Brunsdon died of cholera within the first few months of their arrival in India.)

On October 17, 1799, the *Criterion* docked in India with its British cargo and the new missionaries for William Carey's work. To Carey's surprise, he found that the Baptist Missionary Society had not sent two missionaries but eight adults and five children, for whom he would now be responsible. Carey was especially delighted to hear that William Ward, the printer he had met six years earlier, was among them.

Once again, the British East India Company fought the arrival of these new missionaries. Someone reported that the missionaries were French Papists, and the British government immediately accused them of being French spies! The group fled during the night to Danish-controlled Serampore to escape British capture and prison. There was no way they could join Carey in Mudnabatti; their only option was to stay in Serampore.

Who Likes to Move?

Now Carey faced a difficult decision. Should he stay with his work at the indigo factory and use his printing presses there, or should he move his family once again and set up the mission in Serampore? Carey desperately needed the expertise of William Ward, and he was longing for Christian fellowship. His decision was made, and on January 10, 1800, the Carey family took up residence at Serampore, their final move in India.[112]

God's ways are wondrous when we put our trust in Him! What the enemy meant for evil in their flight to Serampore, God meant for good! In His divine providence, He had placed William Carey in the most densely populated area of India, where he could be used mightily by the Lord for the next thirty-four years.

Carey had always envisioned a Christian community of missionary workers. In Serampore, he and his fellow missionaries set up their living quarters in one large house with a chapel in the center and separate family rooms on either side. They made a voluntary agreement that everyone's earnings would be deposited into a common account, and would be used for the mission's needs above anything else. After seven years of lonely labor, Carey saw his vision of a God-honoring mission settlement finally coming to pass.[113]

An Unbeatable Team of Firsts

William Ward and Joshua Marshman had been handpicked by the Lord to join Carey's ministry. They would serve beside him and encourage him—as Timothy and Titus blessed Paul in the New Testament—for the next three decades.

William Ward was a kindred spirit who shared Carey's vision for printing Bibles and Christian tracts in as many dialects as possible. He set up the first large printing press in India, and they quickly published, separately, each of the four Gospels in Bengali. Carey planted God's Word by giving away copies of the Gospels to the curious natives.

Ward was also a mentor for Carey's sons. The four boys, ages four to fourteen, would run wild in the mission compound because their father was too busy and their mother was too ill to care for them. Ward and the Marshmans worked together to bring stability to the children's lives. God especially used William Ward in Felix Carey's rebellious young life; Ward taught Felix how to run the printing presses and eventually led him to Christ. Later in life, Felix spoke fondly of his mentor: "How often he has upheld me when my feet well-nigh slipped! He was my spiritual father."

Joshua Marshman was the other spiritual partner in Carey's missionary work. Marshman, Ward, and Carey became known in India, England, and America as the Serampore Triad, because of how well they worked together under the direction of the Holy Spirit. Joshua was gifted in translation work and learned Bengali quickly, so he joined Carey in preaching the gospel.

Marshman and his wife, Hannah, understood the importance of education. Shortly after arriving, they opened two boarding schools for English children and one free school for Indian children. Over the next seventeen years, the Serampore Mission would found more than one hundred schools to educate thousands of English and Indian children throughout India.

Hannah Marshman was officially the first woman missionary to India. She served as a "mother," taking care of mentally ill Dolly and all of the staff working at the Serampore Mission. Along with William Ward, Hannah disciplined and loved the unruly Carey children, and she was loved by everyone who knew her.[114]

Carey exhorted this team at the beginning of their work together:

> Let us often look at David Brainerd in the woods of America, pouring out his very soul before God for the perishing heathen....Prayer, secret, fervent believing prayer, lies at the root of all personal godliness....Let us give ourselves unreservedly to this glorious cause. Let us never think that our times, our gifts, our strength, our families, or even the clothes we wear are our own. Let us sanctify them all to God and His cause.[115]

The First Indian Convert

By 1800, Carey had served in India for seven years without a single Indian convert. Carey was not only a man of unfathomable zeal but also one of "unconquerable persistence." He often referred to himself as a "plodder," but his companions knew his tenacity brought powerful results.

For seven years, Carey had preached God's Word to the Indian people and prayed for their salvation. Finally, his prayers were answered. Dr. Thomas, who had returned to work at Serampore, led the mission's first Indian convert to the Lord.

Finally, his prayers were answered. Dr. Thomas, who had returned to work at Serampore, led the mission's first Indian convert to the Lord.

Krishna Chandra Pal was working near Serampore as a carpenter. One day, while bathing in the nearby river, Krishna Pal slipped, fell, and dislocated his right shoulder. Knowing that Thomas was a medical doctor, he sent to the mission for help. While Thomas took care of his shoulder, he talked to Krishna Pal about the healing of his soul and offered him a tract in Bengali. After the accident, Carey and Thomas often discussed Scriptures with Krishna Pal at the mission.

One morning, Krishna Pal confessed to Dr. Thomas, "I am a great sinner; but I have confessed my sin and I am free!" Rejoicing, Dr. Thomas replied, "Then I call you my brother. Come and let us eat together in love." This was an unheard-of invitation at the time—a Hindu eating with a non-Hindu would be breaking caste, which was culturally forbidden. The caste system in India did not allow Hindus to mix with members outside of their caste status or with foreigners.[116]

In the following days, Krishna Pal was attacked by his fellow villagers and accused of being a traitor. Despite the pressure, on December 28, 1800, he was baptized in the Hooghly River, along with Felix Carey.

"Yesterday was a day of great joy," William recorded. "I had the happiness to baptize the first Hindu, Krishna, and my son Felix. Krishna's coming forward gave us very great pleasure. We have toiled long, and have met with many discouragements; but, at last, the Lord has appeared for us."[117]

Soon after, Krishna Pal led his wife, sister, and four daughters to Christ, followed by his neighbors. Petumber Singh, an educated Hindu, came to Christ and accepted the job of a schoolmaster at the Mission schools.

The long-awaited harvest had begun!

The Word of God...in Bengali

March 5, 1801, was a day to remember in Serampore. The complete Bengali New Testament was finally printed and bound in special black leather. This New Testament was the heart of eight years of labor for Carey and months of work from the printing staff. Carey had also learned Sanskrit, the language of the educated people of India. While studying it, Carey said it was "the hardest language in the world."[118] But, before long, he mastered it and then began working on a Sanskrit New Testament.

That same year, Fort William College was founded in nearby Calcutta to train young Englishmen to lead in finance and government. They needed to learn Bengali and Sanskrit to be successful. Who was better equipped to teach them than William Carey? He was the only Englishman fit to be a professor of Bengali and Sanskrit in India.

With no textbooks, Carey wrote a grammar book for both languages to use in the classroom. With little formal education and no college background, Carey was first an instructor, then a professor, and finally dean of the department of native languages in this prestigious British college, where he would work for the next thirty years.

William Carey, engraved by J. Jenkins.[119]
(Ken Welsh/Bridgeman Art Library)

Carey knew the job was God's provision for his real work: translating the Bible and spreading the Word. With his salary, he purchased additional printing equipment and paper, and he hired workers for the presses. Through the college, Carey also became so well-connected to British leaders that he was allowed greater freedom in his evangelizing and translating work.

Soon after, Carey and Ward wrote and printed the first Bengali dictionary for use by college students and government leaders alike. Within two years of his new position, Carey excitedly wrote to Fuller, "We have opened a place of worship in Calcutta where we preach on Sunday, Wednesday, and Thursday in English and Bengali."[120] For the next thirty years, Carey spent as much time in Calcutta as he did in Serampore, spreading the gospel of Christ in the bustling Indian city.

In the fall of 1801, Dr. Thomas contracted a raging fever and died on October 13 at forty-four years old. His health had been steadily failing. In spite of Thomas's difficulties in handling finances, he had been loyal to the missionary vision to the end of his life, and Carey greatly missed his friend.

The Killing Fields of India

Human kindness and social reform were always close to Carey's heart. As a boy, he had secretly cheered for the American colonies to win their freedom from England and refused to pray for an English victory at King George's command. He was outspoken against slavery in the late 1700s, long before it was abolished in England.

Once arriving in India, Carey was sickened by more than one Hindu practice that destroyed innocent lives. Newborn babies were sacrificed to the Ganges River god to bring good luck or to appease the false god's anger. Carey wrote to the British governor-general, Lord Wellesley, pleading for this practice to be put to an end. The decree to ban infanticide was finally written into law in 1802.

Another horrific Hindu custom, called *sati*, or "method of purity," took many more years of prayer, petitions, and pleading before the British governor-general finally banned the practice. Sati was the practice of burning widows alive on the funeral pyres of their deceased husbands. According to the Hindu clerics, the widow was promised that "if she will offer herself on the funeral pile, she shall rescue her husband from misery and take him and fourteen generations of his and her family with her to heaven, where she shall enjoy with them celestial happiness."[121]

To Carey's horror, the widows agreed to the practice, allowing themselves to be tied down to the funeral pyre and burned along with their husband's corpse. It would take nearly thirty years of outrage and prayer by the Christian missionaries before sati was finally declared illegal in India.

The Gift of Charlotte

After twelve years of suffering from delusional paranoia, Dolly Carey died on December 7, 1807, at fifty-one years of age. Carey wrote a letter to his son Felix, who was, by then, a missionary to Burma:

> Your poor mother grew worse and worse from the time you left us, and died on the 7th December about seven o'clock in the evening. During her illness she was almost always asleep, and I suppose during the fourteen days that she lay in a severe fever she was not more than twenty-four hours awake. She was buried the next day in the missionary burying-ground.[122]

There are few diary notes on the tragedy of Dolly's final decade and death, or on how William Carey felt at the end of their twenty-six-year marriage. Perhaps the helplessness he felt concerning his wife's illness accounted for his frequent comments on his own unworthiness and his desperate need for the grace of God to complete his mission work.

For some time, the Serampore missionaries had been friends with Charlotte Emilia Rumohr, a Danish countess who lived in the large home next to the mission. She had joyfully witnessed the baptisms of Krishna Pal and Felix, and had then become a supporter of the missionary work. She was a petite, well-educated woman, fluent in seven languages, and had a heart to serve Jesus Christ.

During her teen years, Charlotte had been burned severely in a fire, which had injured her legs. She moved to India with her family in the hopes that the warm climate would bring healing. Although she spent a good bit of the day lying on her couch, she was still a positive influence for Christ to everyone who knew her.

Six months after Dolly's death, in May 1808, Carey and Charlotte were married. They were both forty-six years old at the time. Even though Charlotte had to spend much of her day resting, she was an enormous encouragement to her husband, helping him with his challenging translation work and the growing ministry. Their thirteen years of marriage were happy ones. Carey shared, "We enjoy the most entire oneness of mind. Her solicitude for my health and comfort is unceasing, and we pray and converse together on those things which form the life of personal religion, without the least reserve."[123] William Carey had been blessed with his soulmate.

During the years of their marriage, three of Carey's sons, Felix Jr., William, and Jabez, were missionaries in parts of India, Burma, and the Spice Islands. Felix became a skilled medical missionary, as well as a scholar and a printer. The young men had been raised in the gospel's power and went out to successfully continue the work for Christ. Jonathan, Carey's youngest son, chose a law profession instead and worked in the city of Calcutta, not far from the Serampore work.

A Devastating Fire

As William Carey's influence in India grew, new Bible translations rolled fresh off the printing presses, and his successes were reported around the world. In 1807, he was given a Doctor of Divinity degree by Brown University in America. In 1808, the New Testament was published in Sanskrit. In 1809, the entire Bible was published in Bengali. In 1811, New Testaments in Marathi and Punjabi were completed. By 1812, the entire Bible was translated into Sanskrit.

The Serampore team also spent five years, from 1807 to 1812, working on what Carey called *A Universal Dictionary of the Oriental Languages.* Derived from Sanskrit, Carey declared it was to help "biblical students to correct the translation of the Bible in the Oriental languages after we are dead." Seen as an astounding triumph, it was finally ready to go to press.

Then disaster struck! On the evening of March 11, 1812, as William Ward sat at his desk completing the day's work, smoke began to pour from the hall from the south side of the print shop. Quickly, Ward closed all the windows and doors, and he, Joshua Marshman, and the native workers poured water through the roof for four hours until the fire appeared to be out.

Tragically, as Ward and Marshman checked for damages, someone (who was never discovered) opened several windows in the print shop, and the fire blazed back to life, sweeping through every corner of the building.[124]

The next day, William gathered his heartbroken colleagues around him and said, "We must stay the course, trusting God, who has brought us safe thus far. We can rebuild and replace what was lost."

In the devastating loss, the final draft of the universal dictionary, ten different versions of the Bible, several other manuscripts, and many hand-cut type fonts were completely destroyed. With tears streaming down his face, Carey walked among the ruins with Marshman and Ward.

"In one evening," he said, "the labours of years are consumed. How unsearchable are the ways of God!"[125] William and Charlotte wept together in anguish over the loss of so many years of work.

Once again, Carey turned to his Savior and left the tragedy in God's hands. He didn't understand, but he trusted the God who was the Author and Finisher of his faith. Fortunately, five printing presses and much of the foundational type had survived. The next day, William gathered his heartbroken colleagues around him and said, "We must stay the course, trusting God, who has brought us safe thus far. We can rebuild and replace what was lost."[126]

Famous Around the World!

To William's astonishment, the Serampore disaster made his mission famous all over Europe and America. When the news of the fire reached Europe, churches throughout the continent prayed for the mission and sent ten thousand pounds to India to fund the replacement of what had been lost. Andrew Fuller had to circulate a letter asking people to stop sending money! Hearing of the mission's success in the gospel, churches in England and the United States requested a portrait of William Carey to place in their halls in his honor.

And so, in His faithfulness, God used the fire disaster for the good. God doesn't cause these things to happen, but He is faithful to make good come from there. *"And we know that all things work together for good to those who love God, to those who are the called according to His purpose"* (Romans 8:28 NKJV).

As British churches took notice of all that the Serampore mission was accomplishing for Christ in India, they petitioned Parliament to immediately end the East India Company's ban on missionaries. William Wilberforce, the dynamic force behind the banning of slavery in England, joined the missionary cause. Wilberforce declared that the fight to allow missionaries in British India was "the greatest of all causes, for I really place it even before the abolition, in which, blessed be God, we gained the victory!"[127]

In 1813, the British Parliament amended the charter of the East India Company to allow missionaries to enter the country at will "to promote the happiness of the Indian people."[128]

Although the cause of the Serampore fire was never discovered, what Satan meant for evil, God used for great good for the Indian people. Within one year of the fire, Carey reported to John Ryland, "Thirteen out of eighteen translations are now in the press, including a third edition of the Bengali New Testament. Indeed, so great is the demand for Bibles that though we have eight presses constantly at work I fear we shall not have a Bengali New Testament to sell or give away for the next twelve months, the old edition being entirely out of print.

"We are going to set up two more presses, which we can get made in Calcutta, and are going to send another to Rangoon. In short, though the publishing of the Word of God is still a political crime here, there never was a time when it was so successful! '*Not by might, nor by power, but by my spirit, saith the* Lord *of hosts*' (Zechariah 4:6)."

Missionary Society Under Attack

With the ban lifted, the Baptist Missionary Society quickly sent additional missionaries to India. The first one to arrive at Serampore, on August 1, 1814, was Eustace Carey, William's nephew. Several new missionaries followed shortly after, and what should have been a great blessing was turned by Satan into a spiritual disaster.

The new missionaries were eager young men with their own ideas of how to run a Christian mission. Carey was grieved as they impatiently disagreed with the more mature missionaries at every turn, eventually complaining to the missionary board back in England. At one point, they even accused Carey of accumulating personal wealth, although all of the money he had ever received for his work had been deposited into the common mission account.

To make matters worse, in June 1814, Carey's staunch mission board supporter, John Sutcliff, had died. The following year, Carey's dearest friend and confidante, Andrew Fuller, became gravely ill and died, as well. The death of Andrew Fuller affected Carey more deeply than any other. For almost a quarter of a century, Fuller had "held the ropes" as he had promised, and there was no other brother in Christ that Carey loved as much.[129]

That year, the leadership of the Baptist Missionary Society passed into the hands of a new generation. Carey had been gone from England for more than twenty years, and most of the new missionary board members had never met him. In an attempt to gain control of its world-famous missionary work, the board issued an order that all of the Serampore mission property must be signed over to their committee at once. Heartsick at this turn of events, Carey quietly refused.

Mission Split

The Serampore Mission had been run by the leading of the Holy Spirit for over two decades. Carey was convinced that it was not God's will that it should be run by a committee from the other side of the world. When a new missionary printer, William Pearce, was sent from the Baptist Missionary Society, he and the other young missionaries deserted the Serampore Mission to set up one of their own.

Carey was heartbroken, especially because his nephew, Eustace, was one of the leading dissenters. To Carey's great disappointment, the young men did not venture out to an un-evangelized part of India but remained in the same area, establishing a rival mission in Calcutta, just fourteen miles away. For Carey, this break in Christian fellowship was one of the hardest things he had ever faced. He wrote, "Nothing I ever met with in my life—and I have met with many distressing things—ever preyed so much upon my spirits as this difference has."[130]

Once again, William remained steadfast in his call. The number of Bible translations increased to twenty-five. In 1818, Carey and Marshman introduced the first newspaper ever printed in an Asian language. The Bengali paper was followed by the first English periodical, *Friend of India*, produced by Joshua Marshman and, later, by his son, John. The periodical was written in both English and Bengali and kept the Indian people informed on important spiritual and secular issues. It was published continuously for the next fifty-seven years. The number of Indian schools continued to explode, with more than 126 native schools containing ten thousand boys and girls educated in Serampore and the surrounding districts.

Serampore College Is Founded

With unconquerable persistence, William Carey prayed that God would give him a new vision for India's future. The answer to that prayer was a school of higher education.

In 1818, Carey established Serampore College, the first nondenominational Christian college in India, where natives were educated in math, science, and biblical studies. The graduates shared the gospel *and* became a successful part of India's cultural development.

The Serampore College began with thirty-seven students—nineteen native Christians, and the rest Hindus. Carey wrote to his son William, "I pray that the blessing of God may attend it, and that it may be the means of preparing many for an important situation in the church of God."[131]

But the college created a new furor in England! The Baptist Missionary Society refused to financially support a school that was nondenominational and not established under the Baptist name. Fortunately, Christians in England and India rallied around Carey and donated five thousand pounds to the school. The Serampore Mission added four thousand pounds of its own. The main building was constructed, and the college was launched!

Serampore's Danish government was eager to support Carey, and the school became the first degree-awarding college in Asia. By 1829, hundreds of Indian citizens were enrolled in classes where Carey taught divinity, botany, and zoology.

For several years following the school's opening, Carey and the Baptist Missionary Society were at odds. In Carey's final years, however, they reconciled, and he relinquished the Serampore property to the mission board with the understanding that he and Joshua Marshman would live and work there for the rest of their lives.

As a confirmation that this was God's work, Serampore College is still open and graduating Indian students today, nearly two hundred years later!

Losing Loved Ones

By God's grace, even as Carey aged, he led a powerful and productive life. However, the life of a missionary is often challenged by the loss of those he holds dear. From the beginning of 1821, Charlotte's frail health began to decline, and, on May 30, 1821, after a thirteen-year-marriage to William, she went home to the Lord. She had been Carey's dearest love, and he mourned her deeply.

Carey could have quit. He had never taken a sabbatical or gone on furlough in all his years of ministry. Yet spreading the gospel was always his all-consuming mission in life.

The following year, Felix Carey was diagnosed with liver disease. He had rejoined the Serampore Mission and was working with Ward and the printing presses when he became seriously ill. On November 10, 1822, at age thirty-six, Felix Carey died. Just seven months later, William Ward was struck with cholera and went home to the Lord.

How Carey mourned: "This is to me a most awful and tremendous stroke and I have no way left but that of looking upward for help."

Carey could have quit. He had never taken a sabbatical or gone on furlough in all his years of ministry. Yet spreading the gospel was always his all-consuming mission in life.

A Thirty-Year Prayer Answered

Following a time of mourning, Carey married again at the age of fifty-nine. His third wife, Grace Hughes, was a forty-five-year-old widow who loved the Lord and faithfully served beside Carey in the ministry. Grace lovingly cared for Carey during their eleven years together.

She celebrated with him when, on December 4, 1829, the British governor-general, Lord Bentnick, signed an order finally declaring the practice of sati illegal throughout India! With tears streaming down his face, Carey read the order in English and then translated it into Bengali at the governor's request. He had fought for and prayed for this edict for *thirty years*! God had been faithful to answer his prayers.

In 1830, India suffered a devastating financial crisis when the banks and holding companies in Calcutta failed. As a result, Fort William College was suddenly closed, and Carey lost his teaching position of thirty years. The financial crisis wiped out all of the Serampore funds as well. Thankfully, with the help of donations, Serampore College remained financially sound, and Carey continued to teach there and to revise the Bengali New Testament once more.

Throughout his years in India, improving the Bengali translation was Carey's dearest project. In June 1832, he completed his last revision of the complete Bible in Bengali. It was his fifth edition of the Old Testament and eighth edition of the New Testament. He walked into the pulpit at the Serampore church with this final edition in his hands and spoke before the congregation, "*Lord, now lettest thou thy servant depart in peace, according to thy word: for mine eyes have seen thy salvation*" [Luke 2:29–30].[132]

"Not the Shadow of a Doubt"

In 1833, at the age of seventy-one, William Carey's health began to fail. In July, he had the first of three strokes, which left him bedridden. Friends and loved ones traveled to visit Carey from across India. His three surviving sons, Jabez and William Jr., both missionaries in India, and Jonathan, an attorney in Calcutta, spent many hours with their father. People flocked to say their good-byes, including the governor-general of India, dignitaries, missionaries, and friends throughout the country.

Carey had become a father to so many who admired him for his unsurpassed dedication and his deep relationship with Christ. Daniel Gogerly, a young English missionary, visited with him and quietly asked Carey the question that lay on his heart:

> My dear friend, you evidently are standing on the borders of the eternal world; do not think it wrong, then, if I ask, "What are your feelings in the immediate prospect of death?"

The question roused Carey from his rest, and, opening his eyes, he earnestly replied, "As far as my personal salvation is concerned, I have not the shadow of a doubt; I know in Whom I have believed, and am persuaded that He is able to keep that which I have committed unto Him against that day; but when I think that I am about to appear in the presence of a holy God, and remember all my sins and manifold imperfections—I tremble."[133]

In the last days of Carey's life, a young Scottish missionary, Alexander Duff, came to visit at his bedside. At the end of that visit, Carey left a final word with Duff: "Mr. Duff, you have been saying much about Dr. Carey and his work. After I am gone, please speak not of Dr. Carey, but rather of my wonderful Savior."[134]

Joshua Marshman daily spent time at Carey's bedside. They had served the Lord together for thirty-four years. He was comforted that Carey was peaceful about entering into the joy of the Lord. With a lingering smile, Carey reassured Marshman, "Friend, I have no fears; I have no doubts; I have not a wish left unsatisfied."

"On Thy Kind Arms I Fall"

On Monday morning, June 9, 1834, William Carey went home to the Savior that he had served so faithfully. He had arrived on India's shores at the age of thirty-one, and, he had left at seventy-two. When Marshman reached Carey's room that morning, "he found that he had just entered into the joy of his Lord." His wife, Grace, and son Jabez were with him.[135]

At his request, Carey was buried beside his beloved wife Charlotte. He had a simple headstone to mark his grave with his name, age, and an inscription from an Isaac Watts hymn, "A wretched, poor, and helpless worm / On thy kind arms I fall." To the very last, Carey trustingly placed himself in the charge of a kind and loving Savior.

Three years after Carey's death, Joshua Marshman, the last of the Serampore Triad, passed away. The very day after his funeral, the British Baptist Missionary Society closed the Serampore Mission.[136] But nothing anyone did could ever diminish the anointing of God that had surrounded Carey's life and fellow missionary workers.

They are inscribed in Christian history as dynamic instruments of the Holy Spirit, opening wide the nation of India to the gospel of Jesus Christ. They set the bar high for future missionaries by creating a Christian environment in which the gospel of Jesus Christ could flourish.

A True Friend of India

William Carey's impact on India was unparalleled in both the spiritual *and* secular world. He was an industrious pioneer in agriculture, horticulture, and education. He founded the Agricultural and Horticultural Society of India, which later became the model for the Royal Agricultural Society of England. He also introduced India's first steam engine to run his presses.

By establishing the great Mission Press, Carey was the driving force in India's initial printing and publishing industry. Not only did Carey and the Serampore mission team translate and print the first Bengali Bible, but they also established the first Bengali newspaper and periodical. Essentially, they formed the foundation for modern Bengali publishing.

An Indian postage stamp in honor of William Carey.

Carey's unrivaled passion for cultural and social reform ended the horrific practices of infant sacrifice and sati and made the Sanskrit language available to the less-educated members of Indian society.

His Baptist Missionary Society was the model for missionary organizations formed all over Europe and America, including the London, Glasgow, Anglican, and American Baptist unions. Within fifty years of his death, this one ordained English missionary became a band of 20,000 men and women sent out by 558 Christian agencies to lands throughout the world.

By the end of his life, Carey and his team had translated and printed the complete Bible into six languages, and portions of the Bible into twenty-nine additional languages, including Bengali, Hindi, Marharashtra, Sanskrit, Mandarin, Cochin Chinese, Oriya, Telinga, Bhutan, Persian, Malay, Tamil, and Tongkinese.

Throughout his journey with Christ, William Carey never lost his faith. Whether life was heartbreaking or joyful, he had learned as had the apostle Paul, to be content in whatever circumstances he found himself. (See Philippians 4:11–12.) Fulfilling the call on his life and bringing the gospel of Jesus Christ to India was the primary purpose of his existence. There was nothing of importance to Carey beyond this call.

Not only did Carey and the Serampore mission team translate and print the first Bengali Bible, but they also established the first Bengali newspaper and periodical.

✯✯✯✯✯

Sixty years earlier, because of Carey's daydreams of foreign adventures, he had been nicknamed "Columbus" by his childhood friends.

> Little did they imagine that he would become greater than Columbus, a discoverer of worlds which seemed to have eluded the famous Italian, an adventurer who crossed the seas, not seeking to dispossess others of their gold, but to distribute as lavishly as possible "the unsearchable riches of Christ."[137]

Declare His glory among the nations, His wonders among all peoples.
(Psalm 96:3 NKJV)

Will you declare the greatness of God among the nations?

Chapter 4

Adoniram Judson

America Sends Her First Missionary

Walking up the icy plank on a winter's day in Salem, Massachusetts, Adoniram Judson boarded the British ship *Packet* bound for England. It was January 1811, and Great Britain was at war with France; but, like many American citizens, Adoniram never gave the war a thought.

Two weeks out to sea, Judson's Bible reading was interrupted by anxious cries: "It's a French privateer! We must outrun her!" In a few short hours, the was captured by the French ship *L'Invincible Napoleon*. Judson was immediately taken aboard the new vessel and thrown into the dark, dank hold with the British sailors. The ship tossed harshly in the wintry Atlantic, and the hold was filled with the unbearable smells of sick and unwashed men. Never before had twenty-two-year-old Adoniram experienced such fear and hopelessness. God's training had begun in earnest for his future missionary life.

Adoniram Judson

After several weeks at sea, *L'Invincible Napoleon* docked in Bayonne, France. Adoniram was dragged down the gangplank in irons on his way to prison. Fearing he would never see another day of freedom, he began to shout in English, "This is a mistake! I am an American! I am not British!" Minutes later, a stranger jostled against him and whispered hoarsely, "Lower your voice!"

Hastily Judson explained that he was an American who had been aboard a British ship captured by the French. The stranger, an American officer from Philadelphia, promised a way of escape but warned, "You had better go on your way quietly now."

The French prison was underground, dark, and dismal. Adoniram was revolted by the vermin-covered straw spread over the damp floor. He paced for hours, wondering if his rescuer would ever come. As he leaned against a column to rest, the cell door swung open, and in walked the American officer in a black, floor-length military cloak; he never once looked in Judson's direction.

Suppressing a cry of joy, Adoniram pretended to be indifferent to the entire scene. As the American sauntered past the column, he swung his great military cloak around Judson, whose slender figure was almost lost in the folds. Judson crouched as low as possible while walking awkwardly ahead. How would they ever get past the guard? Then he heard the jingling of silver coins; the American officer wisely slid silver into the jailer's hand as they walked through the open gate.

Once the heavy metal doors clanged shut behind them, the American cried, "Now, run!" The men raced through the city to the wharves and onto an American merchant ship, where Judson shed tears of relief.[138]

For the first time in his life, Adoniram Judson had experienced the despair of captivity and the glory of freedom; but it wouldn't be the last time, for he consecrated his life to serving the Lord on hostile foreign soil.

Devoted for Life!

"The motto of every missionary, whether preacher, printer, or schoolmaster ought to be 'Devoted for life!'"
—Adoniram Judson

As a brilliant scholar in the early nineteenth century, Adoniram Judson seemed destined for a prestigious career as a United States statesman. Instead, for the love of Christ, Judson renounced worldly success and surrendered all that he had—his academic standing, his fame, his earthly possessions, and his precious family—to spend thirty-eight years sharing the good news of Jesus Christ

During his tireless ministry in Burma, Judson experienced both the triumph and the tragedy of mission life: he saw thousands of lives transformed in Christ yet faced years of persecution, imprisonment, and family tragedy.

with the people of Burma (present-day Myanmar, located just east of India). Adoniram became "the father of American missions," the first American citizen to become a foreign missionary.

"Devoted for life" was the cry of Judson's heart. To the eighteenth- and nineteenth-century missionaries, this devotion meant spending the rest of one's life ministering the gospel in a foreign country, sometimes without a single furlough home. There were no short-term missions for these men and women. This was the description of Judson's heart for ministry.

Judson's vision was to translate the Bible directly from the Hebrew and Greek into the Burmese language. He knew that there was no greater hope for the Burmese people than having the Word of God in their hands. Empowered by the Holy Spirit, he worked on the translation for twenty-eight years, using such precision that his translation is still used in Myanmar today.

During his tireless ministry in Burma, Judson experienced both the *triumph* and the *tragedy* of mission life: he saw thousands of lives transformed in Christ yet faced years of persecution, imprisonment, and family tragedy. Not all missionaries are called to make the sacrifices that Adoniram made in Burma, suffering much for the cause of Christ. But Judson was an overcomer. *"And they overcame* [Satan] *by the blood of the Lamb, and by the word of their testimony; and they loved not their lives unto death"* (Revelation 12:11). Never giving up the "fight of faith," he was known for his famous quote "The future is as bright as the promises of God!" An uncompromising disciple of Jesus Christ, Adoniram has earned a compelling place as one of God's missionary generals.

At the Birth of a Nation

Adoniram Judson came into the world during the birth of a nation. On August 9, 1788, the same year that the Constitution of the United States was ratified, Adoniram was born in the small town of Malden, Massachusetts. His father, Adoniram Sr., was a thirty-six-year-old Congregational pastor who had married young Abigail Brown just two years earlier. Adoniram Jr. was the eldest of four children; he had two sisters, Abigail and Mary (who died as an infant), and a brother, Elnathan.

It was obvious from a very early age that Adoniram was a gifted child. When he was just three years old, his mother taught him to read while his father was away on a preaching tour. Imagine his father's surprise when Adoniram read an entire chapter of the Bible aloud when he returned home! The senior Judson was a stern man who required obedience in his household, but he was proud that his namesake was brilliant at such a young age.

It is important to recognize the power of parents in developing the gift of a child. Today people talk about a "village" raising a child; they want the church, the school, or even the television to do it. Yet the Bible speaks in more than one place of the parents' role: *"For I have chosen him, so that he will direct his children and his household after him to keep the way of the Lord by doing what is right and just"* (Genesis 18:19 NIV). The role of the parent is to give a child a foundation for his character and to help him to develop his gifts. Judson's parents recognized this truth.

"Old Virgil—Academic Genius"

By the time Adoniram was ten years old, he had read most of the books in his father's library and gained a growing reputation in academics, especially in mathematics. His father enrolled him in Captain Morton's College of Navigation in Wenham, where Adoniram advanced quickly and became so accomplished in his Greek studies that his classmates nicknamed him "Old Virgil" in honor of the ancient Greek scholar. His father was increasingly proud and often boasted, "Son, you will be a great man someday!"

At sixteen, living with his family, now in Plymouth, Massachusetts, Adoniram was accepted to Rhode Island College (later renamed Brown University) in Providence, Rhode Island. Although most New England Congregationalists attended Harvard or Yale, by 1804, those schools had strayed from conservative biblical teaching and were steeped in Deism and the French Enlightenment.

Deism is the belief that there is a creator but that he never intervenes in human affairs. It was almost as if they were saying, "God made you, and then He went on vacation!"

The Enlightenment introduced the philosophy that man didn't need God or institutionalized religion. He was a "freethinker" who had the ability to reason about the deep things of life for himself. The freethinkers challenged the legitimacy of the Bible as the Word of God and rejected all miracles, choosing *reason* in place of *revelation*. This errant teaching led the young college students far from their Christian roots.

Adoniram was an ambitious student who was able to skip his freshman year and enter Rhode Island College as a sophomore. He worked doggedly, resolved to become the great man that his father expected him to be. For three years, Adoniram's foremost goal was to graduate as the valedictorian of his class. As soon as he learned that he had attained this high honor, he sent a note to his proud father, saying, "Dear father, I have got it! Your affectionate son, A. J."[139] Unfortunately, unknown to Adoniram Sr., young Judson had learned more than advanced academics at school. The heresies of the Enlightenment were not just running rampant at Yale and Harvard; they had seeped into Rhode Island College, as well.

"I Don't Believe in Your God!"

Jacob Eames was Adoniram's closest friend, an intelligent and polished student who was a confirmed Deist. They developed a strong friendship and spent hours discussing how they would make their marks on the world. They could become lawyers, politicians, or playwrights—there was no limit to where their talents could take them! By the time they parted company at Adoniram's graduation in September 1807, Judson no longer believed in the God of his parents; he was a confirmed Deist, too.

After returning home to Plymouth, Adoniram opened a private school for young girls, Plymouth Independent Academy, where he taught for a year and published two textbooks: *The Elements of English Grammar and The Young Lady's Arithmetic*. But he was restless; it was time to launch on a "personal discovery tour."

Arguing with his parents over his plan to leave, Adoniram's anger seethed until he finally shouted, "Stop! I don't want to be a teacher or a pastor! I don't believe in heaven or hell or your God! I am a Deist!"[140] Silence followed. Adoniram Sr. was stunned and became furious. How could his successful son, the apple of his eye, turn his back on his Christian faith? Using Scriptures, he reasoned with his unyielding son for hours. "Point by point, the intellectual Adoniram demolished every thesis his father set out to prove."[141] His mother and sister wept bitterly; they prayed and pleaded with him, but to no avail.

Saddling his horse, Judson first rode to Albany to see the latest "wonder of the world," Robert Fulton's newly invented steamboat, the *Clermont*. He embarked on the *Clermont* and traveled to New York City, where he joined a group of young actors to experience theater life as an actor and a playwright. But the actors were just delinquents with little income and, within weeks, "living a reckless, vagabond life" had lost its glamour; Judson turned his horse toward the west to continue his journey.

Lost and Dead

Soon after, Adoniram stopped at a country inn for the night. The landlord led him to a room. "I am sorry," he said, "but all I have left is this room next door to a young man who is deathly ill."

"It is no matter," Judson replied. "I will have no trouble sleeping." But he was wrong!

Throughout the long night, Adoniram tossed on his hard cot, listening to the young man's desperate groans and his caretakers' hasty footsteps. Adoniram was tortured by thoughts of the dying young man. *Am I prepared to die?* he wondered. Immediately, Adoniram felt ashamed of himself. What would the clearheaded, witty Jacob Eames say to his weakness?

Still, Judson couldn't help himself. *Was the dying man a Christian? Did he have a praying mother at home?* Thankfully, the biblical words sown in him by his parents were still at work. It is a good reminder: plant the Word in the heart of your children and loved ones. If they go astray for a time, don't be discouraged; the Word of God still resides in their hearts. (See Proverbs 22:6.)

Finally, at four in the morning, the room next door to Judson's became eerily quiet, and he drifted off to sleep. With the sunshine of morning, Adoniram felt embarrassed about his "superstitious illusions" of the night before. As soon as he had dressed, he went in search of the landlord.

"How is my ill neighbor this morning?" he inquired. "He is dead, I'm afraid" was his sad reply.

"Do you know who he was?" Judson questioned warily.

"Why yes; he was a young man from Rhode Island College—a very fine fellow—his name was Jacob Eames."[142]

Judson was stunned! *Jacob!* Those dying groans had come from Jacob! Adoniram had been lying just a few feet away as his friend perished! For hours, Adoniram sat in the inn, overwhelmed with grief and confusion; he mounted his horse unsure of where to go next. "Jacob was lost in death!" The single thought occupied his mind, and the words *Dead! Lost! Lost!* continually rang in his ears. In his heart, Adoniram knew that salvation in Christ was true. In despair, he turned his horse toward Plymouth and home.

A Not-So-Dramatic Conversion

Adoniram arrived at his parents' home in Plymouth on September 22, 1808. He had experienced so much disillusionment in just six weeks of travel. He wept bitterly as he recounted Eames's death and his own fear and confusion. Adoniram and Abigail welcomed their son home with tender embraces and forgiveness.

The Holy Spirit continued to draw Adoniram to Christ. On December 2, 1808, "he made a solemn and complete dedication of himself to God." From that moment, he never turned back.

Within a few weeks, even though he was still uncertain what he believed, Adoniram was invited to enroll in Andover Theological Seminary, where he could closely study the Bible and renew his faith. He immersed himself in the Word and biblical teachings, and, steadily, his doubts and questions began to fade away. "While I had no sudden lightning conversion," he wrote, "I began to entertain a hope of having received the regenerating influences of the Holy Spirit." The Holy Spirit continued to draw Adoniram to Christ. On December 2, 1808, "he made a solemn and complete dedication of himself to God."[143] From that moment, he never turned back.

Following the Eastern Star

A year passed at Andover. Judson began to ask himself, *How shall I so order my future as best to please God?*[144] He came across a sermon entitled "The Star in the East" by Dr. Claudius Buchanan, a chaplain of the British East India

Company. The message was based on Matthew 2:2: *"For we have seen his star in the east, and are come to worship him."* Buchanan shared his personal experiences of the power of the gospel to change lives in Asia. His sermon "fell like a spark into the tinder of Judson's soul."

Within a short time, Adoniram had made his decision. "It was during a solitary walk in the woods behind the college, while meditating and praying on the subject,...that the command of Christ, 'Go into all the world and preach the Gospel to every creature,' was presented to my mind with such clearness and power, that I came to a full decision,...resolved to obey the command at all events."[145] Somehow, Adoniram Judson would bring the message of Christ to the lost in Asia!

The Haystack Missionaries

Just as the missionary call was emblazoned on Adoniram's soul, four young men from Williams College in Massachusetts enrolled at Andover Seminary. They shared the story of their missionary call in connection with the "Haystack Prayer Meeting."

Four years earlier, on the campus of Williams College, Samuel J. Mills, Harvey Loomis, James Richards, Francis Robbins, and Byram Green had gathered outdoors in Sloan's Meadow for their weekly prayer meeting. When a sudden rainstorm split open the skies, the students fled for shelter under a nearby haystack. Huddled together, they began talking and praying about their growing desire to bring Christ to foreign nations by founding an American missionary movement focused on eastern Asia.

Haystack Monument in Mission Park at Williams College.

That Saturday afternoon in August 1806, under the leadership of Samuel Mills, the young men consecrated themselves "to send the gospel to the lost of Asia." They named their student missionary group "The Society of the Brethren." Soon, other students from Williams College joined their ranks. Today, in Williamstown, Massachusetts, on the exact spot of that decision to launch American missions, stands the famous Haystack Monument, commemorating that momentous decision.

"I Have Much Farther to Go"

God's timing is never a coincidence. In 1810, while Adoniram was still a Bible student, several of "the brethren" from Williams College arrived at Andover Seminary full of excitement about God's call to become American missionaries. Adoniram quickly formed a bond with the men: Samuel Newell, Samuel Nott, Gordon Hall, and Samuel J. Mills. As they began to quietly plan what they hoped would become the first American missionary society, Judson was unanimously selected as their missionary candidate.

But, as Adoniram's graduation was quickly approaching, his parents had different expectations for their brilliant son. The tension grew when he was offered a prestigious Congregational position: assistant pastor of the Park Street Church, under the Reverend Edward Griffin, the first pastor of the now historic Boston church. This was quite an honor for the seminary graduate. Park Street Church had the fastest-growing congregation in Boston at the time and was influential in the nation's political and social affairs as well. Just a few years later, the head pastor was Edward Beecher, brother of Harriet Beecher Stowe, who wrote *Uncle Tom's Cabin*. The church became an early birthplace of the abolitionist movement in America.

Ecstatic over the news of Adoniram's job offer, his father swelled with pride, and his mother embraced him exuberantly, saying, "Adoniram, you will be so near home!"

"No!" came Adoniram's swift reply. "Mother, I shall never live in Boston! I have much farther than that to go." Once again, the senior Judson was shocked by his son's plans. His ambitions for Adoniram to be an influential man in the fledgling nation were overthrown. Adoniram's mother and sister broke down in sobs of fear and grief.

But he was convinced that his life and intellectual gifts would not be wasted doing missionary work. As one biographer noted, "It is a mistake to suppose that a dull and second-rate man is good enough for the heathen. The worst-off need the very best we have. God gave His best, even His only-begotten Son, in order to redeem a lost world. Christianity will advance over the earth with long, swift strides when the churches are ready to send their best men, and the best men are ready to go."[146] Judson was ready to go, but how would he get there?

America's First Missionary Society

The young missionary hopefuls wrote a proposal to the Congregational Board of Ministers in Boston with their vision for an American missionary society. Adoniram stood before the board and read in a clear, commanding voice that "they considered themselves as *devoted* to this work *for life*, whenever God, in His providence, shall open the way." It was signed by Adoniram Judson Jr., Samuel Nott Jr., Samuel J. Mills, and Samuel Newell. (The names of Luther Rice, Gordon Hall, and James Richards were added later.)[147]

The General Association held a follow-up meeting in Bradford, Massachusetts, and the decision to form the American Board of Commissioners for Foreign Missions (ABCFM) was unanimous. American missionary work overseas would finally become a reality!

Enthralled by the events taking place right before their eyes, the young men accepted an invitation for lunch at the home of John Hasseltine, a Congregational deacon. Seated at the table, engrossed in their missionary plans, Adoniram's attention was drawn to the lovely face and wavy black hair of Hasseltine's youngest daughter, Ann. His heart skipped a beat as Ann served his food while laughingly catching his eye. In that brief moment, Adoniram's life was changed forever.

Caught His Eye

Ann "Nancy" Hasseltine was born in Bradford, Massachusetts on December 22, 1789. She was the youngest of five children and a lively little girl who grew to be a young woman more interested in parties than in God. Her parents' home had a large ballroom, and Ann was a natural hostess with a fondness for social gatherings and laughter.

At sixteen, Ann's life changed. "I began to discover a beauty in the way of salvation by Christ. He appeared to be just such a Saviour as I needed. I committed my soul into His hands."[148] Now, at twenty years old, Ann—or, Nancy, as many friends called her—was teaching school, pouring her love of life and of Christ into her students. Her personality was very different from Adoniram's intense, intellectual manner, but Adoniram Judson loved Ann Hasseltine at first sight.

A Shocking Letter

After a brief courtship of Ann, Adoniram sent a letter to her father asking his permission to marry her. The courageous young man painted a clear picture of future missionary dangers:

> I have now to ask whether you can consent to part with your daughter early next spring, to perhaps see her no more in this world? whether you can consent to her departure to a heathen land, and her subjection to the hardships and sufferings of a missionary life? whether you can consent to her exposure to the dangers of the ocean; to the fatal influence of the southern climate of India; to every kind of want and distress; to degradation, insult, persecution, and perhaps a violent death? Can you consent to all this, for the sake of Him who left His heavenly home and died for her and for you; for the sake of perishing, immortal souls; for the sake of Zion and the glory of God?"[149]

The letter caused John Hasseltine and his wife, Rebecca, great pain, but Hasseltine gave his consent. Ann was always a woman of courage and determination. She confided to a friend,

> I feel willing and expect to spend my days in this world in heathen lands. I have come to the determination to give up all my comforts and enjoyments here and go where God, in His providence, shall see fit to send me....He has my heart in His hands, and when I am called to face danger, He can inspire me with fortitude, and enable me to trust in him. Jesus is faithful; his promises are precious.[150]

A Momentous Decision

Before the marriage could take place, Adoniram was sent to London to ask the London Missionary Board to partner with the new American Missionary Board. It was then that he was captured by the *L'Invincible Napoleon* and taken to France, then set free by his American military rescuer. His meeting with the London Missionary Board was not successful.

On September 18, 1811, the American Missionary Board made a momentous decision. It would formally appoint Adoniram Judson Jr., Samuel Nott Jr.,

Samuel Newell, Gordon Hall, and Luther Rice as the first American missionaries to eastern Asia. The American missionary movement was born!

That year, Adoniram wrote to Ann with high hopes for their future. "May this be the year in which you will change your name; in which you will take a final leave of your relatives and native land; in which you will cross the wide ocean, and dwell on the other side of the world, among a heathen people. What a great change will this year probably effect in our lives!"[151]

Married, Anointed, and Sent

As 1812 began, Massachusetts was bursting with rumors of war between England and the United States. The young missionaries were determined to set sail before a naval conflict would put a stop to all sea travel.

On February 3, 1812, Adoniram said his final good-byes to his family in Plymouth. The rest of the month was a blur of activity. On February 5, Adoniram and Ann were married by Parson Allen in her home in Bradford. The next day, he and the other young missionaries were ordained in Salem.

On February 19, 1812, an icy, windy day in New England, Adoniram and Ann set sail aboard the brig *Caravan*, destined for Calcutta, India, along with Samuel Newell and his new bride Harriet Atwood. Harriet had just turned seventeen and was a frail young woman; she and Ann were childhood friends and were facing the future missionary life together. Samuel and Roxana Nott, Gordon Hall, and Luther Rice followed a few days later on the sailing ship *Harmony*.

The Water Baptism Controversy

Through the long sea voyage, Adoniram had much on his mind. When men and women came to Christ in foreign lands, they would be water baptized into their faith. But should he baptize their children as well? Was infant baptism truly the right answer according to the Bible?

Judson was also thinking of his upcoming meeting with William Carey and his fellow Baptists in Calcutta. With his usual intensity, Adoniram immersed himself in studying every Bible reference to water baptism. At one point, he told Ann, "Baptism is always linked with believing. I am afraid the Baptists may be in the right!"[152] Slowly and quietly, Judson became convinced that baptism by immersion was for the believer. But leaving the doctrine of infant baptism meant leaving the support of the Congregational Mission Board, as well. It was a frightening prospect.

Ann was confused by Adoniram's growing conviction, so he wrote her a simple letter, addressing it to her pet name, "Nancy." "Thus, my dear Nancy, we are confirmed Baptists, not because we wish to be, but because truth compels us to be."[153] Adoniram and Ann kept quiet about his changing doctrine during the voyage while he prayed for God's leading.

Advice: "Forget Burma!"

After four months at sea, the Judsons and Newells arrived in Calcutta, India, on June 18, 1812, and traveled up the Hooghly River, just as William Carey had done twenty years earlier. Ann described her first sight of foreign soil: "I have never witnessed nor read anything so delightful as the present scene. This city is by far the most elegant that I have ever seen."[154]

Unfortunately, the East India Company was not happy to see them. The Judsons met with the same harsh treatment that Carey had years earlier. As soon as they arrived, the missionaries were required to check in at the local police station and were bluntly told that they could not stay in India.

What a sharp contrast to the warm welcome they received from William Carey, who met them in Calcutta and invited them to stay in beautiful Serampore until the *Harmony* arrived and the missionaries could make their future plans.

Adoniram had felt a call to Burma ever since reading Michael Syme's book *Embassy to Ava* while it Andover. However, when he spoke about his desire to go to Burma, the missionaries in Calcutta responded with a unanimous cry, *"Forget Burma!"* The nation of Burma was ruled by a despotic emperor who hated Western culture. Beheadings and crucifixions were common punishments for small crimes. Although William Carey's oldest son, Felix, had founded a mission station there, he'd had no missionary success. The cry "Forget Burma!" continually echoed in Adoniram's ears![155]

Cast Out of India

While in Serampore, the Judsons and Newells received an order from Calcutta. "You must return to America aboard the *Caravan*!" the British commanded. With the help of Joshua Marshman of Serampore, the American missionaries received permission to sail for the Isle of France (present-day Mauritius) instead. The first ship available, the *Colonel Gillespie,* could take only two passengers. The Newells would be the first to leave since Harriet was expecting their first child.

Four days after the Newells' departure, the *Harmony* finally arrived in Calcutta with Hall, Rice, and the Notts on board. It was a happy reunion after seven months of separation, but the merriment soon turned to concern. Adoniram finally confessed his conviction concerning water baptism. By this time, after studying the Scriptures, Ann supported her husband's decision. Hall and Nott were shocked.

"But Adoniram," they protested, "this will mean an end to our mission together! We cannot run a unified mission with two conflicting denominations. And your financial support from the American Board will cease." Only Luther Rice remained oddly silent during the heated discussions. Ann was terrified; she had never considered sacrificing their mission together while so far from home.

Adoniram was resolute. It was God's Word; he must be baptized and become a Baptist. After writing a letter to Serampore with his desire for baptism by immersion, he and Ann were baptized by William Ward in Calcutta on September 6, 1812. Two months later, Luther Rice was also immersed in baptism. John Marshman wrote to several Baptist ministers in Boston with the exciting news: "There are now three American Baptists on the missionary field!" Soon after, the American Baptist Missionary Union was born.

What a blessing resulted from the missionary passion of a handful of Andover students. Their desire to send American missionaries to the foreign field resulted in two societies: the American Board of Commissioners for Foreign Missions and the American Baptist Missionary Union—the first, an outreach of the Congregational Church, the other, an outreach of the Baptists of America. The message of Jesus Christ was spreading across the globe.

A Tragic Loss

Saddened by the change of circumstances, Samuel and Roxana Nott and Gordon Hall left Calcutta to begin a mission work in Ceylon. The Judsons and Rice stayed behind. Losing all patience with the missionary "intruders," the East India Company ordered them to immediately board a ship bound for England.

Desperately searching for another possibility, the Judsons found *La Belle Creole* about to sail for the Isle of France. Adoniram secretly approached the captain of the *Creole*. "Will you take us on board without a passport?" he inquired hopefully. "Yes!" the captain answered. "There is my ship; you can go on board if you please!"

The Judsons and Rice hurried aboard. Ann could hardly wait to be reunited with Harriet and see the new baby. But when they reached the Isle of France, they were met with horrifying news! Harriet's baby girl had been born during a terrible storm at sea; both mother and child had caught pneumonia, and the baby had died just five days later. After landing, Harriet had succumbed to her fever as well and passed away. Devastated, Samuel Newell left the Isle of France to join the Notts' mission in Ceylon.

"We Shall Go to Rangoon!"

Where would Adoniram and Ann go? Luther Rice, already fighting health problems, decided to sail back to America. He pledged to the Judsons that he would not desert their missionary work; his role would be to travel to the American Baptist churches and raise money and missionaries for their work in Asia.

Desperate to find a place to start their missionary enterprise, Adoniram searched for a ship leaving the Isle of France immediately; he found one—the creaky old *Georgiana*, bound for Rangoon (Yangon), Burma! Secretly, Adoniram had never given up the idea of Burma. On June 22, 1813, a year after their arrival in Calcutta, Adoniram and Ann were bound for the port of Rangoon on Burma's southern coast.

Standing on the deck of the Georgiana *as she slipped out to sea, Adoniram couldn't help but rejoice! This was the opportunity he had been waiting for!*

Standing on the deck of the *Georgiana* as she slipped out to sea, Adoniram couldn't help but rejoice! This was the opportunity he had been waiting for! He wrote later, "Dissuaded by all our friends against Burma, we commended ourselves to God." He had little idea of the trials and triumphs that awaited them.

The *Georgiana* was a small vessel, and it was a difficult voyage, especially for Ann, who was eight months pregnant. During a raging storm at sea, she went into premature labor and gave birth to a stillborn son. Cold and seasick, the grieving parents turned to the Lord for their hope. After a treacherous three-week voyage, on July 13, 1813, the Judsons stepped ashore at Burman—the country that would become their home for life.

The American Baptist Society Is Born

Curious onlookers lined the docks—women dressed in bright tunics, and little children, naked and smoking small cigars—all fussing over Ann, the first white woman to visit Rangoon.[156] Adoniram and Ann were taken by bamboo chair to Felix Carey's mission house. Shyly opening the mission door at their knock, Felix's young Portuguese wife welcomed the Judsons warmly into their home. A medical missionary, Felix had traveled to Ava, the capital, to vaccinate the royal family against smallpox.

Within a few weeks, Felix made a decision to leave the mission for good with his family and accept a position in Emperor Bodawpaya's royal government. The Judsons, who knew nothing of the Burmese language and culture, were sad to see them go. Tragically, while the Careys were traveling up the Irrawaddy River on their way to Ava, their boat capsized, and Felix's wife and children drowned. In a fog of grief, Felix roamed the countries of southern Asia for several years before returning to his father's ministry in Serampore.

The Judsons ministered alone for the next three years. In the meantime, Luther Rice returned to America and traveled extensively, telling the thrilling story of the pioneer missionaries. Adoniram wrote a letter to Luther that November, encouraging him to choose missionaries for Burma with great care: "Choose men with some natural aptitude to acquire a language; men who live near to God and are willing to suffer all things for Christ's sake, without being proud of it."[157]

The Baptists in Boston were invigorated by the news of the Judsons' arrival in Burma and immediately organized the Baptist Society for Propagating the Gospel in India and Other Foreign Parts.[158] Southern and western Baptist churches soon joined them, and missions became the rallying point for the fledgling Baptist denomination; its members became dedicated to spreading the gospel around the globe.

Burma and the "Golden Face"

Ann was enchanted with the beauty of Burma. They were surrounded by a colorful landscape, lush vegetation, and gently rolling hills. But the city of

Rangoon was dirty and impoverished. Rangoon's highlight was the Shwedagon Pagoda, the most sacred of the Buddhist temples, with its gold-plated spire that towered above the city.

Just as the Calcutta missionaries had warned, Burma was led by a tyrannical emperor who was referred to as "The Golden One" or "The Golden Face." He ruled with an iron hand, and the people lived in fear of his displeasure.

Buddhism was the only religion allowed. To the Buddhists, there is no god or supreme being; there is no human soul to be forgiven or saved. Buddhists believe in the continuous life cycles of birth, death, and rebirth as they progress from lower life forms to human beings. In this country that knew nothing of Christ and His sacrifice for mankind, Adoniram and Ann Judson stood alone as beacons of light.

Just Go Out and Speak

"My only object at present," Judson wrote to Luther Rice, "is to prosecute, in a still, quiet manner, the study of the language, trusting that for all the future 'God will provide.'"[159] Conquering the Burmese language, with its series of half circles and small curlicues, was the only hope of reaching millions of lost natives with the gospel. Working for hours each day, Adoniram became an expert on the technical knowledge of the language.

Ann's role, on the other hand, was to become acquainted with her new countrymen. Just as she had in America, Ann exercised her gift of hospitality in Burma. She ran the house, directed the servants, went to the market to purchase food, and visited with the wife of the viceroy; as a result, she became more fluent in understanding and speaking the Burmese of the common citizen. Both of the Judsons went out and did what they needed to do; they hit the ground running.

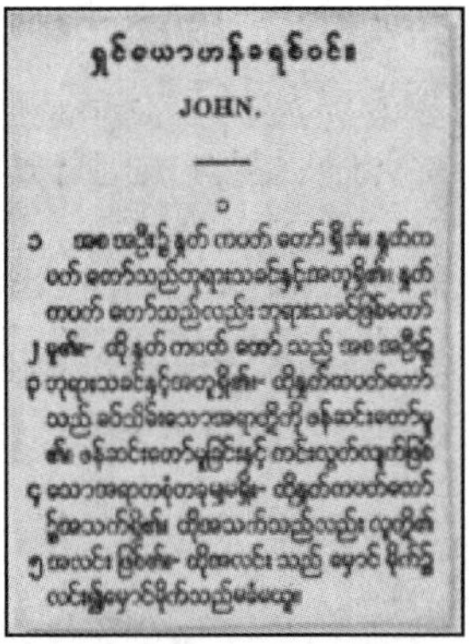

An image from the Burmese Judson translation of the book of John.

"I am frequently obliged to speak Burman all day," Ann wrote home. "I can talk and understand others better than Mr. Judson, though he knows more about the nature and construction of the language."

On December 11, 1813, she recorded, "Today, for the first time, I have visited the wife of the viceroy. She received me very politely, took me by the hand, seated me upon a mat, and herself by me. She was very inquisitive whether I had a husband and children and whether I was my husband's first wife—meaning by this, whether I was the highest among them!"[160]

Ann had no way of knowing that her warm relationships with the Burmese officials would save them from death in the years ahead.

The Birth of "Sweet" Roger Williams Judson

The next two years were filled with busy Burmese life and the happy news that the Judsons were expecting their second child. On September 11, 1815, with only Adoniram to help with the delivery, Ann gave birth to a healthy baby boy. Overjoyed, they named him Roger Williams Judson, in honor of colonist Roger Williams, the American Baptist who founded Rhode Island as a colony of true religious freedom.

Baby Roger was a continual blessing to his parents, a sweet, smiling, alert, blue-eyed boy. As he grew, he was happiest when he was in the same room with his father as he worked. During this time, Adoniram wrote home, "Thanks be to God, not only for 'rivers of endless joys above, but for 'rills of comfort here below.'"

But in the spring of 1816, baby Roger developed a fever and a cough that seemed to worsen with each passing day. Without any medical assistance, Ann and Adoniram cared for him as best they could. But on May 4, 1816, baby Roger closed his eyes and died in his sleep at just seven and a half months old.

Adoniram and Ann were gripped with grief, especially being so far from family and friends. It was the viceroy's wife who reached out to them and showered them with sympathy during this painful time.

Help from William Carey

On July 13, 1816, three years after their arrival in Burma, Adoniram completed a book on Burmese grammar. Two weeks later, his first Burmese tract, *A View of the Christian Religion,* was completed as well. Now, how to have them printed?

The Burmese loved literature and were waiting to read about this Jesus who was called "the Son of God." Then Adoniram received a gift—a printing press and

The Burmese loved literature and were waiting to read about this Jesus who was called "the Son of God."

Burmese typeface sent by William Carey. He wrote to the society at home: "It is with great pleasure that we announce the valuable present of a press and Burman types, made to us by the Serampore brethren."[161]

To make the blessing complete, the American Baptists sent a missionary printer, George Hough, who arrived with his family in the fall of 1816. Within a few weeks, one thousand copies of Judson's first tract and three thousand copies of a Burmese catechism written by Ann were published and distributed throughout Rangoon. Immediately, the inquisitive Burmans came to the mission house clamoring for more. The message of Christ was finally being heard!

It is hard to overemphasize the importance of the written word to the gospel missionary. If I hand out a gospel tract while ministering in the Philippines today, the people there will treasure it. I have watched young men sit down on the curb to read it the very moment they receive it. In Western nations, we do not value gospel material as we should; it has become too common to us and has lost its preciousness to our hearts and minds.

"Of how much real happiness we cheat our souls by preferring a trifle to God!" Adoniram proclaimed.

Telling the "Christ Story"

"Ho! Everyone that thirsteth for knowledge come in here!" These words of encouragement rang from Adoniram's lips as he sat beside the road in Rangoon. He and a newly arrived Baptist missionary, James Colman, had built a Burmese *zayat*, or open-air chapel, where religious and political men gathered to share their ideas. Adoniram would sit under the zayat all day, calling out in Burmese fashion to passersby, welcoming any who would stop and listen to him as he preached the gospel of redeeming grace.

On April 4, 1819, six years after arriving in Rangoon, Judson conducted the first public Christian service in the zayat. Years later, his son Edward would write, "To Adoniram Judson, the most important work was the oral preaching of the gospel—this was his first love."

Moung Nau was a young Burmese man who came to that first service and listened with an open heart to the Christian message.

"I think that the grace of God has reached Moung Nau's heart," Judson joyously recorded on May 5. "He expresses repentance for his sins, and faith in the Saviour. He professes that from the darkness and sins of his whole life, he has found no other Saviour but Jesus Christ; and he proposes to adhere to Christ, and worship Him all his life long....Praise and glory be to His name forevermore! Amen."[162]

A Trophy of Victorious Grace

The Spirit of God was moving among the people of Rangoon. Six long years of planting and watering for Adoniram and Ann, but the seed of Christ's sacrifice had finally taken root!

Several more young men joined Adoniram and Moung Nau in their Bible discussions. Judson sent for five thousand copies of his tract to be printed by the Houghs, who had temporarily moved to Serampore. Hundreds of curious Burmese clamored for new tracts every day.

On Sunday, June 27, 1819, the first Burmese converts to Christianity were baptized—Moung Nau, Moung Byaa, and Moung Thahlah. (*Moung* is "young man" in Burmese.) That evening, in the mission house, Adoniram and Ann rejoiced with "joy unspeakable and full of glory!"

"This event," Ann wrote in her journal, "this single trophy of victorious grace, has filled our hearts with sensations hardly to be conceived by Christians in Christian countries. This event has convinced us that God can and does operate on the minds of the ignorant with the truth of His own Word!"[163]

Appeal to the "Golden Face"

No sooner were the baptisms held than the black clouds of persecution appeared on the horizon. Fearing retaliation from the government for this public display of Christianity, the once-curious Burmese began to avoid Adoniram and the new converts.

Judson was determined to end their fear. "I'm going to travel to the capital to see the Golden Face himself," he told Ann, speaking of the Burman emperor. Only a few European men had ever been in the "Golden Presence." The old emperor had recently died and his grandson, Emperor Bagyidaw, had assumed the throne after a bloodbath that had taken the lives of thousands. It was this cruel man that Adoniram was determined to face.

"Our business must be laid before the emperor," Adoniram wrote home. "If he frowns upon us, all missionary attempts within his dominions will be out of the question. If he favors us, none of our enemies can touch a hair of our heads. But there is One greater than the emperor, before whose throne we desire daily and constantly to lay this business. O Lord Jesus, look upon us in our low estate, and guide us in our dangerous course!"[164]

In late December 1819, Judson and Colman traveled the treacherous 350 miles up the Irrawaddy River to Ava, where they petitioned the governor's office for an audience with the emperor "to behold the Golden Face." The night before, Judson solemnly recorded, "Tomorrow's dawn will usher in the most eventful day of our lives. Tomorrow's eve will close on the bloom or the blight of our fondest hopes. Yet it is consoling to commit this business into the hands of our heavenly Father—to feel that the work is His, not ours."[165]

"Our Fate Was Decided"

The Golden Palace appeared to be on fire! As Adoniram and Colman approached the capital, the palace's golden dome appeared ablaze from the sun's glistening rays. Adoniram and Colman prayerfully entered the great palace hall with Ava's governor. The spacious hall was filled with golden idols, golden-inlaid furniture, and bejeweled tapestries. They had entered the domain of a ruler who believed he was divine.

At the announcement of the emperor's approach, everyone in the court cast themselves prostrate on the floor. The two American missionaries knelt down to show their respect. As Emperor Bagyidaw entered the room in a white tunic and robes, he glared at the two Western visitors.

"Who are these men?" he demanded.

"We are the religious teachers you have heard about, O great one!" Judson answered in Burmese.

The Emperor was shocked. "You speak like a Burmese man. How can this be? What have you come for?"[166]

The governor presented the emperor with Adoniram's petition to teach the Christian religion without persecution and included Judson's Christian tract. After hearing the petition, the Golden Face read the first line of the tract: "There is only one eternal God and besides Him there is no other God." In disgust, he threw the brochure onto the floor and walked away.

"In that brief moment," penned Judson, "our fate was decided."[167] It was time to return to Rangoon, but they had lost all hope that the gospel would ever flourish under the emperor's condemnation.

"The Emperor Cannot Stop It!"

Was it time to leave Rangoon? Judson wondered. Things looked bad, but God was still bringing in a harvest. Before Adoniram and Coleman even arrived back home, Moung Shway-gnong, a well-respected Burmese teacher, had confessed his allegiance to Christ. The Lord was giving them new believers in the face of the emperor's disapproval. *But how can we escape the emperor's wrath?* Adoniram worried. The simple answer was that they could move to Chittagong, a region of Burma under British control (now in Bangladesh), and share Christ free from the emperor's eye.

To Adoniram's surprise, the new Burmese Christians stood strong in the face of persecution.

To Adoniram's surprise, the new Burmese Christians stood strong in the face of persecution. "Do not leave!" they pleaded with Adoniram. "Stay at least until a little church of ten is collected, and a native teacher is set over it. This religion of truth will spread of itself. *The emperor cannot stop it!*"[168] The heroism of these disciples kept Judson and Ann in Rangoon.

James Colman and his wife moved to Chittagong to begin a new mission there. And the church of Jesus Christ continued to grow to fifteen...twenty...and then twenty-five believers.

Awakening Missionary Fire

Ann was setting sail for America. After nine years, the tropical climate of Burma had taken its toll on her. In the nineteenth century, with few advanced medicines, doctors believed that the air of a sea voyage could heal patients of many illnesses.

On September 5, 1821, Adoniram posted a letter soon after Ann's departure: "Dearest Ann, Oh! how consoling it is to give up myself, and you, and the interests of the mission, into the faithful hands of Jesus....The Lord reigns, and I feel, at times, that I can safely trust all in His hands, and rejoice in whatever may betide. If we suffer with Christ we shall also be glorified with Him."[169]

For the feisty Ann Judson, a time of "rest" in America was anything but that! In her two-year stay, she traveled throughout New England sharing the testimonies of the Burma mission. At the encouragement of Christian friends, she published a book entitled *An Account of the American Baptist Mission to the Burman Empire.*

Ann's vibrant testimony awakened missionary enthusiasm in America, especially among the Baptists. She returned to Rangoon in December 1823 with two new missionaries, Jonathan and Deborah Wade, who served faithfully in Burma for the next twenty-five years.[170]

Completing the Burmese New Testament

While Ann was in America, a medical missionary, Dr. Jonathan Price, and his wife, Hope, arrived in Rangoon. Dr. Price was welcomed with open arms for his medical skill, especially in cataract surgery. When his reputation reached the emperor's ears, Price was summoned to appear at the royal court. Since the doctor's Burmese was very poor, Judson accompanied him. Perhaps the Golden Face would allow the men to plant a mission in the capital city after all.

On August 28, 1822, Judson made his second trip up the Irrawaddy River to Ava. Because of Dr. Price's medical knowledge, the emperor openly welcomed the two men and invited them to move to the capital, where they could live under his protection. "It will be an opportunity to spread the gospel in the capital," Judson rejoiced. "Perhaps the emperor will change his mind concerning freedom of religion in the country!"

Adoniram returned to Rangoon to await Ann's return from America, and Dr. Price remained in Ava, looking for a new direction to his ministry since the death of his wife to cholera months earlier.[171]

It was a time for great rejoicing of another kind for Adoniram. On July 12, 1823, the manuscript for the Burmese New Testament was finally completed after ten long years of diligent and difficult labor.

Accused as Spies

Shortly after Ann returned to Burma, in January 1824, the Judsons moved to Ava, leaving the Wades to continue the mission in Rangoon. Adoniram's hopes rang high as he looked around the beautiful capital city and envisioned the lives that could be transformed for Christ. Ann wrote home, "We have worship every evening in Burman and a number of the natives assemble, and every Sabbath Adoniram preaches in Dr. Price's house. We feel it an inestimable privilege."[172]

But within weeks, the favorable atmosphere of Ava took a 180-degree turn. And, with it, the Judsons' lives changed forever.

The threat of war between the British and the Burmese emperor had the capital in an uproar. They were fighting over control of the borderland between Burma and Bengal. The emperor had no conception of the size and power of the British Empire. He foolishly commanded his forces to attack Chittagong; the British shelled Rangoon; war had begun!

Suspicion fell immediately on the white foreigners living in Ava. Henry Gouge, a rich, young British merchant, was first imprisoned, then had all his gold and property seized. Once the authorities saw that Gouge had donated funds to Judson and Price, the American missionaries were immediately accused of being paid spies for the British!

Seventeen-Month Hell

Just as the Judsons sat down to supper on June 8, 1824, the door of the mission house flew open, and a dozen Burmese officials rushed in! One was a "spotted face," a criminal and prison executioner who had a small red spot branded on each cheek. The "spotted face" criminals served as cruel guards in the Burmese dungeons.

"Where is the teacher?" called one official gruffly.

"Here." Judson stepped forward, standing as a shield in front of Ann.

"You are called by the king!" said the officer—the dreaded Burmese words spoken at the arrest of a criminal. Immediately, the Spotted Face seized Adoniram, threw him roughly to the floor, and wrapped a metal chain around his arms so tightly that blood began to flow.[173]

"Please, stop! Please don't take him," Ann pleaded with the Spotted Face. "I will pay you money."

"We should take her, as well," came the reply. But the officer in charge ignored the remark and took Adoniram alone, leaving a weeping Ann Judson behind.

Dirty and bleeding from the fetters, Judson was thrown into a dark prison cell along with one hundred other prisoners.

Adoniram was dragged to the dreaded *Let-may-yoon*, or "death prison," where three pairs of iron fetters were riveted to his ankles. Dirty and bleeding from the fetters, Judson was thrown into a dark prison cell along with one hundred other prisoners. The stench of unwashed bodies, rotting food, and human excrement was unbearable, and Adoniram retched from the smell alone.

"Horror of horrors, what a sight!" Judson wrote later. "Never to my dying day shall I forget the scene: a dim lamp in the midst, just making darkness visible, and discovering to my horrified gaze sixty or seventy wretched objects, some in long rows made fast in the stocks, some strung on long poles, some simply fettered; but all sensible of a new acquisition of misery in the approach of a new prisoner."[174]

As his eyes grew accustomed to the darkness, he saw Gouger; Dr. Price; a Scotsman, Captain Laird; and several other white foreigners already fettered in a corner of the room. Prison, deprivation, and the unceasing threat of death would be their companions for the next seventeen months.

"The man who loves his life will lose it, while the man who hates his life in this world will keep it for eternal life" (John 12:25 NIV). Never had this Scripture seemed more real to Adoniram than now.

Tortured in the Death Prison

The death prison was a large rectangular wooden "box" with no ventilation, except through the chinks between the boards and through the door. A thin tin roof separated the wretched prisoners from the rays of the tropical sun, as the daily temperatures reached over 100 degrees Fahrenheit. Vermin scuttled from all corners of the room and found homes in the prisoners' clothing. Food was not provided by the prison. Friends from the outside had to bring food each day, or the prisoners would starve to death.

Each night, the *aphe*, or "father," of the prison would approach Judson and the other foreigners with an evil grin. Together, the prisoners were strung up on a bamboo pole that was lowered from the ceiling. The pole was passed between their fetters, and they were hung by their feet until only their heads and shoulders touched the ground. The tortuous position gave much pain and little sleep, but they did not die. In the morning, they were lowered to the ground once again.

Each day, at three o'clock in the afternoon, a powerful gong would resonate through the outside courtyard; the guards would march into the deathly quiet room and approach one or two prisoners. Without a word, the chosen ones would follow the guards out of the room, shuffling in their iron fetters to their executions. Each day, the question hung in the air, which prisoners would be chosen next?[175]

A Wife's Fight for Justice

Ann ran to the prison door; she hadn't seen Adoniram since his arrest days earlier. Tears coursed down her cheeks, and she hid her face in her hands as her haggard, ashen-faced husband crawled to the gate, still bleeding from his ankles. Leaving the prison later that morning, the courageous Ann was determined; by God's grace, she would fight for justice for her innocent husband.

Resolutely, Ann visited as many government officials as possible throughout the long months of imprisonment, pleading for Adoniram's release.

Finally, the governor of Ava agreed to see Ann and expressed some sympathy: "I cannot release them from their fetters or from prison, but I can try to make them more comfortable." But the weeks wore on and nothing changed. With each visit, Adoniram looked more like the living dead.

Daily, the prisoners heard the guards sharpening their knives for beheadings or talking of hangings in the courtyard. And, daily, Ann arrived with food, reports from the outside, and encouragement for the desolate men.

Silver and the Buried Bible

One morning, the officials informed Ann, "We will be visiting your house tomorrow." Ann hurried home to hide valuables before they arrived. "I secreted as many little articles as possible," she wrote later, "together with considerable silver, as I knew, if the war should go on, we should be in a state of starvation without it."[176]

Carefully carrying the bag of silver to bury in the backyard, Ann remembered their greatest treasure and ran back into the house. She wrapped Judson's completed manuscript of the Burmese New Testament in a piece of muslin. Ann would not let ten years of Adoniram's hard work be destroyed in a moment! She buried the bag and prayed for God's divine protection over the contents.

At the prison, in hushed whispers, she told her husband what she had done. He praised her ingenuity, but they knew that the manuscript would not survive underground. Digging it up in the dark of night, Ann followed Adoniram's directions. She sewed the manuscript into an old, hard pillow and brought it to him in the death prison. For the next few months, Adoniram slept each day with his head securely nestled on the Word of God.[177]

Keeping Adoniram Alive

The next months were a blur of petitions, pleadings, and dashed hopes. Ann's work to free the prisoners and to provide for their needs was relentless. For a short time, she and Adoniram were permitted to spend a few hours a day together in a small hut in the prison yard—a blessing, since she was eight months pregnant. But then, without warning, the hut was destroyed, and the white foreigners were sent to the dark inner prison. The guards ripped Adoniram's pillow away with no idea of the treasure it held.

"What crime has he committed to deserve this additional punishment?' Ann sobbed to the elderly governor of Ava.

The old man's heart melted as he spoke between his own tears. "I was ordered to execute them, but I refused. The least that I can do is to put them out of sight....I promise you, I will never execute your husband. But I cannot release him from his present confinement, and you must not ask it."[178]

Ann visits Adoniram in prison

Despite Adoniram's agony in prison, God was faithful to move on the hearts of Burmese officials to keep him alive!

For the next three weeks, Ann did not visit. On January 26, 1825, she delivered a baby girl, Maria Elizabeth Judson. When she returned to see Adoniram, Ann looked fragile and worn as she carried the tiny baby in her arms. Looking at the helpless child, Adoniram wondered, *What will the future hold for her now?*

Within weeks, the foreigners were seized and forced to walk seven miles to a new prison. The hot gravel seared Adoniram's feet and made walking unbearable. Finally, the men were thrown into carts to complete the journey to Oung-pen-la prison, outside of Ava. For seven months, the prisoners lived in another death camp, close to starvation and with the continued threat of execution. If it hadn't been for Moung Ing, one of Judson's earliest converts, the prisoners and Ann, who had followed Adoniram to Oung-pen-la with baby Maria, would have starved to death.[179]

"If I had not felt certain that every additional trial was ordered by infinite love and mercy," Adoniram wrote, "I could not have survived my accumulated sufferings." There, in the valley of the shadow of death, God's hand would still comfort and provide. For the Judsons, the words of Psalm 23:4 were life: "*Yea, though I walk through the valley of the shadow of death, I will fear no evil; for You are with me; Your rod and Your staff, they comfort me*" (NKJV).

The New Testament Miracle

The war had been going badly for the Burmese. Panic reached the city of Ava as the British army approached the capital. On November 5, 1825, the long-awaited orders finally came. A treaty had been signed! Adoniram was released from prison! The little Judson family, all three of them emaciated and ill from seventeen months of sacrifice, was transported to the capital so Adoniram could translate government documents. Their bodies were nearly depleted of all strength, but their hearts were full of joy!

Adoniram was still a prisoner of the Burmese government, but he was allowed to go to his house in Ava with Ann and little Maria. There, a miracle was waiting for them! Moung Ing had found Adoniram's old pillow lying discarded in the prison yard. Carrying it home, Ing was astounded to discover the hidden treasure inside—the Burmese New Testament had been protected from discovery or destruction, purely by the grace of God! Adoniram was moved to tears by God's goodness in the midst of the cruel persecution they had suffered.[180]

In March 1826, Adoniram was finally released to the English; overcome with joy, he wrote, "It was on a cool, moonlight evening, in the month of March that, with hearts filled with gratitude to God and overflowing with joy at our prospects, we passed down the Irrawaddy, accompanied by all we had on earth. Our feelings continually soared: What shall we render to the Lord for all His benefits toward us?"[181]

After all of this pain and suffering, the Judsons were still serving God and one another; they were a living testimony to the value Christian couples should place on their commitment to God and to each other. Their marriage covenant was consecrated to Him and not prone to the breakups we see so often today due to selfishness on the part of one or both parties.

After all of this pain and suffering, the Judsons were still serving God and one another; they were a living testimony to the value Christian couples should place on their commitment to God and to each other.

The Terrible Price of Peace

Adoniram and Ann stopped for a brief time in Rangoon to see if they had any possessions left, but the mission house had been destroyed by the war. Thankfully, the Wades and the Houghs had escaped unharmed to Calcutta.

Leaving Burmese territory behind, the Judsons met the Wades at Amherst, a jungle village under British control near the west coast of Burma. They would begin their new mission in Amherst with fresh hope. But first, the British and Burmese governments insisted that Adoniram use his translation abilities to negotiate the final peace treaty.

Ann was in fragile health; she was still recovering from a life-threatening bout of typhus. She longed for Adoniram to refuse the order and remain with her and Maria. But the British government had promised to negotiate for a "freedom of religion" clause in the treaty. Religious freedom for Burma! It would be worth the sacrifice of a few more months apart. On September 30, 1826, Adoniram arrived in Ava to begin serious translating work. Within days, he realized that the emperor was not going to grant the religious freedom he had promised.

In the first weeks that Adoniram was gone, Ann cheerfully supervised the building of a bamboo house and two schoolrooms for the new mission. She wrote delightedly to Adoniram, "I have this day moved into a new house and for the first time since we were broken up at Ava, feel myself at home. The house is large and convenient, and if you were here, I should feel quite happy!"

"Our parting was much less painful than many others had been," Adoniram wrote later to Ann's mother. "We had been preserved through so many trials and perils that a separation of three or four months seemed a light thing. We parted, therefore, with cheerful hearts."[182]

But without warning, Ann collapsed from a raging fever. Perhaps the typhus was returning? Even with the careful attendance of British doctors nearby, her body had suffered so much from the year and a half of deprivation that she couldn't fight the ravages of fever again. On October 24, 1826, at just thirty-seven, Ann Hasseltine Judson passed away.

Her Spirit Is Rejoicing

On November 24, Adoniram received a letter from the British superintendent at Amherst. He opened it hurriedly, concerned that something had happened to Maria. With a broken heart, he read the stark words on the page: "To sum up the unhappy tidings in a few words, 'Mrs. Judson is no more. She died the other day at Amherst of remittent fever, eighteen days ill.'"

Ann was no more? How could this be? In anguish, he recalled his beloved Ann, "who had given him her heart in her girlhood, who had faithfully followed him for fourteen years, over land and sea, through trackless jungles and strange crowded cities, with a heroism unparalleled in the annals of missions...dearest Ann."[183]

Inconsolable, Adoniram could not bear that he had not been there for her as she had been for him while in prison. He cried before the Lord for days, "with bitter, heart-rending anguish;" he wrote of his surrender to "the comfort which the Gospel subsequently afforded—the Gospel of Jesus Christ, which brings life and immortality to light....While I am writing...these lines, her spirit is resting and rejoicing in the heavenly paradise."[184] But his heart was broken.

Tragedies and Triumphs

Adoniram returned to the mission in Amherst and to little Maria. He preached in Burmese for the first time since he had been dragged into prison nearly two years earlier, and he welcomed the natives who had accepted Christ without fear of Burmese persecution. A new missionary couple, George and Sarah Boardman, arrived from America, and their commitment to Christ encouraged Judson in his grief.

When ministers need time to heal, we need to love them, support them, and pray for them, or we will lose them.

But one more tragedy awaited him. Maria, who had never been a very healthy baby, became seriously ill with dysentery. No amount of care from Mrs. Wade or the doctors could overcome this newest onslaught. Adoniram wrote home to Ann's mother, "On April 24, 1827, my little daughter Maria breathed her last, aged two years and three months, and her emancipated spirit fled to the arms of her fond mother."[185]

Shortly after, Adoniram joined the Boardmans and the Wades in a new mission in Moulmein. Villagers flocked to the mission house to hear messages of salvation through the blood of Christ. But for Adoniram, it was a season of grieving and prayer. He built a hut that he named "the Hermitage" in the jungle near Moulmein, and lived there alone. Other than short spurts of missionary work, Adoniram spent hours walking through the jungle, praying for the Lord's comfort and direction, asking for a renewal of the joy of his salvation.

As mature Christians, we need to realize that it is okay when someone who has been wounded emotionally or spiritually needs time to heal. It doesn't mean that they are walking away from the Lord or from their call. Sometimes, we don't give people enough time to process the pain; time is necessary to get over disappointment, loss, and grief. When ministers need time to heal, we need to love them, support them, and pray for them, or we will lose them.

For Adoniram, it was a quiet time, but God was at work in the deep wells of his soul. The fields for Christ were white for harvest in Burma, and Adoniram was being prepared to reap those souls for the kingdom of God.

"Are You Jesus Christ's Man?"

When he came out of his solitary time, Judson was on fire for the gospel once again. He set out for the Shwedagon celebration in Rangoon, where tens of thousands of Burmese would flood the city to worship at the gold-covered spire. Judson wrote to Cephas Bennett, their new missionary printer, "Send me all of the tracts and Scripture pamphlets that you can get your hands on, as quickly as possible!" The Burmese would be ripe for God's planting; on festival days, the missionaries would scatter all of the seed that they could.

"During the festival," he wrote to Jonathan Wade, "I have given away nearly ten thousand tracts, giving to none but those who ask. There have been six thousand requests at the mission house alone. Some Burmese have come three months' journey, from the borders of Siam and China—'Sir, we hear that there is an eternal hell. We are afraid of it. Do give us a writing that will tell us how to escape it.'

"Others come from the interior of the country, where the name of Jesus Christ is a little known—'Are you Jesus Christ's man? Give us a writing that tells about Jesus Christ.'"[186]

God was opening doors that had been sealed shut. Ann would have been so excited!

When he returned to Moulmein, the little church had grown with the baptism of many Burmese and Karens—an ethnic group near the Thai-Burma border. Two million pages of tracts and Scriptures had been printed and distributed. George and Sarah Boardman had moved inland to Tavoy to set up a mission in the heart of the Karen population. By the end of 1830, Adoniram sent a report to the American Baptist Mission: "Two hundred and seventeen people have been baptized this year alone, one hundred and thirty-six at Moulmein, seventy-six at Tavoy, and five at Rangoon!"[187] It was the fruit of God's faithfulness.

"The Best of All, God Is With Us"

The greatest barrier to mission work in the tropics was the very real threat of disease. In February 1831, after leading countless Karen natives to Christ, George Boardman passed away from tuberculosis. His wife, Sarah, continued to minister in the jungle, taking her young son, George Jr., with her. (The other two Boardman children had passed away from jungle fevers.) Adoniram began making more frequent trips to Tavoy to help with the growing revival.

The Karens shared a miraculous story of how God had prepared them for the gospel message:

> My lord, your humble servants have come from the wilderness to lay at your feet a certain book, and to inquire whether it is good or bad, true or false. We Karens have no books, no written language; we know nothing of God or His law. When this book was given to us, we were charged to worship it, which we have done for twelve years. But we knew nothing of

its contents, not so much as in what language it is written. We have heard of the gospel of Jesus Christ, and are persuaded of its truth, and we wish to know if this book contains the doctrine of that gospel.

Amazingly, it was *The Book of Common Prayer with the Psalms,* published at Oxford University, England. "It is a good book," Adoniram told them, "but it is not good to worship it. You must worship the God it reveals."[188]

Within six weeks, Judson had baptized twenty-five Karens, including an elderly man who had embraced the gospel of Christ and now wanted to be water baptized before he died. "The old man went on his way," Judson wrote, "rejoicing aloud, and declaring his resolution to make known the eternal God and the dying love of Jesus....'*The best of all is,*' the old man shouted, '*God is with us.*'

"Yes," Adoniram continued, "the great Invisible is in these Karen wilds....He is present by the influence of his Holy Spirit, and accompanies the sound of the Gospel with converting, sanctifying power. '*The best of all is, God is with us.*'"[189]

Today, there is still a great love and desire for the gospel among the Karen people of Myanmar. I had the honor of preaching among the Karens in the northern forests of former Burma, and they were a very kind and humble people, hungry for the gospel of Christ.

It Is Done!

Throughout 1832 and 1833, Adoniram spent weeks secluded in a small hut in Moulmein, working on the translation of the Old Testament. Finally, on January 31, 1834, at the age of forty-six, Adoniram could shout the victory "The Bible is done!"

"Thanks be to God, I can *now* say I have attained. I have commended it to His mercy and grace; I have dedicated it to His glory. May He make His own inspired Word, now complete in the Burman tongue, the grand instrument of filling all Burma with songs of praise to our great God and Saviour Jesus Christ! Amen."[190]

Twenty-one years earlier, a youthful Adoniram and Ann Judson had stepped on the shores of Burma; now, a seasoned missionary of God could rejoice that the Bible translation he had longed to write was finally complete. Adoniram was ready for the next phase of his life in Christ to begin.

Adoniram Judson

God Brings Sarah

Eight lonely years had passed since Ann had died in Amherst. In the years that followed her death, as Adoniram made trips to Tavoy, his relationship with Sarah Boardman became more personal. As a young widow, she had worked among the Karens for three years. Once again, Adoniram had fallen in love with an accomplished, godly woman wholly committed to serving Christ.

On April 10, 1834, Adoniram and Sarah Hall Boardman were married in Tavoy among the people she loved. They moved back to Moulmein the following day with little George, her son.

Adoniram and Sarah began a vibrant ministry life together. At forty-six, Judson still had a full head of auburn hair and was in robust health. He walked vigorously two miles a day over the hills of Moulmein to keep himself strong for ministry. He preached seven sermons a week in Moulmein and spent his days revising the Old Testament while Sarah wrote catechisms, taught Bible studies, and translated *The Pilgrim's Progress* into Burmese. They ministered together as kindred spirits, free from the persecution of the Golden Face.

When Adoniram traveled to Calcutta, and they spent a few months apart, he wrote to Sarah of his desire to return home quickly: "How joyfully do I hope to embark…to see the hills of Moulmein…and how joyfully do I hope to see your dear face and to take you in my loving arms."[191]

On October 31, 1835, Sarah gave birth to their first child, Abigail Ann Judson. She was a special joy to her mother, who had sent young George home to America the year before to begin his formal education. A year and a half later, on April 7, 1837, Sarah gave birth to a son, Adoniram Brown Judson. In the next three years, she gave birth to two more boys, Elnathan and Henry.

Great Praises and Deep Pain

"Every morning we come around the family altar," Adoniram described in a letter to his stepson, George, "your mother and myself, your sister, and your brothers; it is our earnest prayer that all our children may *early* become partakers of divine grace. I hope you will never neglect the duty of *secret prayer*…praying to God, in the name of Jesus Christ" (March 3, 1839).[192]

In 1840, Adoniram's revision of the Old Testament was complete, and by October, the entire Bible was in print. He had labored to translate directly from the Hebrew "to make every sentence a faithful representation of the original." His early passions were accomplished: the Bible was complete and the Burmese church was flourishing. "There are now above a thousand converts from heathenism, formed into various churches throughout the country," he recorded.[193]

On the heels of these days of praise followed months of pain. The next year, in March 1841, Sarah delivered Luther, a stillborn son. Shortly after, she and all four children were struck with dysentery, and the Judsons were forced to sail to Calcutta to recuperate. While they were there, little baby Henry, just a year and a half old, succumbed to illness and was buried beside the graves of William Carey and his associates. How different India was now that the Serampore Triad had gone home to heaven.

Christ Above All

In the next three and a half years, Sarah gave birth to three more sons, Henry Hall in 1842 (named for his brother), Charles in 1843, and Edward in 1844. Just three months after Edward was born, forty-one-year-old Sarah was fighting a losing battle with the dysentery that had plagued her off and on over the years. The doctors insisted that her only hope for recovery was a sea voyage to America away from the oppressive heat and parasites of the tropics.

On April 26, 1845, Adoniram and Sarah boarded the ship the *Paragon* with their three oldest children, Abby Ann, Adoniram, and Elnathan. The children would join George Jr. in America and continue their education there. The three youngest children remained with missionary families in Moulmein until their parents could return.

Adoniram was heartsick at the breakup of his family. "These rendings of parental ties are more severe...than any can possibly conceive who have never felt the wrench. But I hope I can say with truth that *I love Christ above all*; and I am striving, in the strength of my weak faith, to gird up my mind to face and welcome all His appointments."[194]

"Let the Will of God Be Done"

In the Isle of France, the Judsons transferred to the *Sophia Walker*, bound for the United States. For a few weeks, Sarah appeared to be recovering, but then she took a turn for the worse.

Sarah was in perfect peace through her final sickness. She longed to see George Jr. again after a ten-year separation, but she was at rest with the Father's will. "I am in a strait betwixt two—let the will of God be done." At three in the morning on September 1, 1845, after a final kiss for Adoniram, she fell asleep and woke up in heaven. Later that day, her body was buried on the British island of St. Helena in the South Atlantic, in "a beautiful, shady spot." By evening, the *Sophia* had put out to sea once again, while the grieving husband and children clung to the Lord for comfort and understanding.[195]

Sarah Boardman Judson had faithfully served the Lord in Burma—writing, preaching, translating, and ministering beside two missionary husbands. She had also given birth to eleven children, three with George Boardman and eight with Adoniram; six of her children survived to adulthood. She lived a life fully surrendered to Jesus Christ.

A Hero's Welcome

Six weeks later, after thirty-three years in Burma, a reticent Adoniram Judson stepped on the shores of Massachusetts once again. For the past three decades, the stories of his victories and his sacrifices had been circulated throughout America, and he was considered a hero far and wide. Yet, because of a recurring throat ailment, when asked to speak, he could barely talk above a whisper.

A welcome meeting was set up at the Bowdoin Square Church in Boston, and Adoniram sat on the platform with the church dignitaries, feeling humbled and out of place. As one pastor stood to speak of Judson's missionary accomplishments, an older man walked down the center aisle and slowly mounted the platform. As he approached, Adoniram gasped and reached out to embrace the gentleman. It was Samuel Nott![196]

Adoniram had thought that all of the original members of the first missionary group were gone. He knew that Newell, Rice, and Hall had all died of tropical diseases and that Samuel Mills had been lost at sea. He had never heard that Samuel Nott had become ill while serving in Ceylon, had returned to America, and had been a pastor in Massachusetts for the past thirty years. They had been mere boys when they'd left America's shores to spread the gospel of Jesus Christ to the lost; now, they stood before the body of Christ as seasoned and honored men of God.

Raising a Storm

While attending a missionary meeting in Philadelphia, Adoniram was introduced to a young writer, Emily Chubbock, who wrote fanciful stories under the pen name Fanny Forester. Adoniram was searching for a biographer to write Sarah's life story, and Emily had a great deal of writing talent.

As they worked together on Sarah's biography, Emily confessed a little-known secret to Judson—since girlhood, she had harbored a desire to become a foreign missionary. Although she was only twenty-seven years old, half Judson's age, a difficult home life had made her wise beyond her years. Adoniram was surprised at their compatibility.

Within a month, the "famous Burman missionary" shocked the Christian world by proposing marriage to the "fiction writer" Emily Chubbock. She equally stunned her friends in the literary world by saying yes.[197] Despite of raising a storm of protests from all directions, Adoniram and Emily planned to marry the following June.

Adoniram worked to complete a Burmese-English dictionary for the new missionaries pouring into the Burmese nation. By this time, there were thirty-six thriving Baptist churches in the coastal lands of Burma.

The month before the wedding, Judson tearfully left ten-year-old Abby Ann in Plymouth, and eight-year-old Adoniram and six-year-old Elnathan with their stepbrother George in Worcester, so that they could live and grow in the safety of America. On June 2, 1846, in a small, quiet wedding, Adoniram and Emily were married in her parents' home in Hamilton, New York, and set sail for Rangoon a month later.

At fifty-seven, Adoniram realized that he would never see his native land again. That day, he recorded, "Although I feel sadness, I have no regrets. I am returning to my home."[198]

"The Happiest Year of My Life"

Adoniram was overjoyed to see four-year-old Henry and two-year-old Edward when they arrived in Moulmein. Sadly, little Charlie had died a year earlier from a tropical fever. The boys could not remember Sarah, and they shyly embraced Emily as their new mother.

After a brief but unsuccessful stay in Rangoon, the Judson family traveled back to the mission in Moulmein. Emily finished Sarah's biography, and Adoniram worked to complete a Burmese-English dictionary for the new missionaries pouring into the Burmese nation. By this time, there were thirty-six thriving Baptist churches in the coastal lands of Burma. Adoniram continued to preach the message of Christ's love among them.

In June 1847, Adoniram and Emily celebrated their first anniversary. In the midst of mothering the little boys and enjoying a loving husband, Emily wrote to her sister, "It has been by far the happiest year of my life!"[199]

Six months later, on December 24, 1847, she gave birth to a beautiful, healthy baby girl, Emily Frances Judson. The little boys were delighted with their pink-skinned baby sister. Their home was filled with love for Christ and for one another. It was a short season of refreshment for Adoniram.

"O the Love of Christ!"

Two years later, at sixty-one years old, Adoniram was still walking the hills of Moulmein. "He continues his system of morning exercise, started as a student at Andover," Emily wrote home, "and is not satisfied with a common walk on level ground, but always chooses an uphill path, and then goes bounding on his way with all the exuberant activity of boyhood!" Emily was not able to join him as she was battling a persistent cough.

Daily, Judson's fervency for the gospel seemed to increase still more. "Every book we read, every train of thought, seems to me that, more than ever before, 'Christ is all his theme,'" Emily wrote home.[200] "What deep cause have we for gratitude to God!" Judson exclaimed to his wife. "O the love of Christ!"[201]

Shortly after, Adoniram caught a severe cold, accompanied by a high fever. He was sure he wozuld recover quickly, but, instead, the illness settled in his chest, and dysentery followed soon after. For the next few months, Adoniram spent most of his time in bed.

With a great deal of time to pray, he exclaimed to Emily one night, "I have gained the victory at last! I love every one of Christ's redeemed as I believe he would have me love them. And now I lie at peace with all the world, and what is better still, at peace with my own conscience."[202]

Steadily, Adoniram grew worse, and his doctors insisted, as always, that his only hope was a sea voyage, to transport him from the suffocating tropical air of Burma to fresh ocean winds. With apprehension, Emily booked Adoniram on the French ship the *Aristide Marie*, due to sail for the Isle of France. She could not accompany him because it was late in her second pregnancy.

"I Feel So Strong in Christ!"

"I am not tired of my work," Adoniram confided to Emily before sailing, "neither am I tired of the world. Yet when Christ calls me home, I shall go with the gladness of a boy bounding away from his school....Death will never take me by surprise; I feel so strong in Christ!"[203]

On April 6, 1850, the *Aristide Marie* put out to sea with Adoniram on board and fellow missionary Thomas Ranney as his companion. Within days, Adoniram's strength was gone. As Ranney sat beside his bed, the missionary spoke in barely a whisper, "I am glad you are here. I do not feel so abandoned. You are my only kindred now—the only one on board who loves Christ; and it is a great comfort to have one near me who loves Christ."[204]

"Adoniram's death," Ranney told Emily later, "was like one going to sleep. The gentle pressure of his hand showed the peacefulness of his spirit about to take its homeward flight." On Friday afternoon, April 12, 1850, "Adoniram Judson reached his golden shore."[205] Because the ship was far from any shore, he was buried at sea in the Bay of Bengal, a few hundred miles west of the country that he loved.

Three weeks later, Emily gave birth to a son she named Charles, but the baby did not live beyond the first day. Her consolation was in Christ and in the three precious children she had with her at all times. Three months later, word finally reached her of Adoniram's death; she lovingly packed all of their personal belongings and returned to the United States with their little ones.

At home, Emily was well-received by the Baptist community; she worked tirelessly to gather papers for an official biography of Adoniram to be written by Dr. Francis Wayland, the president of Brown University. Sadly, many of Judson's personal writings had been destroyed through the hardships of life in Burma. As often as possible, she reunited all six of the Judson children and George Jr. so that they could remember their father and share as one big family.

Tragically, Emily never recovered from the persistent cough that had overtaken her in Burma. On June 1, 1854, at the early age of thirty-six, Emily Chubbock Judson passed away from tuberculosis and joined the missionary saints in heaven.

Judson's Legacy—Larger than Life

Adoniram Judson left a legacy that is larger than life.

At his death, he left the Burmese Bible, a Burmese grammar book, and a Burmese-English dictionary, all of which are in print and used widely in Myanmar today. His Bible translation remains the most popular in the nation; every dictionary and grammar book written in the last two centuries has been based on the one he originally created.

When Adoniram set sail on the *Aristide Marie*, there were 100 churches and 8,000 believers in Burma as a result of his missionary call. Today, despite fierce government opposition, the Christian church continues to flourish with nearly four million believers, half of which are Baptists; many are descendants of the Karen tribe.

Today, despite fierce government opposition, the Christian church continues to flourish with nearly four million believers, half of which are Baptists; many are descendants of the Karen tribe.

Each July, the churches in Myanmar celebrate "Judson Day," commemorating his arrival with his young bride on that long ago July afternoon. On the campus of Yangon University (once named Judson College) stands Judson Church. In that same city (formerly Rangoon), where Adoniram and Ann labored so tirelessly, a Baptist seminary was founded that still operates today as the Myanmar Institute of Theology, open to all Protestant denominations. In a final triumph to God's faithfulness, the Judson Baptist Church and Ann Hasseltine Judson Memorial Chapel stand on the very site of the Oung-pen-la prison.

In the United States, Judson is considered a significant catalyst for the formation of the American Baptist Associations. There are more than thirty U.S. churches named after him, as well as Judson University in Illinois; Judson College in Alabama is named in honor of Ann. During World War II, a ship, the *SS Adoniram Judson*, was named in his honor, and Judson Press, in Valley Forge, Pennsylvania, publishes Christian books under his name.

"Resolve to Send the Day into Eternity!"

Adoniram suffered untold persecution and tragedies. But he had the honor of marrying three exceptional women whose faithful commitment to Christ and diverse talents helped him spread the gospel of Christ throughout Burma.

Of Adoniram's thirteen children, seven survived to adulthood. His four sons and stepson all attended his alma mater, Brown University. George Jr., Adoniram Brown, and Edward all became distinguished ministers. Edward founded the Judson Memorial Baptist Church in Market Square, New York City, which still welcomes a large congregation today. Abby Ann became the director of a girl's school, and little Emily Frances became a wife and a mother of eight children who continued the Judson line.

In Malden, Massachusetts, a tablet was placed in the first Baptist meeting house that reads:

IN MEMORIAM
REV. ADONIRAM JUDSON
BORN AUG. 9, 1788
DIED APRIL 12, 1850
MALDEN, HIS BIRTHPLACE.
THE OCEAN, HIS SEPULCHRE.
CONVERTED BURMANS, AND
THE BURMAN BIBLE HIS MONUMENT.
HIS RECORD IS ON HIGH.

In December 1810, before his ministry had begun, Adoniram penned the following words. By the time he was laid to rest in the ocean forty years later, he had emblazoned them on the soul of Christian history:

> God is waiting to be gracious if we would not run away from Him.... A few days, and our work will be done. And when it is once done, it is done to all eternity. A life once spent is irrevocable. It will remain to be contemplated through eternity.

The same may be said of each day. When it is once past, it is gone forever. How we wish to see each day marked with usefulness! It is too late to mend the days that are past. The future is in our power.

Let us, then, each morning, resolve to send the day into eternity in such a garb as we shall wish it to wear forever. And at night let us reflect that one more day is irrevocably gone—indelibly marked. Good-night."[206]

Adoniram Judson had indelibly marked the Christian church for eternity.

Ask of Me, and I will surely give the nations as Thine inheritance, and the very ends of the earth as Thy possession. (Psalm 2:8 NASB)

Are you praying for the unsaved of the nations as a part of your inheritance?

Chapter 5

The Hawaiian Revival

When Heaven Kissed Paradise

"Who is in charge of this country?" Lieutenant John Percival, commander of the U.S. naval ship *Dolphin,* defiantly demanded of Queen Ka'ahumanu.

"It is I," the Hawaiian queen responded calmly.

"You are then king," he answered. "I am also a chief. You and I are alike. You are the person for me to talk with. Are you the one who has made it taboo for your women to come and spend the night on our ships?"

"Yes," she replied. "It was by me."

He laughed contemptuously and retorted, "It was not by you! It was by Hiram Bingham!"

"The decision was by me," she insisted. "By Bingham, God's Word is made known to us."

"Take heed!" Percival responded furiously. "My men will come! If the women are not forthcoming, the men will not obey my word. By and by, they will come to get women, and if they do not obtain them, they will fight! We are ready to battle; my vessel is just like fire!"

"We love the Word of God and, therefore, hold back our women," Ka'ahumanu answered firmly. "Why then would you fight us without cause?"

"It is not good to taboo the women. It is not so in America," Percival said. Of course, this was a lie; and prostitution is still "taboo" in America today. He argued that the queen had freely given women to English sailors who had anchored in the harbor, but she told him that was no longer true.

"It is for us to make the decisions respecting our women. They will not come to your men."

"The missionaries are not good!" Percival cried. "They are a company of liars; the women are not taboo in America! Declare to me the man who told you the women must be taboo, and my men will pull his house down. If the women are not released from the taboo tomorrow, my men will come and pull down the house of the missionaries!"

The next morning, Lieutenant Percival allowed twice the usual number of sailors to have shore leave in Honolulu. The men rushed with wooden clubs into the church where the Hawaiians had gathered for daily worship and demanded, "Where are the women? Remove this taboo and let us have your women on board our vessels or we will pull your houses down! There are one hundred fifty of us!" Raising their clubs, they broke the windows of the meeting place.

Racing toward Hiram Bingham's home, the sailors cornered him as he stood on his porch, trying to open the front door. His wife, Sybil, had locked it to protect herself and the children from the angry sailors. One man grabbed and held Hiram by the shoulders, while the others used their clubs to smash in the missionary's windows. The children cried with fear from within the house.

As a sailor raised a knife in front of Hiram, declaring, "You are the man," several Hawaiian Christians came running from the church in their pastor's defense. One of the *Dolphin's* men raised his club to strike Hiram across the head and was restrained by the muscular arms and penetrating blows of the Hawaiian natives. Only Bingham's plea for mercy saved the sailors from being beaten to death.[207]

The Christian revival on the Hawaiian Islands in the early nineteenth century brought peace to the hearts and souls of thousands of Hawaiian natives, but it brought anger and vengeance from those who defied God's message to the Hawaiian people. In that spiritual battle, several consecrated American missionaries made their stand for Christ and His Word.

What Happened in Hawaii

Among the many missionaries who were influential in Hawaii's revival, there are three I would like to introduce in this chapter, two men and one woman, who were used by the Holy Spirit to bring the gospel to the Hawaiian people: Hiram Bingham, Betsey Stockton, and Titus Coan. These three missionaries were significant in Hawaii's introduction to Jesus Christ in very different ways.

The introduction of Christianity in Hawaii didn't happen without a great struggle. Any time the Holy Spirit is at work on the earth, Satan is also on the move.

Bingham was the first missionary sent from the United States to the "Sandwich Islands" (Hawaii); he spearheaded the overwhelming adoption of Christianity and education in the Hawaiian nation. Betsey Stockton was a rarity in early mission work. Not only was she the first *single female* missionary from America, but she was also a freed African-American slave. Finally, Titus Coan was God's instrument to carry the anointing of the Holy Spirit and a great awakening to the Hawaiian Islands. Together, they brought Jesus Christ to a nation.

The introduction of Christianity in Hawaii didn't happen without a great struggle. Any time the Holy Spirit is at work on the earth, Satan is also on the move; he "*prowls about like a roaring lion, seeking someone to devour*" (1 Peter 5:8 NASB).

One thing we can say for certain: God loved the people of the Hawaiian Islands (as He loves them today), and He sent His missionary generals to bring them a new foundation for life: their first written language; hundreds of schools to regenerate their minds, resulting in the highest literacy rate in the world at the time; freedom from alcoholism and forced prostitution; and, most important, the eternal Word of God.

Hiram Bingham: First Missionary to Hawaii

On a beautiful farm in the hills of Bennington, Vermont, Hiram Bingham was born on October 30, 1789. One of thirteen children born to Calvin and Lydia Bingham, Hiram and his siblings grew up in a staunch Congregational home, performing daily farm chores and obeying the rules laid out by a disciplinary father. Like most of the children in eighteenth-century New England, the seven boys in the family attended school sparingly, going to class only in the winter months when the farmwork was buried under the New England snow.

Hiram Bingham
(From *Portraits of American Protestant Missionaries to Hawaii* Published by the Hawaiian Mission Children's Society, 1901. Public domain.)

Of all of the Bingham boys, Hiram was the one his aging parents presumed would take care of them and the family farm in their old age. By the time Hiram was twenty-one, his father was in his seventies. But farming in Vermont was not in Hiram's plans. During his twenty-first year, there was a revival in Bennington, and Hiram committed his life to Jesus Christ, joining the Congregational Church. Even though his education had been minimal throughout his childhood, he was determined to attend a college in New England and prepare for a future life in the ministry.

Duty and Work Ethic

Before Hiram could continue his schooling, he needed to catch up on his Greek and Latin studies. It was common at the time to hire a personal tutor, so he hired the Reverend Elisha Yale to prepare him for the rigors of higher education. Two years later, at twenty-three years of age, he entered Middlebury College in Middlebury, Vermont, as a Bible student. Bingham's strong personality, relentless sense of duty, and "work ethic" pushed him to the top of his class.

His gift of leadership was evident in the classroom and on the campus. Bingham became a member of the Andover Tract Society and the Corban Society (to help needy residents in the area), and he helped to create a Bible Society to encourage his classmates in their faith. In 1816, he and fellow student David Root asked the local Congregational Church for an early Sunday morning study of the Bible; these classes would eventually become New England's first official Sunday school.[208]

After his graduation from Middlebury, Hiram applied to Andover Theological Seminary, the same institution that, just four year earlier, had sent the first American missionaries, including Adoniram Judson, to India and Burma. At Andover, the American Board of Commissioners for Foreign Missions (ABCFM) was still interviewing candidates to send as missionaries overseas to bring the message of Christ to the world. In addition to studying the Scriptures for hours each day, Bingham devoted his time to excelling in Hebrew and Greek. Every missionary candidate knew that translating the Bible from the original Hebrew and Greek into a native language would be a vital part of their missionary work.

Bingham was well-known for his unrelenting fervor in studying the Word of God. He was uncompromising in his love for the Lord but was also "puritanical" in his protest against all things "worldly," pronouncing judgments against "dancing, card playing, and all frivolity." He had been raised as a young man of "duty and responsibility," and he carried those traits into his Christian faith. That stalwart, unrelenting personality would be both his greatest strength and his prevailing weakness through twenty-one years of spreading the gospel in the Hawaiian Islands.

Unusual Students in New England

While Hiram was at Andover, he met five young men who were unusual students for early nineteenth-century New England. Henry Obookiah, Thomas Hopu, William Kanui, John Honolii, and George Tamoree were "Hawaiians," or natives of what was then called the Sandwich Islands. They had left their Pacific island homes as young boys, eager to experience adventure on United States naval ships as they headed out of Honolulu Bay.

Since 1809, they had been living in America, where the young men had accepted Christ as Savior and enrolled as Bible students at the Foreign Mission School in Cornwall, Connecticut. One young islander in particular, Henry Obookiah, had a burning passion to share Christ with his people; he shed tears as he spoke of taking the Word of God back to his homeland. "May the Lord Jesus dwell in my heart and prepare me to go and spend the remaining part of my life with them. But not my will, O Lord, but thy will be done."[209] Unfortunately, as Obookiah was organizing a missionary team to travel to the Islands, he became critically ill and passed away.

During those same months, Hiram was praying for the Lord's guidance in his missionary destination. When he realized that Obookiah's missionary team to the Sandwich Islands was now without a leader, he approached the American board. "Feeling a new impulse to become a pioneer in the enterprise of spreading the gospel in that portion of the Pacific Isles, I freely offered myself to the American Board for that purpose."[210] After a time devoted to prayer, he wrote, "The language of the Holy Spirit seems to be, 'Go quickly to the rescue of the dying heathen, and I will go with you.'" At the encouragement of his older brother Amos and some friends, Hiram applied and was accepted as a missionary to the largely unknown Sandwich Islands. He graduated from Andover in the early fall of 1819 and looked forward to his ordination a few weeks later.

Married in Three Weeks

Bingham had made up his mind; he was ready to dedicate his life to the unsaved natives halfway around the world. But then his fiancée, Sarah Shepherd, decided that a life of service in the wild islands of the Pacific Ocean was not for her and broke off their engagement. Now what would Hiram do? The American mission board had decided that all missionaries must be married before leaving for the field; a wife would provide companionship for his lonely work and protection from sexual temptation while he was so far from home. Where would Bingham find a wife before it was time to depart?

On September 29, 1819, the day of Hiram's ordination in Goshen, Connecticut, he met Sybil Mosely, a young lady who stopped to ask him for directions to the ordination service. He offered to drive her there in his carriage. Along the way, they discovered their mutual desire to serve Christ on the foreign mission field. There was no time for a courtship; within days, Bingham proposed to Sybil, and, three weeks later, on October 11, 1819, they were married in Hartford, Connecticut. By the end of the month, the newlyweds, still relative strangers, began their journey to a new world together.[211]

An Eighteen-Thousand-Mile Journey

The Binghams sailed from Boston Harbor on October 30, 1789, on the ship the *Thaddeus*, along with another missionary couple, Asa and Lucy Thurston; Asa had graduated from Andover and had been ordained with Hiram. "Though leaving my friends, home, and country," Bingham recorded later, "as I supposed forever, and trying as was the parting scene, I regarded that day as one of the happiest of my life."[212]

The pioneer missionary company consisted of two ordained preachers and translators (Bingham and Thurston), a physician, two schoolmasters, a printer, a farmer, the wives and children of the seven men, and three Hawaiians returning home from America. They also had a printing press on board, as there were prepared to imitate William Carey's success in printing the Bengali Bible for the natives of India.

It was a five-and-a-half-month journey from Boston, sailing south in the Atlantic Ocean, around Cape Horn at the southern tip of South America, then northwest to the Sandwich Islands, across eighteen thousand miles of open ocean. During the arduous journey, Hiram's natural leadership propelled him to a position as the head of the missionary company.

On first sighting the Islands in March 1820, Hiram wrote, "The lofty Mauna Kea lifted its snow-crowned summit above the dark and heavy clouds wrapped around its waist. The natives with us shouted for joy at this sight of home from eighty miles out in the ocean."[213]

Captain Cook's Death on the Sandwich Islands

What did Bingham and Thurston know about the Sandwich Islands, where they had committed to spend the rest of their missionary lives?

Forty-two years earlier, on January 18, 1778, British Captain James Cook was the first European to sight these lustrous Pacific lands. This was Cook's third voyage exploring in the Pacific Ocean; he arrived first at the island of Oahu. Impressed by the majesty of the volcanic mountains and crystal clear beaches, he named the island chain the Sandwich Islands, in honor of John Montagu, Fourth Earl of Sandwich, one of his most devoted sponsors. That name was used until the 1840s, when the local name *Hawaii* gradually took its place.

For ten years, Cook had been writing exciting journals about his sea adventures, published as *Captain Cook's Voyages.* (They were the same journals that captivated William Carey as a young boy, enticing him to dream of visiting exotic foreign lands.) Now the British captain would have the honor of introducing the Sandwich Islands to the entire Western world. When Captain Cook arrived at the Islands, he estimated that there were about 300,000 natives living there. Although he was initially received warmly by the island natives, their excitement soon turned into suspicion. On February 14, 1779, at fifty years of age, Captain

Cook was stabbed and killed during a fight over a stolen boat on the beaches of Kealakekua Bay.

Although their sea hero was dead, once the Western world heard about the Sandwich Islands, whaling vessels and sailing ships from many nations hastened to the harbors to establish a new trading port in the Pacific. The sailors on shore leave visited the islands and began to spread "trader's disease"; these were the illnesses inflicted on the native population by foreigners, particularly measles, smallpox, and sexually transmitted diseases.

The Violent Hawaiian King

The missionaries also knew of King Kamehameha I, the Islands' most famous king, who was known for uniting the eight main Sandwich Islands under one government. He was celebrated for this historic accomplishment, but it had not come without a great deal of fighting and bloodshed.

For centuries, each of the islands had its own king and several chiefs who governed the people. Kamehameha was determined to be the supreme king over all. Through deception, betrayal, and hand-to-hand combat between the island leaders and Kamehameha, thousands of native lives were lost. "He was a man of violence," the people said of their king. "Nothing could pacify his wrath."[214]

In an attempt to guarantee his victory, Kamehameha built a temple to the war god, Kūkā'ilimoku, and, at times, offered human sacrifices at his altar. He also worshipped his Polynesian gods by keeping the code of laws called *kapu*, or taboos. The Hawaiian people faced death if they broke any of these taboos. For example, if any men and women ate a meal together, they would be sentenced to death; if a commoner's shadow crossed a chief or a prince—death; if women ate certain foods, including bananas, coconut, pork, and various types of fish—death. After years of bloodshed, with ten thousand victims of war and taboo executions, Kamehameha finally became master of the entire Hawaiian Islands chain in 1810.[215] A critical outcome of both the bloodshed and the "trader's diseases" was a rapid depopulation of the Islands. By the time the American missionaries arrived in 1820, there were only 130,000 natives left of the 300,000 Captain Cook had estimated just forty years earlier.[216]

Destroy the Temples

Kamehameha's land of bloodshed and taboos was what Bingham and the other missionaries were expecting to face on their arrival. But on May 8, 1819, five months before the missionary team even left Boston Harbor, King Kamehameha I died. During his final illness, the king decreed that his favorite wife, Queen Ka'ahumanu, would be the queen regent, and her stepson, Liholiho, would serve as the new king—"they would share the land together."

After years of war and taboos, the new leaders were tired of Kamehameha's culture of death. The king and queen regent met with Hewahuwa, the royal high priest; together, they agreed that it was time to end the kapu system. One night, during a royal banquet with many island chiefs in attendance, the queen entered the men's building and sat with Liholiho and his younger brother to eat dinner, breaking the kapu system and ending the taboos forever.

"When the feast was ended, the king issued his commands that all the idols should be overthrown, the temples destroyed, and the priesthood abolished."[217] According to a missionary account, the high priest himself confessed, "I knew that the wooden images of deities carved by our own hands could not supply our wants.... My thought has always been, there is only one great God dwelling in the heavens."[218]

The Hawaiian people were thrown into a state of confusion. There was no longer a "religion" to follow—no stability, no set of rules, and no kapus. The priests had deserted their altars and given up their taboo system, and the people did not know where to turn. Of course, God knew what was happening in the Hawaiian Islands! Into this religious void, He sent the American missionary team with the message of eternal salvation through Jesus Christ.

"How our hearts were surprised," Bingham wrote, "and encouraged beyond every expectation to hear the astonishing report! Kamehameha is dead—his son Liholiho is king—the taboos are abolished—the images are destroyed—the temples of idolatrous worship are burned....The hand of God! How visible in already answering the prayers of His people for the Hawaiian race!"[219]

"Aloha"

In addition to hearing the wonderful news of the end of the taboo religious system, the missionaries were greeted by excited natives who rowed out to the *Thaddeus* in their canoes. The natives cried, *"Aloha!"* a greeting that is translated "goodwill and peace," then offered the missionaries some island fruit. The Americans had biscuits to give in return.

The natives were especially delighted by the missionary wives. They had seen scores of Caucasian sailors, but no white women before. Landing on shore, the missionaries viewed the large village of thatched houses, towering coconut trees, and blue ocean bays. They were enchanted with their new surroundings but overwhelmed by the natives who crowded around without giving them a moment of privacy.

The natives were especially delighted by the missionary wives. They had seen scores of Caucasian sailors, but no white women before.

Still, Bingham ended the day by recording, "Praise the Lord for His goodness and for His wonderful works to the children of men." When the missionaries met the king a few days later, Bingham wrote, "I made the offer of the gospel of eternal life and proposed to teach him and his people the written, life-giving Word of the God of heaven."

King Liholiho listened politely but declined; he was not interested in giving up his five wives or the pleasure of drinking rum. He granted the missionaries his royal permission to remain on the Islands but asked that they set up one mission in Honolulu, Oahu, (where Bingham remained), and another in Kailua, on the big island of Hawaii. The latter location became Asa and Lucy Thurston's home and mission for the next forty-seven years.

Queen Ka'ahumanu met the missionaries with an air of haughtiness and self-confidence as coruler with the young king. There was no way that Bingham could know that Ka'ahumanu would be the most instrumental person in Hawaii to extend the kingdom of God.

Thirsty to Learn

One month after their arrival, Bingham was able to open his first school in Honolulu. He announced to the king and his chiefs that education was available to anyone who would make the effort to learn. They would also "be sharing the Christian gospel, which was free to all people and a guide in the way of righteousness, temperance, and salvation."

The king didn't want the common people to learn before he did, so he attended school immediately, studying first under Asa Thurston at Kailua, along with his wives and younger brother. While the missionaries worked feverishly to develop the Hawaiian written language, they and their wives also taught the natives the English alphabet, so that they would be accustomed to recognizing how letters form sounds and then words.

Missionaries preaching under kukui groves, 1841.
(Drawn by Alfred T. Agate / Engraved by J. A. Rolph / Public domain)

The king and his chiefs gladly welcomed the education for their people. Within three months, the school in Honolulu, led by Sybil Bingham, had grown from ten adult students to forty attending five hours a day. The combined efforts of Asa Thurston, the two American school teachers, their wives, and many well-trained native teachers allowed them to open schools on every one of the islands. Over the next ten years, hundreds of schools would be established throughout the Hawaiian Islands, and more than 50,000 natives would become students of both the written Hawaiian language and the Word of God.

As the numbers increased, Asa Thurston wrote to the ABCFM for help: "We want men and women who have souls—who are crucified to the world and the world to them—who have their eyes and ears fixed on the glory of God in the salvation of the heathen—who will be willing to sacrifice every interest but Christ's....to such we say, 'Brethren, come over and help us.'"[220]

Creating a Hawaiian Alphabet

When the missionaries arrived in 1820, the Hawaiian people had no written language, no alphabet of any kind, and no literature to communicate their island history. They had oral traditions alone to convey the events of the past.

The Hawaiian Revival

One interesting portion of the oral history was a prophecy that someone would come to them from "heaven" to tell them of "the real God," something entirely different from anything they had ever known; and, the taboos of the country would never be followed again.[221]

Bingham's object was not to change the language of the Hawaiian nation but to develop a simple alphabet so that the written language could be easily understood. "We want to give them the Bible in their own tongue—with the ability to read it for themselves," Bingham wrote.[222] Another goal of the missionaries was to give the natives the necessary tools to write their own literature and to record their oral history on paper so that it would be available to future generations.

Studying the spoken Hawaiian language while they were still aboard the Thaddeus, Bingham and Thurston discovered that there were just a few vowel sounds in the native tongue and that every word ended in a vowel sound. In order to make the reading and writing of the language as easy as possible, they devised an alphabet of five vowels and seven consonants (a, e, i, o, u, h, k, l, m, n, p, w) to express every sound in the pure Hawaiian dialect. An additional nine consonants were introduced later for foreign words that were added to the Hawaiian language.[223]

"We began," Bingham recorded, "by applying ourselves to the acquisition of the Hawaiian language, reducing it to a written form and preparing books for instruction for the nation, teaching all classes to use them as speedily as possible."[224]

January 7, 1822, was a joyful day! Just twenty months after the missionaries had arrived on the Islands, the printing press was humming, printing the first page of the Hawaiian language! It was accomplished, Hiram wrote, "in order to give them letters, libraries, and living oracles in their own tongue that the nation might read and understand the wonderful works of God."[225]

That day, the Binghams handed out the first spelling sheets to seventy pupils who could hardly contain their excitement! In a few months, there were five hundred new students in the Honolulu school alone. At Kamehameha II's (Liholiho) request, one hundred copies of the first Hawaiian spelling book were printed for him, his chiefs, and their families, to learn the written language. In spite of her original resistance, Queen Ka'ahumanu entered the schoolroom as a pupil, as well; and, at the age of fifty, she eagerly learned how to read and write in her native language.

Queen Ka'ahumanu Finds Jesus

It took longer to reach the natives with the message of Christ than it did to get them excited about learning. Slowly, as they heard of Christ's love and redemption in the schools and the church services, more and more of the Hawaiians accepted Christ as Savior. Bingham believed that his personal role was to reach out to the royal family and the other Hawaiian leadership with the gospel of Christ. Then, they could help to introduce their people to God's truth.

One of the first leaders to embrace Christianity was John Ii, a special counselor to the king. Before leaving Honolulu to travel with the king, Ii spoke to Bingham about his new faith.

"I am going away from you," Ii said to the missionary. "I want you to pray with me first. I do not know how to use the words, but I pray in my thoughts."

"God can understand your thoughts," Bingham responded, "when your words are few or broken or even without words."

Queen Ka'ahumanu

John Ii responded with this prayer: "Our Father in heaven, we love Thee. We desire Thee to take care of us. Take care of the king and all the queens. Take care of the land...."[226]

Queen Ka'ahumanu still had little interest in the "new faith" until December 1821, when she became critically ill. The Binghams rushed to her house to pray for her, and Sybil compassionately spent days by her side, offering physical comfort and prayers. After her recovery, the queen regent walked into her first church service to hear the gospel message. Bingham rejoiced that the influential queen, who truly loved her people, was willing to at least listen to what the gospel had to offer. "The Lord had a great work for her to accomplish," Bingham recorded later. "She was to become a humble disciple of Christ and a reformer of her nation."[227]

A Strange Path to Revival

Kamehameha II

Young King Liholiho was still not interested in hearing the gospel. He spent his life in daily festivities with his five wives and his chiefs. Drinking a great deal of rum, which had been introduced by the foreign sailors, had become a way of life for many Hawaiians.

"I cannot repent at once," the king confided to Bingham one afternoon. "My wickedness is very great. But in five years, I will turn and forsake sin."[228]

The king's mother, Keōpūolani, had accepted Christ and tried to persuade her son to listen to the missionaries, but her pleas went unheeded. As she approached death, she whispered to Bingham, who was sitting at her bedside, "Great is my love for the Word of God. It is true—it is good. A good God is Jehovah. The gods of Hawaii are false. I have love to Christ. I have given myself to Him....Great is my desire that my children may be instructed in Christ and know and serve God."[229]

After his mother's death, Kamehameha II became even more restless, moving about from island to island. Desperate for an exciting adventure, he was assured by the British sea captains that King George would welcome him in England. So, the Hawaiian king rashly decided to travel across the world to visit England and King George IV. After that, he would sail on to the United States to meet with President James Monroe. Captain Starbuck, an American captain of the whaling ship *L'Aigle*, offered the king and his party a free passage to England. Liholiho took his favorite wife and several of his chiefs and sailed from Honolulu Bay on November 27, 1823.

With the freedom to reign alone, Queen Ka'ahumanu began to reform Hawaii.

The Queen's Public Conversion

On December 5, 1825, one of the most notable events in Hawaiian Christian history occurred. Queen Ka'ahumanu; her new husband, Kaumualii; and five of her chiefs were "accepted into Christ's church and sat at the Lord's Supper for the first time."

The Queen announced that "it was her determination to attend to the instructions of the missionaries, and to observe God's laws herself, and have her people instructed in letters and in the new religion."[230] She proclaimed, "This is my word and my hand—I am making myself strong—I declare in the presence of God that I repent of my sins, and believe in God our Father." There were five hundred Hawaiian people, both royalty and commoners, present in the service and listening to the queen's announcement. Turning to them, she asked, "Are you willing to unite with me in this good work?" Many responded, "Yes."[231]

From this point, the customs of Hawaii began to change rapidly, mostly for the good of the nation. It is in regard to these areas that Hiram Bingham has received the most criticism for his personal influence in the Hawaiian government. His intention was to bring the gospel of Christ and His commandments to the Hawaiian people. He just did it through his Puritan view of what a "Christian nation" should look like. He had grown up in a faith that reflected "work-based" Christianity, expressing your love for Christ by what you did and didn't do. At times, it was rigid, but it certainly wasn't all bad.

As Bingham taught the Word of God, the queen recognized that some of the practices of the country needed to change. An enormous amount of alcohol was being consumed by the Hawaiian people; the prostitution of Hawaiian girls to foreign sailors was rampant; and adultery, polygamy, murder, and even infanticide still went unpunished in the culture.

The queen's new understanding of the gospel changed all of that. With Bingham's influence, the government established Sunday as the Lord's Day; no work, outdoor competitive games, or alcohol were permitted on that day. Bingham believed that temperance, or the complete rejection of all alcoholic beverages, was an important part of the Christian's commitment to Christ.

The pervasive selling and drinking of rum was shut down on the Sabbath and eventually declared illegal during the rest of the week as well. Bingham often spoke to the chiefs, "If a ship cannot be well commanded by a drunken captain, how much less a nation by a drunken ruler?"[232] Although many of the natives had formerly lived lives of drunkenness and idolatry, the missionaries shared the Scriptures of freedom, such as this: *"And such were some of you. But you were washed, but you were sanctified, but you were justified in the name of the Lord Jesus Christ and by the Spirit of our God"* (1 Corinthians 6:11 NKJV).

Bingham has been condemned in some historical accounts for encouraging the Hawaiians to abolish the hula dance; but, at the time of his arrival at the Hawaiian Islands, the hula was a sensual celebration in honor of *Laka*, the goddess of fertility. Therefore, he did not see it as a cherished Hawaiian tradition but as a form of worship to a false god.[233]

By 1825, the congregations in many of the island churches numbered between 600 and 1,000 natives each Sunday morning. There were 3,000 to 4,000 people meeting for services in Honolulu.

In spite of any controversy over the new laws established by the queen, the Christian church was flourishing. By 1825, the congregations in many of the island churches numbered between 600 and 1,000 natives each Sunday morning. There were 3,000 to 4,000 people meeting for services in Honolulu. Eventually, Bingham designed a large and permanent stone church for Honolulu. It was named Kawaiaha'o Church and still stands today as the oldest church building in the Hawaiian Islands. That same year, 16,000 spelling books were printed and used by the student-filled nation.

In the midst of the positive reports from the Hawaiian people came the sad news that one year earlier, on June 13, 1824, Kamehameha II (Liholiho) had died of measles in England. He and his wife had both been infected soon after arriving in Great Britain, and within days they both passed away without ever meeting the British king. Bingham remembered Kamehameha II's earlier proclamation that he wanted to live five more years for himself before he came to Christ; but he had not lived halfway through the five years. Bingham was saddened by the news of the king's death. "How clear it is that education and civilization without a firm belief in God's Word will accomplish little or nothing for the lost."[234]

Lusting Sailors Angered

The Hawaiian Islands were not only the favorite stopping port for sea captains to have their ships refitted or to purchase new supplies, but they were also infamous for their plenteous young virgins or prostitutes, who were sold for their services on the ships while they were anchored in port.

Lucy Thurston wrote with great sadness of the behavior of the Hawaiian women when a ship pulled into the harbor: "A sisterhood of fifteen or twenty assembled and took seats in a conspicuous part of the village to display themselves. Their own relatives, perhaps fathers or brothers, or even husbands, then paddled the whole company of women and girls to spend the night on board that ship specially for the gratification of the sailors."[235] For their services, the women were "rewarded" with a piece of foreign clothing.

The illicit behavior was the catalyst for the spread of venereal disease throughout Hawaii. The missionaries were disgusted and grieved by the violation of God's commandments by the captains and sailors who claimed to be from "Christian" nations.

All of that changed with the arrival of the gospel of Christ and the resolute leadership of Hiram Bingham.

The *Dolphin*, a U.S. naval ship commanded by Lieutenant John Percival, docked in Honolulu Bay in January 1826 for some repairs before returning to America. Percival and his men came onto Honolulu's shores in search of "purchasing vile women" for the sailors while they were at anchor.[236] Queen Ka'ahumanu responded with a note to the lieutenant that her country had established new laws forbidding prostitution and that the men could not purchase the women's services.

Percival's written response to the queen was, "I will come and have a talk with the queen. If Mr. Bingham comes, I will shoot him. Though my vessel is small, she is just like fire!" Ka'ahumanu read the note to her chiefs and then encouraged them, "Let us be firm on the side of the Lord, and follow His Word."[237]

The next day, Percival visited the queen; their meeting ended in Percival's defiant argument with Ka'ahumanu, and the sailors' later assault on Bingham's house, incidents that were described in the opening pages of this chapter.

After he was repeatedly denied women for his ship, Lieutenant Percival complained to the seaport authorities in Honolulu: "Mr. Bingham has interfered with the civil regulations of this place and has deprived my sailors of the enjoyment they have always participated in when they visit this island!"[238]

The American Board of Commissioners for Foreign Missions heard of the incident and respectfully asked the U.S. naval authorities to investigate the claims. There was a naval inquiry in Charleston, South Carolina, and Lieutenant. Percival was disciplined for his actions.[239]

Revival Explodes

By the end of the 1820s, the church grew such that the missionaries had to preach outdoors, at times to crowds of 10,000 natives. There were six large churches in the Islands with 12,000 in attendance; there were 26,000 students in the schools, and 440 native Hawaiian teachers.

Bingham wrote home to the American Board: "Your hearts would leap for joy, and you would give thanks to God for having ever put into the hearts of any to come over the wide waters that divide us and to preach salvation to this people."[240]

The British and the American sea commanders still brought accusations against the missionaries, and particularly Bingham, for the changes in Hawaiian law, not just concerning the prohibition of prostitution but also the Sabbath restrictions and the lack of available rum and of gambling.

The British and the American sea commanders still brought accusations against the missionaries, and particularly Bingham, for the changes in Hawaiian law, not just concerning the prohibition of prostitution but also the Sabbath restrictions and the lack of available rum and of gambling. Eventually, in support of the missionaries, President John Quincy Adams stepped in by recognizing Hawaii's sovereign right to set up her own laws, which must then be obeyed by all U.S. naval personnel: "Our citizens who violate your laws, or interfere with your regulations, violate at the same time their duty to their own government and country...."[241]

Queen Embraces First Hawaiian New Testament

In 1832, the Honolulu mission printed a total of seven million pages in the Hawaiian language! Also, after twelve years of translating work, the Hawaiian New Testament was finally complete!

At the same time, the mission was saddened; Queen Ka'ahumanu's health was failing. She was sixty-four years old and fighting an illness that the doctors couldn't diagnose. In spite of being bedridden, after seven years of leading her nation in Christ's love, she continually proclaimed that she had "an unshakable reliance on Jesus as her Friend and Savior."

Hiram took a freshly bound New Testament to the queen's bedside. "She took the sacred prize into her hands as she lay upon her lowly couch, glanced through it to assure herself it was really the Bible, and pronounced it *maikai*—excellent!"

In her final days, Bingham spoke gently to the queen, "Elizabeta [her baptismal name], this is perhaps your departure. Stay yourself on Jesus; He is your Physician, your Savior. We wish you to stay with us; that would be our joy; but we think the Lord will soon take you from us."

"I will go to Him," she replied, "and I shall be comforted." Ka'ahumanu died just before dawn on June 5, 1832.[242]

The Hawaiian nation felt the shock of losing their beloved queen; and the body of Christ in Hawaii, their strongest supporter. No one could fill her place. "She was a distinguished reformer of her nation, a kind friend of the missionaries, and a firm supporter of their cause," Bingham wrote to the ABCFM. She could truly say with the apostle Paul, *"I have fought a good fight, I have finished my course, I have kept the faith: henceforth there is laid up for me a crown of righteousness, which the Lord, the righteous judge, shall give me at that day: and not to me only, but unto all them also that love his appearing"* (2 Timothy 4:7–8).

The new king, Kauikeaouli (Kamehameha III), was too young to rule alone, so his older sister Kinau was named the queen regent. She desired to still "follow the ways of Jehovah, the God of Abraham, Isaac, and Jacob, the God of the living and not of the dead."[243] But the young king had become more interested in rum and in the frivolity of Hawaii's former years, before the missionaries had arrived. He overturned the restraints on the manufacture and sale of alcohol, allowing the reestablishment of the rum-selling houses. Although the missionaries were saddened at this turn of events, they dedicated themselves to the preaching, teaching, and publishing of the Scriptures, concentrating on the translation of the Hawaiian Old Testament.

Revival Sweeps the Islands

In Bingham's last ten years on the Hawaiian Island, every area of ministry continued to grow. The number of pupils in the schools reached as many as 50,000, and the country of Hawaii was known to have the highest literacy rate in the world at that time. Millions of pages of Hawaiian text were printed and distributed throughout the Islands.

The Hawaiian Revival

Societal standards may have lowered in Hawaii after Ka'ahumanu's death, but the Holy Spirit was still moving among the people with His anointing power. A great awakening swept the Hawaiian Islands through the prayers and ministry of the Reverend Titus Coan, who arrived from the United States in June 1835. We will read more about Coan's place in the Hawaiian church in a later section of this chapter.

Bingham was truly blessed by the new revival through Coan's ministry:

> Indeed there was a shaking among the dry bones throughout the nation. The Spirit of God most manifestly hovered over the islands. The gospel proved to be the power of God and the wisdom of God for the recovery of the lost.
>
> Our ears were allowed to hear and our eyes to see glorious things in our Hawaiian Zion. Thousands of the liberated appeared to be coming to Zion and celebrating the praises of the Deliverer.
>
> This gracious visitation of the Spirit of God from on high led unusual thousands to crowd the doors of the sanctuaries, where they were addressed with unusual earnestness and where the united cry of many ascended into heaven."[244]

Over 7,000 people were added to the Hawaiian churches in a matter of a few months, 600 of them children and teenagers. The revival continued for the next seven years.

On May 10, 1839, the last page of the completed Bible, including both the Old and New Testaments, came off the printing press. Bingham responded, "The entrance of God's Word giveth light." (See Psalm 119:130.)

Hiram Bingham Never Returned

Hiram and Sybil Bingham decided to sail to New England for a short furlough in 1841. Hiram didn't really want to leave Hawaii, but Sybil was ill and needed some rest; she also longed to see their four children, who were completing their education in the United States.

Hiram Bingham never returned to Hawaii. Even after Sybil passed away from her illness, the ABCFM would not allow him to return to the field because of the controversies surrounding his influence on the Hawaiian government.

Foreign residents and sea captains regularly filed complaints against the missionaries, Bingham in particular. Any investigations always found the Christian men innocent of the charges, leading lives that benefited the natives. But, in the end, the mounting criticism concerning Bingham's close contact with the Hawaiian royal family became too much for the American Board of Commissioners, and they refused to reinstate him as a foreign missionary.

To me, their action reflected a weakness that can be found in some Christian institutions that bow to criticism instead of following the leading of the Holy Spirit. If you have a man or woman in ministry who is making a mistake, you take him or her aside, explain the situation and the need for change, bathe the situation in prayer, and then allow the person to continue in the calling. But the commissioners didn't do that; they didn't even give Bingham a second chance. Who knows what other work God may have had for Hiram Bingham to complete in Hawaii?

The missionary pioneer was initially distraught over the decision, but he was determined to continue to serve the Lord. He published a memoir entitled *A Residence of Twenty-one Years in the Sandwich Islands* in 1847. In 1852, after several years as a widower, he married Naomi Morse, the principal of a girl's school. He spent the remainder of his life pastoring an African-American church in Connecticut, an interesting choice of ministry, since he has so often been accused of racial prejudice. My research did not uncover the name or exact location of that ministry.

Hiram Bingham died on November 11, 1869, at the age of eighty and was buried in Grove Street Cemetery in New Haven, Connecticut, beside his longtime helpmate, Sybil.

The Bingham Name Lives On

Bingham's son, Hiram Bingham II, returned to Hawaii as a missionary in 1857 and successfully preached the Word of God in the Pacific Islands for more than twenty-five years. Bingham's grandson, Hiram Bingham III, was a renowned explorer who is credited with "discovering" Machu Picchu, an Inca estate located in the mountains of Peru. Bingham III later became a U.S. Senator, representing the state of Connecticut. Bingham's great-grandson, Hiram Bingham IV, was the U.S. vice consul in France during World War II, and organized the rescue of thousands of Jews from the Holocaust. In addition, the World War II U.S. liberty ship, *S.S. Hiram Bingham,* was named in the missionary's honor.

Influencing Hawaii for Good

There is very little "good press" in modern history books concerning the pioneer missionary Hiram Bingham I. He was caricatured in James Michener's epic novel *Hawaii* as a self-righteous, intolerant New England Puritan with little love for God or the Hawaiian people. The 1966 movie *Hawaii,* based on the Bingham caricature, sealed modern opinion in disfavor of the missionary. However, both Hollywood and historians are guilty of presenting a one-dimensional assessment of this nineteenth-century missionary.

It is true that Hiram Bingham viewed the gospel through the eyes of Puritan doctrine; as a result, he could be harsh in his judgment of the Hawaiian natives. He also exhibited some of the condescension toward native people that existed in the Western world in the nineteenth century, and still exists among some people today. However, very little credit is given to what this resourceful Christian man actually did accomplish for Hawaii.

It was Bingham who spearheaded the creation of the Hawaiian alphabet to bring literacy to the Hawaiian nation. That alphabet is still used for the native language today.

It was Bingham who spearheaded the creation of the Hawaiian alphabet to bring literacy to the Hawaiian nation. That alphabet is still used for the native language today. Between 1828 and 1839, he published a Hawaiian speller and dictionary. He was determined to see the completion of the Bible in the Hawaiian language, personally translating several books of the New Testament.

Bingham and his colleagues wrote and printed the first *Hawaiian Almanac* in 1835 and published the Islands' first newspaper, *The Hawaiian Teacher,* "supplying the people [as Carey had done in India] with useful knowledge of the arts, sciences, history, morals, and religion."[245] He initiated daily prayer meetings attended by three hundred natives, who rose an hour before sunrise to pray for God's blessings on each of the Hawaiian Islands.

Bingham and his wife set up the first school on the islands and provided the model for the other missionaries, spreading the educational movement throughout the Hawaiian Island chain. By 1831, there were 52,000 students in 1,100 schools, bringing literacy to over 70 percent of the population. The missionaries trained the natives to be teachers, and, in that way, the number of schools was multiplied throughout the islands.

Determined to teach the Hawaiian people to be self-sufficient, Bingham and his colleagues introduced the plough for farming, the wheel and loom, scissors, needle and thread for making clothing, simple blueprints for building sturdier houses, and printing presses and bookbinding for publishing literature; they also recognized that the natives could earn a living with these tools as they were instructed in their use and became skilled with them.

Bingham never sought financial gain from the Hawaiian Islands, as some descendants of these early missionaries are accused of doing in following decades. He did not buy land or accumulate great wealth at the expense of the native people. Nor did he pave the way for annexation of Hawaii by the United States, since he consistently befriended the royal family and supported Hawaiian sovereignty and independence.

In more than one way, this often-criticized missionary was a man of determination who went to the Hawaiian people and brought them the freedom of education and the hope of eternal life in Jesus Christ. Although today we understand more clearly that the kindness of the Lord does more to bring the lost to Christ than a Puritan fear of His judgment, Hiram Bingham moved in the light that he had at the time to introduce Christ to the nation of Hawaii.

"As our great aim has been to win the nation to Christ," Bingham wrote, "we believe we have begun right in preaching the gospel, translating the Scriptures, making books, establishing schools, and by their means giving the people access to the Bible and other means of knowledge. A great change has been affected in the religious views of the nation...."[246]

Betsey Stockton: America's First Single Female Missionary

Betsey Stockton was a brave young woman who was called by God to sail from the shores of America as the first unmarried female missionary. What made her astounding was that she was not only the first single female to go forth in mission work, but she was also an African-American. While there is not a great deal of detail available about her life and ministry, she has earned our respect for having the courage to break society's racial barriers and, as a former slave, to take on the challenges of missionary life in the early nineteenth century. Although Betsey was denied her individual right to liberty during the first twenty years of her life, she spent the next fifty years bringing freedom to those in spiritual captivity.

Betsey Stockton

Betsey Stockton was born a slave in Princeton, New Jersey, probably in the year 1778. (There are no records of her actual date of birth.) As a child, she was owned by a Richard Stockton and therefore was given his last name. Because slaves were considered property, Betsey was "a present" for Stockton's daughter, Elizabeth, on her marriage to the Reverend Ashbel Green, who became the eighth president of the College of New Jersey (later renamed Princeton University).

It was in Dr. Green's home that a whole new and unexpected world was opened up to Betsey. During the summer of 1816, a revival swept through the town of Princeton and the college. Betsey sat in the gallery of the First Presbyterian Church of Princeton and listened to the Word of God concerning the forgiveness of sins and salvation in the name of Jesus. During the revival, she surrendered her life to Jesus Christ. In September 1816, Betsey applied for and was accepted into membership in the First Presbyterian Church of Princeton.[247]

In earlier years, the Green family had shown Betsey love and respect by opening their library to her; she had been tutored by both Reverend Green and his son, James, in reading, writing, geography, math, and literature. Shortly after Betsey surrendered her life to Christ, Ashbel Green, who had become an antislavery advocate, honored her new freedom in Christ by granting her freedom from slavery. She continued to work in the Green home but now as a paid employee.[248]

Grateful beyond words for the Greens' love, Betsey longed to be used in service to the Lord. She wondered if perhaps she might work as a teacher to train other African-American children. But deep in her heart was a growing desire to travel to a foreign mission field and teach the Word of God.

Accepted to the Sandwich Islands

A recent Princeton Seminary graduate, Charles S. Stewart, was a friend of the Green family. He visited Green in 1821 and shared his desire to go to the Sandwich Islands to share the gospel of Christ. Hiram Bingham and his missionary party had sailed to the Islands two years earlier.

The point of the contract was that while Betsey would do the domestic jobs required of any of the missionary women, she would not be in Hawaii to work as a servant. She would be free to teach and to proclaim the gospel of Christ among the lost.

Overhearing their conversation, Betsey inquired about the possibility of accompanying the Stewart and his wife on their missionary journey. Both men thought it was an excellent idea and encouraged her to apply to the American Board of Commissioners for Foreign Missions for a position on the next missionary team. On September 3, 1821, the Reverend Green mailed a letter of recommendation to the ABCFM, promoting Betsey's abilities as a nurse, a teacher, and a committed disciple of Christ.

Both the Stewarts and Betsey were immediately accepted for the mission. While Charles was raising money to pay his portion of the expenses for the journey, Betsey was saving every penny possible from her servant's wages to pay part of her own expenses, as well. Before the missionaries could leave for Hawaii, the ABCFM insisted that a contract be written to protect Betsey from being taken advantage of in her new environment.[249]

Her contract stated that she was not to be treated as a servant but as a teacher: "She is to be regarded and treated neither as an equal nor as a servant—but as a humble Christian friend, embarking in the great enterprise…to bring to the heathen the saving knowledge of the truth as it is in Jesus."[250] The point of the contract was that while Betsey would do the domestic jobs required of any of the missionary women, she would not be in Hawaii to work as a servant. She would be free to teach and to proclaim the gospel of Christ among the lost. Reverend Green, Charles Stewart, Betsey, and the secretary of the ABCFM each signed the contract, which marked another step toward Betsey's lifetime work as a teacher.[251] Betsey Stockton, a single, free, African-American woman in the early nineteenth century was now officially an American missionary!

The Hawaiian Revival

Rough Sailing but Happy

On November 19, 1822, Charles and Harriet Stewart, Betsey, and eleven other missionaries embarked on the ship the *Thames*, destined for the Sandwich Islands. They were the first reinforcements to be sent to the Pacific Islands since Bingham and Thurston had arrived three years earlier.

The day after they left New England, Betsey began to record her daily experiences in a journal that she then mailed to Ashbel Green. Green published portions of her writings in installments in the periodical *Christian Advocate* in 1824 and 1825. Unfortunately, the original diary was lost. From the beginning of the journey, Betsey wrote that she was treated with kindness and respect by the other missionaries on board.

Within the first week at sea, even though a gale had sent ocean water rushing into her cabin, Betsey wrote praises to the Lord: "The Lord reigneth, let us all rejoice!" (November 23).

As the weather changed from week to week, through calm and stormy seas, Betsey expressed her similar feelings, sometimes happy and sometimes lonely: "My soul longed again for the house of the Lord. I endeavored to find Him present with me and soon found indeed that He was near to all who call on Him" (December 1).

On the final day of 1822, she wrote, "I must finish this year by saying with the psalmist, 'When I consider the works of thy hands, Lord, what is man that thou art mindful of him?'"[252]

There were some very rough days at sea for the missionary party. In the Atlantic, they experienced three weeks of gale-like storms, and rounding Cape Horn, the seas were so rough that they often feared for their lives. On February 9, 1823, Betsey recorded, "At times I have seen the waves rise like mountains high before us; and it appeared that we must inevitably be swallowed up; but in a moment our ship would rise above the wave, and it would be seen receding at the stern."[253] Once again, God was merciful.

On April 11, two weeks before their first sighting of Hawaii, Harriet Stewart gave birth to a baby boy they named Charles. Betsey was the midwife at the birth and became instantly attached to the little one who was partly in her charge. She would remain close to Charles and be lovingly referred to as his "Aunt Betsey" for the rest of her life.

"The Sight Chilled Our Very Hearts"

On April 24, 1823, the *Thames* came into sight of Oahu and the Honolulu Bay. Betsey recorded a great deal that day. "At the first sight of the snow-capped mountains, I felt a strange sensation of joy and grief. It soon wore away and as we sailed slowly past its windward side, we had a full view of all its grandeur."[254]

Betsey's first impression of Hawaii's beauty was soon replaced by her graphic description of their initial sighting of the natives. "Two or three canoes, loaded with natives, came to the ship: their appearance was of half man and half beast—naked—except a narrow strip of *tapa* round their loins. When they first came on board, the sight chilled our very hearts. The ladies retired to the cabins and burst into tears; and some of the gentlemen turned pale...my every nerve trembled."[255] But soon after, the response of Betsey's conscience was, "They are men—and they have souls."

In order to ease the nerves of everyone on board, both missionaries and natives, Betsey went below deck and brought the newborn baby—two-week-old Charles Stewart—to the top deck. The natives were delighted: "Some of them took him in their arms and in ecstasy exclaimed, *'aloha maitai'*—very great love to you—and kissed him." The missionaries were ready to serve the people of Hawaii.

Betsey's Maui School

In response to these new missionaries who had arrived at the Islands, Queen Ka'ahumanu inquired after them, sending fresh fruit and meat out to the ship while they were still anchored in the harbor. The missionaries were relieved to be welcomed with such hospitality.[256]

On May 10, the missionary party left the ship and joined Bingham in Honolulu. Soon after, the Stewarts and Betsey were assigned to begin a new mission in Lahaina on the island of Maui. On May 31, they reached their beautiful, tropical home, and, at the request of the natives, they started their missionary school the next day.

The church in Lahaina was an open beach area that was visited at times by Kamehameha II and his wives. After the royal family met Betsey, one of the king's sons came to her the next morning requesting that she teach him English. From the start, Charles Stewart put the Lahaina school in Betsey's capable hands. She began with four English students and six Hawaiian students. She wrote to Ashbel Green in 1824, "I have now a fine school of the... lower class of people, the first I believe that has ever been established."[257]

Betsey Stockton, a former slave, became known for establishing the first school for the common natives on the Hawaiian Islands. Before long, there were thirty students meeting with her each afternoon in the church chapel.

Most of her students were farmers from the island of Maui, so Betsey Stockton, a former slave, became known for establishing the first school for the common natives on the Hawaiian Islands. Before long, there were thirty students meeting with her each afternoon in the church chapel. Betsey became "quite familiar with the Hawaiian language" and taught them with ease.[258]

Unfortunately, Stockton's time in Hawaii was cut short. After just two and a half years, Harriet Stewart became too ill to remain on the Islands any longer. She and Charles, with their two children (a baby girl had been born the year before), made plans to return to America. Although Betsey appears to have enjoyed her season of ministering in Hawaii, she left with the Stewarts on October 17, 1825, never to return.

Founding the First African-American Presbyterian Church

Although she was no longer a foreign missionary, Stockton's service to the Lord was far from over. She spent the next several years working for the Stewart family in the care of their children. Harriet Stewart never fully recovered from her illness, and, in 1830, after bearing her third child, she passed away. Charles was now a Navy chaplain and often out to sea, so "Aunt Betsey" moved to Cooperstown, New York, to take care of the Stewart children. During the five years in which she served as their paid nanny, Betsey took them with her to Princeton, New Jersey, so that she could be back in her home city. Once Stewart remarried in 1835, however, he moved the children back to New York, while Betsey remained in Princeton, where she would dedicate the rest of her life to serving the Lord and others.

Returning to her true love of teaching, Betsey opened a public, or "common," school for African-American children in Princeton, where she served as teacher and principal for more than twenty-five years. She also helped to establish the first Presbyterian church for a black congregation; her name is listed at the top of the founding members of the First Presbyterian Church of Colour, later renamed the Witherspoon Street Presbyterian Church of Princeton.[259]

Young Charles, who remained dear to her for the rest of her life, rose to the top of his class at West Point and became a Brigadier General in the United States Army. He bought Betsey her own home in Princeton, where she could live in comfort for the remainder of her life.[260] "Aunt Betsey grew to be one of Princeton's most admired and beloved figures, though unassuming and gentle in spirit. She had a quiet, steady Christian influence, particularly on young people, with whom she was always surrounded in week-day school and in Sunday school."[261] Her mission work as a compassionate teacher had continued throughout her life.

When Betsey Stockton passed away in 1865, her funeral was conducted by Dr. John Maclean, who was then president of Princeton University. She was buried in Lakewood Cemetery in Cooperstown, New York, in the Stewart family plot. The remarkable nineteenth-century female missionary had made her mark in America and halfway around the globe in Hawaii, as well. She earned her place as a missionary general in the kingdom of God.

Titus Coan: Hawaii's Revival Preacher

Titus Coan
(Hawaii Historical Society / Public domain)

Titus Coan was born on February 1, 1801, in Killingworth, Connecticut, the youngest of seven children born to Gaylord and Tamza Coan. Unlike the rigid upbringing of Hiram Bingham, Titus had a happy childhood growing up on a New England farm, with some duties but still plenty of opportunities to attend school. Coan was an excellent student and spent hours devouring any books he could find. After he had successfully completed every class in the local district school, his parents provided him with private tutors and then sent him on to a boys' academy in Madison, Connecticut, to be challenged and better prepared for his future education.[262]

In 1819, when Coan was just eighteen years old, there was a revival in Killingworth led by New England evangelist Asahel Nettleton. "He came," Titus wrote, "and 'the Power of the Highest' came with him!"[263] There were conversions in every service, and the bars in town were closed, while the churches were filled with people singing hymns of praise. Unfortunately, Titus was out of town during the revival, but 110 of his friends and relatives came to Christ as Lord and Savior. Disappointed that he had missed the messages of faith, Titus began to search the Scriptures on his own, slowly recognizing the salvation Christ had provided for him on the cross.

Revival Meetings with Charles Finney

In the next ten years, Titus spent time in the military, opened a school near Salisbury in northern Connecticut, and worked in the mercantile industry with his brother. All the while, he was searching his heart for a permanent profession and praying for a stronger personal relationship with Jesus Christ. There were three offers on the table for Coan's future: his brother wanted Titus to join him in his successful mercantile business; a widely-respected physician in Rochester believed that he had the intelligence and ability to become a distinguished physician; and his Christian friends were certain that the ministry was his calling. Which potential endeavor was from the Lord?

Each of these professions stirred Titus's interests, but only one pulled at the strings of his heart. He wanted to minister for the Lord, but he felt so unworthy. After months of fighting a severe illness that nearly cost him his life, Coan was convinced that he should go into the ministry and trust the Lord to use him as He saw fit. "Lead me, Savior," he prayed fervently. "Tell me where to go and what to do, and I will *go* and *do*."[264] From there, he enrolled in Auburn Theological Seminary, a training school for Presbyterian ministers located in upstate New York.

During the months before he entered the seminary, a divinely appointed relationship changed Coan's life. He spent the summer of 1830 living near Rochester, New York, with a friend, the Reverend Lewis Cheeseman, and his family. The Second Great Awakening was at its height, and the primary revivalist in New York at the time was Charles Finney. That summer, Finney spent months traveling throughout northern New York State, preaching in the power of the Holy Spirit to bring men and women to Christ. Titus and Rev. Cheeseman attended and sometimes assisted in those meetings.

The Holy Spirit was evident wherever Finney spoke; the Spirit swept through the congregation night after night, with repentant sinners dropping to their knees in tears, and redeemed Christians filling the church halls with their praises. Titus Coan's heart and spirit were revived and inspired at those meetings. He saw what prayer and preaching could accomplish when the man of God was surrendered to the leading of the Holy Spirit. During those months, Coan learned of the relationship in Finney's ministry between fervent prayer and the power of revival:

> Prayer is an essential link in the chain of causes that lead to a revival, as much so as truth is. Some have zealously used Bible truth to convert men, and laid very little stress on prayer. They have preached, and talked, and distributed tracts with great zeal, and then wondered that they had so little success. And the reason was that they forgot to use the other branch of the means, effectual prayer. They overlooked the fact that truth, by itself, will never produce the effect, without the Spirit of God, and that the Spirit is given in answer to prayer....
>
> A revival may be expected when Christians have a spirit of prayer for a revival. That is, when they pray as if their hearts were set upon it. When Christians have the spirit of prayer for a revival. When they go about groaning out their heart's desire. When they have real travail of soul.[265]

A Missionary Calling Begins

After two years at Auburn Seminary, on April 17, 1833, Coan was licensed to preach as a Presbyterian minister. Shortly after, the American Board of Commissioners for Foreign Missions contacted him. Would he consider being ordained as a missionary and traveling to Patagonia in the Andes Mountains of South America as a missionary for a year?

Titus and Fidelia Coan

In the spring of 1834, after the year's commitment was finished, Coan returned to New England. The time spent in Patagonia had convinced him that he was called to be a missionary, but he didn't want to go alone. He proposed to twenty-four-year-old Fidelia Church, a young woman he had been in love with for six years. They were married in Churchville, New York, on November 3, 1834, and, one month later, on December 5, they sailed with six other missionaries on the merchant ship *Hellespont* bound for the Sandwich Islands.

After a month's delay in Chile for ship repair, the new missionaries landed in Honolulu on June 6, 1835. Coan wrote that he was honored and excited to meet Hiram Bingham, whom he called, along with the other early Hawaiian missionaries, "apostolic; the fathers and mothers in Israel, an honored and happy family."[266]

The Doors of Revival Burst Open

Hiram and Fidelia were assigned to a small church of only twenty-three members in Hilo on the island of Hawaii. They joined another ABCFM missionary couple, David and Sarah Lyman, who had been assigned to Hilo on their arrival three years earlier. Hilo was one of the most picturesque areas on the big island of Hawaii; it was blessed with dramatic waterfalls, fertile rain forests, flourishing gardens, and snowcapped volcanoes.

While Titus and Fidelia worked diligently at night to learn the Hawaiian language, they taught English, Bible, and other subjects in the Lymans' school for the native children during the day. Within two years, the school grew so large that David Lyman asked to be released from his duties as Coan's copastor in order to administrate the school. The preaching was left to the capable and anointed ministry of Titus Coan. The most important thing that occurred during this time is that both missionary couples, along with their twenty-three native converts, spent hours in fervent prayer for revival to fall on the Hawaiian Islands.

While Titus and Fidelia worked diligently at night to learn the Hawaiian language, they taught English, Bible, and other subjects in the Lymans' school for the native children during the day.

The population of the Hilo district was about 16,000. By the end of 1836, after eighteen months on the islands, Titus was fluent enough in the Hawaiian language to share the gospel without an interpreter. On November 29, 1836, he began his first tour of the island of Hawaii, preaching for thirty days to a large number of natives along one hundred miles of shoreline. The answer to the missionaries' prayers had come—the doors of revival burst open before this anointed man of God!

Forty-Three Messages in Eight Days

As Titus moved through the small villages along the Hawaiian coast, the natives responded enthusiastically to his messages of repentance and life in Christ:

> I preached three, four, five times a day....The people rallied in masses and were eager to hear the Word. Many listened with tears and after the preaching, when I supposed they would return home and give me rest, they remained and crowded around me so earnestly that I had no time to eat. In places where I spent my nights, they filled the house to its entire capacity, leaving scores outside who could not enter. All wanted to hear more of the Word of Life.[267]

Coan moved on to preach in Kau, a village at the southernmost tip of the island of Hawaii. He sent a report of the visit to Hiram Bingham in Honolulu:

> From the time I arrived in Kau, until I reached home, a period of eight days, I preached forty-three times. And often to congregations that listened with much interest and many tears...hundreds of natives pressed upon me afterward to receive instruction....There was so much interest that I found myself preaching three times before breakfast, which I ate at ten o'clock. I could not move out of doors, in any direction, without being thronged by people from all sides, who could find no other opportunity to converse with me [about Christ]. Some followed me from village to village to hear the gospel. Many were pricked in their hearts and asked what they should do to be saved![268]

Among the true converts during Coan's first tour of the island was the high priest of the volcano. The priest was over six feet tall, with a regal bearing; however, he was not only guilty of idolatry but also of adultery, robbery, and murder. After listening to the truth of God's Word, he humbled himself in repentance and sought forgiveness from the one true God. Years later, he was still a part of the Hilo congregation.[269]

Both Bingham and Coan realized that this revival was a result of both the fervent prayer of the Christians of Hilo and the toil of the previous fourteen years of missionary planting and watering.

There Is Always Room in God's House

Coan remained in Hilo, and the natives came from miles away to hear him preach. He recorded many occurrences when the Spirit of God moved among the people.

> The meetings were full and solemn. Many came from 50 or 60 miles way. The Holy Ghost came at the commencement of the meeting and many were awakened to Christ under the first sermon, "Now the time is coming and now is when the dead shall hear the voice of the Son of God and they that hear shall live."
>
> The church seemed much aroused and to have an unusual spirit of prayer poured upon them....How many souls were born again, we know not. Some we believe are—we hope many!
>
> During that week we preached the gospel three times a day. Lyman and myself divided all of the labor. We sent out church members in all directions to bring the aged and decrepit, that we might tell them that God's house is not full—there is room for them....They listened with attention and some seemed to be affected. What the fruit will be the Judgment will reveal.[270]

One doctrine that was prevalent among the early Congregational and Presbyterian missionaries was the "waiting period," which occurred before new converts were baptized and allowed to be admitted into the church. This required waiting time was to prove that their commitment to Christ was sincere. Coan kept a notebook on the native converts and then baptized them into the church when he felt they had proven their readiness. "The admission of many was deferred for the more full development of their character, while they were to be watched over, guided and fed as sheep of the Great Shepherd."[271] Of course, Bingham held to even higher standards of inquiry before a convert was welcomed as a true disciple of Christ. During this time period, some Christians in the church waited for behavioral signs that someone had become a Christian. If they didn't see those life changes, the "convert" couldn't be water baptized.

Coan's doctrine evolved somewhat as he spent years in ministry to the Hawaiian natives. He began to shorten that waiting period, realizing that it left new converts without enough support from the body of Christ and therefore easy prey for the enemy for temptation or backsliding. He wrote that he didn't agree with "leaving the people to wander in darkness, uncertain as to their own character, exposed to every temptation of earth and hell, unknown and unrecognized as the sheep and lambs of the Lord Jesus, and in danger from the all-devouring lion."[272]

Hilo Church: From Twenty-three to Ten Thousand

Throughout 1838, Coan continued to record the great blessings of revival:

> Many came once again from sixty miles to hear the gospel. It was a season of deep and solemn interest. God's Word was with power, and His work was glorious. Multitudes wept and trembled, and hundreds were converted. How many will come bearing forth fruits for repentance remains to be seen. Of one thing we can be sure, that God is in this place, and that He has spoken to many hearts. We expect to return with many sheaves for Christ.[273]

Coan had an expectation that God would move as a result of their prayers and the proclamation of God's Word, which never returns to Him void!

"During all of the years of 1837–1838," Coan wrote in his autobiography years later, "Hilo was crowded with strangers; whole families and whole villages in the towns and in the country were left empty. Little cabins studded the place like the camps of an army and we estimated that our population had increased to 10,000 souls. The sea of faces, all hushed except when sighs and sobs burst out here and there, was a scene to melt the heart."[274] At this point, Titus Coan actually had the largest Protestant church in the world—ten thousand avid seekers and believers attended meetings at his congregation.

Titus Coan actually had the largest Protestant church in the world—ten thousand avid seekers and believers attended meetings at his congregation.

On their own initiative, the natives of Hilo built a second meeting house so that Coan could move from one place to another on Sunday mornings and afternoons, and all of the people could hear his message from the Scriptures without exposure to the sun or rain.

When Coan preached during the Hilo services, "the Word fell with power, and sometimes as the feeling deepened the vast audience was moved and swayed like a forest in the mighty wind."[275]

"I had seen great and powerful awakenings under the preaching of Charles Finney," he wrote, "and like doctrines, prayers, and efforts seemed to produce like fruit among the people."[276]

Saved from a Devastating Tsunami

On November 7, 1837, during the evening prayers, the people of Hilo "were startled by a heavy thud and a sudden jar of the earth." Cries from natives on the beach were heard throughout the village, and the missionaries raced from the prayer house to the beaches nearby to see what had gone wrong. They came upon a scene of terror.

"The sea, moved by an unseen hand, had all of a sudden risen in a gigantic wave, and this wave, rushing in with the speed of a race-horse, had fallen upon the shore, sweeping everything not more than fifteen or twenty feet above high-water mark into indiscriminate ruin. Houses, furniture, calabashes, fuel, timber, canoes, food, clothing, everything floated wild upon the flood."[277] About two hundred people were struggling to swim through the sweeping waves to the shore. Frantically, husbands, wives, mothers, and children called out to find lost loved ones. As desperate as the moment was, most of the people were saved with the help of the strong native men who had trained all of their lives to survive in the surrounding Pacific Ocean. Undoubtedly, what they were experiencing was a tsunami, probably caused by an underwater earthquake.

Although thirteen people drowned that day on the shores of Hilo, there was still a reason for great rejoicing. If it had happened during the night while they slept, hundreds of people would have been swept out into the ocean. God had been their protection. The people turned to Him in even greater numbers.[278]

Outstanding Works of God

It was a day to be remembered. In early July 1838, there were 1,705 Hawaiians lined up in the church at Hilo to be water baptized "in the name of the Father and the Son and the Holy Spirit." There was great rejoicing in the church on that day. In 1839, at the height of the revival, 5,244 people from Hilo were baptized into the body of Christ. In 1840, another 1,499 converts were added to the church.[279] Although revival moved throughout the Hawaiian Islands in the years 1836–1842, three-fourths of the new Christians on the islands lived in the Hilo region under Titus Coan's ministry.[280]

In 1838, Fidelia Coan opened up a boarding school for girls, located near the established boys' school run by the Lymans. The young people of Hilo were growing by leaps and bounds in their knowledge of the Word of God and other subjects. Coan also began a separate ministry for the officers and crews of the ships that anchored in the Hilo Harbor. Thousands of tracts were distributed among the seamen who would come ashore from the nearby bay; a church service was also established at 3:00 PM every Sunday afternoon for all of the seamen who wanted to attend. Coan estimated that 40,000 sailors put into port in Hilo during the forty-seven years of his ministry there, and thousands were turned to Christ.

Science Comes to Hilo

In 1840, Charles Wilkes, commander of the United States Exploring Expedition, arrived in Hilo Bay on the ship *Vinccunes*. Since the Mauna Loa volcano was located just thirty miles from Hilo, a group of scientists intended to spend the next three months on the summit to conduct geological tests and make observations of the volcanic activity. They offered to pay one thousand of the local men to assist them in various ways on the long expedition to the summit.

There were two unexpected results of this activity. One was the unfortunate slowing down of the revival in Hilo. The native men who were hired could no longer set aside work on the Lord's Day, because the expedition required them to work seven days a week. Fortunately, Coan reported that most of the Christians "held fast" during this time and didn't fall away from the Lord or His church.

A more positive outcome of the science expedition was that a friendship was established between Coan and James D. Dana, a young scientist who was also a Christian. The two became lifelong friends, and Coan supplied Dana with scientific and seismic information concerning the activity of the Hawaiian volcanoes for the next several decades.[281] Coan's account of the eruption of Mauna Loa in February 1852 was published in *The American Journal of Science and Arts* that September.[282]

Even though the revival began to slow down in Hilo, the Word of God was still alive and active among the people. At one point, there were as many as fifty churches and sixty schoolhouses in the district. All of these were led by mature native converts whom Coan was training to take over the ministry after him.[283]

The Hawaiian Revival

Hawaii: The Book of Acts

Titus Coan trained hundreds of native missionaries during his forty-seven years of ministry.

> Sometimes ten, twenty or forty men were sent out, two by two, through all Puna and Hilo, into all highways, hedges, jungles, and valleys, to "seek and save the lost," the sick, the ignorant, the stupid, the timid, or the "remnant of the giants" in idolatry. And they were drawn out by hundreds into the light of the Gospel and the love of the Saviour.... They...went out two and two into all the villages, exhorting, persuading, weeping, and praying, and their influence was wonderful for good.... With these [native] helpers every village became a guarded citadel of the Lord.[284]

The native Christians taught through the power of the Word and of the Holy Spirit, and the work flourished wherever their feet tread. Before the great revival, Coan thought the people's prayers had seemed to be mechanical and cold, but when the Holy Spirit fell upon them, this all changed. "They took God at His Word; their faith was simple....They went '*boldly unto the throne of grace*...[to] *obtain mercy, and find grace to help in time of need*' [Hebrews 4:16]. They were praying with melting fervor for the Spirit, and He came, sometimes like the dew of Hermon or the gentle rain, and sometimes 'like a rushing mighty wind,' filling the house with sobbing and outcries for mercy."[285]

A pastor serving in Hawaii today has noted, "The revival that occurred in Hilo was a Pentecostal revival that happened sixty years before the famous Pentecostal revival in the United States at the start of the twentieth century."

The spirit of repentance and godly fervor that accompanied Coan's preaching was much different from the earlier record of Bingham's ministry in Hawaii. Bingham was more task-oriented than he was sensitive to the needs of the people. As one eyewitness noted, "I think it true that the severer forms of Calvinism presented by the earlier missionaries were less adapted to facilitate the work of the Divine Spirit, than were the *gentler* and *sweeter* forms in which the Gospel was presented by those more lately arrived [like Coan] who had been in the wonderful revival under Finney's preaching."[286]

Changes in Hawaii

During the early 1840s, changes were taking place throughout the Hawaiian Islands. By 1841, Hiram Bingham was gone. That same year, Kamehameha III, encouraged by the Reverend William Richards, wrote the nation's first constitution. Of his own accord, the king began the document with the words "God has made of one blood all races of people, to dwell upon this Earth in unity and blessedness." Later, Hawaii's new motto, first spoken by Kamehameha III, was added to the state constitution: "The life of the land is perpetrated in righteousness." In 1843, the Reverend Richards made a trip to England and France to obtain a signed commitment that those nations would respect Hawaii's independence.

For a time during the revival, Kamehameha III returned to his love of the Lord and visited Hilo often to join in the joyous elements of the revival; he stayed with Coan in his home and ate at his table. The king even gave up alcohol and put a halt to the production of rum on the islands.[287]

But soon after, the French and English, who had settled on the islands, threatened the king and his crown if he did not repeal the ban against alcohol. The foreign sailors and citizens living in Hawaii wanted to be free to do as they pleased. They called the king a fool for listening to the missionaries. Kamehameha yielded and, soon after, returned to his old ways. His thirst for alcohol was rekindled, and he died on December 15, 1854, at the early age of forty-one.[288]

When I read of this decision by Kamehameha III, it reminded me of the Old Testament account of Rehoboam, who inherited the kingdom of Israel when his father, King Solomon, had died. The people approached the new king and pledged their faithfulness but asked that he would lighten their heavy tax load. His father's wise counselors advised him, "*If you will be a servant to these people today, and serve them, and answer them, and speak good words to them, then they will be your servants forever*" (1 Kings 12:7 NKJV). Unfortunately, Rehoboam did not choose to follow the godly counsel; instead, he turned to his young, arrogant friends who had no experience in leading the Hebrew nation. Their counsel was that he should show no weakness to the people, that he should "increase their yoke and their punishment." (See 1 Kings 12:11.) Rehoboam foolishly followed the unwise counsel of his friends. As a result, the northern part of the kingdom rebelled, ten Hebrew tribes formed their own nation of Israel, and Rehoboam was left with the small kingdom of Judah. How much wiser it would have been for King Rehoboam, and for King Kamehameha III, to have followed the wisdom of godly counsel.

End of His Missionary Work

For the next forty years, Titus Coan faithfully served the Hawaiian people at Hilo. Other than a short furlough to the United States, Coan remained in ministry in Hilo for the rest of his life. He lived through the short reigns of Kamehameha IV and Kamehameha V. After that, the Hawaiian kings were chosen by election.

In spite of political unrest, the Hawaiian church continued to grow. Coan considered the common bond that all Christians had on the islands of Hawaii: "Our Hawaiian churches are not called Episcopal, Presbyterian, or Congregational, or by any other name than that of the Great Head, the Shepherd, and Bishop of souls. We call them *Christian churches*."[289]

"Controversies among Christians always sadden me," Coan wrote. "Our warfare is against sin and Satan; and Heaven's 'sacramental host' [the body of Christ] should never fall out by the way, or spend an hour in their conflict with Hell fighting one another. Grasping and defending *vital truths*, and allowing kind and courteous discussions of outward forms, the whole Church of Christ should clasp hands and march shoulder to shoulder against the common foe."[290]

Coan was still serving in Hilo when young Hiram Bingham II and his wife stopped to visit them before going on to their first mission field in Micronesia, a region in the Pacific consisting of thousands of small islands. In 1860, Titus and Fidelia visited the Marquesas Islands in the South Pacific to plant a new church there.[291]

During Coan's long ministry, the Hilo church donated more than one hundred thousand dollars to mission work on other Pacific islands, such as the Marquesas Islands and Micronesia.

During Coan's long ministry, the Hilo church donated more than one hundred thousand dollars to mission work on other Pacific islands, such as the Marquesas Islands and Micronesia.[292] Native Hawaiian missionaries were sent out to other islands throughout the Pacific to spread the gospel of Jesus Christ. Eventually, Coan established six other churches in the Hilo region.

The years moved on. After a time of illness, Fidelia Coan passed away on September 29, 1872. Titus commended his beloved wife for freely choosing the life of a missionary and for being his faithful companion to the end. One year later, on October 13, 1873, Coan married Hiram Bingham's youngest daughter, thirty-nine-year-old Lydia Bingham. Over the next nine years, he called her "my faithful helpmeet, who is the strength and support of my age." During the last two years of his life, Titus recorded his outstanding ministry in his autobiography *Life in Hawaii: Mission Life and Labors,* published in 1881. Three and a half months later, on December 1, 1881, Coan died and was buried in Hilo, the village of his heart's work.

He is remembered in Hawaii today as a man of great faith and compassionate spirit who dedicated his entire adult life to the people he loved on the island of Hawaii, near the base of the majestic Mauna Loa. Historian Gaven Daws characterized Coan's ministry as one of love: "Love was the driving force in Coan's life; he loved his wife, he loved Christ, and he loved his work."[293]

I am very appreciative of men like Titus Coan, who took the time to write down the works of God that took place through his ministry. Future generations can learn from both the victories and mistakes of Christian men and women. For those of you in ministry today, please record what God is doing in and around you. The impact on the kingdom of God may be immeasurable.

Blaming the Hawaiian Missionary Movement

The last quarter of the nineteenth century in Hawaii was filled with tumultuous change.

As Hawaii became a rich nation, some Christians deserted their faith when opportunity arose to make large fortunes.

In the 1870s, the American Board of Commissioners for Foreign Missions decided that Hawaii no longer needed their direct support. They would not send any new missionaries; instead, they encouraged all churches to set up native pastors as the foreign ones retired or passed away.[294] This was a good decision for the native Christian church in Hawaii. The missionaries had left behind a Hawaiian college, several seminaries, and a network of schools to be used throughout the islands.[295]

Unfortunately, many modern accounts of Hawaiian history do not present the American missionaries in a favorable light. Today, we live in a revisionist culture in which history can be rewritten to present the past in a way that reflects the views of those who are writing it. Although there were less than one hundred Protestant missionaries sent from America to Hawaii over a fifty-year period, these Christian men and women are often blamed for all of the difficulties that occurred on the islands in the following decades.

Any negative results from the introduction of Western commerce, the growth of sugar cane and fruit plantations, and the onslaught of Chinese and Japanese immigrants in Hawaii are often blamed on the early Christian missionaries. Before the nineteenth century was over, the United States annexed Hawaii on the premise that it was protecting the islands from a takeover by other foreign countries, such as Japan or Great Britain. In some circles today, this violation of Hawaii's sovereignty is also blamed on the presence of Christian missionaries on the islands.

The Hawaiian nation and the Hawaiian church suffered from the aforementioned events. By the end of the nineteenth century, largely as a result of disease, the number of native Hawaiians had been reduced to less than forty thousand people. As Hawaii became a rich nation, some Christians deserted their faith when opportunity arose to make large fortunes. In addition, some of Hawaii's larger church denominations supported the annexation by United States, which alienated the native Christians, who felt betrayed.

How should the body of Christ answer these accusations? None of the pioneer missionary men and women who arrived on Hawaii's shores with the gospel of Christ was perfect. However, those who launched the earliest missionary quests came to bring the Word of God to a people who had only false gods that could not answer their prayers or bring them eternal life. They were not responsible for the decisions of following generations, who might have had a different motivation. The early missionaries went with the love of Christ in their hearts and the desire to see the Hawaiian nation enveloped by the Spirit of God.

Titus Coan wrote of his fervor upon his first arrival in Hawaii:

> When I came to these islands, and before I could use the Hawaiian language, I often felt as if I should burst with strong desire to speak the word to the natives around me. And when my mouth was opened to speak of the love of God in Christ, I felt that the very chords of my heart were wrapped around my hearers, and that some inward power was helping me to draw them in, as the fisherman feels when drawing in his net filled with fishes.[296]

These men and women arrived with the prayer to see souls saved for eternity by the love of Christ. And, for tens of thousands of Hawaiian people, that prayer was answered.

Then [Jesus] *said to them, "Follow Me, and I will make you fishers of men." They immediately left their nets and followed Him.*

(Matthew 4:19–20 NKJV)

Will you answer the call?

Will you follow Jesus to become a fisher of men?

Chapter 6

David Livingstone

Africa's Greatest Missionary

The cry of "*Tau! Tau!*" ("Lion! Lion!") rang through the African village. Danger was on the prowl once again. Racing up the hill with spears in hand, the Bakgatla natives came upon their small herd of sheep lying on the ground, scattered and bloody. It was the middle of the day, but the lions had nothing to fear.

Engraving from *Missionary Travels and Researches in South Africa* by David Livingstone (London, 1857)
(Image Asset Management Ltd.)

Grabbing his rifle, David Livingstone ran through the tall grasses of the Mabotsa mission in answer to their cries. Beating the underbrush with their spears, the natives had discovered a huge male lion and were slowly encircling him, ready to kill. David and his rifle would provide backup if their spears failed.

Suddenly, the Bakgatlas panicked, frightened that, according to legend, the lion might be "bewitched." Sensing the hunters' fear, the beast sprang past their circle and escaped into the undergrowth. Walking back toward the mission, David heard a loud rustling in the bushes behind him; as he spun to his left, the terrified cry "Tau!" rang out once again. The massive lion was crouched just a few steps away, his tail erect in anger, ready to pounce.

Raising his rifle, David squeezed the trigger and fired; the lion reared back in pain. "He is shot! He is shot!" the natives cried as they raced toward the missionary. "Wait, let me load again," David called. As he rammed another bullet into the chamber, the enraged lion sprang forward. It clenched its jaws on David's shoulder, and the heavy weight propelled the missionary violently to the ground.

"Growling horribly close to my ear," David wrote later, "he shook me as a terrier dog does a rat. The shock produced a stupor similar to that which seems to be felt by a mouse after the first shake of the cat."

Livingstone saw rather than felt the lion's teeth tear into his shoulder. It was as though he was trapped in a dream, "in which I had no sense of pain or feeling of terror, though I was conscious of all that was happening. The shake annihilated fear, and allowed no sense of horror in looking round at the beast. It seemed a merciful provision by our benevolent Creator for lessening the pain of death."[297]

Mebalwe, the native schoolmaster, raised his rifle and fired at the lion at close range. The animal sprang onto his new attacker, driving his fangs into his thigh, and then spun away and fell dead. "Everyone has survived the lion's attack," David muttered, before he slipped into unconsciousness.

Something supernatural happened in David Livingstone's spirit that day. His shoulder and arm had been scarred for life, but, miraculously, he had survived. From that day on, Livingstone was fearless in the wilderness, exploring the wild interior of his adopted land, certain that God would keep him alive as long as He had work to be completed. Likewise, every great leader has an "inner knowing" that God will keep him alive until he fulfills his destiny in Christ. David Livingstone's inner knowing was unshakeable.

Where No Man Has Gone

"God, send me anywhere, only go with me. Lay any burden on me, only sustain me. And sever any tie in my heart, except the tie that binds my heart to Yours."

—David Livingstone

David Livingstone

David Livingstone is celebrated as the most famous of the nineteenth-century British explorers. His heroic role as a missionary/explorer yielded astonishing results in the geographical mapping of Africa's interior. In his lifetime, he was an honored missionary, pioneer, botanist, and physician. He was recognized by the British, French, Italian, American, and Viennese Geographical Societies as one of the most successful explorers who ever lived.

In the nineteenth century, the interior of Africa was shrouded in mystery; European maps of central Africa were still largely blank.

History praises his exploits, not just because he was the first European to travel over forty thousand miles in Africa, crisscrossing the continent's interior, but because he did it largely on foot and with no prior knowledge of what was hidden in the "vast wasteland." He was undaunted by fears of the unknown and had an unyielding tenacity to complete whatever task lay before him.

In the nineteenth century, the interior of Africa was shrouded in mystery; European maps of central Africa were still largely blank. With his sextant and telescope, Livingstone measured and recorded the position of every village, river, mountain, waterfall, and valley along his way. He faced lions, crocodiles, cannibals, slave traders, malaria, dysentery, and looming death. Yet, for thirty years, God led him, protected him, and revealed Africa's deepest secrets to him—this follower of Christ who strove to open the heart of Africa to the gospel. "The end of the [geographical] exploration," he would often quote, "is the beginning of the [missionary] enterprise."

Among his contemporaries, he was often seen as a controversial missionary, for he was not a conventional gospel messenger. Even though he was dedicated to opening Africa for Christianity, some people later accused Livingstone of having only one true convert, not recognizing the millions who came to Christ after his explorations were completed. His initial goal to personally lead the natives to Christ was supplanted by his insatiable desire to explore and unveil the interior of Africa for the sake of the gospel and civilization.

Dependent on divine guidance, Livingstone became one of God's missionary generals who committed his life to his three Cs: Christianity, civilization, and commerce. He was convinced that advancing these three objectives would ultimately bring Christ to Africa. And he was determined to succeed—no matter the cost.

His relentless driving force was based on the same vision of apostle Paul: *"So have I strived to preach the gospel, not where Christ was named, lest I should build upon another man's foundation"* (Romans 15:20). His labor in Africa was a seed that was planted him, and which was later watered by others. Ultimately, by God's grace, it has led to the present-day African crusades by which millions of people are coming to Christ and establishing the huge African churches of the twenty-first century.

The Shire of Scotland

David Livingstone was born on March 19, 1813, in the industrial town of Blantyre, Scotland, eight miles from Glasgow. He was the second of seven children born to Neil and Agnes Livingstone, a poor family living in a one-room tenement apartment.

How David Livingstone longed to learn! In spite of his fatigue, he attended school each night; there was nothing he wanted more than to study everything, from the smallest insect to the most complicated machine.

By the tender age of ten, David rose each day at 5:00 AM for morning prayer and then, along with his older brother, John, went to labor in the local cotton mills. For fourteen hours a day, they worked as "piecers," standing under the spinning machinery to piece together broken strands of cotton that had snapped. With a portion of their wages, the brothers helped the family to survive.

After the long day, workers who wanted to attend school had to go at night from 8:00 to 10:00 PM. How David Livingstone longed to learn! In spite of his fatigue, he attended school each night; there was nothing he wanted more than to study everything, from the smallest insect to the most complicated machine. He spent his first week's wages on a Latin grammar book and propped it up on the machinery to read whenever he could steal a moment.

At the age of nineteen, two things happened that changed his world. After nine years of labor, he was finally promoted to be a cotton spinner at the mill, which meant more money. Second, and most important, he and his family left the authoritative Church of Scotland to attend an independent Congregational church. For the first time, David heard the message of salvation in Christ based on faith alone, rather than on perfect conduct. He accepted Christ's gift of salvation and became a believer. Livingstone wrote, "I saw the duty and inestimable privilege to immediately accept salvation by Christ. Humbly believing that through His sovereign mercy and grace I have been enabled to do so…to His glory."

Science and God

To David Livingstone, the most fascinating things in the world were science and the natural world. Science fired his imagination! Unfortunately, he had to read his books on botany and chemistry in secret, because his father was vehemently opposed to them, convinced that science led Christians away from God. David struggled with guilt until he was introduced to the book *The Philosophy of a Future State*, by Dr. Thomas Dick, an eighteenth-century Scottish astronomer and Christian.

"Science and creation both come from God," the author claimed. "The study of His world will draw the Christian closer to Jesus Christ." The book became the greatest influence in Livingstone's life after the Bible. How could he help his father to understand?

One Sunday morning, as the Livingstone family sat together on a church bench, the pastor read a letter to the congregation from Dr. Charles Gutzlaff, a German missionary to China. Gutzlaff's plea to European Christians was to consider becoming medical missionaries in order to bring the Chinese both physical aid and spiritual salvation.

David was enthralled! Here was the perfect blend of God and science. It was the answer to a dream; he could become a medical missionary. After hearing the letter, his father willingly admitted that Jesus could use even science to reach the lost. David had his father's blessing to pursue his dream of medicine.

Livingstone assured his father, "It is my desire to show my attachment to the cause of Him who died for me by devoting my life to His service."

David had heard God's call, but how would he get from the cotton mills of Scotland to the medical mission field of China? Only God could answer that question.

Looking at his salary (which had just been raised), his family obligations, and the cost of tuition at Anderson College in nearby Glasgow, David calculated his expenses. If he saved every penny, it would take three years to accumulate the twelve pounds he needed for tuition. With the determination that defined his entire life, David did just that! Three years later, at the age of twenty-three, he walked the eight miles to the city of Glasgow to begin his medical training.[298]

Absorbing knowledge like a sponge, David finished his studies in two years by September 1838. Because he had excelled in every class, the college offered him a teaching position with the "astronomical" salary of 150 pounds a year. But David turned down the job; he knew that his destiny was in the lands where the gospel had gone unheard for too long.

"The Smoke of a Thousand Villages"

The bustling city of London was the next stop for the young Scotsman. David applied for a missionary post with the nondenominational London Missionary Society (LMS).

He was accepted, and he had begun his preparation to serve in China when his missionary plans came to an abrupt halt. The British East India Company had been selling Indian opium in China. As a result, thousands of Chinese men and women had become hopeless addicts. When the Chinese government demanded that the East India Company immediately cease selling the opium, the British refused, unwilling to give up the exorbitant profits. The result was the first Opium War in China; entering the country now would be suicide.

Undaunted, Livingstone sought God for another open door.

One evening, in the fall of 1840, David took a break from his missionary studies to attend a meeting of the African Civilization Society in London's Exeter Hall. Prince Albert, Queen Victoria's young husband, was giving his first speech before the British public.

The next speaker was Sir Thomas Buxton, a member of Parliament and a fierce abolitionist, who believed that presenting *Christianity* and *commerce* together to the people of Africa was the two-pronged attack that would end slavery. For many people, human slavery was an evil—but easy—way to make money. The continent had other products than slaves to sell to the world, but the natives had no knowledge of these markets. This two-part plan of providing both the knowledge of Christ and the knowledge of commerce became Livingstone's lifetime mission.[299]

The final speaker to step onto the platform that evening was Robert Moffat, a celebrated LMS missionary with a flowing white beard. Livingstone listened transfixed as Moffat spoke passionately of his twenty years among the natives of South Africa: "I have sometimes seen, in the morning sun, the smoke of a thousand villages where no missionary has ever been."

That momentous night, a fire for Africa was lit in David Livingstone that would not be extinguished until his final breath decades later. What a reminder that we never know who our words are reaching. Be encouraged to speak your heart and mind, and don't hold back. Thank God that Robert Moffat's heartfelt words moved Livingstone to answer the call to Africa.

Africa: "The White Man's Grave"

With his heart beating wildly, Livingstone wrote to the London Missionary Society, requesting to be sent to Africa as a medical missionary. The Board immediately agreed and assigned him to Robert Moffat's Kuruman Mission in South Africa, six hundred miles north of Cape Town.

Elated, David hurried home to Scotland to spend a day with his family before leaving Britain. Neil and Agnes Livingstone were proud of their son's commitment to serve Christ, but it broke their hearts to see him travel such a long distance to the continent referred to as "the white man's grave."

At 5:00 AM the next morning, David led the family prayer for the last time from a favorite Scripture passage: "*The LORD is thy keeper: the LORD is thy shade upon thy right hand. The sun shall not smite thee by day, nor the moon by night. The LORD shall preserve thee from all evil: he shall preserve thy soul. The LORD shall preserve thy going out and thy coming in from this time forth, and even for evermore*" (Psalm 121:5–8).[300]

One last time, Neil Livingstone walked the eight miles to Glasgow with his son. Within days, on December 8, 1840, David stood on the sailing ship the *George* bound for South Africa and an adventure beyond his wildest dreams. "*Lo I am with you alway*" (Matthew 28:20) was the promise of God he carried in his heart. Livingstone recorded in his diary, "This is a promise I can rely upon, for it is the word of a Gentleman of honor!"

No Waiting! Explore Now!

After three months at sea, David arrived in Cape Town, South Africa, in early March 1841. He stayed there just long enough to purchase four wagons and twelve oxen to travel the six hundred miles to Moffat's mission at Kuruman.

Another missionary, William Ross, and his wife traveled with him. When he arrived at Kuruman, David was ready to begin his life's work, but he was disappointed to find that Robert Moffat and his family were still on furlough in England with no planned date of return.

Kuruman was a beautiful mission station, with luscious vegetation and low-built adobe houses. There were two missionaries already at the station, and a few hundred African natives were living there. But the zealous Livingstone was anxious to be on the move. What would four missionaries do with their time? Two could suffice for the work; he wanted to begin discovering those "one thousand villages" to the north.

David convinced a fellow missionary, Roger Edwards, to travel north with him. On September 24, 1841, two months after his arrival in Kuruman, David Livingstone launched his first expedition into Africa's interior—by oxcart!

Reaching the closest village of the Bakgatla tribe, Livingstone and Edwards heard the women cry a warning from the fields. The male villagers descended on Livingstone's cart with spears raised high, more curious than threatening. Livingstone's native guide and interpreter, Pomare, offered beads and gifts to the chief.

When the natives asked to trade for rifles, David cleverly diverted their attention by showing them his mirror. They were wild with excitement over their reflections, and eagerly welcomed the men into their camp. When they discovered David was a "white shuman" (doctor), they brought their sick, and he spent days applying poultices and distributing medicine. What a promising first experience! With each step of the journey, he checked his compass and kept a log of their location—an early routine that lasted his entire lifetime.[301]

Excited that new lands were so easily opened, Livingstone and Edwards continued north to the village of the Bakwains and Chief Sechele. The chief would become one of Livingstone's closest allies and his most committed convert in Africa. Spending weeks among the Bakwain people, David slowly learned the Bantu language. The young missionaries headed back to Kuruman with a sense of victory, arriving by Christmas of 1841. Moffat still had not returned.

A New Mission plus a Wife

Itching to share Christ among these new tribes, Edwards and Livingstone wrote to Robert Moffat for permission to establish a northern mission. Moffat's answer was a definitive yes, so the two young missionaries moved to a site several miles north of Kuruman, called Mabotsa, inhabited by the Bakgatla tribe. With rich vegetation, grazing lands, and water, the mission was certain to be a success.

Shortly after the main mission building was completed, the lions of Mabotsa began preying daily on the sheep and cattle. Not afraid of taking a stand against them, Livingstone one day encouraged the natives to encircle the lions for the kill. It was then that David was violently attacked and mauled by the angry male lion described in the chapter opening. Lying with a mangled left arm, Livingstone painfully coached Edwards on how to reset his arm and bandage his open wounds. For the remainder of his life, Livingstone's left arm hung stiffly by his side.

David Livingstone saved from a lion by Mebalwe, a native school master.
Engraving from *Missionary Travels and Researches in South Africa* by David Livingstone (London, 1857)
(Image Asset Management Ltd.)

For two months, he rested in the mission compound as his arm healed. When word reached Mabotsa that Robert Moffat was finally on his way to Kuruman, the impatient Livingstone impulsively jumped on his horse and raced to join the Moffats on their journey. Arriving at their caravan, he soon met twenty-three-year-old Mary, the eldest of Robert Moffat's ten children. They spent several weeks together while his shoulder continued to heal in Kuruman. By the time he rode back to Mabotsa, David had decided to ask Mary Moffat to be his wife.

She Is All I Want

Mary Moffat was not known as a pretty girl, but she had spent nineteen of her twenty-three years in Africa and had a true missionary's heart. The thirty-year-old muscular and high-spirited Livingstone suited her well.

On the other hand, the idea of marriage was a strange one for David. Staying single in the wilds of Africa had been his plan from the beginning! On his

London missions application five years earlier, he had emphatically declared, "Unmarried; under no engagement related to marriage, never made proposals of marriage!" David and Mary were married in January 1845.

Writing in his daily journals, Livingstone described his new wife in a few words: "[Mary is a] plain common sense woman, not a romantic. Mine is a matter of fact lady, a little thick black haired girl, sturdy and all I want."

As his love for Mary grew, though, his letters revealed a more tender heart: "I never show all my feelings; but I can say truly, my dearest, that I loved you when I married you, and the longer I lived with you, I loved you the better."

After their wedding, the Livingstones didn't remain long in Mabotsa. Roger Edwards and his wife had become cold toward the Livingstones because of their family relationship with Robert Moffat; Edwards wanted to run the mission in his own way. Livingstone was happy to move with his new wife further into the interior and settled upon Chonuane, a village near Chief Sechele of the Bakwain tribe.

"These Words Make My Bones to Shake"

From the beginning, Chief Sechele was interested in the Christian message David preached. When the chief heard the gospel would bring him salvation for all eternity, he told Livingstone, "You startle me: these words make all my bones to shake; I have no more strength in me."

Sechele and the Bakwains spoke the Sechuana dialect of Bantu, and in God's perfect timing, Robert Moffat had translated and published the New Testament in the Sechuana language. When the chief was presented with the Bible, he pored over its pages, trying to understand Livingstone's God. Before long, he rejected his worship of false deities and accepted Jesus Christ as his Savior, the Redeemer of his sins.

When the chief was presented with the Bible, he pored over its pages, trying to understand Livingstone's God. Before long, he rejected his worship of false deities and accepted Jesus Christ as his Savior, the Redeemer of his sins.

During the two years that David spent in Chonuane teaching the chief the good news of Christ, Mary delivered their first two children: Robert, born in

1846, and Agnes, born in 1847. When the water at Chonuane began to run out, the Livingstones, their children, and the entire Bakwain tribe relocated further north at Kolobeng and established a new settlement there.

The Chief's Five Wives

While discipling Sechele, Livingstone discovered the greatest barrier to the spread of Christianity among African tribes—*polygamy*. An African man was esteemed for the number of wives and children that he had in his immediate family. Sechele struggled for months with what to do about four of his five wives. Finally, he decided he would follow Jesus and the Bible's teachings rather than his traditions. Sechele broke the marriage bond with four of his wives and, after showering them with gifts, sent them home to their families.

What an uproar among the Bakwains! The rejected wives were distraught, the young women's fathers were furious, and the other African men emphatically proclaimed, "We will never follow your new God, Sechele! He made you give up your beautiful wives!"

In spite of the other natives' protests, Chief Sechele and all of his children were water baptized into the body of Christ as his tribe looked on in curiosity and amazement.

Crossing the Kalahari Desert

"You cannot cross the Kalahari Desert to the tribes beyond; it is utterly impossible even for us African men, except in certain seasons. No white man could survive!" Sechele issued this challenging warning as David talked of traveling across the arid desert near Kolobeng to search for a better water source. *Impossible* was not a word David Livingstone would accept!

Water had become scarce in Kolobeng, so David was determined to find a path across the Kalahari Desert and possibly a new location for the mission. But more than that, he was eager to push forward, to discover what was really on the other side of the desert in Africa's "vast wasteland."

Not having enough money for supplies, he wrote to Captain Thomas Steele, a friend and wealthy British safari hunter, requesting a financial sponsor for the trip. Steele wasn't available, but he recommended Cotton Oswell in his place. It was a divine answer to prayer, for Oswell and Livingstone began a God-ordained partnership that lasted for decades.

Cotton Oswell, a wealthy Englishman living in India, longed to explore Africa and jumped at the opportunity to join Livingstone's expedition. In addition to oxen laden with all the food and supplies they would need, Oswell arrived with a sextant and a telescope, instruments David could use to verify his geographical locations now and on future explorations. Oswell also hired thirty Bakwain natives with the promise to pay them in the elephant tusks he would accumulate throughout the journey.[302]

On June 1, 1849, after kissing Mary and the three children good-bye (by this time, Thomas Steele Livingstone had been born), David launched his first major exploration. He had heard rumors of Lake Ngami, a beautiful body of water just north of the desert, but no European had ever seen it. He was determined to be the first one!

Traveling the first one hundred miles through parched lands, Livingstone and Oswell finally entered territory that no white man had ever walked across. David Livingstone was officially an explorer! Yet, despite their careful planning, within a month in the desert, the expedition was in desperate need of water for the men and their oxen.

First Discovery

On July 4, 1849, Cotton Oswell spied a sparkling ribbon in the distance that he thought might be a mirage. Traveling toward it in excitement, the men discovered it wasn't a mirage at all but a beautifully wooded waterway, the Zouga River, which was unknown to all but the few natives who lived near the Kalahari. The explorers, the natives, and the oxen all splashed into the shallow waters of the Zouga to drink their fill and wash away the dust.

Surely this river will lead to the mysterious Lake Ngami, thought Livingstone. Leaving the desert and following the Zouga north for over two hundred and fifty miles, the adventurers finally looked out on a wide, dazzling blue lake teeming with African wildlife. On August 1, 1849, David Livingstone, Cotton Oswell, and a

Although Europe had feared that central Africa was one large desert wasteland, Livingstone had discovered the first of what he believed was a string of lakes in Africa's interior.

A year after discovering Lake Ngami, Livingstone returns with members of his expedition and his wife and family.
Engraving after drawing made on the spot by Alfred Ryder. From *Missionary Travels and Researches in South Africa* by David Livingstone (London, 1857)
(Image Asset Management Ltd.)

third British guide, Mungo Murray, stepped along the shores as the first Europeans to view the clear Lake Ngami.

Returning by the route Livingstone had painstakingly recorded, the explorers reached Kolobeng to announce their discovery. Although Europe had feared that central Africa was one large desert wasteland, Livingstone had discovered the first of what he believed was a string of lakes in Africa's interior. The native guides who had accompanied them on their journey reported that there were other large rivers and lakes to the north of the Zouga. Africa's interior was no arid wasteland! It was teeming with rivers, lakes, native villages, and exotic wildlife!

Barely able to contain his excitement, Livingstone wrote home to the London Missionary Society and the Royal Geographical Society of the lush vegetation and beautiful waterways he had already discovered in central Africa. He was certain that Christian settlements could eventually be established in these inner regions, as well. The gospel would come to central Africa!

In a letter to Arthur Tidman of the London Missionary Society, David wrote, "I hope to be able to work as long as I live beyond other men's line of things, and plant the seed of the gospel where others have not planted."[303]

Family Explores Together

Within a few months, David was ready to travel beyond the Kalahari Desert once again. This time he would follow the Zouga River to the south. Mary

Livingstone, in spite of being pregnant with their fourth child, insisted that she and the children would come along.

Overconfident after the success of his first trip, David agreed. In July 1850, the Livingstones and several Bakwain workers set out across the Kalahari. Following David's detailed hand-drawn maps, they reached the Zouga without trouble, but shortly after their arrival, four-year-old Agnes and two-year-old Thomas contracted malaria. Although Agnes recovered quickly, Thomas became very ill. Fearing for his life, the Livingstones turned back to make the two-month return trek to Kolobeng.

Thankfully, both children recovered completely, but, a month later, tragedy struck the young family. During the delivery of their new baby girl, Mary suffered a stroke that resulted in minor paralysis on her left side. Although the paralysis cleared up, a few weeks later, baby Elizabeth came down with severe bronchitis and passed away. The family mourned the loss of their "sweet, blue-eyed girl" and buried the baby at Kolobeng.

David decided that a trip to Kuruman and time with Mary's parents would speed her recovery. While they were there, he received two unexpected letters from England. In honor of discovering Lake Ngami, the Royal Geographical Society (RGS) had awarded Livingstone the Gold Medal, their highest honor for a British explorer. He was astounded! The London Missionary Society also sent him a letter of praise and pleasure; he was opening a whole new world for the gospel of Jesus Christ!

As Long as It Is Forward

Returning to Kolobeng, Livingstone became restless and began to plan his next trip to the Zouga. As Mary packed for her and the children to accompany him, Cotton Oswell protested, "Are you sure this is a wise move? There are so many dangers where we will be traveling!" David replied grimly, "I can't leave my family here at Kolobeng. There is disease, and I am their doctor. And the Boers [Dutch descendants and slave traders] are threatening to attack the village. They can't stay here!"

Just before the expedition set out, David received a letter from his furious mother-in-law, Mary Moffat, in protest: "O Livingstone, what do you mean? Was it not enough that you lost one lovely babe, and scarcely saved the other, while the mother came home threatened with paralysis? How can you go?"

Livingstone did not respond to her letter. He was convinced that he had not been called by God to settle in one place, to establish a mission post as Robert Moffat had done with such success in Kuruman. God had placed in his soul the desire to be a *pioneer* missionary, always moving toward the next frontier. "I will go anywhere," he wrote, "as long as it is forward!" I believe that it was an apostolic spirit given to him by God that carried him always onward.

At thirty-one years old, Mary Livingstone was a strong woman and absolutely determined not to be left behind, even though she was pregnant with their fifth child. Once again, Livingstone ventured into the wilds of Africa, with his beloved wife and children riding in the largest of his wagons. Cotton Oswell went along, thrilled to join another Livingstone expedition into the heart of Africa. Livingstone had convinced him that with each remote exploration, they would discover a new African waterway; it was an explorer's dream.

Pregnant Mary's Discovery

On June 18, 1851, two months after leaving Kolobeng, the Livingstone expedition made a new discovery: the wide Chobe River of central Africa. Mary Livingstone had finally become an official explorer on one of her husband's expeditions! They set up camp along the Chobe River and, after meeting with a local tribal chief, learned that there was a mighty rushing river, the Sheshke, that would take the explorers "across central Africa."

Livingstone could scarcely contain his excitement at the thought of a navigable river through Africa's interior. Mary looked at him with sad but understanding eyes as he explained how important is was to his mission work to find the powerful Sheshke. There was enough food and protection for his family in camp, so he left his pregnant wife and children camped beside the Chobe River, protected by their African guides. Livingstone and Oswell rode out together on horseback, navigating through crocodile-infested swamps, looking for the mighty river the natives had described so proudly.

The Mighty Zambesi

After nearly a month of crossing swamplands, on August 4, 1851, Livingstone and Oswell pushed through the African undergrowth to behold a wondrous sight. Before them ran the swiftly flowing Sheshke—now the Zambesi

River—four hundred yards wide, and with an unknown depth. An expansive, glorious waterway right in the middle of Africa; no European record or map had even hinted of such a river before!

Was this the answer Livingstone had been looking for? If the Zambesi flowed east all the way to the Indian Ocean, could it be the water highway linking the outside world to Africa's interior? How David longed to forge ahead, following the river's winding course, uncovering its mysteries, but Mary was within weeks of having their fifth child. He had to return to the wagons.

The entire expedition headed south, back toward the Zouga River on their way to Kolobeng. Mary Livingstone, a brave missionary/explorer in her own right, endured the journey well, even though she had reached her ninth month of pregnancy. On September 15, 1851, camped on the shores of the Zouga, she gave birth to their fifth child, a healthy baby boy.

The relieved parents named the infant William Oswell Livingstone, in honor of their fellow explorer. Inspired by his surroundings, David nicknamed the baby "Zouga," and the name stuck with him for the rest of his life.[304] Little Thomas was also a healthy boy, but he was struck with malaria once again. David ministered quinine, a natural, fever-reducing, anti-inflammatory painkiller made from the bark of the cinchona tree. Livingstone was the first medical doctor known to use quinine in just the right doses to fight malaria. The family quickly resumed its journey back to Kolobeng.[305]

Open Africa or Perish

David Livingstone's conscience was stricken. What was he thinking, taking Mary and their young children into the swamps and jungles of Africa? It was time to send Mary and the children to a place of safety and go on with his explorations without them.

It was a continuous struggle for eighteenth- and nineteenth-century missionaries to reconcile their call from God with their families' lives. Their choices were limited; either take their wives along and place them in grave danger or leave their spouses to years of loneliness while they fulfilled their call in Christ. It was never an easy decision, and one that rested between each missionary and God.

David Livingstone was a driven man; he was driven to forge ahead into Africa's interior, but it was too risky for the children. "I at once resolved," he wrote, "to save my family from exposure to this unhealthy region by sending them to England, and to return alone, with a view to exploring the country in search of a healthy district that might prove a centre of civilization, and open up the interior by a path to either the east or west coast."

It was a continuous struggle for eighteenth- and nineteenth-century missionaries to reconcile their call from God with their families' lives. Their choices were limited; either take their wives along and place them in grave danger or leave their spouses to years of loneliness while they fulfilled their call in Christ.

How would he break the news to Mary?

"Mary, you and the children must go to your parents in Kuruman or to my family in Scotland. I won't risk your lives any longer." Mary begged to stay with her husband, but he could not be persuaded otherwise. Mary was too independent to live under her parents' roof again, so she chose to go to Scotland.

When they arrived in Port Elizabeth, Cotton Oswell was there to greet them with a traveling gift. He provided the money for Mary and the children to purchase new clothes to travel back to Europe. It was a bittersweet blessing, for the Livingstone family did not want to leave Africa.

For David Livingstone, the next four years would make him a renowned explorer and bring him worldwide fame—but it was at a great cost to his family. He couldn't know that Mary would struggle greatly in Scotland and that the children would grow distant from their father. But on this day, Africa was all that was on his heart and mind.

Mary and the children sailed from Port Elizabeth on the *Trafalgar* on April 23, 1852. Setting his face toward the continent's deep interior, Livingstone recorded, "As for me, I am determined to open up Africa or perish!"

Attacked by the Slavers

Riding toward Kolobeng, David received a tragic letter from Chief Sechele, delivered by the chief's wife, Masebele. She handed him the letter while crying. It read, "Two of my sons were carried away. Sixty of our people were shot and killed. The cattle and oxen are all gone, and they burned all of our crops in the field."[306] Chief Sechele and his wife had barely escaped with their lives.

Six hundred Dutch Boers had savagely attacked the Kolobeng mission. Although claiming to be Christians, the European descendants ruthlessly shot men, women, and children as they ran from their homes. Canons mounted on wagons leveled the buildings within minutes. The Bakwains never had a chance. In addition to the deaths, hundreds of natives had been captured as slaves. The Boers ransacked Livingstone's home and destroyed his medical equipment and medicines, his books and papers.

Livingstone was heartbroken at the loss of his Bakwain friends and angered by the evil that existed among the Boers and all of Africa's slave traders. He vowed to end the savagery of the slave trade, but he would never return to Kolobeng or build a permanent mission settlement again.[307]

At the time, his journal read, "O Jesus, fill me with your love now, and I beseech you accept me and use me a little for your glory. I have done nothing for you yet, and I would like to accomplish something...."

Preaching to Six Thousand

David Livingstone reading the Bible to the natives in the Rwanda-Urundi region, Africa, in the nineteenth century.
Artist unknown.

In December 1852, Livingstone's legendary drive to uncover Africa's secret interior reached a new fervor. He traveled with a number of African porters to Linyanti (in current Botswana) and met with the Makololo tribe and their eighteen-year-old chief, Sekeletu.

While living there with six thousand Makololo, David preached the gospel in Bantu and displayed pictures of Bible stories with his new slide projector, which he called his "magic lantern."[308] Their interest in the Bible and Jesus was developing, but slowly. Their desire to have multiple wives always stood in the way of accepting the gospel message.

When Livingstone told Sekeletu that he was planning to travel northwest across central Africa all the way to the great ocean (the Atlantic), the chief protested the foolishness of such a dangerous trip. Realizing David was determined, the chief shook his head and replied, "I will honor your wish to go north to your death." He sent twenty-seven of his best warriors to accompany him.

Because a cross-continent expedition had never been attempted by a white man before, David sent a farewell note to his father-in-law, Robert Moffat. He wrote, "My blessing on my wife. May God comfort her....Please be a father to the fatherless for Jesus' sake."

First to Cross Africa

All of their supplies for the long trek to the west coast were loaded on oxen; they carried canoes for the times they could navigate rivers. Always combating the slave trade in Africa, Livingstone challenged one African chief along the way to release the Balonda natives he had just captured. Knowing it was a dangerous position to take, David repeated to himself, "I trust God, and God doesn't make mistakes."[309] Once released in their village, the Balonda chief and villagers gratefully thanked Livingstone for his courage.

Crossing West Africa, Livingstone traveled over nine months, encountering dense forests, flooded rivers, crocodile-infested swamps, and wild beasts. At times, he met with friendly natives; other days, he had to pay tribute to savage chiefs to receive safe passage through their lands. But the company was never assaulted!

David Livingstone had a gift: an ability to reassure and even befriend tribal chiefs throughout his journeys. Whether they were friendly or hostile, they learned to trust this European explorer who loved their land and was never a threat to their safety. Livingstone respected the natives and worked relentlessly to prevent their villages from being destroyed by slave traders. Livingstone's gift was a blessing from God that preserved his life over and over again.

David Livingstone had a gift: an ability to reassure and even befriend tribal chiefs throughout his journeys. Whether they were friendly or hostile, they learned to trust this European explorer who loved their land and was never a threat to their safety.

On May 31, 1854, David Livingstone and his men arrived safely at the port city of Loanda on the Atlantic Ocean. He had traveled more than two thousand miles from Kuruman, through the Kalahari Desert to Sekeletu at Linyanti and then on to the western coast. The Makololo workers gazed in wonder at the Atlantic with its swells and crashing waves—and there seemed to be no end to it beyond the horizon.

Immortal Until I Am Done

What a feat for Livingstone! He had successfully traveled through African lands that no other white man had seen before. He had meticulously recorded every landmark and drawn detailed maps for the geographical society. But the trip had taken its toll.

Just before they left Linyanti, Livingstone had his first attack of malaria. With his strong constitution, he had avoided the disease for years. On this trip, he recorded thirty-one feverish attacks, which had reduced him to "a bag of bones." He arrived at Loanda riding on the back of an ox and in desperate need of a physician. He rested for months in the port city, quietly working on his journals and maps, before he could make the return trip to Linyanti.

A British captain ready to set sail for England offered David free passage on the *Forerunner* to reunite with his anxious family. But Livingstone would not leave his faithful Makololo workers behind. They would never make it back to Linyanti through hostile tribes and swamplands without his maps. Livingstone gratefully gave the captain letters for Mary, and detailed maps of his discoveries for the Royal Geographical Society in England.

In September 1854, Livingstone had not gone far in his return travels when a messenger brought the tragic news: the *Forerunner* with her cargo and crew had gone down in the Atlantic. The expedition stopped while David redrew his maps and rewrote a few letters to send back with the messenger for England.

Once again, the Lord had rescued him from death so that he could complete God's purposes!

"I am immortal till my work is accomplished," Livingstone wrote. "And although I see few results, future missionaries will see conversions following every sermon. May they not forget the pioneers who worked in the thick gloom with few rays to cheer, except such as flow from faith in the precious promises of God's Word."

Chief Sechele and the villagers were astonished when Livingstone and all twenty-seven of the Makololo arrived safely back in Linyanti. The trip had taken nearly two years, but not one man had been lost to disease, desertion, or tribal murder.

David Livingstone

The Thunder of "Sounding Smoke"

The success of the expedition drove Livingstone to further discoveries. Instead of taking time to rest, within a month, he planned a similar excursion to Africa's east coast. Arab traders in Loanda had told him that following the Zambesi River would take him all the way to the Indian Ocean. This time, Chief Sekeletu trusted him with one hundred warriors to aid in the journey.

While attempting to find this new route to the east, Livingstone wrote, "Cannot the love of Christ carry the missionary where the slave-trade carries the trader? I shall open up a path to the interior or perish."[310]

Throughout the journey, Livingstone took the opportunity to preach to native tribes along the way. "What effect the preaching of the gospel has at the commencement on such individuals, I am unable to tell," Livingstone recorded, "except that some have confessed that they first began to pray in secret. As that great Redeemer of the guilty seeks to save all He can, we may hope that they find mercy through His blood."

Throughout the journey, Livingstone took the opportunity to preach to native tribes along the way.

By November 13, 1855, Livingstone's men were following the Zambesi River, some in canoes, others driving the oxen along the riverfront.[311] Days into the journey, the men started talking of "the smoke that thunders." While they were still several miles away, David saw columns of "white smoke" rising high above the trees. A faint rumble soon turned to a deafening roar as they approached the rushing water. The natives skillfully maneuvered the canoes to an island that protruded over the falls (known today as Livingstone Island). Stepping out of the boat, David and his oarsmen carefully crawled to the overhang.

David gasped. What a work of God's creation! Before him, the Zambesi River plunged in flat sheets of water three hundred feet into the gorge below. After feasting his eyes on the falls, he wrote in his diary, "Five columns [of smoke or mist] now arose....The whole scene was extremely beautiful; the banks and islands dotted over the river are adorned with sylvan vegetation of great variety of color and form....Scenes so lovely must have been gazed upon by angels in their flight." Livingstone was the first European to view the largest waterfall in the world, two thousand yards wide; he named it Victoria Falls in honor of his queen.

Because of the waterfall, the expedition left the river and traveled for one hundred miles by land. In this northern plateau region, David found a paradise of lush vegetation and a vast supply of game and water. To him, this seemed a perfect place for a Christian mission. He wrote home to the London Missionary Society, describing the area in glowing terms.

Livingstone's next stop was Tete (in Mozambique), a Portuguese colony that was nothing more than a city of slaves. In much of Europe, slavery had been abolished by now, but the Portuguese continued to sell slaves on both coasts of Africa. Abhorring the practice, David still had to rest in Tete for several weeks because his malaria had returned. While there, he asked the Portuguese about the hundred miles of the Zambesi that he had bypassed by traveling on land. "The Zambesi is navigable from Victoria Falls all the way to the Indian Ocean," they assured him; he had avoided only a small section of rapids. Their statement would haunt his next expedition. Leaving the Makololo natives in Tete, David canoed the last section of the river with five Portuguese escorts.

In May 1856, David Livingstone reached the mouth of the Zambesi in the port city of Quilimane (Mozambique), at the Indian Ocean. He had done it! He had crisscrossed Africa's interior from west to east, and drawn detailed maps for all of Europe to employ. He was convinced that the Zambesi River was "God's highway"—a passage for missionaries and tradesmen from the Indian Ocean into the interior of Africa!

Now it was time to go home to England.

A Hero's Welcome

It had been four and a half years since David had watched Mary and the children sail away to Great Britain. By ship and across land, the forty-six-year old missionary took the fastest route possible to return home.

Mary was waiting anxiously for him in Southampton. While the children felt shy around their father, Mary threw herself into David's arms. She shared a loving poem with him that said, in part, "A hundred thousand welcomes, how my heart is gushing o'er / With the love and joy and wonder thus to see your face once more." She had missed her husband more than he could ever understand.

To Livingstone's astonishment, England showered him with a hero's welcome! Reports of his African discoveries had filled the newspapers and the halls of British society. Roderick Murchison, president of the Royal Geographical Society, declared his trip to Loanda "the greatest triumph in geographical research in our time!"[312]

The RGS had a lavish meeting to present him, once more, with the Gold Medal, its highest annual honor for geographical discoveries. David and Mary entered the ballroom greeted by the upper crust of British society, as well as the warm and welcoming face of Cotton Oswell. Murchison spoke in glowing terms of Livingstone's work, and then David was asked to step to the podium and speak.

After sixteen hard years in Africa, Livingstone was a suntanned, weathered man. He had wrestled with malaria for the past four years, often wondering if he was losing the fight. As he groped for words, he realized that all the years of speaking Bantu rather than English had made his speech awkward. But he spoke with passion of his work in Africa: "I am only doing my duty as a missionary in opening up a part of Africa to the sympathy of Christ. I am only just now buckling my armor for the good fight. I have no right to boast of anything. I will not boast until the last slave in Africa is free and Africa is open to honest trade and the light of Christianity."

Applause filled the room as David returned to his seat. He received offers to speak around the country and was persuaded to write a book on his African adventures. He spoke at Oxford and Cambridge Universities, mesmerizing the students with accounts of Africa's beauty and pleas for new missionaries to join him in bringing Christ to the lost. He ended his speech, "Do you carry on the work I have begun? I leave it with you!"[313]

In February 1858, David was invited to a private audience with Queen Victoria in Buckingham Palace and awarded an honorary doctorate from Oxford University. Other honors flowed in from countries throughout the continent. It was a whirlwind of praise and awards.

But not all the news Livingstone had received since arriving in England was positive.

Conflict and Decision

David's homecoming was met with some bad tidings as well. His father, Neil, had not lived long enough to see his son return triumphantly from Africa, and his mother was too ill to remember her family any longer. David mourned the time he could not share with his parents.

David Livingstone, missionary and traveler, circa 1870.

Worse yet, he was heartbroken when Mary shared the sad story of her life over the past four years. She had not felt welcome in her in-laws' home, and harsh words had been spoken between them. The London Missionary Society had been unwilling to give her David's salary to live on, as the Livingstones had expected. Destitute, Mary had left the children in Scotland with David's sisters and moved to London, living with friends of her parents. Sobbing, Mary confessed how she had grieved during their years of separation and had become overly fond of brandy during that time.[314]

Livingstone was distraught. How could he forgive the London Missionary Society for its thoughtless neglect of his wife and family? He had built mission stations with his own salary and had worked relentlessly to open Africa to the gospel as a partner in its foreign work. Why had it deserted his family members during their time of need?

This should be a reminder to mission organizations today that there must be love and support for the family of every missionary. Even if the family members are not on the mission field themselves, they are still sacrificing without the husband and father at home.

The London Missionary Society had become single-minded; its directors said that they were disappointed at what they saw as Livingstone's lack of Christian converts. Actually, they had lost their apostolic spirit. They had become caught up in the home organization and all of the paperwork and had forgotten that it was not about them and their "numbers." It was about the man on the field who was fulfilling the call of Christ to the lost.

Sometimes, I compare thoughtless decisions like this to a football game. It is easy for the guys in the stands to yell at the players on the field about how to run a play. But they are not the ones who are standing their ground while a 300-pound-man tackles them at full speed and knocks them to the ground. The London Missionary Society had turned into a mean group on the sidelines who could not see what was happening on the field. They were not there in the heat of the moment, in the midst of the battle. They should have given David Livingstone, "the guy on the field," the benefit of the doubt!

The London Missionary Society had turned into a mean group on the sidelines who could not see what was happening on the field. They were not there in the heat of the moment, in the midst of the battle.

When they urged Livingstone to return to Africa to set up a mission station among the Makololo and to discontinue all of his explorations, he decided that it was time to end their relationship. Roderick Murchison of the Royal Geographical Society was certain that the British government would provide the finances needed for his next exploration. David's decision was made. He would become an official explorer for Great Britain.

A Runaway Best Seller

For the next six months, Livingstone worked on his first published book, *Missionary Travels and Researches in South Africa of 1857,* which became an instant best seller. It established Livingstone as a heroic explorer who had made successful contributions to geography, medicine and science, the abolition of the slave trade, and the gospel of Christ. "If Christian missionaries and Christian merchants can remain throughout the year in the interior of the continent," Livingstone wrote of his purpose in exploring Africa, "the slave trader will be driven out of the market place."

The book's publisher, John Murray, offered Livingstone more than the usual 50 percent of the profits to write the book. The royalty money was enough to provide for his family in the years to come. The first edition of twelve thousand copies sold out immediately, and Murray ordered the printing of another eight thousand copies of the 689-page volume. Within months, Murray announced that twenty-five thousand copies were in print. The book is still in print today.

At the time of the book's publication, a special book review was written by British author Charles Dickens, who proclaimed Livingstone's work "a narrative of great dangers and trials, encountered in a good cause by as honest and courageous a man as ever lived!"

The Zambesi Expedition

After fifteen months of celebrations, speeches, and writing, it was time to return to Africa. Robert, Agnes, and Thomas would stay in Scotland with Livingstone's sisters, while Mary and five-year-old Zouga would return to Africa with him.

The British government had commissioned Livingstone to explore the Zambesi River as the waterway into Africa's interior. It was to be a two-year expedition and included six other members: navy officer Norman Bedingfield; botanist John Kirk; geologist Richard Thornton; storekeeper Thomas Baines; ship engineer George Rae; and David's brother, Rev. Charles Livingstone, who was to be the spiritual support for the journey.

On March 10, 1858, with "the cheers of England ringing in their ears," the Zambesi Expedition sailed from England on the *Pearl*, hopeful that they would discover a waterway into the heart of Africa. They would travel a thousand miles from the mouth of the Zambesi River on the east coast to Victoria Falls. The only thing standing in their way was the Kebrabasa Rapids, which Livingstone had been told was nothing of great concern. They had little idea of the danger and disappointment that lay ahead.

Life would change for the brilliant and determined missionary/explorer. He would travel from the fame of London to the most difficult and often tragic years of his life. After stopping in Cape Town to drop off Mary and Zouga for a visit with her parents, the *Pearl* rounded the tip of Africa and unloaded the expedition at the mouth of the Zambesi.

The Zambesi Disaster

Unfortunately, *nothing* went as planned. The team had brought a special riverboat, the *Ma-Robert*, from England to help in the exploration; it was to be assembled in Africa. However, it wasn't shallow enough to travel the Zambesi and continually ran aground. Eventually, they had to abandon it.

When they finally reached the Kebrabasa Rapids, David was speechless at the number of boulders that jutted from the riverbed of the Zambesi, with the rushing water foaming and twisting downriver. Docking on the shore, he and John Kirk continued to follow the river on foot to see how soon the rapids improved. Looking down from an overhanging ridge, David cried in horror, "I believe now these rapids extend for thirty miles!" His worst fear had been realized. The middle Zambesi River was impassable.[315]

David Livingstone was stunned. He had been so certain the Zambesi would be "God's highway" into the interior. In desperation, he made one last attempt to travel the rapids by canoe. Although questioning Livingstone's sanity, Kirk agreed to join him. At the rapids, their canoes were "twisted about like twigs," and Kirk's canoe overturned. The doctor was saved, but he lost all eight of his botanical journals.

Sometimes, what we think is the right direction for our lives is a mistake. When that happens, we need to stop before the Lord and discover what is wrong. We need to have the inner stillness to hear His voice and to deal with the problem. If things are consistently going wrong for us, we need to start asking the Lord, "Why is this happening?" and then be certain to listen for His answer.

Big Challenges

Although he had been wrong about the Zambesi River, Livingstone refused to admit defeat. The expedition moved on to explore the Shire River north of the Zambesi. In 1859, following the river to its source, he and John Kirk discovered Lake Shirwa and Lake Nyassa, the third largest lake in Africa.

But problems beset the crew of the *Ma-Roberts* on every side. The British crew was petty and continually bickering. It was unfortunate that the Geographical Society hadn't let Livingstone choose his own men. You must have the right team with the right focus in order to achieve success. Nothing was going right, so David dismissed all of the men except Kirk, his brother Charles, and engineer George Rae.

Returning to Tete, Livingstone received a surprising letter. Unbeknownst to either of them, Mary had been pregnant with their sixth child when he left her with her parents two years earlier. Mary had given birth to a baby girl, Anna Mary, but none of her other letters with this news had reached him. Mary was restless to join her husband, but he urged her to wait a little longer until he felt it was safer.

Another letter brought a disturbing message: His fiery speeches in England about Africa's needs had led three zealous missionary families to join his cause for Christ in Africa's interior. The families were already headed to the Makololo tribe.

"It is too soon," David cried. "We are not ready for men with families." Rushing as quickly as they could to Linyanti, he and Kirk discovered they were too late; with the exception of one adult and two children who had already returned to Kuruman, the missionaries had all succumbed to malaria. Livingstone blamed himself for not being more careful in his plea for help. Missionaries are visionaries, and his rousing speeches in England led people to believe Africa was already safe enough for women and children to join the work.

"I Feel Willing to Die"

Just months later, David received another disturbing letter from Kuruman; Mary was on her way to meet him. She had waited as long as she could and wanted to join him in his work. Since writing her last letter, she had taken Zouga and little Anna Mary back to Scotland and had returned to join her husband in exploring the depths of Africa. It had been another four long years since they had been together.

Within six short days, on April 27, 1862, Mary Livingstone was dead at just forty-one years of age. In the seventeen years of their marriage, she and David had lived together for only four of them.

On January 1, 1862, Mary finally reached David in Quilimane (a seaport in Mozambique). She arrived on the same ship that brought his new riverboat, the *Lady Nyassa*. He had personally designed the boat and paid six thousand pounds with his royalty money. He hoped to explore the lakes and rivers of Africa with ease.[316]

Mary was delighted to be reunited with her husband, and she worked diligently by Livingstone's side. While they waited for the boat to be assembled, they planned their future expeditions with excitement, listing all the discoveries he wanted her to see. But secretly, David was worried. The lower Zambesi was a swampland noted for malaria. Mary was in danger until they could move to a drier area.

Before they had time to leave the swamplands, in the village of Shupanga (in modern-day Mozambique), Mary contracted the dreaded disease. Without warning, she became violently ill. None of David's tender care or the quinine he administered eased her pain. Within six short days, on April 27, 1862, Mary Livingstone was dead at just forty-one years of age. In the seventeen years of their marriage, she and David had lived together for only four of them.

The grieving husband buried her body under a giant boabab tree in Shupanga. For once, the always optimistic Livingstone was overcome with despair; he sobbed at her graveside. That night, he wrote in his journal, "I wept over her who well deserved many tears. I loved her when I married her and the longer I lived with her I loved her the more. God pity the poor children....For the first time in my life I feel willing to die."[317]

Mary Moffat Livingstone's gravestone[318]

Sometime after Mary's death, David wrote in his journal, "I will place no value on anything I possess or anything I may do, except in relation to the kingdom of Christ." Although he grieved for his wife, Livingstone was able to turn his grief into a motivation for the future rather than to allow it to be an end to his work. This is something that is essential for those serving in the ministry.

Two Thousand Five Hundred Miles for a "Side Trip"

Everything had gone wrong with the expedition; now Mary was gone.

In 1863, the Zambesi Expedition was recalled by the British government after five years of labor. The original two-year exploration had gone far beyond its limits, and, still, no waterway had been mapped from the ocean to the interior. Charles Livingstone and John Kirk asked to be released, and Livingstone continued his explorations with only George Rae left from the original party.

In four hundred years, beginning in 1400 until Livingstone's time, an estimated twelve million slaves had been taken from the continent of Africa by nearly every nation in the world. Livingstone's passion was to see it abolished worldwide—forever.

As Livingstone traveled the Shire River in the *Lady Nyassa,* he saw the ravages of the slave trade in Africa. Villages were deserted or burned to the ground. Corpses of murdered slaves floated past their boat. In horror, he realized that, to some extent, his discoveries had opened the way for Portuguese slave traders to move with greater ease through Africa's interior.

"We were made the unwilling instruments of extending the slave trade," he mourned. Livingstone became increasingly angry and outspoken against the Portuguese and now avoided their settlements for fear of retaliation.[319]

Exhausted and discouraged, it was time to go home to visit his children. But what would he do with the *Lady Nyassa*? If he left her in Africa, she would be stolen by slave traders. Coming up with a shocking solution, he announced, "I will sail her to the British Navy in India." "Across 2,500 miles of open ocean?" George Rae asked incredulously. "You will never make it. It is a suicide mission."

But make it he did! Livingstone set out on April 30, 1864, with a crew of twelve, none of whom had sailed before. Forty-five days later, the undaunted Livingstone anchored in India. He left his boat with British naval officers in Bombay and boarded the next ship for England.

Why did Livingstone make such a dangerous and illogical decision to embark on a 2,500-mile "side trip" to India with an inexperienced crew? I believe that his grief over Mary's death and his disillusionment over the rising slave trade led him to reject wise spiritual guidance. Thanks be to God, they didn't die on their way across the open ocean! The devil would have had a victory, and David's future purpose in God would have been thwarted.

Denouncing the Slave Trade

David arrived in London in July 1864. There he met with mixed reviews; some criticized him for the Zambesi failures, others still gave him a hero's welcome. The Royal Geographical Society and Murchison were excited by his discovery of Lake Nyassa and his unveiling of Africa's interior through his detailed maps.

Livingstone spent considerable time on this trip to England denouncing the role of Portugal in the African slave trade. He pleaded with the British government to intervene to stop the death and destruction of the African people.

England had banned the slave trade in the British Empire nearly sixty years earlier, in large part due to the Christian abolitionist William Wilberforce and his work in the House of Commons to bring about the Slave Trade Act of 1807. Slavery was abolished in the British Empire in 1834. Though Portugal had banned transatlantic slave trading in 1836, greedy Portuguese slave traders were still immersed in the capture and sale of slaves in Africa.

In four hundred years, beginning in 1400 until Livingstone's time, an estimated twelve million slaves had been taken from the continent of Africa by nearly every nation in the world. Livingstone's passion was to see it abolished worldwide—forever.

When David left England for Scotland to see his children, he found them well; he held the youngest child, Anna, in his lap for the first time. But, the oldest, Robert, wasn't there. After hearing of his mother's death, Robert, with David's drive for adventure, had traveled to Africa in search of his father. When he couldn't locate him, Robert had sailed on to America and joined the Union army to fight slavery in America's Civil War. He was currently in a Confederate prisoner-of-war camp.[320]

In London again, David wrote and published his second book, outlining the details of the Zambesi Expedition, called *Narrative of an Expedition to the Zambesi and Its Tributaries.* While it was not as wildly popular as the first book, it was still well-received in England.

Britain's Holy Grail: Finding the Source of the Nile

The passion of the Royal Geographical Society and of Great Britain itself had become finding the source of the Nile River in Africa. Murchison of the RGS offered to send Livingstone on another expedition into Africa, this time to locate the elusive origins of the world's longest river.

Slowly, this quest became Livingstone's obsession as well. Although he still kept a diary of his prayers, his primary goal seems to have shifted from opening Africa to the gospel to the thrill of discovering what no man had found before.

The funds that Murchison raised were matched by the British government. Livingstone would return to Africa.

In September 1865, he arrived in India, sold the *Lady Nyassa,* and returned to Africa. He traveled first to Lake Nyassa and then moved further west, exhilarated at being back "home." In his journal, he confessed, "The mere animal pleasures of traveling in a wild, unexplored country are very great."[321]

Livingstone started out with sixty porters, but after six months, all but twenty had deserted him. The guides had been unruly from the start, except for two faithful African workers, Susi and Chuma, who had traveled with Livingstone before. During 1866, he discovered two more lakes, Lake Moero and Lake Bangwelo. He recorded the geographic measurements carefully, remembering his prediction years earlier that Africa's interior contained a series of lakes stretching nearly to Egypt. Each year, more discoveries proved he was correct.

Livingstone continued his explorations, but the Nile's source remained a mystery. By 1869, he was extremely ill, suffering from repeated bouts of malaria and dysentery, which caused extensive bleeding. Nine more African guides ran off with supplies, including his most precious commodity, his medicine box containing his quinine to fight off the attacks of malaria.

Chuma, David Livingstone's servant. From *Africa,* by Keith Johnston, published 1884.

"This loss," he wrote, "is like a sentence of death." The dishonest guides, headed by a wily native named Musa, traveled east to Zanzibar and announced to Dr. John Kirk, now the British consul there, that Livingstone had been murdered. Kirk promptly sent the report to England, but no one knew what to believe.

Growing increasingly weak and disoriented from illness, Livingstone rested in the village of Nyangwe, a post of Arab slave traders frequented by cannibals. One afternoon, while resting in the marketplace, he witnessed a horrifying massacre of four hundred native villagers, mostly women and children, by the Arabs simply because they wanted to show their power. Livingstone screamed at the

Arab murderers for their senseless cruelty, but they laughed or simply ignored him. He cried out to the Lord, "O let Thy kingdom come! No one will ever know the loss on this bright, sultry morning. It gave me the impression of being in hell."[322]

Shattered and nearly alone, Livingstone, Susi, and Chuma fled to the village of Ujiji on the banks of Lake Tanganyika (in modern Tanzania). David collapsed in exhaustion in a small hut. Malaria was still ravaging his body, and he had lost most of his teeth due to chewing the hard corn he had to eat to survive. It was here in Ujiji that he cried out to God to send him a deliverer.

Little did he know that, for the last year, a rescuer had been crossing Africa from the east coast, driving forward with no other goal than to find and rescue David Livingstone!

"Dr. Livingstone, I Presume?"

While Livingstone was fighting malaria and slave traders in Africa, James Gordon Bennet Jr., owner of the *New York Herald*, was looking for a new sensation to sell newspapers. There were rumors of Livingstone's death, but no one was certain what had happened to the explorer. Bennett decided to secretly send his most adventurous reporter to Africa. His choice was Henry Morton Stanley. Stanley's directive—"Find David Livingstone, dead or alive, and don't return without news of his fate!"[323]

For nearly all of 1871, Stanley traced Livingstone's journeys from Quilimane through Tete and Linyanti. He suffered the same illnesses as Livingstone and struggled through the same crocodile-infested waters; he bribed savage native chiefs and tricked wily Portuguese slave traders. And, just like the determined explorer he eagerly searched for, he stubbornly refused to give up!

When the journey seemed impossible, Stanley wrote in his journal, "No living man shall stop me. Only death can prevent me; but death—not even this. I shall not die; I cannot die; I will not die. Something tells me that I shall find him. And I write it larger, *find him, FIND HIM.*"[324]

On November 3, 1871, as Livingstone rested in his hut, Henry Stanley approached the village of Ujiji. Hearing a sudden commotion, Susi ran to look and then rushed back into David's hut, crying, "A white man is coming!" Livingstone walked out of the hut to see a white man walking toward him holding an American flag, with the entire village following behind in excitement. The thirty-year-old Stanley, who now looked like a seasoned African explorer, had just traveled 975 miles in 236 days to find the bent, white-haired man who stood before him.[325]

As Stanley approached Livingstone, he spoke the legendary words "Dr. Livingstone, I presume?"

"Yes," David answered quietly.

"I thank God, Doctor, I have been permitted to see you," Stanley said in relief.

"Thank God, I am here to welcome you," was Livingstone's smiling reply.

Stanley had done it! He had found Dr. Livingstone!

An illustration from Henry Stanley's book *How I Found Livingstone.*

My Work Is Not Done

Over the next four months, the relationship between the two explorers became much like father and son. Together, they paddled a canoe three hundred miles to explore the northern end of Lake Tanganyika together.[326] Stanley admitted that he came to Africa to rescue Livingstone on behalf of an American newspaper but that the doctor had come to mean so much more to him than a news story.

Stanley also confessed to Livingstone what no other man knew. He was actually not an American citizen but British and had been born John Rowlands. Because of a troubled family life in Wales, he had migrated to the United States and adopted a new name. He had fought on both sides of the Civil War and become a newspaper correspondent.

After they had explored the region near Ujiji together, the aging Livingstone made Stanley promise that, after his death, the young man would continue the search for the source of the Nile. Repeatedly, Stanley begged Livingstone to leave Africa with him. His answer was always the same: "No, my work is not yet done."

Later, Stanley wrote of Livingstone, "I challenge any man to find a fault in his character....The secret is that his religion is a constant, earnest, and sincere practice."

In February 1872, Stanley and Livingstone, with their guides, traveled east to Tabora, where Stanley had built a hut on his earlier journey; there, he provided Livingstone with much-needed supplies for his continued explorations. On March 14, 1872, Stanley reluctantly left his dear friend and mentor in the village of Tabora, taking with him all of Livingstone's journals and letters to England to be published and shared with the world.

Livingstone escorted Stanley partway out of the village as they sang together, holding back tears before they finally parted company. Livingstone spoke these last words to his young friend and rescuer: "I am grateful for what you have done for me. God guide you for what you have done for me. God guide you safe home and bless you, my friend. Farewell."[327]

Stanley was the last European to see David Livingstone alive.

My Birthday Prayer

Five days later, March 19, 1873, was Livingstone's sixtieth birthday. He recorded, "My birthday! My Jesus, my King, my Life, my All. I again dedicate my whole self to Thee. Accept me and grant, O gracious Father, that ere this year is gone, I may finish my task. Amen."[328]

For the next year, Livingstone traveled south of Tabora toward Lake Bangweolo, exploring modern-day Zambia, where he believed the Nile bubbled up in fountains of fresh water from under the ground. His body was becoming more ravaged by illness with each passing month, and he had to rest for weeks at a time. Finally, in April 1873, Susi and Chuma set up camp in Chief Chitambo's village in the Congo wetlands, sixty miles south of Lake Bangwelo. Livingstone's faithful guides built him a small hut, and he lay inside on his straw cot, fighting the pain.

On April 30, 1873, when David went to bed, he was once again feverish with malaria and bleeding from dysentery. Sometime after midnight on May 1, he knelt quietly by his cot in prayer. In the early morning hours, when Chuma went in to check on the doctor, he found him dead. At sixty years of age, Livingstone had gone home to His heavenly Father while still on bended knee in prayer.

His Heart Belonged to Africa

Chuma and Susi had been Livingstone's closest companions for the last seven years of his life. They knew the great missionary explorer would want to be buried with his own people in England. But his heart belonged to Africa.

> *"You can have his body, but his heart belongs to Africa!"*

As part of the African tradition of embalming, they cut his heart out and placed it in the tin box where he had kept his journals safe from the rain. They buried his heart under a large mvula tree in Chief Chitambo's village. In 1899, the Livingstone Memorial was built by the British to mark the spot where Livingstone's heart is buried. Today, the memorial still stands in a meadow near the edge of the Bangweulu Swamps in modern Zambia.

After burying his heart, Chuma and Susi dried Livingstone's body in the sun, bound him in sailcloth, and sealed it with tar. Susi, Chuma, and Jacob Wainwright, an educated African native, placed Livingstone's body in a sack and attached a note in honor of their dear mentor and friend: "You can have his body, but his heart belongs to Africa!" Then they started their journey to the east coast of Africa so that their beloved leader and friend could return to England. It took them nearly a year to walk more than one thousand miles to Bagamoyo and turn Livingstone's body over to the British consul there. Wainwright, who spoke English fluently, accompanied the body to Great Britain.

David Livingstone

Photo of Jacob Wainwright, a student from one of Livingstone's mission schools, who accompanied Livingstone's body all the way back to England.

The English wept when they heard that their hero-explorer was dead. On April 18, 1874, David Livingstone was buried with a twenty-one-gun salute and a hero's funeral at Westminster Abbey. His pallbearers were men who had faithfully served with him in Africa: Thomas Steele, Cotton Oswell, Henry M. Stanley, Jacob Wainwright, and Dr. John Kirk. Livingstone's father-in-law, Robert Moffat, who was still alive at ninety-two, sat in the front row of the abbey with the Livingstone children—all but Robert, who had died of his wounds in the Confederate prison camp.

David Livingstone's tombstone, set among the heroes and royalty of England, reads:

> Brought by faithful hands over land and sea, here rests David Livingstone, missionary, traveller, philanthropist....For 30 years his life was spent in an unwearied effort to evangelize the native races, to explore the undiscovered secrets, to abolish the desolating slave trade....

The inscription closes with Livingstone's own words:

> All I can add in my solitude, is, May heaven's rich blessing come down on every one, American, English, or Turk, who will help to heal this open sore of the world [slavery].

Africa Opened for Good and for Evil

David Livingstone had opened the interior of Africa to the whole world for the good of spreading the gospel of Christ.

A positive of Livingstone's influence was that, within a year of his death, the British government closed Africa's largest slave trade center, located on the island of Zanzibar. Slavery slowly became illegal across the entire African continent.

The tragic side of Livingstone's explorations and maps of Africa was the evil that came when countries used his discoveries for greed and power in what became known as the "Scramble for Africa."

Chief Sechele lived years beyond the attack at Kolobeng and became a dedicated missionary of Christ to his people. European and American missionaries poured into Africa, as well, including Mary Slessor, Alexander Mackay, and Peter Cameron Scott, who founded the Africa Inland Missions (AIM) and pioneered the idea of setting up Christian centers throughout Africa. AIM's mission is "Christ-centered churches established among all African peoples."

By 1900, just twenty-seven years after Livingstone's death, the number of Christians in Africa totaled nine million! In 2012, this number reached five hundred million, or 20 percent of the African population. David Livingstone's persistence had truly opened Africa to the gospel of Christ.

Henry Stanley fulfilled his promise to Livingstone, as well, returning to Africa as an explorer. He traveled the circumferences of Lake Victoria and Lake Tanganyika, followed the Congo River to the Atlantic Ocean, and explored the Congo regions. However, he never discovered the mysterious source of the Nile.

It would be one hundred years before satellite imagery would finally pinpoint "God's well-kept secret" in the middle of Africa: the fact that the Nile bubbles out of the ground like a fountain from springs in the mountains of Burundi between Lake Tanganyika and Lake Victoria. Its waters then flow down in streams into Lake Victoria. Although he was searching too far south, Livingstone's prediction was nearly correct—as always.[329]

The tragic side of Livingstone's explorations and maps of Africa was the evil that came when countries used his discoveries for greed and power in what became known as the "Scramble for Africa"—a term used to describe the invasion, occupation, and colonization of African territory by European powers that fought for control of Africa's rich resources. The world's richest diamond and gold mines were discovered near Robert Moffat's original mission in Kuruman. Shortly afterward, the continent was carved into British, Portuguese, French, German, and Belgian colonies. It would be decades before those African colonies would gain their rightful independence.

David Livingstone

A Missionary Hero

David Livingstone went to Africa as a missionary to spread the gospel of Jesus Christ and to open the interior to both Christianity and commerce. Time and his passions transformed him into more of an explorer, but he always sought to glorify God in his explorations. Some have said that Livingstone's obsession made him reckless and even insane. His reply to his critics was always, "Remember us in your prayers that we grow not weary in well doing. It is hard to work for years with pure motives, and all the time be looked upon by most of those to whom our lives are devoted as having some sinister object in view....We should have grace to follow in Christ's steps."[330]

David Livingstone was certainly driven, in spite of grave illness, to press on in his work until he died upon his knees before his Savior. But the Lord protected him and led him through many dangers, and, in the end, used him mightily to help put an end to the horrific slave trade in Africa and to open the continent to the gospel of Jesus Christ for thousands of dedicated Christian missionaries who would come after him.

Above all else, David Livingstone was a man who made a difference: He transformed the continent of Africa. His iron will and his tenacity to endure beyond his own strength has provided a role model for Christian missionaries for the last one hundred fifty years.

David Livingstone memorial at Victoria Falls.

David Livingstone is still honored in the Africa he loved. As mentioned earlier, in Chief Chitambo's village in Zambia, there is the Livingstone Memorial, marking the site of his death. The cities of Livingstone in Zambia and Livingstonia in Malawi still proudly bear his name. A life-sized bronze statue of Livingstone stands overlooking the world's largest waterfall, Victoria Falls, in Zimbabwe.

Years before his death, when Livingstone was asked by his brother, Charles, to leave Africa, his reply was clear: "I am a missionary, heart and soul. God had an only Son, and He was a missionary and a physician. I am a poor, poor imitation of Him, or wish to be. But in this service I hope to live; in it I wish to die!"[331]

> *Then He said to His disciples, "The harvest is plentiful, but the workers are few. Therefore beseech the Lord of the harvest to send out workers into His harvest."* (Matthew 9:37–38 NASB)

Will you be a faithful end-time harvester that God can count on?

CHAPTER 7

J. HUDSON TAYLOR

China Must Be Saved!

She could only peek out of the darkened window. "How will we escape?" Maria Taylor silently cried. The streets of Yangchow, China, teemed with thousands of screaming protesters demanding the lives of the missionaries trapped inside the clapboard house. Someone screamed, "The foreign devils have eaten twenty-four of our children!" The Chinese mob threw rocks and mud balls, pressing against the locked gate of the courtyard.

It was August 22, 1868, and the day before, a note had been smuggled into the mission house: "Get out! The crowd is out of control and is planning to burn the house to the ground. Escape or face certain death!"

J. Hudson Taylor

Hudson Taylor now crumpled the note and solemnly looked at his pregnant wife, Maria, who had her arms around their four small children huddled against her. Among the nine missionaries in the house, there were none more vulnerable than his own family. After barricading everyone in a back room, Hudson spoke hurriedly, "Our best hope is to get to the mandarin quickly and ask for his help. He is the only one who can stop this."[332]

With a fervent prayer for God's protection, Hudson and George Duncan slipped out the back entrance and moved quietly in the direction of the quarters of the *yamen,* or mandarin. Wearing their customary Chinese dress, with long black queues (pigtails), Hudson prayed that he and Duncan would not be recognized as they rounded the corner and hurried away from the house.

Hearing pounding feet and clamoring voices rushing up behind them, the men broke into a run, dashing toward the open gates of the yamen. With seconds to spare, they ran into the front hall, crying, "*Kiu-ming! Kiu-ming!*" ("Save life! Save life!"), a request for asylum that the Chinese official was required to grant.

In fluent Mandarin Chinese, Hudson hastily explained the situation to the waiting official; the hostile crowd was threatening their lives because of posters circulated throughout the city depicting horrible crimes the missionaries had supposedly committed.

"Well, where *are* the children you have captured?" the Mandarin asked quizzically.

Frustrated, Hudson replied, "We have not captured or harmed any children!" Fearing for his family's life, he pleaded, "Would you please stop the riot and check on these facts later?"

For two hours, the anxious men waited as the mandarin sent his guards to dispel the angry crowd; they were finally released to return to the mission house. Arriving breathless, they found the front gates broken in two and the house ransacked. Where were the other missionaries, and Maria and the children? Had they been dragged away to their deaths?

Compared with other British missionaries arriving in nineteenth-century China, Taylor was not well-educated, not ordained, not a licensed doctor, not well-funded, only twenty-one years old, and alone.

Thankfully, in the darkness of night, the missionary party had snuck upstairs and opened a bedroom window. Hurling blankets and pillows to the ground to cushion their fall, the men, women, and children leaped to safety and hid in the darkened house next door. Maria had jumped while five months pregnant but suffered only some cuts and bruises; missionary Emily Blatchley had a broken elbow. They were all grateful to be alive.

J. Hudson Taylor

Weeks earlier, Hudson Taylor and his party had traveled four hundred miles from the port of Shanghai to Yangchow, finally reaching inland China to minister for Christ. Although some Chinese had met them with hostility and rioting, God had met them with protection and peace, and He would continue to protect and guide them as they brought Christ's message of salvation to China.

A Passionate Focus

"How often do we attempt work for God to the limit of our incompetency rather than to the limit of His omnipotency?"
—Hudson Taylor

One chapter in a book could never do justice to the inspiring faithfulness and Christlike love of Hudson Taylor. Although he was a short, slender man, he remains a giant among God's missionaries. Answering the call to China while still a teenager, Taylor graciously poured out his life, bathed in prayer, honoring Christ at every opportunity. With his unflinching commitment to present the gospel, he overcame persecution, famine, and heartache to pioneer a mission that changed countless Chinese lives for eternity.

J. Hudson Taylor, age twenty-one.

Compared with other British missionaries arriving in nineteenth-century China, Taylor was not well-educated, not ordained, not a licensed doctor, not well-funded, only twenty-one years old, and alone. But within his heart burned such a passion for the lost millions of China that he dedicated his life in faith—believing in the God who would empower him and provide for him in the midst of his call.

It was Hudson Taylor who popularized the term "the Great Commission" when he spoke of Christ's command to the disciples: "*Go therefore and make disciples of all the nations, baptizing them in the name of the Father and of the Son and of the Holy Spirit, teaching them to observe all things that I have commanded you*" (Matthew 28:19–20). Hudson was determined, saying, "In the Bible we aren't told to try anything—we are told to obey Him."

And obey he would, investing his life, money, prayers, and toil to bring the gospel to China's four hundred million lost souls. Beginning as a solitary voice in Shanghai, he eventually founded the China Inland Mission, the largest Protestant mission society of the time, with over a thousand missionaries across all twelve of China's provinces. Taylor crisscrossed the world's oceans on behalf of China's cause, proclaiming the motto he made famous: "Christians must recognize the truth that Christ is either Lord of all or He is not Lord at all!"[333]

Through his witness, Hudson Taylor is still challenging Christians today to be used as God's instruments of hope in a lost and dying world.

A Flash of God's Lightning

In 1831, in the village of Barnsley, England, James Taylor, a young chemist (pharmacist) and lay preacher married Amelia Hudson, the pretty daughter of the Methodist pastor. Together, they shared a sincere longing to serve Jesus Christ in some way beyond their own small village. James was captivated by the journals of missionaries to China, a vast country where one fourth of the world's population lived and died without Christ.

One evening, James was stirred by the Holy Spirit to pray: If God would give the Taylors a son, they would consecrate him to serve the Lord in China. God was faithful, and their answer came with the birth of their first child, James Hudson Taylor, on May 21, 1832.

Hudson grew up with two younger sisters, Amelia and Louise, hearing about a powerful God who answers prayer. But by his teen years, he had become rebellious and bored with the constant reminders of Christian life. Working at a bank with several other young men, he became envious of their wild and carefree lifestyles. A sudden illness required him to reluctantly give up his bank position and return home to rest and recover.

A sullen seventeen-year-old, J. Hudson Taylor walked into his father's study one warm afternoon in June 1849 looking for something interesting to read. He found a short gospel biography and decided to read the personal testimony at the beginning and skip over the end concerning Christ's offer of salvation. "Little did I know at the time," he wrote later, "what was going on in my mother's heart seventy miles away."[334]

Hudson's mother, Amelia, had been visiting her sister for several weeks when she had a sudden overwhelming burden to pray for her wayward son. Kneeling beside her bed in the guest bedroom, she cried out with a mother's impassioned prayers for the Lord to save her firstborn. Hour after hour, she prayed until she had a peaceful assurance from the Holy Spirit that her prayers were answered.

At the same time, while reading, Hudson came upon the unusual phrase "*the finished work of Christ*." Puzzled, he stopped and questioned, "*What* is finished?" and then he remembered his parents' teachings of Christ's sacrifice on the cross.

"Of course," he exclaimed. "It is the full and perfect satisfaction for my sin."

In that moment, Hudson wrote, "a light was flashed into my soul by the Holy Spirit, that there was nothing in the world to be done but to fall down on my knees and, accepting this Savior and His salvation, praise Him forevermore!"[335]

Although they were miles apart that afternoon, both mother and son praised a Savior who knows us and loves us and calls us by name. That summer day in 1849, J. Hudson Taylor's name was whispered by the Holy Spirit, and the young man became a new creature in Jesus Christ. "God became unutterably real...and a deep consciousness that I was no longer my own took possession of me from that day forward."[336]

"No Longer My Own"

In December 1849, just six months after Hudson experienced new life in Jesus, he became discouraged. What was his real purpose in Christ? Would he be able to keep himself from falling into sin? Could he measure up to Christ's expectations for him? Lying prostrate before the Lord, Hudson pleaded to be set free from his fear of failing, offering his life to God's will and service. Almost as if spoken out loud, he clearly heard the words, "Then go for Me to China!"

"Never shall I forget the feeling that came over me then," he wrote. "I felt I was in the presence of God, entering into covenant with the Almighty....And from that time the conviction never left me that I was *called to China*."[337]

Lying prostrate before the Lord, Hudson pleaded to be set free from his fear of failing, offering his life to God's will and service. Almost as if spoken out loud, he clearly heard the words, "Then go for Me to China!"

Hudson Taylor was now a man set apart, and going to China in the name of Jesus Christ became the reason for his existence. God has always worked His earthly plans through covenants with men and women. Within those covenants, certain geographical regions become their place of ministry. That is where their greatest spiritual authority comes into play. Taylor had discovered that China was his geographical calling, and he accepted it with great joy. Do you know your covenant? It is the "agreement of destiny" between you and God.

A Hard Floor and Exercise

At seventeen, Hudson was too young to travel halfway around the world as a missionary, but he was not too young to prepare for it. Dr. William Medhurst, the first Protestant missionary in China, had written a book called *China: Its State and Prospects*, and Hudson eagerly devoured the descriptions of the people, customs, and lands. With a Chinese copy of the gospel of Luke, he began a self-study of the language, comparing the Chinese characters with English words in his own Bible. And he began his medical studies by working with his father, dispensing medicine to the sick. Providing medical assistance was the quickest way to open the gospel to people in need in any nation.

Hudson Taylor was not a strong young man; he was slender with fair hair and blue eyes. Knowing that missionary life would be strenuous, he decided to prepare his body, as well as his mind. He removed the feather bed from his room and began sleeping on the hard floor. He also started exercising regularly.

Yet building his faith was the most vital step in his preparations. Hudson spent hours studying the Word of God and reading the testimonies of men of faith. He was especially drawn to the missionary/evangelist George Müller, director of the Ashley Down Orphanages in Bristol, England. Müller had an unshakable faith in *God alone* to provide for the care of thousands of English children. He never asked for financial support but took his needs privately to the Lord in prayer, and the provision was always there. Müller's faith walk struck a chord in Hudson's heart.

Hudson Taylor was a wise young man to realize that preparation is never lost time. He understood its importance. He knew that he needed to be physically, mentally, and spiritually ready for the work God had placed ahead of him. We bear much more fruit is we follow God-directed preparation.

Learning About Healing and Prosperity

Hudson asked himself an important question: *Would he really have the faith to trust God alone when he began to travel through the unopened provinces of China?*

He decided to put himself to the test: Before even leaving England, he would "learn to move man—through God—*by prayer*."[338]

Taylor had just moved seventy miles from Barnsley to Hull to work as a doctor's assistant to Dr. Robert Hardey, a distant relative. With the little money that Hudson earned from his job, all he could afford was a small room in "Drainside," the poverty-stricken area of town. Dr. Hardey paid Hudson's salary just once a quarter, so he would have to budget his money carefully for the three months between payments. Everything he learned, Hudson noted, was God's preparation for the work in China.

Dr. Hardey was a busy man, and he told Taylor he should remind him when his pay was due. *This,* Hudson decided, *would be his test.* He would not tell the doctor directly when it was payday, but instead "ask that God would bring the fact to the doctor's recollection, and thus encourage me by answering my prayer."[339] It would be a much greater challenge than he imagined.

When payday approached, Hudson prayed and waited for God to remind Dr. Hardey—but it didn't happen. Five days passed, and then two weeks. After paying his monthly bills, all that Hudson had left was one coin, a single half-crown (worth two-and-a-half shillings, or 60 cents). *I have enough for a few more days,* he thought, then prayed harder.

That Sunday night, after a late church service, Hudson was stopped on his way back to Drainside by a poor, desperate man whose wife lay dying. "Please come and pray for her, sir," the man cried. Hudson followed him in haste.

Entering the room, he found four emaciated children standing in the corner, and a dying mother lying with a helpless infant in her arms. Hudson was heartsick and silently cried, *If only I had a shilling or two instead of this one single coin, I would gladly give them a portion of my money.*

Overwhelmed by their needs, he knelt beside the bed to pray. "Our Father, who art in heaven…" he began, but the words caught in his throat. He could hear the Lord chastising him, "Do you mock God? Dare you kneel down and call him Father with that half-crown in your pocket?"[340] Feeling ashamed, Hudson finished the prayer for the woman's healing.

When the grieving husband asked again for help, the young missionary remembered Jesus' own words, "*Give to him that asketh thee*" (Matthew 5:42). Hudson gladly offered the family his last coin. Walking home with a peaceful heart, he laid his needs before the Lord. He had obeyed God's Word and could trust Him to be faithful.

The next day, while eating breakfast, Hudson received his Monday morning mail. Wrapped in a blank sheet of paper was a half-sovereign, a coin worth $2.40. He stared at the coin in amazement; God had returned four times his offering to the family the night before! The Lord had done exceedingly beyond all that the missionary-in-training had imagined!

Hudson Taylor's faith for finances was established that day. He often remembered the incident and the promise that "if we are faithful to God in little things, we will gain experience and strength for the more serious trials of life."[341]

Within days, there were more miraculous answers to his prayers. The once-desperate husband came to find Hudson at Dr. Hardey's offices. His wife was up from her bed and completely healed of her deathly illness![342] And, without being reminded, Dr. Hardey paid Taylor's salary by the end of the week, the night before his rent was due.

How much more can be accomplished in God when we lay all of our concerns before Him in prayer! Prayer had brought Hudson into God's kingdom, and it was sustaining him now as he prepared for his life's work. Hudson Taylor was ready for China!

"You Would *Never* Do for China!"

For some time, Taylor had been writing letters to George Pearse, the Foreign Secretary of the newly founded Chinese Evangelization Society (CES). He wanted to go to China as one of their first European missionaries. Although the answers from Pearse were slow in coming, Hudson was convinced the time had come to move forward.

Finally, Mr. Pearse invited him to visit London for an interview with CES and to meet William Lobscheid, a missionary who had just returned from China. The red-haired Lobscheid took one look at the slight, blonde man. "'Why, you would *never* do for China,' he exclaimed, drawing attention to Hudson's fair hair and grey-blue eyes. 'They call *me* "red-haired devil" and they would run from you in terror! You could *never get them to listen at all.*'"

"'It is God who has called me,' replied Hudson Taylor quietly, 'and He knows all about the color of my hair and eyes.'"[343]

Not the least put off by the missionary's insensitive comment, Hudson wrote to his sister Amelia, "I have a stronger desire than ever to go to China. That land is ever in my thoughts. Think of it—400 million souls without God or hope in the world!"[344]

A Miracle Wind

After a full year of studies at London's Royal Hospital, on September 19, 1853, Hudson Taylor stood on the deck of the sailing ship the *Dumfries*. On his way to China at last, he rejoiced in God's faithfulness!

The Taiping Rebellion, led by Chinese rebel Hong Xiuquan, had arisen in China three years earlier. Xiuquan claimed that he was seeking to reform the Chinese government with education, equality for women, and open doors for Christian missionaries. The CES saw this as God's timing to send someone to China immediately and offered the first opportunity to Taylor. Even though it meant leaving his medical studies before they were complete, he was eager to go. After a tender good-bye to his parents and sisters, Hudson Taylor was sailing off to his newly adopted country.

Even though it meant leaving his medical studies before they were complete, he was eager to go. After a tender good-bye to his parents and sisters, Hudson Taylor was sailing off to his newly adopted country.

Satan must have suspected that millions of lives would be changed for eternity through the ministry of this unassuming young man. On more than one occasion during the long journey, the *Dumfries* was nearly lost at sea. The first time was during a horrific storm in the English Channel before they had even reached the open sea. For twelve days, the ship was dashed about, nearly crashing against the rocky shore of Wales, before the winds finally calmed. The second occasion was even more dangerous.

As the *Dumfries* neared the end of her journey, just north of the island of New Guinea, the winds disappeared for days; the sailing ship was becalmed at sea. The *Dumfries* was being carried along by a strong ocean current into the path of a sunken reef ahead. Without wind, the ship's rudder was useless to move them away from danger—the ship would break up in the middle of the South Pacific.

One afternoon, the Captain spoke solemnly to the passengers and crew, "We have done everything that can be done. We can only await the result."

"No, there is one thing we have not done yet," Taylor replied to the captain. "Four of us on board are Christians. Let us each go to his own cabin and agree together to pray and ask God to give us wind right away."[345]

Above everything else in his short lifetime, the young missionary had learned the incomparable *power of prayer.* Taylor sought the Lord's help and then climbed back up on deck, assured by God's peace that their prayers were answered. Within minutes, the *Dumfries* sails began to fill. By the grace of God, the wind had come just at the right time. Over and over again, God was saying to Taylor, "Bring every need to Me in prayer."

Stepping onto China's Shore

After five and a half months at sea, on March 1, 1854, twenty-one-year-old Hudson Taylor stepped onto mainland China at the port city of Shanghai. The years of preparation were finally over! "My feelings on stepping ashore," he wrote, "I cannot attempt to describe. My heart felt as though it had not room and must burst its bonds, while tears of gratitude and thankfulness fell from my eyes."[346]

In spite of his initial joy, loneliness quickly followed. The Chinese Evangelization Society had no other missionaries in China for him to team with, and they had promised that a letter of credit would be waiting for him when he arrived to pay all of his expenses. But the promised letter of credit was not waiting at the Shanghai post office. This was Hudson's first of many disappointments concerning the CES.

Thankfully, the London Missionary Society, which was well-established in Shanghai, graciously took Hudson under its wing, offering him a place to stay within the LMS compound. He was excited to personally meet Dr. Medhurst, author of the book he had read on China, who gave Hudson sound advice for his first step in China: *learn Mandarin Chinese as quickly as you can!*

In each town in China, there was a government-appointed "mandarin," or "mayor," who had the power to protect citizens from unlawful behavior. All of the mandarins were required to speak a specific dialect, commonly known as Mandarin Chinese, so that government orders could be communicated throughout every province of China. Once Hudson learned Mandarin, he would be able to communicate with officials and citizens across the country—and so he did.

J. Hudson Taylor

The Horrors of War

On his first arrival in China, nothing was as Taylor had expected. The Taiping Rebellion against the Qing Dynasty had evolved into a bloody civil war, with thousands of Chinese dying all around him, and there was little sign that the country was more welcoming to Christian missionaries. Although the Europeans were protected from gunfire by living in the special International Settlement of Shanghai, they were not immune to the horrors of war.

The wounded, diseased, and poverty-stricken were suffering all around him, and Hudson's heart broke at the enormity of their pain. He pressed harder into his language studies so that he would be able to reach out to those who were suffering.

While waiting anxiously for a letter of credit from England, Hudson received the startling news that only a small amount of money would be coming. Instead, the society was sending another missionary, Dr. William Parker, with his wife and three children, who would soon arrive in Shanghai. Since Hudson was already "established" in China, he was expected to find adequate housing for all of them—three adults and three children—to live in the pressingly overpopulated city.

Writing home to his mother, the inexperienced Hudson showed the first signs of discouragement, saying, "Pray for me, for I am almost pressed beyond measure, and were it not that I find the Word of God increasingly precious and feel His presence with me, I do not know what I should do."[347]

Fortunately, when Dr. Parker and his family arrived in November 1854, the men were immediately knit to each other as Christian and missionary brothers. The CES had not sent Parker's promised letter of credit with his funds, either, and so the two men began to seek God's direction for their new ministry together.

Traveling by Boat and Wheelbarrow

Twelve years before Hudson arrived in China, in 1842, the First Opium War was fought between Britain and China over opium imports. With superior strength, Britain won the war, and the two countries signed the Treaty of Nanking. The Chinese agreed to open five "treaty ports"—Shanghai, Canton, Ningpo, Fuchow, and Amoy, where foreign tradesmen and missionaries could live without threat of harm from the Chinese government. But the rest of inland China was off-limits to anyone but Chinese citizens.

Both Taylor and Parker had traveled to China to bring Christ to the lost, but the Holy Spirit had a divinely chosen direction for each of them. In the treaty port of Ningpo was a thriving mission settlement; the two missionaries traveled up the Yangtze River to visit and preach in the chapel. There they found the answer to Parker's missionary quest. Ningpo needed a medical clinic, and Dr. Parker needed a place to minister medicine and the Word of God. He and his family settled in Ningpo with Hudson's blessing.

Hudson Taylor believed the "treaty ports" already had enough missionaries. His heart's cry was for the millions in China's interior who had never heard the name of Jesus. For the next year, he traveled inland, by boat or by wheelbarrow (pushed by hired coolies), sometimes with other missionaries, other times alone, spreading Bible literature and preaching through translators. Far too often, the crowds fled in fear or protested against his illegal presence. When he traveled in his dark overcoat, they called him the "Black Devil." Somehow, things had to change.

While other British missionaries were careful to maintain their English culture and often pressured the Chinese to accept it, Hudson was not interested in promoting any culture other than the kingdom of God and the good news of Jesus Christ.

Hudson Taylor received revelation from God that would transform his relationship with China's vast population forever.

Chopsticks and Pigtail

The thing that I need the most, thought Taylor, *is a closer identification with the Chinese people.* While other British missionaries were careful to maintain their English culture and often pressured the Chinese to accept it, Hudson was not interested in promoting any culture other than the kingdom of God and the good news of Jesus Christ. None of the rest of it was important to God or to him.

The idea became clear; to win the Chinese, he would follow the example of the apostle Paul, who said, "*I am made all things to all men, that I might by all means save some*" (1 Corinthians 9:22). "Let us in everything not sinful become like the Chinese," Hudson declared, "that by all means we may save some."

This meant adopting Chinese food, using chopsticks, and wearing Chinese dress, including the black queue. Not just when he was traveling inland but in the treaty ports, as well. What a shock he would be to the British establishment in Shanghai. But winning the confidence of the Chinese people was the only thing that mattered.

"I resigned my locks to the barber [shaved the front off]," the blonde-haired Taylor wrote, "dyed my hair a good black, and in the morning had a proper queue plaited in with my own."[348] The transformation was complete when he dressed in Chinese silk clothing and shoes. All that betrayed him were the smiling blue eyes peering out from under his black Chinese cap.

Hudson Taylor in native attire.

It was scandalous behavior to the European missionaries in the Shanghai settlement. Decrying Hudson's "foolishness," they would often cross the street to avoid him. But for Hudson, it was a joyful transformation; immediately, he saw welcoming changes on the faces and in the hearts of the Chinese people. He reached out to them as one unashamed of the people he wanted to befriend.

An Abundant Harvest

Hudson pushed into the interior, even though it was against Chinese law. Traveling by boat up the Yangtze River, he visited nearly fifty-eight cities and villages by the end of 1855. Adopting Chinese dress and extending medical care made him welcome in many towns.

"Oh, what an abundant harvest may soon be reaped here!" he rejoiced. "The fields are white and so extensive around us, but the labourers are few! I do thank God that He has given me such opportunities. I sometimes wish I had twenty bodies, that in twenty places at once I might publish the saving name of Jesus!"[349]

Since the Lord sends His disciples out in pairs for their mutual encouragement, God brought a strong spiritual partner to Hudson for 1856. William Chalmers Burns was a Scotsman and a seasoned missionary with the English Missionary Society. Together, they answered a call to go to Swatow, a Chinese port filled with immorality, poverty, and opium trade.

It was in Swatow that Hudson Taylor's eyes were opened to the insidious practice of opium trade. The addicting drug flooded the Chinese black market,

William Chalmers Burns

sold by greedy Indian and British tradesmen. He saw the despair of drug abuse and the rising slave trade of poor Chinese men shipped to the East Indies as laborers. Taylor and Burns faced much hatred and scorn from the Chinese and British merchants in Swatow, but, in the power of God, the men went door-to-door daily, sharing gospel tracts in Chinese and praying for the needs of the suffering population.

Slowly, lives began to change in Swatow. With the work growing, Hudson traveled back to Ningpo to get medical supplies from Dr. Parker before returning to Swatow. But it was not to be. Burns was arrested by Chinese authorities, and the Swatow ministry was closed to them. Although the two men ministered in China for years, they never saw each other again.

God had other plans for Hudson in Ningpo; a part of his destiny waited for him there.

Loving Maria

Mary Ann Aldersey, the first female Christian missionary to China, had established China's first school for girls in Ningpo. On her staff were Mrs. Bausum and her two wards: twenty-year-old Burella Dyer and her eighteen-year-old sister, Maria. The girls had been raised in China and were the orphans of missionary parents, Samuel and Maria Dyer.

Soon after arriving in Ningpo, Hudson met the lovely Maria. From the first, he was intrigued by the young woman, who was quiet but fervent in her commitment to the work of Christ among her Chinese students. It was obvious that soulwinning was the center of her life. At twenty-five, and growing lonely in his travels, Taylor saw Maria as an answer to prayer, but what could he offer any woman in marriage? His travels and financial needs were all directed by faith alone.

Unknown to Hudson, Maria had quickly recognized that he "shared her longings for holiness, usefulness, and nearness to God." She didn't admit her growing affection for him to another soul but prayed fervently to the One who cared the most. "The love of her life had come to her, and nobody knew but God."[350] Both of the young people secretly turned their desires to the Lord in prayer.

While on a trip to Shanghai, Hudson revealed his intentions in a letter and proposed to Maria. She read it with tears of joy. However, when she shared the letter with her school "family," Miss Aldersey was incensed. The feisty sixty-year-old missionary, used to voicing her opinions about everything, stubbornly insisted that Hudson Taylor was "a ridiculous little man" who was unfit to be anyone's husband. She insisted that Maria write him a letter of rejection.[351] The heartbroken Maria obeyed in tears, and the downcast Hudson gave his desires over to the Lord again. Deep in his heart, he suspected that Maria was not the sole author of the letter.

When Hudson returned to Ningpo in May 1857, a fellow missionary arranged a meeting between the two young people, with Mrs. Bausum as a chaperone. Before the meeting was over, with Mrs. Bausum's blessing, Hudson and Maria were engaged to be married.

More than forty years later, Taylor spoke tenderly of that moment: "We sat side by side on the sofa, her hand clasped in mine. It never cooled—my love for her. It has not cooled now."[352] On January 20, 1858, at the ages of twenty-five and twenty-one, they became husband and wife.

Chinese Soulwinning

One year before the marriage, Hudson had officially resigned from the Chinese Evangelization Society. Its support had been very erratic, but worse than that, the society was a thousand pounds in debt, borrowing the money that was sent to their missionaries each month. With his own unshakeable belief that Christians should "*owe no man any thing, but to love one another*" (Romans 13:8), Hudson sent in his resignation letter.

The Lord was still providing. Taylor had been receiving monthly donations from two godly supporters in England: William T. Berger and George Müller. Berger was a wealthy businessman whose heart was stirred by the gospel mission to China, and George Müller believed that God would do mighty things in China through Hudson Taylor's life.

After the wedding, the Taylors settled in the Bridge Street Church in Ningpo, and a rich time of soulwinning among the Chinese became their joy! Hudson's vision was to spread the gospel through native Chinese missionaries who could reach their fellow countrymen for Christ.

Their first convert was Mr. Nyi, a businessman in Ningpo, who came to inquire about "this Jesus." After listening to the message of Christ's salvation, Nyi exclaimed, "I have long sought the Truth, as did my father before me, but without finding it. In Confucianism, Buddhism, Taoism, I have found no rest; but I do find rest in what we have heard tonight. Henceforward, I am a believer in Jesus."[353] Immediately, he began to evangelize among his own people.

Hudson and Maria Taylor

Soon after, through Nyi's preaching, Feng Neng-kuei, the basketmaker, came to Christ. The spirit of evangelism continued to pick up steam. Feng refused to weave baskets to be used for idol worship and, while explaining his new love for Christ to his customers, Wang Lae-djun, a young painter, overheard the conversation and pleaded to hear more. Within days, Wang accepted the love of Christ, as well, and became a fellow missionary with Hudson for the next forty years.

Joy continued to flow in Ningpo when, in July 1859, the Taylors were blessed with their first-born child, a precious little girl they named Grace.

Unfortunately, tragedy became a part of the mission work. James Parker's wife was suddenly stricken with cholera; within days, she was dead, leaving four little children and an inconsolable husband. After five years of serving in China, and feeling the loss deeply, Parker decided to return to Scotland with his little ones.

Hospital Miracles

What should Taylor do with the hospital that Parker had run so successfully? Hudson had not completed his medical degree. He could not treat the European patients whose fees had paid for the medical treatment of the poor Chinese. Should the hospital be closed? After days of fervent prayer, Hudson reached a decision: He would keep the hospital open and rely on God's faithfulness for its support. He had no way of knowing that the provision was already on its way—God had heard him before a single prayer had been uttered! But first came weeks of trusting.

All of Ningpo's hospital staff would now have to live by faith. It was an opportunity for the new Chinese believers to serve without promise of financial provision, waiting on the Lord alone to meet their needs. Whatever happened, Hudson Taylor would not go into debt.

"In Confucianism, Buddhism, Taoism, I have found no rest; but I do find rest in what we have heard tonight. Henceforward, I am a believer in Jesus."

Soon, the entire community, including the patients at the hospital, heard about the Taylors' stand of faith. Everyone waited in anticipation. Would his Christian God move on behalf of Hudson's prayers?

The Sign: The Last Bag of Rice

One morning, Keuei-hua, the cook, opened the last bag of rice at the hospital. He went to Hudson with the bad news. "Then the Lord's time for helping us must be at hand," Hudson confidently replied.[354]

Before the bag of rice was depleted, they received God's answer. William Berger had sent his monthly donation of 50 pounds, but with it came a letter explaining that he had just received a substantial inheritance. The Lord had clearly told him the money was for the Chinese work; but how would Hudson like the funds to be used? Rejoicing in God's perfect timing, a letter was swiftly sent to England detailing the needs of the hospital ministry. That night, the Bridge Street Church and hospital were filled with songs of praise from European and Chinese believers alike![355]

Throughout the coming months, the joy of the Lord and answered prayers flowed through the mission hospital. Severe illnesses were healed, and patients were coming to Christ and being baptized each week. In February 1860, Hudson wrote home to Amelia, saying, "If I had a thousand pounds, China should have it—if I had a thousand lives, China should have them. No! Not China, but Christ. Can we do too much for Him? Can we do enough for such a precious Saviour?"

The blessings of the Lord were rich, but God had a much larger plan for Hudson Taylor than Ningpo, and returning to England for a while was a part of that plan.

The Birth of a Vision

Working day and night in the hospital, as well as preaching Christ's love to the Ningpo people, began to take its toll. In June 1860, an exhausted Hudson Taylor, along with Maria, little Gracie, and the painter, Wang Lae-djun, boarded the *Jubilee* clipper ship headed for England. After six strenuous years in China, it was time for Taylor, just twenty-eight years old, to recover his strength and seek the Lord for the next step in reaching China's millions.

While recuperating in England, he began to work with Wang and fellow missionary Frederick Gough on a Mandarin translation of the New Testament using Roman letters instead of Chinese figures. In addition, Hudson returned to the Royal London Hospital to complete his medical training.

The months of work turned into years. By 1864, Wang returned to China with the completed New Testament, and Taylor turned his heart and prayers to finding new missionaries for inland China. In addition, between 1860 and 1864, Maria gave birth to three little boys: Herbert, Howard, and Samuel. At twenty-seven years old, she had her hands full taking care of four little ones and aiding her husband in his work.

The year the Taylors had left China, the Treaty of 1860 was signed, giving Europeans more freedom to minister in China. Taylor traveled widely throughout Scotland and England, trying to convince the missionary societies that the time was ripe to send gospel workers to the interior. None of the missionary societies caught his vision.

Hudson was conflicted. The societies were not willing to commit new missionaries to China, but he was praying for God to send fifty more workers. Who would be responsible for these new workers? He could pray for them, but if they came and then lost their lives in serving, how could he bear such grief and responsibility?

"I knew God was speaking. I knew evangelists would be given and their support secured, but there unbelief came in. Suppose the workers are given and go to China: trials will come; their faith may fail; [they may lose their lives]....For two or three months my conflict was intense."[356]

Revelation at Brighton

On June 25, 1865, a quiet Sunday by the sea at Brighton, God spoke to Taylor's heart. If men should go to China and then lose their lives for Christ, they would go straight into the Father's arms in heaven. If even one person could be saved, it would be worth the cost. *Why, if we are obeying the Lord,* he thought, *the responsibility rests with Him, not with us!*

"Thou, Lord," Hudson cried with relief, "Thou shalt have all the burden! At Thy bidding, as Thy servant, I go forward, leaving results with Thee!"[357] Taylor rejoiced at receiving such a clear answer from the Lord. They could proceed into inland China, knowing that God would be there with His grace and power.

Hudson had conceived a daring plan to place workers in every province of China. He began by asking the Lord for two missionaries for each of China's eleven provinces and two for Tibet.

Hudson had conceived a daring plan to place workers in every province of China. He began by asking the Lord for two missionaries for each of China's eleven provinces and two for Tibet. Opening his Bible on the beach, he wrote these memorable words: "Prayed for twenty-four willing skillful labourers at Brighton, June 25, 1865." And in those moments, the China Inland Mission was born.

Over the next weeks, Hudson and Maria finished writing *China's Spiritual Needs and Claims*. Under the Holy Spirit's anointing, this book influenced thousands of Christians to give financially to mission work, and hundreds to give their lives to the missionary call.

It Is Not Convenient

Just before leaving to return to China, Hudson stood before a large crowd at the Perth Christian Conference in Scotland. At thirty-three years of age, the young, blonde missionary described the unique needs of China, a land of seekers who were ripe for harvest. As the audience listened in rapt attention, he ended his message with a curious tale.

"I was traveling by a native junk from Shanghai to Ningpo on the Yangtze River," he began. He continued with the story of meeting a Chinese man named Peter on the boat. Peter had spent a few years in England, and he had heard the gospel preached often but had never accepted the saving power of Christ. Approaching Shanghai, Hudson heard a splash. He looked around the small deck and discovered that his new friend was missing. "Where has Peter gone?" he cried to the fishermen standing nearby. One of them pointed to the boat's railing. He had gone over the side!

"Come quickly!" Hudson implored. "A man is drowning! Help me rescue him; bring your nets!" "*Veh bin*" was the response. "It is not convenient." After losing precious moments arguing, the fishermen finally agreed to rescue the man in exchange for money. Fishing Peter from the water, they pulled him on board, but Taylor's efforts to resuscitate him failed, and Peter was declared dead. He had drowned simply because the men at hand were too indifferent to save him!

Angry murmuring spread through the audience at the unnecessary tragedy until Taylor spoke again: "Is the body then of so much more value than the soul? We condemn those heathen fishermen…but what of the millions in China whom we leave to perish eternally? What of the plain command '*Go ye into all the world, and preach the gospel to every creature*' [Mark 16:15]?"[358]

The audience sat in stunned silence as Taylor reminded them that Jesus Himself commanded that they go, and, if not able to go, that they send their prayers and resources. To do everything possible to save the perishing millions in China. To never have to stand before the Lord with the excuse "It is not convenient." Word of Hudson Taylor's powerful sermon spread throughout Scotland; it was as though a prophet had risen among them.

China Inland Mission: Breaking Old Traditions

In order to go forward in our ministry to the Lord, it is important to have the wisdom of God. Some traditions are biblically based, tried and true. Those traditions we hold on to. But sometimes breaking old traditions reflects the will of God and how He wants us to change the way we minister His gospel. As he established the China Inland Mission, Hudson Taylor needed to break some traditions, especially concerning formal Bible training and the role of women in ministry. Those changes were a reflection of Taylor's heart before God. The main articles were clear:

- There would be no pleas for money except to God. All of their needs would be met by Him as they walked in faith.
- Missionaries no longer had to face rigorous years of education and Bible training; lay Christians who believed they were called by God to the mission field could apply.
- Unmarried Christian women could answer God's call. (Although many people considered it scandalous for single women to venture into inland

China, if they heard God's call, Hudson would give them the opportunity to obey. Zinzendorf had followed the same principle one hundred and thirty years earlier.)

- The China Inland Mission would be strictly nondenominational. Hudson recorded, "After prayer, we decided to invite the cooperation of fellow believers irrespective of denominational views who fully held to the inspiration of God's Word and were willing to prove their faith by going to inland China!"

"Depend upon it," he proclaimed, "God's work, done in God's way, will never lack God's supply."[359] All donations were to be sent to Mr. Berger, who would run the home office from England. The missionaries pledged to minister in Chinese dress, unarmed and equipped with only a Bible, as they entered China's vast mission field.

Twenty-four men and seven women answered this first call. As they readied for China, Hudson spoke to them passionately, saying, "We have undertaken to work in the interior of China, looking to the Lord for help of all kinds. This we can only do in His strength. And if we are to be much used of Him, we must live very near Him."[360]

The Lammermuir Party

Six long years after the Taylors had left China, Hudson and Maria, along with their four young children and sixteen missionaries, set sail on May 26, 1866, on the *Lammermuir*. Nine of the missionaries were unmarried women headed for the unknown trials of China, including Emily Blatchley and Jennifer (Jennie) Ferguson, who would be instrumental in the Taylors' lives for many years. Eight missionaries had been sent beforehand to begin the outreach into China's provinces.

After nearly sinking in the midst of a typhoon, the *Lammermuir* finally anchored at Shanghai in late September 1866. The *Lammermuir* Party, as they came to be called, walked onto Chinese soil ready to pour their hearts and lives into the people of inland China.

The *Lammermuir*

The *Lammermuir* Party

Within days of landing, the new missionaries were initiated into the China Inland Mission by changing their hair and clothing to resemble their Chinese brothers and sisters. While other European missionaries objected, sometimes accusing Taylor of being mentally unbalanced, he was convinced that the pure gospel was all the Chinese needed, not the foreign element of European culture and traditions.

"Why should a foreign aspect be given to Christianity?" he wrote to Mr. Berger in London. "The Word of God does not require it. It is not the denationalization but the Christianization of these people that we seek. We wish to see Chinese Christians raised up—men and women truly Christian, but truly Chinese in every sense of the word."[361] Hudson's perspective was a far cry from that of the foreigners who desired to colonize the nation.

In early 1867, the party made its first move inland to Hangchow, where the missionaries quietly studied Mandarin and conducted small meetings that quickly grew to services of fifty or sixty Chinese. New missionaries arrived from England, including Dr. John McCarthy, who would become Hudson's right-hand medical man for the next forty years.

The Strength of Our Heart

The year 1867 was a roller-coaster ride of blessing and tragedy. The Taylor's fifth child, Maria, was born in Chinkiang, and the family welcomed the fair-haired little girl. Hudson Taylor loved his children and would spend time with them as often as he could, especially the eldest, eight-year-old Gracie. She had given her heart to Christ while they were crossing the ocean in the *Lammermuir* and was a sweet blessing to the sailors with her innocent faith. But now, for the first of many painful times, Hudson would learn what it meant to give his all to serve his Savior.

In the intense heat of the summer, little Gracie fell ill with a high fever that couldn't be controlled. After days of Gracie's battle with the illness, in anguish, Hudson told Maria, "There is no hope of Grace getting better. She has meningitis, and there is no cure."[362] How I wish that these powerful missionary men, so faithful to the Word of God, would have had a spiritual understanding of the healing power of Jesus. They walked in unyielding faith for the salvation of thousands of people, but they did not have an understanding of healing prayer.

A grieving Taylor wrote home to Berger in England, "I am trying to pen a few lines by the couch where my darling little Gracie lies dying. Dear brother, our flesh and our heart fail, but God is the strength of our heart and our portion forever."[363]

Hudson had consecrated his own life, as well as the lives of his wife and children, to the Lord, and he knew that God could be trusted. But, after burying his daughter in a little cemetery by the Yangtze River in Chinkiang, he would often say, "Our dear little Gracie! How I miss her!"

The mission work moved on, with the missionaries separating to move inland. James Meadows and George Stott from Ningpo settled in Taichow and Wenchow; George Duncan went to Nanking. In Hangchow, Wang Lae-djun became the missionary/pastor, and his little church grew rapidly. The women missionaries were establishing work among Chinese women and were well-accepted. Emily Blatchley ministered with the Taylor family in Yangchow, while Jenny Faulding remained in Hangchow with John McCarthy and his wife.

In Yangchow, the Taylors found that Chinese hearts were slowly opening to the gospel. But soon after, a group of dissenters came into the city and spread lies that the foreign missionaries were devils—that they were kidnapping and eating the children of Yangchow! The result was the Yangchow Riot described in the chapter opening. The missionaries left the city for a while until things calmed down. Shortly after they returned, in 1868, Maria gave birth to their sixth child, a boy they named Charles Edward.

The Exchanged Life

In spite of his growing ministry among the Chinese people, Hudson Taylor felt there was something missing from his Christian walk. He had an unsatisfied longing to abide more fully in Christ. He knew that everything he needed was in Christ, but how would he get it?

It was a letter from fellow missionary John McCarthy that opened Taylor's spiritual eyes. McCarthy wrote, "But how do we get faith strengthened? Not by striving after faith, but by resting on the Faithful One."

"As I read it," Taylor wrote in a letter to his sister Amelia, "I saw it all! Suddenly my spiritual eyes were opened and I could see. I looked to Jesus and saw that He said, 'I will never leave you.' *Ah, there is the rest,* I thought. 'I have striven in vain to rest in Him. I'll strive no more! For has He not promised to abide with me—to never leave me, never to fail me?

"Christ liveth in me. How great the difference! Instead of bondage, liberty; instead of failure, quiet victories within; instead of fear and weakness, a restful sense of sufficiency in Another. O my dear sister, it is a wonderful thing to be really one with a risen and exalted Savior!"[364]

Hudson had exchanged his life to dwell completely in the life of Christ. It no longer mattered where God called him to go or what He called him to do.

Hudson had exchanged his life to dwell completely in the life of Christ. It no longer mattered where God called him to go or what He called him to do. He was one with the Master; he could rest in His grace and His strength. It was God's strength he would need for the sacrificial road ahead.

More Precious than Life

"China is not to be won for Christ by self-seeking, ease-loving men and women," Hudson Taylor wrote. "The men and women we need are those who will put Jesus, China, souls, first and foremost in everything at all times; life itself must be secondary—nay even those more precious than life."[365] How the words "those more precious than life" tried his soul!

In the spring of 1869, the Taylors decided that their older children—Herbert, Howard, Samuel, and Maria—should be sent to England to escape the heat of China and to acquire an English education. But baby Charles would remain with his parents.

Five-year-old Samuel had always been a fragile little boy, his body very susceptible to China's diseases. On their way down the Yangtze River, from Yangchow to Shanghai, Samuel fell extremely ill; within hours, he slipped into a coma and died. In a state of shock, bearing their little boy in their arms, the Taylors anchored their boat at Chinkiang to find someone to aid in his burial. They buried Samuel in the little cemetery beside his sister Gracie.

With great sadness, the Taylors saw their oldest children off to England in the care of Emily Blatchley, who was going home to be the children's guardian and to help the Bergers in the home office.

Life moved on swiftly, and the next year, the mission work seemed to explode with converts. Taylor spent most of his time traveling through eastern China and encouraging each team in the inland missions. Maria, who was now pregnant with their seventh child, remained in Hangchow, caring for a young missionary woman who was gravely ill. Unknown to Hudson, who was thoroughly engrossed in the growing mission work, Maria was battling cholera.

Maria Dies

On July 7, 1870, in Chinkiang, Maria gave birth to their seventh and last child, a boy whom they named Noel. The child appeared to be healthy, but Maria was not. At first, Hudson thought she might be experiencing some internal bleeding. Maria had little strength or nourishment for herself or her baby, and their early attempts to find a nurse for Noel failed. Within ten days, the little boy was dead. In spite of Hudson's fervent prayers and medical knowledge, Maria was too weak to fight the cholera that was raging through her body.

At dawn, on July 23, 1870, Hudson knelt beside Maria's bed and tearfully thanked her for the years of love and companionship she had given him. Clasping her husband's hand, she answered, "I cannot be sorry to go to Jesus; but it does grieve me to leave you alone at such a time. Yet He will be with you and meet all your need."[366]

By mid-morning, at thirty-three years of age, Maria Taylor had passed quietly away to heaven. Her funeral was a large one, with the mourners clothed in white, the Chinese color of mourning. With a disconsolate heart, Hudson buried her in Chinkiang beside Gracie, Samuel, and baby Noel. How much he had lost in just a few short months.

Through the next lonely year, without the presence of Maria, Taylor worked tirelessly in Hangchow and beyond, encouraging the thirty workers scattered throughout China.

"No matter how intricate my path, how difficult my service," he penned, "no matter how sad my bereavement, how far away my loved ones, no matter how helpless I am, how hopeless I am, how deep are my soul-yearnings—Jesus can meet all, all, and more than meet."[367]

Knit Together in Ministry

In the summer of 1871, aching for his family, Hudson decided to travel to England with young Charles to see his other three children once again. Taylor, Jennie Faulding, and James and Elizabeth Meadows sailed for England on furlough. Jennie's ministry among the Chinese women at Hangchow had been blessed, but after six years of strenuous work, she was ready to visit her family.

During the long voyage, Hudson and Jennie prayed and talked for long hours about God's love for China and the Christless millions that must still be reached. Before reaching England, Taylor realized that his heart was knit to hers through their life's work. As their feelings for each other moved beyond friendship, the dedicated missionaries decided to marry and continue to serve Christ together. Jennie, at twenty-eight, was a perfect fit as a helpmeet and comforter to the thirty-nine-year-old missionary widower. They married with her parents' blessing on November 28, 1871, in Regent's Park Chapel in London.

God was bringing about change in the British home office. The Bergers were nearing seventy and could no longer handle the work for the growing China Inland Mission. They retired, and the way was made to expand the vision once again. A council of Christian friends was formed in 1872, and duties that the Bergers had done alone would now be spread among several workers, with Emily Blatchley in the primary office role.[368] But one thing would never change: All decisions for the China Inland Mission would come from the ministry on the field in China itself and never from the offices in England.

In addition to his compelling ability to preach the gospel, Hudson Taylor had been naturally gifted as a coordinator and delegator. He could readily see who would fit in different areas of the ministry. Some of us learn how to organize things through trial and error and or over time. Don't be ashamed of how you acquired a particular gift. Dedicate it to the Lord and use it for His glory.

"Give Me a Hundred More"

In October 1872, Hudson and Jennie returned to China on the *MM Tigre,* leaving from Marseilles, France, and traveling east through the Mediterranean Sea. The Suez Canal had opened in 1869, and steamships had rapidly replaced the sailing vessels of the past. Now, the Taylors could travel to China in just over a month, a far cry from the five-and-a-half-month trip Hudson had taken eighteen years earlier when he'd first journeyed to Shanghai.

"We are going into the interior," Hudson wrote back to England concerning all of the CIM missionaries. "If anyone is not prepared to rough it, he had better stay at home. The only persons who are wanted here are those who will rejoice to work—really to labour, not to dream their lives away; to deny themselves; to suffer in order to save."[369]

Over the next couple of years, the Taylors traveled throughout China as the Lord led. Everywhere, the work was rapidly expanding. "Lord, what would you have me do?" was Hudson's continual prayer.

Early in 1874, while in Taichow, Taylor asked God for one hundred more Chinese evangelists to further the work in distant provinces. Some money was coming in, but not nearly enough for the work he had in mind. Journeying into one of the interior missions alone, he wrote to Jennie, "The Lord reigns. Herein is our joy and confidence. We have twenty-five cents and all the promises of God!"[370]

China's Millions

Between 1874 and 1877, many changes occurred for the China Inland Mission and in the Taylors' personal life. After a successful year establishing a new mission far inland in Hankow, they traveled back to England once more, for news had reached them of Emily Blatchley's death due to illness. Her death left a large hole in their hearts and in the home office ministry, as well. Gratefully, Hudson welcomed his sister Amelia and her husband, Benjamin Broomhall, along with their ten children, to take over the full management of the ministry in England.[371]

In these fruitful years at home, Jennie gave birth to two children—Ernest, born in January 1875, and Amy, born in April 1876. Her time was now divided between helping with the China Inland Mission work and caring for all of the Taylor children.

At the same time, the CIM published its first issue of the periodical *China's Millions* to let the world know of China's missionary needs. (The magazine would continue in publication for the next seventy-seven years, until 1952.)

Under the title "Appeal for Prayer," Taylor sent out a plea for Christian workers on behalf of more than one hundred eighty million Chinese in the unreached inland territory. Taylor was adamant about the spiritual commitment of missionary candidates: "While thankful for any educational advantages that candidates may have enjoyed," he wrote, "we attach far greater importance to spiritual qualifications! We desire men [and women] who believe that there is a God and that He is both intelligent and faithful, and who therefore trust Him; that believe He is a Rewarder of those who diligently seek Him, and are therefore men of prayer....We desire men who believe in eternity and live for it."[372]

The Door Swings Open

In September 1876, Britain and China signed yet another agreement, the Chefoo Convention, which guaranteed that all foreign missionaries would be protected by the Chinese government—an agreement that was broken in the years to come. In the following eighteen months, CIM missionaries traveled over thirty thousand miles, crisscrossing China, preaching the gospel, distributing tracts, and developing relationships with the Chinese peasants.[373]

Within a few months, Hudson received reports of a great famine that was devastating northern China. Tens of thousands had died, and there were countless orphans who needed new homes. It was an opportunity to shower the Chinese children with the love of Christ.

In late 1876, Hudson made his fourth trip to China, while Jennie stayed in London with all of the children, including Hudson and Marie's three older children and George Duncan's orphaned daughter, whom they had recently adopted.

Now that travel between the two countries was much easier, Taylor's stay in China could be limited to a year. He returned to England again in 1877, seeking to raise thirty more missionaries as reinforcements. Within a few months, Hudson received reports of a great famine that was devastating northern China. Tens of thousands had died, and there were countless orphans who needed new homes. It was an opportunity to shower the Chinese children with the love of Christ.

"Send us two or three female missionaries" was the urgent request from China. "We need women for orphanage work and we have no one to spare." Jennie Taylor's heart was pierced. She had the dauntless faith and the experience to travel deep into China and provide for the motherless children who needed Christ's love. "But, Lord, who will take care of my children?" she prayed. Amelia was quick to answer the need. "If Jennie can go to China," she said without hesitation, "I am called to care for her children!"[374] With her ten children plus the six Hudson children now under her care, Amelia had dedicated her life to the cause of China, as well.

Days before Jennie left, a thousand-pound donation came in the mail, making it possible for her to buy necessary supplies when she reached China. God was continuing to provide in answer to their prayers.

Having left Hudson and the children in good hands, Jennie arrived in Shanghai in early 1878 and, along with two other courageous young women, traveled to the province of Shansi, further inland than any foreign women had ever gone. Within a year, the orphanages were up and running, and Jennie began the 8,000-mile voyage back to England. It would be nine years before she would see China again.

The Fruit of Intercession

Two years after the orphanages were completed, Dr. Harold Schofield, a promising young physician, left a successful medical practice in England to dedicate his life to China, establishing the first China Inland Mission hospital in Shansi.

The work was grueling, but his heart was fixed on God's Word to "*declare his glory among the heathen, his wonders among all people*" (Psalm 96:3). Tragically, in the midst of the unsanitary conditions, Schofield contracted typhus from his patients and could no longer work—but he could pray.

For hours each day, he asked the Lord for strong young men who would lead the work for China, praying "that God would touch the life of our universities and raise up young men to work among the heathen of the world."[375] God's faithful answer to this prayer was beyond what Schofield or Taylor could have imagined. But the doctor would not live to see the results of his prayer; after just three years in China, he died on August 1, 1883.

In answer to his prayers, the Holy Spirit was breathing new life into a group of seven recent graduates from Cambridge and Oxford Universities. One by one, the young men, well-known athletes and scholars, responded to Taylor's call for men to serve Christ in China. The seven who dedicated their lives became known as the Cambridge Seven and included Stanley P. Smith, captain of Cambridge's rowing team; C. T. Studd, a well-known cricket player; Montagu Beauchamp; W. W. Casels; brothers Arthur and Cecil Podhill-Turner; and D. E. Hoste.

London was shocked when these prestigious young men gave up their bright futures for China. On February 4, 1885, the day before they left England, the Cambridge Seven testified before two thousand students in Exeter Hall of the transformation God had made in their hearts.

"What are we going to do?" Stanley Smith questioned the crowd. "What is the use of great meetings like this if the outcome is not to be something worthy of the name of Jesus? He wants us to take up our cross and follow Him…to leave fathers, mothers, brothers, sisters, friends, property, and everything we hold dear, to carry the gospel to the perishing."

In response to their testimony, hundreds of students pursued service for Christ in different parts of the world. The Cambridge Seven ministered in inland China for a combined total of two hundred fifty years! Five of the seven remained in China for the rest of their lives.

The Student Volunteer Movement

England was not the only place where Dr. Schofield's dying prayers were being answered. The Student Volunteer Movement for Foreign Missions, founded by Dwight L. Moody, John R. Mott, and Robert P. Wilder, had arisen in America—a coalition of young college students who sought God's direction for mission work. Their watchword was "the evangelization of the world in this generation." Thousands of students across the United States pledged to support foreign missions, either with their finances or their lives of service. One of them, Henry W. Frost, first became interested in missions through the preaching of missionary Jonathan Goforth before he left for China. Shortly after, Frost traveled to

London to ask Hudson Taylor to establish an American Council for the China Inland Mission. Taylor's answer was a quiet but firm no.

Disappointed but certain that God had led him to Taylor's ministry, Frost returned to America. He asked Dwight L. Moody to personally invite Hudson to tour America and speak at the summer student conference held at the Mount Hermon School in Northfield, Massachusetts, in 1886.

Taylor accepted the invitation and traveled to the States with his son Howard, who was now serving as a missionary with his father. Hudson was met with an enthusiastic reception wherever he went. Within two months, he had fourteen new missionaries for China and thousands of dollars in American donations. Hudson realized that God was indeed opening a door for an American Council, and the dedicated Henry Frost was named the first director.

Filled with the Holy Spirit

With all of their children grown, in December 1890, Jennie joined Hudson in China again. For years, they had prayed for a great outpouring of the Holy Spirit among their missionary workers.

One young missionary woman, whose name was never recorded, led the way. While in Shanghai, a Christian seaman approached her and boldly asked, "Are you filled with the Holy Ghost?" She knew that the Holy Spirit had resided in her since her conversion, but was she "filled with the Spirit"? The young missionary turned to her Bible to study the personality and power of the Holy Spirit in the believer's life.[376] It was indeed the Holy Spirit that she needed, the fullness of the Holy Spirit to make unseen things real to her and impossible things possible. In the quiet of her room, she prayed that the Holy Spirit would indwell her fully and that the proof would be people turning to Christ as she shared the gospel. Immediately, there were new conversions to Christ wherever she spoke. She shared the power for this change with her colleagues, and the flame of the Holy Spirit spread quickly.

"God is working in our midst," Jennie wrote home in April 1892, "emptying and humbling one and another, and filling us with the Holy Spirit. We are having frequent meetings full of liberty and power."[377] Soon the Chinese Council suspended a scheduled meeting, instead "seeking for themselves, for the whole Mission in China and the Home Councils, the filling of the Holy Spirit."

Hudson Taylor rejoiced in the Holy Spirit's move among them. "The supreme want of all missions in the present day is the manifested presence of the Holy Ghost....Some may think if we had more costly machinery we may do better. But oh, I feel that it is divine power we want and not machinery! Souls are perishing now for lack of this power. God is blessing now some who are seeking this blessing from him in faith."[378]

Over One Thousand Strong

Hudson Taylor and wife with a group of Chinese Christians

By the beginning of the 1890s, after forty years in China, Taylor was supervising four hundred missionaries throughout the provinces. He split his time between ministering in the rich harvest of China and traveling to Europe to inspire more men and women to answer the call. Much like in the book of Exodus when Jethro counseled Moses to appoint seventy elders to help him govern the people, Arthur Broomhall convinced Hudson to appoint superintendents over each of the provinces in China to reduce his workload.

By now, China had tens of thousands of baptized Christians, and the Word of God was spreading to the far corners of the nation. But, never for a moment did Hudson forget the millions of Chinese still dying without Christ.

Taylor had always been fascinated with mathematics, so he determined that if they had one thousand new missionaries who could preach daily to two hundred fifty different people about Christ, in one thousand days, two hundred fifty million people would hear of Jesus' saving grace. However, recruiting the one thousand new missionaries would take a "united simultaneous action of *all* of the mission societies in China who would be meeting at a General Conference in Shanghai."[379] Hudson presented his vision at the conference, and, by the end of the session, all of the societies were committed to raising up one thousand missionaries in the next five years. By God's grace, when the time period was complete, they had not one thousand new workers but 1,153!

Throughout the 1890s, Hudson and Jennie, along with son Howard and his wife, Gwendolyn, crisscrossed the world's oceans—to Australia, the United States, Canada, Japan, and back to Europe—spreading the message of China and obedience to the Great Commission to go into all the world to preach the gospel.

Taylor had always been fascinated with mathematics, so he determined that if they had one thousand new missionaries who could preach daily to two hundred fifty different people about Christ, in one thousand days, two hundred fifty million people would hear of Jesus' saving grace.

At one meeting in Australia, after a long introduction of his accomplishments, Taylor was introduced as "our illustrious guest." As a small man standing before them with a quiet voice, he responded, "Dear friends, I am simply the little servant of an illustrious Master."[380]

The Boxer Rebellion

China was in a state of unrest. The twentieth century was approaching, and tensions between the Chinese people and the Western foreigners were escalating, secretly incited by the Chinese government.

After thirty-two years of protection from death by violence or accident, things tragically began to change. The first martyr of the CIM missionaries was William Fleming, an outgoing Australian who was killed in January 1899 while protecting a Chinese evangelist from a mob as he preached for Christ. With sadness, Taylor wrote, "It seems that God is going to test us with a new kind of trial; surely we need to gird on afresh the whole armor of God."[381]

In the Qing government, the Dowager Empress Cixi, a powerful woman, supported a group of rebels called the "Boxers," whose goal was to exterminate all foreigners in China. With the sanction of the empress, the Boxer Rebellion spread like wildfire. Sixty-eight-year-old Hudson, along with his wife and son, were on a steamship bound for the United States and were unaware that the outbreak of war was so imminent.

In New York's Carnegie Hall on April 23, 1900, Hudson delivered a stirring message to an audience of 3,500 people, including President William McKinley, entitled "The Source of Power": "We are a supernatural people, born again by a supernatural birth, kept by a supernatural power, sustained on supernatural food, taught by a supernatural Teacher, from a supernatural Book. We are led by a supernatural Captain in right paths to assured victories!"

"I Cannot Even Pray, but I Can Trust"

The eternal victory in Christ was assured, but on earth, the spiritual battle was still raging. The Taylors returned to Europe with only fragmented news reports from China. In spite of Hudson's increasing concern for his missionaries, Jennie insisted that they travel straight to Switzerland to rest; Hudson was exhausted from the relentless speeches and travel, and his health was failing.

Because they were located deep within China's interior, the China Inland Mission had endured the greatest missionary loss. Fifty-six CIM missionaries, and twenty-one of their children, had been murdered before the carnage was over.

Soon after their arrival at Lake Geneva, shocking telegrams flooded their home, anguished reports of death and destruction in their beloved China. Lines of communication were disrupted throughout the provinces. Information was sketchy. The Boxers had reached Peking. Hundreds of Protestant Chinese and thousands of Catholic Chinese, as well as missionaries, were being massacred.

Weeping as he read one horrifying report after the other, Hudson could finally endure no more. He cried, "I cannot read; I cannot think; I cannot even pray... but I can trust."[382] Within a year, British soldiers and American Marines had entered China in force, and the Boxer movement was extinguished. The Empress Dowager left Peking secretly, returning only after the furor had died down. Because of foreign pressure, many Boxer leaders were executed by the same government that had encouraged them in their slaughter.

Because they were located deep within China's interior, the China Inland Mission had endured the greatest missionary loss. Fifty-six CIM missionaries, and twenty-one of their children, had been murdered before the carnage was over. Taylor was heartbroken. In tears, he wrote to China of God's love for both the missionaries who had survived and for those who "had been counted worthy to wear a martyr's crown."

✯✯✯✯✯

J. Hudson Taylor

Lake Geneva, Switzerland

Hudson desperately wanted to return to China to console and encourage the missionaries, but his health wouldn't allow it. So he appointed D. E. Hoste, an original member of the Cambridge Seven, to be the acting general director of the mission. He could trust Hoste to care for his missionaries and lead them through this devastating time. In 1902, Hoste traveled to Switzerland, and Taylor placed the full directorship of the mission in his hands.

The Taylors quietly retired near Lake Geneva in Switzerland. Many European Christians came to visit Hudson and to glean from his wisdom. One visitor observed, "It was not so much what he said but what he was that proved such a blessing to me. His strong faith, quietness, and constant industry, even in his weakness, touched me deeply."[383]

In the summer of 1904, the Taylors discovered that Jennie had cancer. She was confined to bed and was peaceful knowing she would soon be with the Lord. Jennie prayed that she would have no pain, and the Lord answered by taking her home quickly. In the following months, Hudson's strength returned, and, at seventy-three years of age, he planned a trip to China with Howard and Gwendolyn. It would be his eleventh and final journey.

"Safe Home at Last"

Docking in Shanghai on April 17, 1905, Hudson was welcomed joyfully by Hoste, CIM missionaries, and Chinese Christians of all ages. The group traveled to Chinkiang so Hudson could visit the cemetery where Maria was buried alongside Gracie, Samuel, Noel, and his adult daughter Mary—a CIM missionary who had died of cholera six years earlier.

How China had changed! Traveling from one mission site to another by train, he could still remember events that had occurred fifty years earlier—being pushed in an unsteady wheelbarrow, bristling with fervor to win China for Christ.

On Saturday, June 3, 1905, there was a reception in Changsha for the "Venerable Chief Pastor," as Hudson was fondly called. He spent a quiet afternoon with both old and new missionary friends. When one young man asked him if he felt as though his small requests bothered God, Taylor replied, "There is nothing small and there is nothing great: only God is great and we should trust Him fully."[384]

That evening, Taylor was too tired to go downstairs to supper. Howard and Gwendolyn sat with him as he quietly read in bed. When they heard a small gasp, they rushed to his bedside, only to realize that he was slipping away. Within moments, he drew his last breath and passed into eternity.

Gwendolyn recorded the event: "Oh, the look of rest and calm that came over his face was wonderful. The weight of years seemed to pass away in moments. He looked like a quiet child sleeping, and the very room seemed filled with unutterable peace."

"Dear Father," she bent over him and whispered, "all the weariness is over, all the journeyings ended—safe home, safe home at last!"[385]

Hudson was laid to rest next to his beloved Maria and four of their children in the Chinkiang graveyard by the mighty Yangtze River.

The Taylors' Graves Found in Communist China

Over the next forty years, all Christian missionaries were slowly evicted from Communist China. By the 1960s, the Communists in Chinkiang (now called Zhenjiang) had built a warehouse over the Christian cemetery. Before the graveyard was destroyed, Hudson Taylor's headstone was preserved in Zhenjiang Museum nearby. It was his great-grandson Dr. James H. Taylor III who found the marker in the museum and helped the local Chinese Christians to erect it within the Zhenjiang Gospel Church in 1999.

What happened in the ensuing years could only have been directed by the Lord. Taylor's great-great grandson Jamie Taylor was contacted in 2012 by a man who claimed to have purchased Maria Taylor's headstone in an antique store in Yangzhou, China, not far from Zhenjiang. When Jamie arrived in China, he bought Maria's tombstone and moved it to Zhenjiang to rest beside his great-great grandfather's marker.

In March 2013, the Taylor family was informed that the warehouse over the cemetery had been torn down, and an apartment complex was to be built in its place. Before construction began, the family had permission to search for the graves of Hudson and Maria. To their astonishment, they found them still intact. The local government permitted the graves to be exhumed and relocated, along with the original tombstones, to the newly built Xuan De Church in Zhenjiang. The Taylors were reburied under the church's belltower, which was constructed to commemorate their years of work for the love of Christ and the Chinese people.

★★★★★

J. Hudson Taylor

My Soul Yearns...

"My soul yearns, oh how intensely for the 180 million souls of these unoccupied provinces. Oh that I had a hundred lives to give or spend for their good!"[386]

Hudson Taylor had more than a hundred lives to give. By recruiting and training over one thousand men and women for China during his lifetime, he replicated his "yearning soul" many times over. For forty-five years after his death, the China Inland Mission remained the largest gospel endeavor in China. It established 300 mission stations, built 125 schools, and baptized more than 200,000 Christians during those years.[387]

By recruiting and training over one thousand men and women for China during his lifetime, he replicated his "yearning soul" many times over. For forty-five years after his death, the China Inland Mission remained the largest gospel endeavor in China.

The CIM missionaries faithfully served in China through the collapse of the Qing Dynasty, the brutal Japanese occupation during World War II, and the final Communist takeover in 1949. By 1950, the CIM made a "reluctant exodus" from the country because of the persecution their presence brought to the Chinese Christians. The mission headquarters moved to Singapore, where it is still located today, extending the ministry to all of East Asia and changing its name to Overseas Missionary Fellowship.[388]

Hudson's two oldest sons, Herbert and Howard, along with their wives, remained in Asia as missionaries, as did their children and their children's children; Hudson's great-great grandson James Hudson Taylor IV still ministers with OMF International today. OMF currently has more than 1,600 workers from 30 different countries spreading the good news of Jesus Christ in Southeast Asia.

Today, China is an atheist country that is technically "closed" to the gospel. However, largely because of Hudson Taylor's radical vision for evangelism, there are nearly 100 million Christians living in China; many are descendants of those Chinese men and women who met CIM missionaries face-to-face 150 years ago. Let us pray that the Lord will continue to protect them from the persecution of their atheist countrymen.

Hudson Taylor was a giant among God's generals. But whenever he was praised for his accomplishments, his response was always the same: "All God's giants have been weak men who did great things for God because they reckoned on *His being with them.*" God was truly with this mighty man of faith.

> *And He said to them, "Go into all the world and preach the gospel to every creature."* (Mark 16:15 NKJV)

The Great Commission is not "the great suggestion"!

Will you follow Christ's command and go to the nations in His name?

Chapter 8

Amy Carmichael

Feisty "Rescuing Mother" of India

A wispy girl of seven years crouched behind the temple pillar, listening to the *sari*-draped women, one of whom whispered, "The child is perfect. We will keep her here until her marriage to the god." The women quickly retreated across the stone floors as little Preena recoiled in terror.

She fled from the temple, and, even though so young, walked the two-day journey to her mother's home in Tuticorin, India. *Even though father is dead,* the little one thought, *mother will let me come back to her.*

The temple women followed Preena. "The wrath of the gods will be upon you if you don't give her back!" they declared to the terrified mother. With sad eyes, Preena's mother grabbed the arms of the clinging child and pulled them from around her neck. "You must go back with the temple women," she murmured. "You belong to them now!" Seven-year-old Preena looked at her mother with eyes of wisdom beyond her years. "I will not stay with them," she said as the eager women pulled her away.

Preena's life at the temple was more terrifying than before she had made her escape. Her small hands were branded with hot irons as punishment. Preena overheard one of the women say, "She must be tied to the gods immediately to keep her from running away!" The child was overcome; in her young imagination, she pictured herself tied with ropes to the statue of the god Perumal and left there with him in his cold, dark cell. Terrified, Preena decided she would risk punishment again and escape.[389]

One day, Preena decided it was time to go. Miraculously, no one saw her walk across the stone floor and slip out the door. No one stopped her as she walked swiftly down the street and past the outside temple walls. No one called her name as she waded across a nearby stream and ran through a grove of palm trees into the next village. There, a kindly woman found the frightened little girl, like a lost lamb, and took her home for the night.[390]

The next day, March 6, 1901, the woman brought the child to Amy Carmichael at the mission house in Pannaivilai, southern India. In God's perfect timing, Amy and her missionary companions had arrived a day earlier for a short stay. Amy opened her arms and her heart to the trembling child.

Years later, Preena recorded the day she met Amy. "When I first came in the early morning, our precious *Ammai* (true mother) was having her morning *chota*. When she saw me, the first thing she did was to put me on her lap and kiss me. I thought, *My mother used to put me on her lap and kiss me—who is this person who kisses me like my mother?* From that day, she became my mother, body and soul."[391]

The courageous Preena became the first temple child rescued in Amy Carmichael's ministry. Amy opened her heart not only to this one little girl, but also to thousands of children throughout southern India—spending a lifetime rescuing them in the love of Jesus.

"You Can't Love Without Giving"

"You can give without loving. But you can't love without giving."
—Amy Carmichael

This famous quote by Amy Carmichael paints the portrait of a woman whose heart and soul were devoted to serving Jesus Christ. Amy was a selfless missionary who dedicated her life to loving the unloved children of southern India. To the children and workers of Dohnavur, she was always "*Amma*" (Tamil for "mother"), for she loved them with a mother's unconditional love, transforming thousands of Indian lives in more than fifty-five years of service.

Amy Carmichael

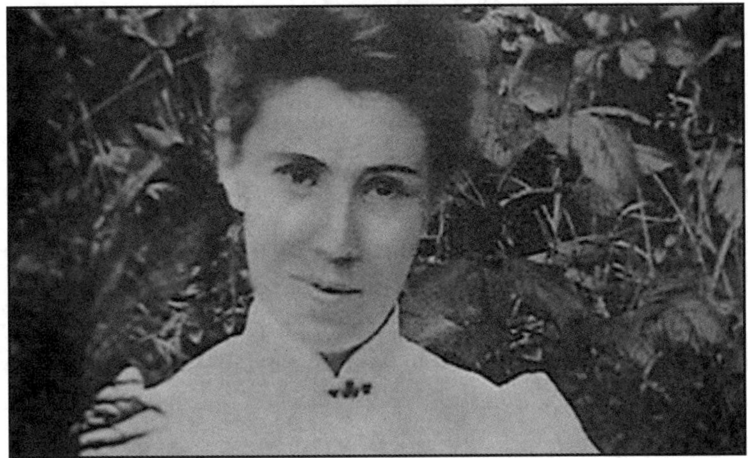

Amy Carmichael

Amy saw the Christian life as "a chance to die to oneself," so that Christ might be revealed. Yet, for Amy, it was not a life of sacrifice, *it was a life of love,* in which the good news of Jesus Christ could shine into unimaginable darkness and rescue the helpless. She loved the people to whom she dedicated her life almost as much as she loved her Lord. And Dohnavur Fellowship became a living, pulsating reflection of that love.

Amy Carmichael was also a trailblazer. No one before her had cared enough to rescue children from a life of moral degradation in the heat and poverty of southern India. There was no model to follow as she built the "family" of the Dohnavur Fellowship except for the example of Jesus, the Word of God, and the guidance of the Holy Spirit. "I would rather burn out than rust out!" Amy often declared about her hardworking toil among the people of India.

In addition to her work at Dohnavur, she was a prolific writer, penning thirty-five books and thousands of letters during her lifetime. Through them, we see an intricate portrait of her unwavering commitment to Christ, along with her struggles, her doubts, and her triumphs.

A longtime friend once wrote, "Amy Carmichael was God's chosen instrument and the glory is His alone, but she was an instrument *amazingly fitted for His purposes* and ready for His hand."[392] Throughout Amy Carmichael's lifetime, God continually "fitted" her for His purposes at Dohnavur Fellowship and molded her into one of His most yielded missionary generals.

"Give Me Blue Eyes"

Amy Beatrice Carmichael was born on December 16, 1867, in the village of Millisle on the northern coast of Ireland. She was the firstborn child of David and Catherine Carmichael, steadfast Presbyterians who loved God and brought up their seven children to love Him, as well.

From the time Amy was a baby, her mother read her stories of Jesus—His power to turn water into wine, to forgive sins, and to answer prayers. At the tender age of three, brown-eyed Amy knelt by her bed and prayed her first earnest prayer: "Lord, please give me blue eyes like my mother and baby Norman." She fell asleep in childlike faith, expecting the answer to come the very next morning!

"I can never tell you my bewilderment," she wrote years later. "Without a shadow of a doubt, I believed my eyes would be blue in the morning. The minute I woke up, I pushed a chair to the chest of drawers on which there was a looking glass and climbed up full of eager expectation and saw—mere brown eyes!"[393]

"God has not answered my prayer," she cried in confusion. But then it was gently explained to her. He *had* answered her—with a loving but firm no. When God says no, it is because He knows something we don't know. We don't need to get angry or sad; we need to trust Him. Trust Him and keep going.

Amy recovered from the hurt of that disappointment, of course. Years later, she smiled at God's wisdom in giving her brown eyes as she walked though the villages of India, disguised in a native sari with her skin darkened by coffee grounds. Blue eyes would have ruined her ministry on the dusty streets of southern India.

Trouble Follows Amy

Young Amy Carmichael was a precocious child who spent her days exploring the rocky beaches of Millisle and leading her brothers, Norman and Ernest, into dangerous escapades. One night, she pushed the boys up through the skylight onto the slate roof of their three-story home and then joined them, walking gleefully on the shingles until they were caught and rescued by their parents. Weeks later, on a dangerously windy day, she hoisted the boys onto the sea wall, where they were drenched to the skin by the spray of the rising ocean tide.

In spite of promises to behave, during a trip to the woods, Amy convinced her little brothers to join her in eating "poison berries." "Let's count how many we can eat before we die," she dared them.[394] Although they suffered from painful stomachaches and foul-tasting medicine, the children survived the ordeal.

Amy's hunger for adventure repeatedly got her into trouble, but it also revealed her indomitable spirit! God was preparing her for a ministry of fearless service, rescuing the lost and frightened from a dark and hopeless life.

Wild Irish Girl

The Carmichael family lived in the largest house in Millisle. David Carmichael and his brother William were well-respected businessmen who ran the Carmichael Flour Mills, the center of Millisle industry for over one hundred years.

In spite of her promise to her mother to "be good," the feisty Amy soon earned the reputation of being a "wild Irish girl," a leader among the girls, both for good and for mischief.

As a young teenager, Amy was sent to Harrogate, a Wesleyan Methodist boarding school in Yorkshire, England. In spite of her promise to her mother to "be good," the feisty Amy soon earned the reputation of being a "wild Irish girl," a leader among the girls, both for good and for mischief.[395]

It was during her time at Harrogate, when she was sixteen years old, that her life changed during a Children's Special Service Mission. At the end of the worship service, the speaker, Mr. Edwin Arrowsmith, asked the girls to sing "Jesus Loves Me, This I Know" and then to bow quietly before the Lord. "During those few quiet minutes," Amy wrote, "in His great mercy, the Good Shepherd answered the prayers of my mother and father and drew me, even me, into His fold."[396] Amy received Christ as her Lord and Savior that day and embarked on a journey of faith from which she never turned back.

Financial Crisis

In a painful turn of events, by the fall of 1884, the Carmichael family business was in a financial crisis; the flood of cheap milled flour from America was threatening to shut down its flour mills. After Amy had been at Harrogate for three years, David Carmichael traveled to England to bring her home. The large family moved from Millisle to Belfast in a desperate attempt to keep the last flour mill open and prospering. But soon it, too, failed.

Within a few months of the last mill failure, David Carmichael came down with a respiratory virus; as the illness progressed, he developed a deep racking cough and then double pneumonia. On Sunday morning, April 12, 1885, he died at the age of fifty-four. From that day forward, seventeen-year-old Amy passed into adulthood, becoming her mother's confidante and a second mother to her younger siblings. In spite of the grievous loss of her father, God was using these years to lay the foundation for Amy's future as a skilled and compassionate leader.[397]

"If Any Man's Work Abide"

God placed clear spiritual guideposts in Amy Carmichael's life to lead her on the road to India. One of the first happened on a cold, misty Sunday morning in the winter of 1885, seven months after her father's death.

As Catherine Carmichael and her children walked home from church, they came upon "a poor, pathetic old woman who was carrying a heavy bundle." Feeling pity for her struggles, Amy and two of her brothers offered to help the woman, taking her package and supporting her as she walked home. Instead of feeling good about their assistance, the Carmichael teenagers turned crimson with embarrassment as several "respectable" church people walked by, staring disdainfully at them and the ragged woman.

"It was a horrid moment. We were only two boys and a girl, and not at all exalted Christians!" Amy admitted in the opening pages of her book *Gold Cord*. But suddenly, as she resisted the urge to run from the embarrassing scene, Amy sensed God's presence.

> This mighty phrase was suddenly flashed at me through the grey drizzle: *"Gold, silver, precious stones, wood, hay, stubble; every man's work shall be made manifest...because it shall be revealed by fire; and the fire shall try every man's work of what sort it is. If any man's work abide..."* [1 Corinthians 3:12–14]
>
> *"If any man's work abide...."* I turned to see the voice that spoke with me....The blinding flash had come and gone; the ordinary was all about us. I said nothing to anyone, but I knew something had happened that had changed my life's values. Nothing could ever matter again but the things that were eternal![398]

Amy went home that afternoon and shut herself in her room, pouring her heart out to God. That day, she "settled once and for all the pattern of her future life."[399] "*If any man's work abide...*" from 1 Corinthians chapter three became the cornerstone of her service to Christ. After that revelation, she would spend her life seeking to do only those things of gold and silver—only those things that would *abide.*

Salvation for the "Shawlies"

"I want to go with you into the city streets of Belfast to find the children who need God's love," Amy announced to the Reverend Henry Montgomery of the Belfast City Mission. Walking with him for the first time into the slums, seventeen-year-old Amy silently prayed, "Oh God, give me the strength and courage to make a difference."[400]

Amy had nothing to fear—working with neglected children on the city streets came naturally to her. During her city visits, she also came in close contact with hundreds of young women who labored in the Belfast factories. They were nicknamed the "shawlies," because they were too poor to buy hats, so they pulled their shawls over their heads during the bitterly cold winters of Ireland.

Amy had nothing to fear—working with neglected children on the city streets came naturally to her.

With the courage that had marked Amy since childhood, she traveled through the slums of Belfast seeking every hurting "shawlie" she could find, inviting them to join her on Sunday mornings in the church hall of the Rosemary Street Presbyterian Church. There, Amy taught the shawlies to read the Word of God, to pray, and to have moral respect for themselves and their bodies. The neglected girls were drawn like a magnet to Amy's love.

While she was thrilled to see God move among the shawlies, Amy was searching for a deeper experience of God's holiness in her life.

Spiritual Power from Keswick

In September 1886, Amy was invited to visit friends who lived in Scotland; she had little idea that God would use the visit to reveal the next *spiritual guidepost* in her Christian journey.

The friends took her to a series of Christian meetings in Glasgow that were "along the Keswick lines." Ten years earlier, in the village of Keswick, England, a six-day conference had been held for Christians who longed for a deeper walk with Jesus. The teachings focused on sanctification as "a second blessing" of power and the indwelling of the Holy Spirit. This sanctification was not earned by works but was granted to believers by God's grace. The Holy Spirit moved with such power for holiness among the believers that the Keswick meetings were still being held throughout the British Isles a decade later. Amy's spiritual life was transformed by those Glasgow meetings.

"Something happened that changed everything for me," she wrote. "I had been longing for years to know how one could live a holy life, a life that would help others. I came to that meeting half hoping, half fearing. Would there be anything for me? Then the chairman rose for the last prayer, 'O Lord, we know Thou art able to keep us from falling.' Those words found me. It was as if they were a light and they shone just for me!"[401]

In the flyleaf of her Bible, Amy recorded: "Thou shalt remember, Glasgow September 23, 1886." And Jude 24: *"Unto him that is able to keep you from falling."* She was revived. The Lord *Himself* would keep her from falling and lead her into a life of holiness and truth.

Belfast with Hudson Taylor

"Every single hour, one thousand souls pass through the gates of death into the darkness beyond—Saviorless, hopeless."[402] Hudson Taylor's words rang through the Belfast Exhibition Hall. It was September 4, 1887, and Amy was attending another series of Keswick meetings, this time in her hometown, accompanied by her mother. Hudson Taylor of the China Inland Mission was one of the keynote speakers.

"Does it not stir our hearts," Amy wrote that night, "to go forth and help them? Does it not make us long to leave our luxury, our exceeding abundant life, and go to them that sit in darkness?"[403]

Amy listened attentively, absorbing every message on sanctification and the deeper spiritual life. At one meeting, she and her mother met the chairman of the Belfast Convention, Robert Wilson, who asked if he could come to visit them in their home.

At sixty years old, Robert Wilson was a large, bearded man with deep blue eyes and a winsome smile. Rather than discussing doctrine with the Carmichael women, Wilson spoke of the immeasurable love of Christ. Amy was inspired by the depth of this giant man's relationship with Jesus Christ. Within a few months, Robert Wilson became a dear friend of the entire Carmichael family and was fondly referred to as the D.O.M., or "Dear Old Man."

Growth = A Bigger Building

Spiritually on fire after the Belfast meetings, Amy moved full speed into her work among the shawlies. The group meetings grew so rapidly that, before long, they had to move from the church hall to a large auditorium. "We need a place like this that will seat 500 people," Amy remarked as she read an advertisement in *The Christian* magazine for the construction of an "iron hall." It cost 500 pounds to build such a hall, which could seat 500 people. Where would she get the money for the building or the land?

Why not ask God for help from those who love Him? she thought. Led by her infectious enthusiasm, the mill girls began to pray for God's provision. Within a short time, they received the money for the new building. Emboldened by God's answer, Amy requested a parcel of land "rent free" from the largest mill owner in Belfast. The owner did even more, handing over the full title to a section of land on Cambria Street for the shawlie building.

In honor of the grand opening of "The Welcome," as Amy called it, on January 2, 1889, Amy sent out invitations that read:

Come one, Come all
To the Welcome Hall,
And in your working clothes!

With a place to call their own, the evenings were filled with Bible studies, choir practice, and night school. The young women adored Amy for replacing the dreariness of their former lives with a future hope in Christ. Today, more than 125 years later, the Welcome Hall stands in the same spot on Cambria Street. It is now called Welcome Evangelical Church, and it is still offering the hope of Christ to the city of Belfast, Ireland.

The Glow of His Love

Soon after, Amy, her mother, and her sisters moved to the northern industrial city of Manchester, England, to begin a similar "Welcome" ministry for the factory girls there. Amy's mother was offered a paid position as the superintendent of the Women's Rescue Mission.

In Manchester, Amy threw herself into her work with the factory girls, living near the mill in a filthy apartment infested with cockroaches and bedbugs. Once again, the Lord was preparing her for a life in which physical comfort was secondary to consecrated ministry. Her prayer during that time was, "Lord, let the glow of Thy great love shine through my whole being."[404]

Determined to show His love, Amy ignored the poor living conditions and worked with boundless energy.

Determined to show His love, Amy ignored the poor living conditions and worked with boundless energy. Unfortunately, she seldom stopped long enough to eat a healthy meal or get a good night's sleep. As the months wore on, she began suffering from severe headaches. Amy was diagnosed with neuralgia, a nerve disease that caused a burning pain along the affected nerves, especially around her head and face. When the neuralgia flared up, Amy had to lie in bed for days waiting for the pain to cease. Before long, it became clear that she had to give up her work with the mill girls. Although saddened, she left the ministry in capable hands and waited on the Lord for His next open door.

Which Blow Broke the Stone?

Robert Wilson, the D.O.M., was a retired coal tycoon and a widower whose only daughter had passed away a few years earlier; his estate at Broughton Grange had become a lonely place. With Amy's work ending in Manchester, Wilson asked if she would live with him and his two sons for a portion of the year as an "adopted" daughter. Both Mrs. Carmichael and Amy graciously agreed. Amy's time with the D.O.M. became her spiritual school.

Wilson had a strong conviction concerning Christian denominations. "We must drop denominational labels," he insisted. "If our precious Lord came tomorrow, what use would He have of such labels?"[405] As cofounder of the Keswick Convention, he had chosen "All one in Christ Jesus" as the Keswick motto, allowing no place for spiritual division in a deeper walk with Christ. Throughout her long ministry, Amy also disregarded all denominational labels.

"Learn to be a deep well, daughter," Wilson often told her. "Thee must never say, thee must never even let thyself think, 'I have won that soul for Christ,'" Wilson counseled in his firm Quaker voice. "If you asked a stone mason as he was breaking a large stone, 'Friend, which blow broke the stone?' his answer would be, 'The first one and the last one and every one in between.'" Each person who shares the gospel with the unsaved, Wilson insisted, contributes to their salvation. Once again, it was "one plants, one waters, and one harvests the increase." It was a lesson on evangelism that Amy never forgot.[406]

Through her association with Wilson, Amy met anointed men of God such as Hudson Taylor, F. B. Meyer, and evangelist Dwight L. Moody. Each one flamed her desire to reach the unsaved world with the gospel of Jesus Christ.

"GO YE!"

"Go ye!" These two small words changed Amy Carmichael's world forever.

On a snowy night, January 13, 1892, twenty-four-year-old Amy spent the evening in her room in prayer, reflecting on the lost and dying millions throughout the world. As clearly as if she heard her mother's voice, she heard the words "*Go ye!*" in her heart. Everything around her seemed to be repeating "*Go ye!*"

The next morning, Amy sent her mother a letter.

> My Precious Mother,
>
> Have you given your child unreservedly to the Lord for whatever He wills? For a long time, the thought of those dying in the dark—50,000 of them every day—has been very present with me, and the longing to go to them and tell them of Jesus has been strong upon me. Everything, everything seems to be saying, "Go!"
>
> Last night...I asked the Lord what it all meant, what did He wish me to do, and, Mother, as clearly as I ever heard you speak, I heard Him say, "*Go ye!*" I cannot be mistaken, for I know He spoke. He says "Go"; I cannot stay.[407]

Her mother's earnest reply was dated two days later:

> Yes, dearest Amy, He has lent you to me all these years....So, darling, when He asks you now to go away from within my reach, can I say nay? No, Amy, He is yours—you are His—to take you where He pleases and to use you as He pleases. I can trust you to Him, and I do....*"Go ye!"*—my heart echoes.[408]

The D.O.M. had hoped that Amy would live at Broughton Grange as his daughter for the rest of his life. With some personal struggle, he also surrendered Amy to the Lord's will for her future.

Both Catherine Carmichael and Robert Wilson avoided the trap that many Christian parents find themselves in today. The parents love their children so much that they want to plan their children's destiny. Instead of wrongly assuming that they know God's direction for their childrens' lives, they should be asking Jesus, "What would You like my child to do, Lord?" Mrs. Carmichael and Wilson got it right; they placed Amy and her future in God's hands.

Not Approved for China

Where should she go? Hudson Taylor had painted a challenging picture of China with his personal stories, so Amy traveled to London and applied to the China Inland Mission. Robert Wilson asked her to change her middle name from Beatrice to Wilson on her application, making her more of an "adopted" daughter in his eyes. For years after, she was known as Amy Wilson Carmichael in missionary circles.

"The doctors have not approved you for China" was the earth-shattering report Amy received a few weeks later. Her neuralgia would be stirred up by the heat of China's summers, the doctors insisted, as they refused to accept her for the CIM.[409]

Amy left London for Broughton Grange, stunned by the setback but still determined to go overseas. Although the D.O.M. longed for Amy to stay in England, his spiritual maturity allowed him to yield to God. Wilson put his own desires in check. Without delay, he searched for another mission field opportunity for Amy. The Keswick leadership had considered sending a "Keswick missionary" to the foreign fields. It was a perfect time for them to choose their first missionary, and, to no one's surprise, it was Amy Carmichael.

Wilson sent a letter to a friend, Barclay F. Buxton, asking if Amy could join him with the Church Missionary Society in Matsuye, Japan. Not wanting to waste another day in England, Amy quickly prepared to sail for Shanghai with three other female missionaries. She wanted to be as close to Japan as possible and asked for Barclay's response to be sent there; she was certain it would be yes!

A Leap into Sunshine

On March 3, 1893, twenty-five-year-old Amy Carmichael finally sailed from England aboard the steamer *S.S. Valetta*. After emotional farewells with her mother and sisters in Manchester, Amy had been seen off at the port of Tilbury by the D.O.M. They had waved and sang hymns to each other across the water as the ship had pulled away from the docks and finally gone out of sight of land.

Amy Carmichael had finally launched out into the foreign mission world.

When she docked at Shanghai, Buxton's letter was waiting, warmly welcoming her to join the mission work in Matsuye. Amy wrote home, "A new province has been opened to them, 1,100 towns and villages, unreached, surround them! This leap in the dark is a leap into sunshine after all!"[410] For Amy, known to everyone as the "Keswick missionary," the next eighteen months would be a time of struggles and miracles.

"They Shall Cast Out Devils"

"God's power in casting out the fox spirit, Matsuye, July 14, 1893." These words were recorded in the margin of Amy's Bible. She had been in Japan for several months, working alongside her interpreter, a Christian woman named Misaki San. She traveled with Misaki from village to village around Matsuye wearing a Japanese kimono and sharing the love of Christ.

On July 14, word reached Amy of an old man in Matsuye who was possessed by an evil spirit, and the situation was desperate. Immediately, Amy recalled Jesus' words "*All power is given unto me in heaven and in earth*" (Matthew 28:18) and "*These signs shall follow them that believe; in my name shall they cast out devils*" (Mark 16:17). Together, Amy and Misaki read the Scriptures aloud and prayed. With a boldness she had possessed since childhood, Amy walked directly into the spiritual battle.

"Full of confidence that the power of the Lord would cast out the fox spirit," Amy wrote, "we asked if we might see the man. We had been told that he was possessed by six fox spirits, and he was held back with cords tied around his body. With confidence, we told the old man's wife, and the relations who crowded around, that our mighty Lord Jesus could cast out the six fox spirits."[411]

As soon as Amy spoke the name of Jesus, the old man raged and cursed, thrashing about uncontrollably. With the room in an uproar, Amy and Misaki were escorted out of the house. Amy turned to the wife, and faith rose in her once more. She said, "Let us know when your husband is delivered from the power of the fox spirit, for our God will conquer, and we shall go home and pray til we hear that He has."

Within an hour, Amy received word from an excited relative: "The foxes are gone; the cords are off; the man is asleep!" The next day, the old man asked to see Amy. "He was sitting quietly in front of me, a well man." She and Misaki shared Christ's redemption with the elderly Japanese couple, and together, they prayed to receive Jesus as Savior. Before the year was out, Amy heard from the wife again. Her husband had passed away from malaria, but he had died peacefully with his New Testament cradled in his hands.[412]

A Birthday Present from Jesus

"The place I really loved in Japan was Hirosi, a largely Buddhist village with only eight Christians shining as stars in the night," Amy wrote.

The day before Amy and Misaki visited Hirosi for the first time, the Lord spoke to Amy's heart, saying, "Pray for *one soul* in the village to receive Me." Amy and Misaki prayed. As small groups of men and women gathered to listen to the gospel message, a young female silk weaver surrendered her life to Jesus. A month later, the Holy Spirit spoke, "Pray for *two souls* in Hirosi." As she shared Christ with a group of Buddhist women, two of them—a friend of the young silk weaver and an old woman with tears running down her face—gave their hearts to Jesus.

Thrilled to see the Holy Spirit moving in a fresh way, Buxton and the other missionaries of Matsuye joined Amy in prayer. Two weeks later, on their third trip to the village, God laid four souls on Amy's heart. For two days, Amy and Misaki shared the Word of God, with no response. As the second day was ending, an elderly woman spoke up: "Help me! I want to believe!" Moved by his mother's confession of faith, her son joined her in praying for new life in Christ. As Christians in the village gathered to rejoice with the two new believers, a third person embraced Jesus as Savior. Amy and Misaki were jubilant!

The final morning, just before they left Hirosi, a woman came forward; she wanted to become a "Jesus person." That last day was December 16, 1893, Amy's twenty-sixth birthday. Four souls were won for Christ—it was Amy's birthday present from Jesus![413]

In January 1894, Amy and Misaki made a final trip to the village. Again, the Lord spoke to Amy's heart: *"Pray for eight people to give their hearts to Me."* The Christians in the village were incredulous. "It is too much to ask; the people will be disappointed when it doesn't happen!" But Amy was convinced that the quiet voice she had heard was the Lord. Within three days, eight Buddhists were won to Christ!

"It was like watching the hand of God at work," she wrote later. "The last [of the eight] was a proud old grandfather who for fifty years had been a slave to sin. Kneeling before all, he prayed, 'Honorable God, deign to forgive me, deign to wash.'"[414] Years after Amy left Japan, Barclay Buxton confirmed that the Hirosi converts were still standing strong in their faith.[415]

Ending So Soon

Soon after the miracles of salvation at Hirosi, Amy's neuralgia came back with a vengeance. "I had a day of bad neuralgia," she wrote to her mother. "I could neither think nor read, was just lying, waiting for it to go."[416] For weeks at a time, Amy was bedridden, unable to do anything because of the unbearable pain. The missionary doctors in Matsuye insisted that she find a change of climate.

After traveling first to Shanghai and then on to Ceylon, Amy found little relief from her pain. In spite of the debilitating illness, Amy wrote home to reassure her mother: "All of life's training is just exactly what is needed for the true Life-work, still out of view but far away from none of us. Don't begrudge me the learning of a new life lesson."[417]

The doctors in Ceylon advised Amy to never return to Japan again. She struggled with confusion. What was God calling her to do? Was her overseas ministry ended so soon?

On November 27, 1894, Amy received a terse letter from England. The D.O.M. had suffered a stroke and was seriously ill. The next day, Amy was on a ship bound for England. Sickness filled her days aboard ship; there were "blank days" when all she could remember was a haze of pain and fever and a doctor's face hovering over hers. She arrived in Manchester and traveled on to Broughton Grange with her mother just before Christmas 1894.

Twenty-seven Years Old: Going for God's Harvest

"I'm determined to go, Mother. It's God's call for my life." It was the spring of 1894; Robert Wilson had recovered from his stroke, and Amy's neuralgia had subsided. Although her time in England had been fruitful (she published her first book, *From Sunrise Land*, recounting her experiences in Japan), Amy was determined to leave again for the mission field.

In God's providence, she received a letter from a friend in Bangalore, India, inviting her to join the Church of England mission there. Amy was delighted with the report that the "climate was healthy, delightful; in fact, it might be possible to live there even if China, Japan, and other parts of the tropics were taboo."[418]

Amy traveled to London and interviewed with the leaders of the Church of England Zenna Missionary Society (CZM) to join the work in Bangalore. Sharing her passion for the lost, she told them, "Missionary work is a grain of sand; the world untouched is a pyramid." Amy longed to go and make a difference in that untouched world. She was accepted by the CZM, and the Keswick board agreed to continue her financial support.

On October 11, 1895, at twenty-seven years of age, ten months after arriving deathly ill from Ceylon, Amy boarded a steamer for India. As she parted tearfully from the seventy-year-old D.O.M., they both secretly realized that she would never set foot in England again. Once she had arrived in Madras, India, on November 9, 1895, the courageous Amy Carmichael would embrace her call to India, without furlough, for the next fifty-five years.

Shocking the British

"The saddest thing one meets is the nominal Christian. I had not seen it in Japan where the mission is younger. The church here is a 'field full of wheat and tares!'"[419] On her arrival in India, Amy realized this spiritual condition was true of many of the British missionaries and Christian Indians she met. Britain had been ruling in India for nearly three hundred years, and most British subjects, even the missionaries, lived there as colonialists, the "entitled ones," set apart from the rest of the population.

Britain had been ruling in India for nearly three hundred years, and most British subjects, even the missionaries, lived there as colonialists, the "entitled ones," set apart from the rest of the population.

In Bangalore, while working at the Church of England Zenna hospital, Amy met a number of "verandah missionaries," as David Livingstone used to call them—British Christians who kept themselves separate from the natives, clinging tightly to their British culture in spite of the barriers it created with the unreached Hindus.

"I long to live as one with the people," Amy wrote in frustration. "'[He] *made Himself of no reputation, and took upon him the form of a servant*' [Philippians 2:7]. I wish to do the same."[420] English dress was the first thing Amy discarded; she adopted the Indian sari in her favorite shade of blue, wearing it with an English blouse underneath for modesty.

In the intense heat of April and May, the British citizens escaped the climate by spending the months at Ooty, a British mountain retreat north of Bangalore. Amy balked at taking a break from the hospital, considering it a terrible waste of time. But once there, at twenty-seven years old and still full of mischief, Amy enjoyed shocking her British acquaintances by racing a horse against the carriage of the British regent and sharing her room at the "British only" resort with an Indian convert named Saral, whom Amy had brought along. Only Mrs. Hopwood, the hostess at Ooty, approved of Amy's antics, and they became fast spiritual friends.

Walker of Tinnevelly

In Ooty, Amy was reminded that every experience of her life was a stepping-stone in God's plan. While there, she met Thomas Walker, a fiery, thirty-six-year-old British missionary who was a dynamic disciple of Christ. When he and his wife met Amy, Walker looked at her with his steely eyes and questioned her plans for ministry among the Indian people. Without hesitation, she replied, "I would much rather live in a mud hut with the people around me than among English people in a bungalow!"[421] Satisfied with her commitment to work among the lost, the Walkers invited Amy to join them.

As Amy prayed about leaving the hospital work in Bangalore, the Lord spoke clearly: *"My presence shall go with thee, and I will give thee rest"* (Exodus 33:14).[422] On November 30, 1896, Amy left Bangalore for the Tinnevelly District, just thirty miles from the southernmost tip of India. There, she would pour out her heart in ministry for the rest of her life.

From the first days in Tinnevelly, Thomas Walker was Amy's trusted friend and mentor; his first task was teaching her the Tamil language. She studied intensely for six hours each day, with Walker serving as a strict taskmaster. They quarreled like brother and sister, both determined, both stubborn, and both sold out to live their lives for Christ. Amy would learn a great deal about trusting in the Lord alone from Thomas Walker.

The Starry Cluster

In 1897, the Walkers and Amy moved into a large house in Pannaivilai, a town in the Tinnevelly District. Amy was now thirty years old, had passed her Tamil "test," and was ready for ministry.

Almost a hundred years earlier, the Tinnevelly District had experienced a powerful revival, and most British missionaries considered it a region full of earnest Christians. Amy's indignant response was, "Nonsense! They are as nominal as Christians as thousands of the people in our churches at home!"[423] Most Indian citizens who claimed to be Christians were second- and third-generation natives who had slid back into Hindu practices and no longer lived for Jesus Christ as their parents had.

What was Amy's response? She formed a Christian group of six Indian women to travel with her to preach the message of Christ from village to village. And so the "Starry Cluster"—as they were called by the natives—was born. Amy's closest companion in the group was Ponnammal, whose name meant "gold." Ponnammal was a young Indian widow who, at age twenty-three, had been cast off by her family for following Christ. She lovingly served as Amy's second-in-command and closest friend throughout decades of ministry.

The Starry Cluster was so committed to showing their love for Christ that they did the unthinkable. They gave up all of their Indian jewelry in service to Him. In southern India, women of high and medium caste were draped in gold and precious jewels, multiple necklaces, bracelets, and rings as a sign of their wealth. When the women eschewed their jewelry, or sold it for the mission work, it created an uproar throughout the Tinnevelly District.

"Nothing is as shameful as no jewelry at all!" one Hindu woman protested.[424] It was never Amy's idea for her companions to sacrifice their customs. But the women of the Starry Cluster were determined to serve in simplicity, as Jesus had served during His life on earth.

Cruel Bondage: India's Caste System

"It should be understood," Amy explained, "that no young man or woman in the antagonistic castes or among Muslims is allowed to live openly as Christians at home in any of the villages or towns in South India."[425] Confession and baptism cost these new Christians their families and, often, their lives, not in open martyrdom, but in secret poisonings or disappearances.[426]

If someone appeared to be drawn to the gospel, his relatives would go to unbelievable lengths to keep them him disgracing the family by breaking caste. They would kidnap their own, spiriting him away, never to be seen again.

If someone appeared to be drawn to the gospel, his relatives would go to unbelievable lengths to keep them him disgracing the family by breaking caste. They would kidnap their own, spiriting him away, never to be seen again. They often would drug perpetrators, a practice that sometimes sent them into a "zombie" state of acquiescence or mental instability.

A high-caste woman who expressed interest in the gospel might be found dead at the bottom of a well. "She couldn't bear the Christian message and decided to end it all," the family would falsely report.[427] As others who wanted to accept Christ considered the potential personal cost of their decision, they would tearfully admit to Amy, "I cannot follow so far."[428]

After a few years of ministering in the dusty villages of India and being rejected by countless Hindus, Amy wrote a book entitled *Things as They Are*, describing the intensity of the spiritual battle and the difficulty of reaching new converts for Christ. Initially, the manuscript was rejected by British publishers because it "discouraged the Christians of Europe" with its brutal honesty. In the end, it was published, and it opened the eyes of European Christians to the real conditions faced by missionaries in the field and to the necessity of unceasing prayer!

"Don't Let Me Go Back to the Dark"

"Refuge! Refuge!" A young girl of eleven ran to the Starry Cluster mission tent, pitched just outside her village; she was requesting sanctuary. The child had seen Amy in her Indian sari sharing Christ in the village square. "I knew if I could only go to her," the young girl confided, "she would have a place in her heart for me....She would be my *Amma* and I would be her daughter and she would teach me to worship Him."[429]

The little girl's name was Arulai. Determined to keep her from Christianity, Arulai's family sent her away to an uncle in another village. But when the Walkers and the Starry Cluster returned to their mission home in Pannaivilai, Arulai slipped away and arrived at Amy's bungalow.

"You are only eleven; we cannot keep you here without your parents' permission," Walker reluctantly told her. Amy invited her to remain with them for schooling, and Arulai was able to stay for a short time before her family spirited her away.

Months later, there was a small sound at Amy's bungalow door. Arulai had escaped once again and threw herself into Amy's arms. For a few weeks, she remained there, until her father, succumbing to caste pressure, came to bring Arulai home once and for all. The night before his arrival, Amy heard Arulai's young voice crying out in prayer, "Don't let me go back to the dark, Lord. Oh, please let me live in the light!"

When her father arrived the following morning, as he reached out to take Arulai's hand, his arm fell lifelessly at his side. Several times, he reached for her, and, each time, his arm became stricken. "It is as if my arm is paralyzed!" he exclaimed fearfully. "It is the one Lord of heaven," Amy told the dazed father. "He has marked this child as His."[430]

Miraculously, Arulai was permitted to remain with Amy; she embraced Jesus as Savior, received her schooling, and ministered with Amy for the rest of her life.

Temple Darkness

"So simply, so without observation, do we turn the corner of the road of life, when as yet we did not know we had turned the corner."[431] Amy was speaking of the countless times God had brought her to a turning point in her life before she realized what was happening. None were more precipitous than her move to the Dohnavur District with the Walkers in 1900.

Thomas Walker had been invited to teach a group of young Indian men in seminary in the village of Dohnavur at the southernmost tip of India, just thirty miles from the sea. When the Walkers decided to make the move, Amy, the Starry Cluster, and young Arulai went with them. A year later, in March 1901, Preena, the temple child introduced in the opening of the chapter, was brought to Amy. It was then that Amy Carmichael realized what was her life's work: rescuing children from the "secret" Hindu practice of temple prostitution.

In the weeks of fighting to keep Preena, Amy heard the horrible stories of the temple rituals for the first time. She discovered that young girls throughout India were sold and groomed for temple prostitution to provide pleasure for the Hindu priests and the village men. The Hindu temples were secretly trafficking the bodies and souls of these girls, a fact that was continuously denied by both the Indian government and the people. Even other missionaries in India refused to believe that the horrific rumors were true. But after Amy's undercover work, the mission world was at last forced to face the dark truth concerning the young girls of India.

Kneeling in the Garden with Jesus

Little girls were dedicated by their families to the temple for one or more of several reasons: their families had made a vow to the gods, it was a family tradition, or their parents were poor and had other family members to provide for. The sale of a child was considered illegal, but the money passed hands in secret just the same. Often, girls were released to prostitution while still very young, and they died painful deaths from mutilation to their bodies.

After learning the truth, Amy searched relentlessly for ways to rescue more temple girls. But the web of secrecy was so entangled that she couldn't break through it. After she met with several devious men who controlled the human trafficking of the little girls, her heartbreak became unendurable.[432]

"At last, a day came when the burden grew too heavy for me. It was unbearable. [I pictured] Jesus; he was under the olive tree, and He knelt alone. And then I knew that it was His burden and not mine. It was He who was asking me to share it with Him, not I who was asking Him to share it with me....And there was only one thing to do...go into the garden and kneel down beside Him under the olive tree."[433]

That is what Amy did. She "knelt in the garden" and prayed that God would give her the children to love; it was three years before the next temple child was rescued. However, in years to come, the saved temple children would number in the hundreds. In the meantime, other neglected babies and young children were also brought to Amy for care, and the Dohnavur ministry began.

"Children Tie the Mother's Feet"

In the Tamil language, there is the saying "Children tie the mother's feet." This means that poor mothers often had no freedom to go where they wanted to go. Amy Carmichael could see some truth in this Indian proverb.

After much prayer, Amy's decision was made—God had called her to the children. Her feet would be tied "for the sake of Him whose feet once were nailed." She would rescue and love all whom God brought to her.

Could it be right to turn from so much that might be of profit [evangelism] *and just become nursemaids?* Amy wondered as the babies began filling up the bungalow in Dohnavur. Then she was reminded of how the Lord had girded Himself with a towel to wash the feet of His disciples. "Is it the bondservant's business to say which work is large and which is small? It was a foolish question, for the Master never wastes the servant's time."[434]

After much prayer, Amy's decision was made—God had called her to the children. Her feet would be tied "for the sake of Him whose feet once were nailed." She would rescue and love all whom God brought to her. She had no idea that, in her lifetime alone, that would number over a thousand children, and that her work would be flourishing in the next century!

As the children arrived, the faithful Starry Cluster moved from being itinerant evangelists to their new roles as teachers and caregivers. A school and nursery were built...and the Dohnavur ministry was in full swing.

By 1904, they had seventeen babies and children under their care, including Firefly, a bright little eight-year-old girl whose father had killed his wife and sold the girl to the temple. For a hundred rupees, which had arrived by mail just in time, Amy was able to buy back sweet Firefly from the priests.

Indian children at the nursery.

On March 1, 1904, the first of the temple babies, just thirteen days old, was placed in Amy's arms; they named her Amethyst. She was followed soon after by a second temple baby named Sapphire. Unsure of her next step, Amy went to the Lord and sensed His encouragement: "Go forward, Amy—do not be afraid!"[435]

The Dohnavur Family

"We grew up from the first very simply—like a family," Amy recorded.[436] Dohnavur was, first and foremost, a family, and Amy was always Amma. Memories of playing with her siblings and other children on the streets of Belfast came rushing back to her. She played games with her Indian charges and taught them songs of joy. She helped them with their Tamil and taught them some English.

At Dohnavur, she celebrated each child's "coming day," the day of their arrival in the family, with a party in the big schoolroom they called the "Room of Praise." Amy, her workers, and the children grew together in prayer, as well. Amy never forgot Hudson Taylor's words of spiritual advice: "Do not be so busy with work for Christ that you have no strength left for praying. True prayer requires strength."[437]

Most important, Amy taught the children the love of Christ, which held them all in His embrace. For years, she kissed each child good-night, until the children numbered in the hundreds. They were her darling children, and she was their precious Amma.

Not a Romantic Life

Amy Carmichael's ministry was not a romantic missionary life. The Dohnavur team faced tragedy and hardship raising fragile children surrounded by a culture of religious bondage. As they freed more children from a temple life of sin and early death, Satan battled hard to stop them. Rejoicing over the baptism of a new believer would often be followed by grieving for a child lost to illness.

Amy Carmichael with Indian children.

Amy remarked that they had no one to give them advice: "No one had ever been this way before—we had crossed an invisible frontier into an unknown land. But in that land, we met our Lord and learned to know Him better....He never let us lose our way, He filled our cup with sweetness, and for the handful of dust that we offered Him, He poured the very gold of heaven into our hearts!"[438]

In 1905, when Thomas Walker returned from a furlough in England, he brought a surprise with him—Catherine Carmichael. Amy's mother came for a visit and remained for more than a year, helping to love and care for Amma's little children. Her mother's presence eased the pain when word came on June 19, 1905, that the D.O.M. had gone home to be with the Lord. Amy named it "Father's Glory Day" and rejoiced that Robert Wilson was with the Lord, whom he had loved so dearly.

Catherine was also there for care and comfort when the first babies of Dohnavur died from a dysentery outbreak. There were few medical supplies to save them. Her presence helped to ease Amy's heartbreak as she watched babies Amethyst and Sapphire breathe their last.

In the meantime, missionaries throughout southern India stayed on the alert for children at risk, slipping away with them over back walls and hiding them in train cars, whisking them to the safety of Dohnavur. By the time Amy's mother returned to England in 1906, the Dohnavur family numbered seventy, including workers, babies, young girls, and a few young boys!

In 1908, Amy's prayer for medical help was answered with the arrival of Mabel Wade, a trained nurse who became a tireless and loving member of the family. With money sent from England, Amy and the Walkers built a new nursery and a small infirmary for the children.

Fleeing to China

While Amy loved all of her charges, some of them were especially dear to her. One of them was Muttammal, or "Jewel."

Sometimes, after temple girls found asylum at Dohnavur, their families would fight to get them back, hoping to return them to the temple or have them marry someone within their caste. Amy and Walker would go to court to prove they had the right to keep the children. The longest and most troubling lawsuit was over little Jewel.

Jewel was a high-spirited child who came to Amy because her father had died and her selfish mother wanted to sell her to the temple. After Jewel's mother signed a *yadast* (a document of release for the girl), Amy promised Jewel that she would never have to go back home. But the fight to keep Jewel became the strongest Dohnavur ever had to face. For two years, Jewel's mother and uncle fought for her return in the courts, bringing additional accusations against Dohnavur each time a new judge was assigned to the case.

Amy and Jewel had a special relationship in Jesus, and Jewel understood Christ's immeasurable love for her. Amy described the night before the final trial: "Before I left [Jewel] I took her hands in mine and looked down into her upturned face, 'Promise me, whatever happens, by His grace, you will never be offended in Him.' And she repeated, 'I promise by His grace, I will never be offended in Him.'"[439]

The next morning, Amy and Thomas were stunned to hear the verdict; the court ruled that Jewel must be returned immediately to her conniving mother and uncle and that Amy would have to pay the court costs for the trial. But, "by God's grace, the courts of heaven intervened."

Unknown to anyone in court that day, the verdict had reached Dohnavur. A female missionary who was visiting devised a daring plan; she dressed Jewel as a Muslim boy and sneaked her out of the village without notice. The child was passed through "an underground railroad" until she finally arrived in mainland

China. Her name was changed, and she lived quietly with a missionary family for the next six years.

Amy was not informed of Jewel's whereabouts for months, and even then, that information was written in unsigned letters so that she could never be implicated. She knew only that her precious girl was safe in China! Six years later, after an arranged marriage was set up by Amma, Jewel returned to India to marry Arul Dasan, one of Amy's most faithful workers.[440] The young couple served together at Dohnavur throughout Amy's lifetime.

A Chance to Die

Without a hint of what lay ahead, August 1912 began a yearlong period of great personal loss for Amy. In early August, Amy received word that Mrs. Hopwood of Ooty had gone home to be with the Lord. Amy had spent fourteen hot summers with her dear friend in the mountain retreat. "She was a part of my Indian life," Amy cried. "She was like a mother to me."[441]

Within ten days, on August 24, Amy received a chilling telegram: Thomas Walker was dead. "He has gone home to see the face of Jesus" was all the first telegram reported. The next day, Amy learned that Thomas had succumbed to food poisoning on a ministry trip to a distant village. The Dohnavur family was in mourning, and Amy grieved for the loss of an irreplaceable brother: "He was such a strong arm at all times, such a wise counselor, such a true friend." Because expressing herself with words was such an important part of Amy's life, she dealt with her grief by writing Thomas's biography, *Walker of Tinnevelly*.

The Dohnavur family slowly recovered from their losses, but the following summer, on July 14, 1913, Amy received the most difficult blow of all—a cable reporting that her mother had died suddenly at her home in Wimbledon, England. Catherine, even though thousands of miles away, had been Amy's closest confidante and strongest prayer supporter; she had sent her daughter a letter of encouragement just a few weeks earlier.

For the first time in her forty-five years, Amy was bereft of close spiritual family for support.

For the first time in her forty-five years, Amy was bereft of close spiritual family for support. They had all gone on to heaven: her "father," Robert Wilson; Thomas Walker; Mrs. Hopwood; and now, her mother. She was an orphan, spiritually and physically, and would need to rely on the Holy Spirit alone for His love and guidance. During the following months of grief, she wrote countless poems that became the Dohnavur songs of praise during their worship services; some of Amy's poetic words are still sung at Dohnavur today.

Visions and Dreams

"For us of the Fellowship," Amy once said, "the gap to which we have been appointed is that unfenced place where so many children have slipped and fallen."[442] The purpose of the Dohnavur Fellowship was to rescue those children and shepherd their souls to a new life in Christ.

But now that her spiritual mentors were gone, who would provide the prayer support and share a common ministry vision? She turned to her Indian sisters-in-Christ who were closest to her, and formed the group "Sisters of the Common Life," named after a fourteenth-century brotherhood known as "Brothers of the Common Life." Amy included Preena, Arulai, and Ponnammal's daughter, Puruppi (precious Ponnammal had died of cancer months earlier). As a group of unmarried women, their motto was, "Whatsoever Thou sayest to me, by Thy grace, I will do."[443] Their purpose was to seek the mind of Christ for Dohnavur together; they received direction from the Lord through His Word and through "shewings" (dreams or visions) from the Holy Spirit.[444]

Throughout the Bible, God used dreams and visions to communicate with His people and give them direction along their way. In the Old Testament, God gave dreams to Joseph, Solomon, and Daniel, to prepare them for their future roles as leaders. In the New Testament, God poured out His Holy Spirit and gave a vision to the apostle Peter to convince him it was acceptable to visit the Gentile home of Cornelius. Both the apostles Paul and John received visions of heaven and the future of the kingdom of God that they shared with the church.

Amy believed that through the fervent prayers of God's handmaidens, the Lord would guide them to His will for the Dohnavur family, using His Word as well as visions and dreams. When she got a word from the Lord, she wouldn't change her mind, and she would fight like a tiger to keep it.

Although all of the women in "Sisters of the Common Life" were unmarried, they were free to marry if they chose. They would simply step out of the sisterhood and be replaced by another single woman whose heart was single-heartedly focused on the Lord Jesus Christ.

Amy had determined years earlier that she was called to serve the Lord as a single woman; however, she was not opposed to marriage, as people sometimes accused her of being. God had simply told her, "No, I have something different for you to do."

Amy had determined years earlier that she was called to serve the Lord as a single woman; however, she was not opposed to marriage, as people sometimes accused her of being. God had simply told her, "No, I have something different for you to do." And when she feared loneliness ahead, His voice spoke to her once again, saying, *"None of them that trust in him shall be desolate"* (Psalm 34:22).

Rescuing the Temple Boys

> It was late evening on January 14, 1918, when a wagon unexpectedly jingled up to the Dohnavur bungalow. A tired woman was crumpled up inside and in her arms was a bundle. It held out thin little arms to me and dropped a weary little head contentedly on my shoulder....I remember thinking, *I wish you were a boy*. Then, Mabel carried off the bundle to the nursery, to return five minutes later, racing breathlessly: "It's a boy!"[445]

Amy and Mabel named the first baby boy Arul, in honor of Arul Dasan. A second baby boy was brought to the compound soon after.

As Amy described the above scene in *Gold Cord,* she admitted, "It was much more difficult than we expected to get on the track of little boys."[446] Handsome Indian boys who were unprotected were sold to actors' guilds to act or sing in sordid performances, or sold to the temples for male prostitution. Just as in her early attempts with the girls, Amy couldn't find a way to reach the boys. Where were they hiding? Even when her workers found them, Dohnavur had few men in ministry to help raise them.

When Amy asked, "Lord, what of the little boys?" she felt His answer came quickly. She was to rescue the boys, as well. When she cried out again, "Lord, what about the men I need?" He promised to provide there, too.

In that very hour, the work for the boys began. Over the next eight years, the number of boys cared for at Dohnavur increased to eighty!

Desperate for Doctors

At fifty-six years of age, Amy was recognized by King George V of Great Britain with the Kaisar-i-Hind Medal "for her services to the people of India." The 1920s were years of rapid growth. By 1924, there were thirteen nurseries teeming with babies, and Amy had published nineteen books introducing Dohnavur to the Christian world.

One positive result of all the recognition was the increasing funds sent to Dohnavur for the construction of nurseries and homes. At the same time, with recognition came difficulties. Prospective missionaries saw Dohnavur as a "success" and applied to join the team there, not realizing they weren't prepared for the "desperately hard work" of life in southern India.

When the number of children grew large and Amy needed consecrated workers to help, she heard the Lord say to her, *"Fear not, little flock: for it is your Father's good pleasure to give you the kingdom"* [Luke 12:32]. *Live not in anxious suspense about the needs that press so heavily. Your Father knoweth: fear not, fear not.*[447]

Amy and her team were especially desperate for doctors. Then, in 1924, came an apparent answer to prayer; three physicians arrived in Dohnavur from Great Britain—Dr. May Powell and two Drs. Neills, a British husband and wife team in their forties. The Neills brought their son, Stephen, an honor graduate from Cambridge, who was working toward ordination in the Anglican Church.

Stealing the Vision

From the outset, the Neills formulated "new and improved" plans for the ministry, in spite of Amy's objections. They proposed that a new hospital be built outside of the compound for the people of the surrounding areas. They pushed for the children to go out into the villages for school and sports leagues, failing to comprehend the danger of rescued children returning to the Hindu population. The Neills were determined to "modernize" Dohnavur. What Amy saw as a refuge given to her by God, the Neills saw as an unhealthy insulation from the real world. To many of the Dohnavur workers, the Neill family appeared to be "on a takeover."

There comes a time when the devil will bring the wrong people into your life to try to divert you from following the vision and Spirit of the Lord, when he can't get you through the sin in your life. You have to be protective of the vision God has given you in your spirit. Amy put her foot down and made some tough decisions, but she saved an entire ministry.

You have to be protective of the vision God has given you in your spirit. Amy put her foot down and made some tough decisions, but she saved an entire ministry.

Amy was certain that God had directed her to go into the evil world and rescue the children. At Dohnavur, she provided them with a strong Christian upbringing, apart from deceptive Hindu influences by separating them from it. She believed that the Neills wanted to make something "lofty" of the Dohnavur work, but her response to them was simple: "We do not live in the clouds—we have never lived there; our way is in the dust of the ordinary road."[448]

Within six months of their arrival, the elder Neills left. Stephen stayed, wanting to become the "bishop" of Dohnavur. He changed the open, nondenominational Sunday church services into formal Anglican liturgies.

"It is a dreadful time of stress," Amy wrote in her diary concerning the constant friction. "Never such stress known here before. I am ready to sink. Lord, save me."[449] Finally, after many sleepless nights of prayer, on November 29, 1925, Amy dismissed Stephen Neill from the Dohnavur ministry.

Thankfully, Dr. May Powell, who had come from England with the Neills, stayed on and remained in leadership over the girls. Stephen also stayed in southern India and eventually became the Anglican Bishop of Tinnevelly. By that time, Amy had severed ties with the Church of England and, therefore, was never under his spiritual leadership.

The Dohnavur Fellowship

The very day after dismissing Stephen Neill, Amy wrote a letter of resignation to the Church of England Zenna Mission. Like so many missionaries before her, including William Carey, David Livingstone, and Hudson Taylor, she could not see any reason to receive spiritual direction from a committee thousands of miles away when the Holy Spirit gave His guidance right on the mission field. The CZM graciously accepted Amy's resignation and donated the two buildings they owned on site to the Dohnavur ministry.

Amy Carmichael had never intended to establish a mission society, but, in order to own the land and other property, the ministry had to become a legal entity. And so the Dohnavur Fellowship (DF) was born. Its mission statement was powerful: "To save children in moral danger; to train them to serve others; to succor the desolate and suffering; to do anything that may be known as the will of our heavenly Father in order to make His love known, especially to the people of India."[450]

During these same years, the Lord laid it on Amy's heart to build a House of Prayer. It would be a place consecrated to worshipping the Lord and praying for His guidance and for one another's needs. After her painful time with the Neills, the need for prayer and God's protection were uppermost in her mind.

The Webb-Peploe Brothers Arrive

The year before the Neills arrived, in 1924, Amy had a special visitor at Dohnavur, Godfrey Webb-Peploe, a British missionary with the Children's Special Service Mission who was on his way to his assignment in Nanking, China. Godfrey stopped first in India and spent three months in Tinnevelly, especially curious to visit Amy Carmichael's ministry. To Amy, he was like a "fresh breeze into our midst straight from home." Their time together was spiritually uplifting, and she was saddened when he had to leave.

A few months later, a letter arrived from Godfrey's mother, thanking Amy for her hospitality to her son. Now a widow, she and her older son, twenty-nine-year-old Murray, wanted to visit Dohnavur before going on to Murray's appointment as a medical missionary at the Church Missionary Society Hospital in Hangchow. On January 30, 1926, when they began their three-month visit, Amy immediately recognized the industrious, cheerful Murray as a kindred spirit.

After meeting both Webb-Peploe brothers, Amma became unusually anxious in prayer. For years, she and the other Sisters of the Common Life had prayed for men who would assume leadership positions at Dohnavur. Now, she believed these brothers were the answer to those prayers. But how could she expect the Webb-Peploes to join her ministry? Wouldn't she be coveting them from their work in China?

There were eighty boys now living in Dohnavur, and the fellowship was getting ready to purchase the land to build a hospital. Amy was certain that the quiet, thoughtful Godfrey and the energetic Murray would be the perfect ministry leaders to the orphan boys and the hospital. In her diary, Amy wrote this prayer: "Still my heart turns to Murray as Thy chosen leader for the hospital and refuses to be forbidden. I cannot quiet myself. Oh, do Thou quiet me. Let me not covet my neighbor's goods—nor his menservants."[451]

On October 8, 1926, Amy had a dream that both Godfrey and Murray were sent to Dohnavur: Godfrey to lead the boys and Murray for the hospital and medical work. She wondered, *Should I simply ask them to come? Do I dare?* Leaning on the Lord for peace, she asked.

Godfrey Webb-Peploe came first; he was ordered out of China because of recurring rheumatic fever. He arrived at Dohnavur on December 15, 1926, one day before Amy's fifty-ninth birthday. The desire of Amy's heart had been answered. "'Seek ye My face,' He was saying to us. And our answer was 'Thy face, Lord, will I seek.'"[452]

The following year, Murray's hospital in China was overrun by Communist rebels. In 1927, two years after Stephen Neill had left Dohnavur, thirty-year-old Murray Webb-Peploe arrived from China.

Murray requested a six-month trial period, to make certain that Dohnavur was God's "directed service" for his life and ministry.[453] "*You are not your own… you were bought at a price*" (1 Corinthians 6:19 NKJV) was his favorite Scripture for prayer. At the end of the waiting period, God's answer to Murray was, "Your work is here; fear not, I have called thee."[454] Murray sent a brief note to Amy, asking, "May I stay?"

It had been a long two years, but Amy's dearest prayers had been answered! She responded to the news with praise from Scripture: "*I had fainted, unless I had believed to see the goodness of the LORD in the land of the living*" (Psalm 27:13).

Place of Heavenly Healing

Within days of Murray's arrival in Dohnavur, the first £100 donation arrived, designated specifically for the new hospital. Amy named the hospital *Parama Suha Salai*, or "Place of Heavenly Healing." Murray's estimation of the cost to build it to modern standards was £10,000, a larger amount than Amy had ever considered. But they prayed, and the money began to come in from Christians around the world. Murray's infectious enthusiasm in everything he did helped to keep the project on task.

The Place of Heavenly Healing was built over several years and served the Tinnevelly community as well as Dohnavur. The children were actively involved, the older children serving those in need and the younger ones blessing the patients with songs. "Our chief evangelistic field," Amy wrote with satisfaction, "is surely the Parama Suha Salai, with all its contacts. Through it, the Lord Himself is bringing to our doors the very people of the villages that we longed so much to reach!"[455]

As the ministry entered the 1930s, things were well at Dohnavur. They had fourteen nurseries filled to overflowing, and, as a family, they numbered more than five hundred. Godfrey and Murray were the leaders on the men's side, with May Powell and Arulai taking the lead on the women's side. John Risk, a former British Naval officer, worked alongside Godfrey as his right-hand man in the discipline and training of the boys.

On August 6, 1931, after a Dohnavur leadership meeting, Amy wrote contentedly in her diary, "Great joy tonight in the sense of moving on together."

The Day That Everything Changed

At sixty-three years old, Amy was still front and center in any new work done by the DF. In addition to the hospital at Dohnavur, the fellowship began to set up local medical dispensaries to reach more people in the mission field.

It was late afternoon on October 24, 1931, when Amy arrived in the village of Kalakadu to inspect the latest dispensary renovation. Curious about every detail, she walked into the new outhouse still under construction. In a design mistake, the workers had dug the hole in the front of the building instead of the back.

It was dusk when Amy was walking toward the outbuilding and, failing to see the hole, fell into it with a cry of pain. After she was rushed to the hospital, it was discovered that she had dislocated her ankle, broken her leg, and twisted her spine.

How the children prayed for a complete recovery for Amma! Each day, they waited for good news. Surely, she would soon be scurrying around the compound, visiting every nursery and classroom with her usual cheerful smile. But as the weeks turned into months and then into years with little improvement, everyone realized much more was wrong. Her leg had never healed properly, and arthritis had settled in her spine.

What had seemed at the time a painful injury for the aging Amy became a life-altering one, and the busy Missie Ammal became an invalid, largely confined to her room for the next twenty years.

Satan had been working to steal Amy Carmichael's ministry her whole life. In the earliest years, he tried to use her neuralgia pain, her gender, and her age to keep her from her missionary calling. Satan had sent the wrong people, the Neills, to try to throw her off course. When he couldn't steal the ministry from her, he handicapped her. By inflicting physical injury, he thought that his attack on her was complete. But, with a determination that comes only from the Spirit of the living God, Amy persevered. On her sickbed, she started writing books to share Christ's salvation with people around the world. Eventually, Satan took even her writing away from her, but she never quit serving the Lord in the face of all the attacks.

What had seemed at the time a painful injury for the aging Amy became a life-altering one, and the busy Missie Ammal became an invalid, largely confined to her room for the next twenty years.

I wish she would have prayed with more understanding for healing. She did her best with her understanding of the will of God and His desire to heal. And she never quit—ever. She just kept on going.

The Room of Peace

Amma was moved into a large bedroom in the main house, and a veranda was built so that she could be wheeled outside her room to see her gardens. A writing desk was placed in front of the large windows so that she could see outside while she wrote. A teakwood plaque was hung over the door that said, "In heavenly places in Christ Jesus." The children were always welcomed, and they often came to sing. She shared stories and prayed for their blessings, still their Amma.

Amy was able to walk a little, sit at her desk, and hold leadership meetings for Dohnavur. She was driven by car to the House of Prayer for services and to

Murray Webb-Peploe's marriage to Oda van Boetzelaer, a Swedish missionary working at Dohnavur.

But things had changed. In the Room of Peace, Amy found sanctuary.

There she used the time of separation from the world to write, as the apostle Paul and John Bunyan had done before her. She began *Dust of Gold*, Dohnavur's monthly letter of Christian encouragement and Fellowship news. Before her fall, she had written twenty-four books, all in longhand; after her injury, she wrote an additional thirteen. Two of her most treasured books were written between 1933 and 1938: *Gold Cord*, about God's cord of binding love in the history of the Dohnavur Fellowship, and *If*, a small book of prose on the depth of Christ's love on Calvary.

Amy often quoted these words from *If*: "If my interest in the work of others is cool; if I think in terms of my own special work; if the burdens of others are not my burdens too and their joys mine, then I know nothing of Calvary love."[456]

The Way of Prayer

Amy Carmichael understood the power of prayer. "Prayer," she said, "is, after all, work—the most strenuous work in all the world."[457] And prayer did "soar on high" from the Room of Peace during the last two decades of her life.

"Perhaps prayer often needs to be followed by a little pause," Amy wrote in *If*, "that we may have time to open our hearts to that for which we have prayed. We often rush from prayer to prayer without waiting for the word within, which says 'I have heard you, my child.'"[458]

Her prayer burden became the heaviest when she received the shattering news that Murray Webb-Peploe would be leaving Dohnavur for England. His wife, Oda, had gone to England with their twin boys to further their education, and she insisted that Murray follow. A painful tug-of-war took place in Murray's heart. Amy expected his commitment to Dohnavur to be for life. His wife and other Christian leaders, including the director of the Keswick convention, insisted he belonged in England with Oda and his sons. After a time of prayer, he wrote home to Oda, saying, "It is absolutely clear that I must come home and make a home for my family."[459]

In 1947, after twenty years of unwavering service, fifty-year-old Murray Webb-Peploe left Dohnavur for home. For the next twenty years, he practiced medicine in southern England and established Webb-Peploe Surgery, which is still flourishing today as a partnership of Christian doctors in Southampton.

As Amy prayed through her painful disappointment, she wrote a note to Godfrey about prayer. "The gates of access into the Father's presence are open continually. There is no need to push—*If the gates are open there is nothing to do but go in.*"[460]

Life Is Continual Change

The year that Murray left was full of change. World War II was over, and the British government finally released the "Jewel of the Empire"—India—to govern herself. The first change instituted by the new government was received at Dohnavur with tears of joy. Temple prostitution was finally outlawed throughout the country! The new Indian government also required that Dohnavur's children get a portion of their education outside the compound in order to receive a school certification (diploma). Amy didn't fight the new law.

In June 1948, while walking in her room, Amy slipped and fell, breaking both her right arm and her femur. Her long days of writing were now over, except for when she dictated to a nurse.

Later that same year, during the Christmas season, Godfrey discovered he had thrombosis, a blood clot, in his leg. The forty-eight-year-old leader of the orphan boys took to his bed for a much-needed rest. Seven weeks later, Mabel Wade walked quietly into Amy's room and said, "Amma, God has trusted us with a great trust. Godfrey is in heaven."[461]

Not Godfrey! One by one, the anointed leaders of Dohnavur had been given to her, and one by one, they had been taken to heaven before her. A few years earlier, Arulai had passed away, and now, precious Godfrey.

"Our God trusts us to trust Him....Let us not disappoint God. Let us rise to that great trust," was Amy's note to the grief-stricken Dohnavur family following Godfrey's death.

"When You Hear I Have Gone, Jump for Joy!"

In 1950, at eighty-three years old, Amy set up the leadership team to guide Dohnavur after she was gone. For the boys, John Risk was teamed with Rajappan,

Arulai's oldest nephew; for the girls, Purripu, Ponnammal's daughter, would assist Dr. May. Amy breathed a sigh of relief that God had placed her beloved Dohnavur in such loving Christian hands.

Amma had spent her final years struggling with the pain of both arthritis and neuralgia. She was more than ready to meet her Lord and Savior face-to-face. Throughout 1950, her health continued to decline. When her New Zealand nurse went home for a furlough, she told her, "Alison, we won't meet again in this world. When you hear I have gone, jump for joy!"[462]

In one of her last notes to the Fellowship, she wrote, "I am very happy and content. Green pastures are before me, and my Savior has my treasure—the DF."[463]

In early January, 1951, Amy fell into a coma. In the last years of her life, she hadn't been able to welcome the children to her room. Now, by the hundreds, they all filed silently through the Room of Peace to see their precious Amma as she slept. Many of them had never seen her face before.[464]

In the early morning of January 18, 1951, Amy Carmichael slipped away in her sleep to dwell in the house of her Lord forever. After the loved ones of Dohnavur celebrated her life in the House of Prayer, she was buried in her special garden outside of her bedroom window. They didn't use headstones in Dohnavur, so they placed a birdbath above her grave on which was engraved *Ammai*—"true mother." Amy Carmichael had completed the race.

Surrounded by a Gold Cord

"There is no force strong enough to hold us together as a company, and animate all our doings, but His one force of Love; and so there is a constant attack upon the love without which we are sounding brass and tinkling cymbal."[465]

The "living bond," or gold cord, that held the Family together was always Christ's love.[466] Amy demonstrated that love by embracing *and* correcting the children in her care. Her love was tough as well as tender. She was strong-willed in dealing with people but always humbly submissive in obeying the will of God.

"If any man's work abide...." Through God's leading, Amy had built a work of gold, silver, and jewels that still abides. The work at Dohnavur Fellowship continues today, directed entirely by Indian leadership. Boys no longer live in the compound due to the difficulty of finding dedicated men to look after them. But there

At the time of Amy's death, over a half million of her books had been printed in English, several titles had been translated into fifteen different languages, and twelve had been imprinted in Braille.

are more than four hundred women and girls living in the homes, teaching or attending the schools where Amy Carmichael once lovingly poured out her life.

At the time of Amy's death, over a half million of her books had been printed in English, several titles had been translated into fifteen different languages, and twelve had been imprinted in Braille. Through the years, Amy had written millions of words in her books and letters to her beloved family at Dohnavur. She had written a letter to each of the nearly 900 people living in Dohnavur at the time of her death to encourage them after she was gone.

Biographer Sam Wellman wisely noted, "Those the world regarded as less than lovely, Amy Carmichael saw with the eyes of God...and gave her life for them."

Over the last one hundred years, since the publication of her very first book, Amy's life of obedience and courage has influenced many others, including missionaries Jim and Elisabeth Elliot. And there is no doubt that her life of passion for the gospel had a powerful effect on the lives of the people of southern India.

Among Amy's favorite prayers were the following verses from Psalm 143:8–10.[467]

> *Cause me to hear thy lovingkindness in the morning; for in thee do I trust: cause me to know the way wherein I should walk; for I lift up my soul unto thee. Deliver me, O Lord, from mine enemies: I flee unto thee to hide me. Teach me to do thy will; for thou art my God: thy spirit is good; lead me into the land of uprightness.*

> *Therefore, my beloved brethren, be steadfast, immovable, always abounding in the work of the Lord, knowing that your labor is not in vain in the Lord.*
>
> (1 Corinthians 15:58 NKJV)

Have you been laboring in the Lord's work?

Be encouraged and remain steadfast! All your efforts to win the lost are never in vain.

Chapter 9

Jonathan Goforth

China's Revival Carrier

"Flee south! Northern route cut off by Boxers!"

It was an ominously hot afternoon as Jonathan Goforth prepared for the day's chapel. "Flee south! Northern route cut off by Boxers!" was the message speeding throughout China, carried by cable, by bike, by boat, by horseback, and even by foot. Jonathan reread the urgent telegram from the American consul in Chefoo, placed it on the table, looked up, and said, "Father, I am in Your hands...again."

The day before, an official Chinese courier heading south on a powerful black steed had raced through the town at breakneck speed. A burnt feather waving from his Chinese cap had signified the fact that he carried a message of life or death from a member of the royal family. Every attempt that Jonathan had made to find what it meant for the Chinese villagers had proved futile.

Jonathan Goforth[468]

Exchanging uneasy glances, Jonathan and his wife, Rosalind, had gathered their four children, ages eight months to nine years, and hastily began packing boxes of food, water, and clothing for their escape. Before sunrise the next morning, they planned to slip out of the Changte mission station with ten carts full of supplies, as well as six missionaries, three Chinese helpers, and four children.

"What route should we take?" the missionaries had asked Jonathan anxiously. The most direct one was south through the capital city, Kaifengfu, and then fourteen days by cart to the Han River. From there, they would travel up the Yangtze to safety in Shanghai. It was a perilous journey, especially for the children.

During the sleepless night, Jonathan had turned to Rosalind and whispered, "Something is wrong; we need to change our plans. I don't believe we are to travel south through Kaifengfu. We are going to journey southwest instead."

"But Jonathan, it will add days to our journey!" she whispered back.

"I know, but I am certain that it is God's will."

What Jonathan didn't know was that the Chinese courier riding through town had carried a sealed packet from the Empress Dowager Cixi directly south to the governor in the city of Kaifengfu. Enclosed was a royal command for the massacre of all foreigners in China—*without exception*!

If Jonathan Goforth had not been listening to the Holy Spirit that night, if his heart had not been sensitive to God's voice, he would have led his family straight into the hands of the bloodthirsty Boxers. Instead, even though there were harrowing days ahead, the Goforths were led by their Redeemer to safety and deliverance.

God's Pioneer Revivalist

> "Brethren, the Spirit of God is with us still. Pentecost is yet within our grasp. If revival is being withheld from us, it is because some idol remains still enthroned; because we still insist on placing our reliance in human schemes; because we still refuse to face the unchangeable truth that it is not by our might, but by His Spirit!"[469]
>
> —Jonathan Goforth

Jonathan Goforth was a pioneer revivalist with a burning passion to win souls for Christ. The quote above is from the closing passage of his book *By My Spirit*. Throughout his ministry, Goforth boldly proclaimed that men's hearts would be drawn to the Savior by the Spirit of God alone. Very early in his ministry, his life verse became Zechariah 4:6: "*Not by might, nor by power, but by my spirit, saith the* Lord *of hosts*." Because of his unshakable faith in the Holy Spirit to change lives for eternity, Goforth was used by God to usher in sweeping revivals in China, reaching tens of thousands of people at the dawn of the twentieth century.

"Jonathan Goforth was a pioneer, through and through," his wife Rosalind wrote. "He always had a forward vision and strong convictions about discerning divine guidance for himself....Jonathan believed in the freedom for each missionary to carry on his or her work as each one felt led by the Holy Spirit."[470]

After witnessing the mighty Korean Revival of 1907, Goforth prayed for the Holy Spirit to fall upon China with a mighty rushing wind, to draw unredeemed men and women to the cross. He was not disappointed, for tens of thousands were won for Christ, and nearly one hundred mission stations were opened throughout northern China and Manchuria.

Through forty-seven years of ministry with Rosalind working by his side, Goforth's zeal for missions and the Word of God never abated. "When [Jonathan] found his own soul needed Jesus Christ, it became a passion with him to take Jesus Christ to every other soul."[471]

Surrendering to the power of the Holy Spirit to win souls for the kingdom of God, Jonathan Goforth became the foremost missionary revivalist in early twentieth-century China and one of God's most anointed missionary generals.

The Study of World Maps

Jonathan Goforth was born on February 10, 1859, in London, Ontario, Canada, the seventh of eleven children born to Francis and Jane Bates Goforth. They were a hardworking farm family of ten boys and one girl, and every hand was needed to keep the farm from failing.

Although Francis Goforth had little time for "religion," his wife taught all of their children the Scriptures from the earliest age, and by the time Jonathan was just five years old, he could read psalms aloud. None of the Goforth children attended school from April to October, as the farm absorbed all of the family's time and energy. During the winter months, Jonathan worked just as hard in school to catch up. His clearest memory was of standing in the front of the classroom, carefully studying the world maps hanging on the walls. As just a boy, he had a stirring in his soul for the far-distant places of the world.

The Smile Said It All

Although Jonathan had six older brothers, when he was fifteen years old, his father entrusted him with running their second property, the Thamesford farm. The elder Goforth gave him specific instructions on clearing a large field that was choked with weeds and underbrush. "Get that field clear and ready for seeding, son. At harvest time, I'll return and inspect."

Years later, Jonathan captivated congregations with the story of his intense daily labor in his father's field. He ploughed and tilled and bought the best seed for planting. When harvest time finally arrived, Jonathan recalled, "My heart filled with joy as I led my father to a high place from which the whole field of beautiful waving grain could be seen. Without speaking, I waited for the coveted 'well done.' My father stood for several moments silently examining the field and then turning to me he just smiled.

"That smile was all the reward I wanted," Goforth stated. "I knew my father was pleased. So will it be if we are faithful to the trust our heavenly Father gives us."[472]

"I Bowed My Head...and Gave Him My Heart"

In 1877, at the age of eighteen, Goforth attended a church service led by his high school Bible teacher, Lachlan Cameron. Jonathan later wrote about that Sunday morning, "Mr. Cameron seemed to look right at me as he pled, during his sermon, for all who had not, to accept the Lord Jesus Christ. His words cut me deeply and I said to myself, I must decide before he is through....As I sat there, without any outward sign except to simply bow my head, I yielded myself up to Christ."[473]

Nearly sixty years later, on his seventy-fifth birthday, Goforth reminisced with his daughter Mary:

> My conversion at eighteen was simple but so complete that ever onward I could say with Paul, I am crucified with Christ: nevertheless I live; yet not I, but Christ liveth in me: and the life which I now live in the flesh I live by the faith of the Son of God, who loved me, and gave himself for me (Galatians 2:20). Henceforth my life belonged to Him who had given His life for me.[474]

Shortly after Jonathan's conversion, his father surrendered his life to Christ, as well.

One warm Saturday afternoon that same year, Jonathan was given a well-worn copy of *The Memoirs of Robert Murray M'Cheyne*, with the challenge: "Read this; it will do you good!" Laying the book on the seat of his farmer's cart, he drove away. Curiosity led him to pull off the road to read the book, and he didn't finish it until darkness fell. In those quiet hours, reading the story of M'Cheyne's spiritual struggles and victories as a missionary, Jonathan Goforth "made the decision which changed the course of his life." He would leave farming forever and dedicate himself to the ministry, sharing the message of God's salvation through Jesus Christ.

Not One Has Heard the Call

Jonathan spent the next year preparing to enter Knox College in Toronto. Around the same time, he heard that a missionary would be speaking in a church nearby. He was spellbound as he sat in the crowded sanctuary and listened to missionary pioneer George L. Mackay describe his ministry to the lost souls in Formosa (modern-day Taiwan). "For two years," Mackay shared, "I have been going up and down Canada trying to persuade some young man to come over to Formosa and help me, but in vain. No one has caught the vision. Now I am going back alone. It will not be long before my bones will be lying on some Formosan hillside. My heartbreak is that no young man has heard the call to come and carry on the work that I have begun."

"As I listened to these words," Jonathan wrote, "I was overwhelmed with shame. Had the floor opened up and swallowed me out of sight, it would have been a relief. There was I, bought with the precious blood of Jesus Christ, daring to dispose of my life as I pleased. I heard the Lord's voice saying in my soul, 'Who will go for us and whom shall we send?' And I answered, 'Here am I; send me.' From that hour, I became a foreign missionary...and set to work to get others to catch the vision I had caught of the unreached, unevangelized millions on earth."[475]

A Rude Revelation at Knox College

In the fall of 1882, at twenty-three years of age, Jonathan left home for Knox College in Toronto with great excitement; he thought he would be spending the

Jonathan's classmates ridiculed him, a country boy with handmade clothes and a naïveté about city life.

next four years bonding with young men whose hearts also burned for Christ's service. But that is not what he found.

Jonathan's classmates ridiculed him, a country boy with handmade clothes and a naïveté about city life. In an attempt to fit in, Jonathan bought new fabric for a more modern suit, but his fellow students stole into his room late at night, tied him up, and cut a hole in his new material. They pushed his head through it and forced him into the hallway to run a gauntlet of ridiculing students. To Jonathan, it was not a boyish prank but a heartrending disappointment.

Humiliated to tears, he fell on his knees, with his open Bible before him, and made a commitment to serve the Lord with greater passion than ever before, even though he had to go it alone. The traumatic experience became a cornerstone in his foundation as a missionary pioneer. Jonathan Goforth would become a trail-breaker for Christ's love, not afraid to go where others would not venture. He could not have foreseen how God would use those scornful young men to help fulfill his missionary call.

The Slums of Toronto

For the next four years, Jonathan regularly evangelized in the slums of St. John's Ward in Toronto. He visited every street, knocking at each door and sharing the gospel of Christ with thousands of impoverished citizens in the inner city. Hundreds responded by accepting the message of Christ's salvation. During these years, he also read Hudson Taylor's book *China's Spiritual Need and Claims*, and felt God draw his heart to China. In each activity, Jonathan was preparing for his future missionary life. Every step a person takes is a preparation for the next one. The season of preparation is never a waste of time. The *journey* is always as important as the *destination*.

Gradually, Jonathan's fellow classmates welcomed the earnest country missionary into their lives. His enthusiasm for the lost was contagious. As a result, the Knox students developed a deep interest in foreign missions and, years later, provided the initial financial support for his missionary journey to China.

Jonathan Goforth

A Well-worn Bible

In June 1885, a group of young men and women sat eagerly at the Toronto Mission Union waiting for the Bible speakers of the day. Goforth, dressed in his usual poor country clothes, sat at one end of an aisle. Just a few seats away, a young lady from a well-to-do Toronto family sat fidgeting in her seat, glancing over at him with increasing curiosity.

When Jonathan was called away to speak with friends, he left his Bible lying on his seat. In a sudden impulse, the young lady stepped over to his chair, picked up the Bible, and scurried back to her place. Quickly turning the pages, she found "the book was near worn to shreds and marked from cover to cover." Silently returning the Bible to Jonathan's seat, Rosalind thought to herself, *That is the man I would like to marry!*[476]

No Engagement Ring

Rosalind Bell-Smith was born in London, England, on May 6, 1864, and moved to Canada with her parents when she was just three years old. Her father, John Bell-Smith, was an accomplished British artist and the founder of the Society of Canadian Artists. Rosalind had spent years in artistic training and was scheduled to leave Canada that autumn to pursue her studies in London—until the day she met Jonathan Goforth.

Rosalind had become a Christian at the age of twelve and had grown steadily in her faith. Now, at age twenty, she was praying earnestly that if the Lord wanted her to marry, He would lead her to a man who was "wholly given up to Christ and His service."

The day of the Toronto Mission meeting, Jonathan and Rosalind were both assigned to the new mission team in the east end of Toronto. By the time autumn arrived, they had fallen in love. When Jonathan asked, "Will you join your life with mine for China?" her immediate answer was yes.

His next question was much more challenging: "Will you give me your promise that you will always allow me to put my Lord and His work first, even before you?" Rosalind gave a little gasp before replying, "Yes, I will, always." Wasn't this the very kind of man she had prayed for?

Her first real test came a week later when Jonathan asked a startling question: "You will not mind, will you, if I do not buy you an engagement ring? We need all of our money to distribute Hudson Taylor's booklet *China's Spiritual Need and Claims* to the Toronto churches."[477]

"As I listened and watched his glowing face," Rosalind wrote years later, "the visions of my beautiful engagement ring vanished." Rosalind always referred to that day as "my first lesson in real values!"

"O God, What Can I Do?"

During this same year, a Believers Conference was held at Niagara-on-the-Lake in Ontario. Jonathan, still an unknown student to many people at the time, was invited to speak on the call to missions. As he presented his appeal for 900 million lost souls in the world, one young man in the crowd was stirred to the depths of his soul.

Henry W. Frost was a Christian and a young American businessman. As he listened to the appeal for China, "Frost cried in his inmost soul, 'Oh God, what can I...what shall I do?'"[478] This was the beginning of Frost's fervent interest in foreign missions. Before long, the young man traveled to England to appeal to Hudson Taylor to open up the China Inland Mission to American missionaries. Taylor eventually recognized the Lord's anointing in Frost's vision and appointed him as the first director of the China Inland Mission of North America. Thousands of Chinese lives were changed for eternity by Frost's commitment to China. And Jonathan Goforth was the match that ignited the flame of Frost's calling.

The Revelation of Feeding the Back Rows

When the China Inland Mission opened up to American missionaries, Goforth became the first North American to apply. After several months of waiting, he was accepted into the organization. But Jonathan's Knox classmates had other plans. They believed that he should be sent to the mission field under the spiritual covering of his home denomination, the Presbyterian Church of Canada. Their financial pledges were enough to launch him on his missionary journey.

In the beginning, the Canadian Presbytery wasn't enthusiastic about adding ongoing mission work to the denomination's budget. Then Jonathan stood up to address them at the annual Presbytery meeting. To Goforth, Christ's command to evangelize the world was crystal clear, and his ringing challenge struck the heart of every minister present.

To Goforth, Christ's command to evangelize the world was crystal clear, and his ringing challenge struck the heart of every minister present.

At the close of his message, Jonathan painted a vivid picture of Jesus and the miraculous feeding of the five thousand from the fourteenth chapter of the gospel of Matthew. He described Jesus blessing the bread and fish and then handing them to His disciples to distribute. Joyfully, the disciples took the food to the first few rows of the hungry multitude.

"Now imagine," Goforth continued, "these same disciples, instead of going on to the back rows, returning to those who had already been fed and offering them more bread and fish until they turned away from it, while the back rows of thousands were still waiting and starving.

"What would Christ have thought of His disciples," he asked his distinguished audience, "if they had acted in this way? What does He think of us today as we continue to spend most of our time and money giving the Bread of Life to those who have heard so often while millions in China are still starving?"[479] When he had finished speaking, the Presbyterian board, without any further discussion, voted unanimously to support the missionary venture.

Quickness in Steps

After that day, things moved quickly. In June 1887, Jonathan was officially appointed a missionary to China. Four months later, he was ordained by the Presbyterian Church of Canada, and on October 25, 1887, he married Rosalind Bell-Smith in Knox Church, Toronto. By early January 1888, reports arrived that a great famine was sweeping across China. The mission board decided that the Goforths should leave as soon as possible to bring needed relief funds directly to the British missionaries already serving in China.

The train station was packed with hundreds of well-wishers as the Goforths prepared to leave for their life's work. Voices were raised in singing hymns as the Goforths were sent off. Who could have known that day that tens of thousands of Chinese lives would be transformed for eternity by the mission of this one man and his devoted wife?

Leave No Stone Unturned

"Let us leave no stone unturned in the effort to spread the message to every creature," Jonathan recorded on February 4, 1888, the night they departed from Vancouver aboard the *S.S. Partha*. "I know that many eyes are fixed on this movement. Let us win ten thousand Chinese souls. It will please Him, our Lord."[480]

Crossing the Pacific Ocean, Jonathan and Rosalind arrived in Shanghai and were welcomed by several missionaries from the London Missionary Society. Goforth handed over the much-needed relief funds, and the seasoned missionaries gave him the mission field assigned to the Presbyterian Church of Canada—the North Honan province (modern-day Henan province) in north central China.

First on the Goforths' agenda would be intensive study of the Mandarin Chinese language at the mission station in Chefoo. Shortly after their arrival for language classes, disaster struck; a fire broke out among the small cabins at Chefoo. The Goforths looked on helplessly as their possessions were consumed by the fire, including Rosalind's precious artwork, as well as their wedding presents and family photographs. Even though Jonathan comforted Rosalind that "they were only things," in her heart, she knew the sacrifices for mission life had only just begun.

The devil throws us these challenges to make our souls weary. He wants to interfere with God's plan, to get us to stop along the way. The Goforths were saddened, but they kept going.

"You Must Go Forward on Your Knees"

"We are asked to do an impossible task, but we work with Him who can do the impossible," Jonathan assured Rosalind; after a year at Chefoo, they were making plans to move closer to North Honan.

Just before they began their journey, Jonathan received a supportive letter from Hudson Taylor that read, "We understand North Honan is to be your field; we, as a mission, have tried for ten years to enter that province from the south, and have only just now succeeded. It is one of the most anti-foreign provinces in China....Brother, if you would enter that province, you must go forward on your knees."[481]

Go forward on your knees! Those words became the motto of the North Honan mission from that time forward!

In the beginning, the governor of Honan refused to grant permission for the mission, so Jonathan crossed into the province just to walk the land and pray. As he gazed at the beautiful countryside and the majestic Shansi Mountains west of the city of Changte, the Lord spoke to his heart.

"Walking ahead of the carts," Jonathan wrote, "I prayed the Lord to give me that section of North Honan as my own field, and as I prayed, I opened *Clarke's Scripture Promises*, my daily text-book, and found the promise for that day read as follows: For as the rain cometh down, and the snow from heaven, and returneth not thither, but watereth the earth, and maketh it bring forth and bud, that it may give seed to the sower, and bread to the eater: so shall my word be that goeth forth out of my mouth: it shall not return unto me void, but it shall accomplish that which I please, and it shall prosper in the thing whereto I sent it." [482] (See Isaiah 55:10–11.)

Goforth was a man deeply immersed in the Word of God. He always found the Scriptures to keep his relationship with the Lord strong and on track with His purposes. Now he believed that this Scripture was God's prophetic word to him; the Lord would answer his prayer and prosper His purposes on that very piece of land.

Many missionaries were geniuses at learning languages, but Jonathan Goforth was not one of them. For him, the Chinese language was indescribably difficult.

Supernaturally Learning to Speak Chinese

The Goforths moved to their first mission station in Linching just outside of North Honan, along with their first child, nine-month-old Gertrude Madeline. Donald McGillivray, Jonathan's closest friend at Knox College, arrived from Canada to join them and spent the next thirty-five years ministering at Jonathan's side. While they preached in Linching, both men worked hard on language study, but with very different results.

Many missionaries were geniuses at learning languages, but Jonathan Goforth was not one of them. For him, the Chinese language was indescribably difficult. When he would preach in chapel, the men often pointed to McGillivray, saying, "You speak to us; we don't understand him!" On the other hand, languages had always been McGillivray's best subject, and he later became known as a brilliant Chinese translator.

Discouragement threatened to sidetrack Jonathan from his work. One day, leaving for a scheduled preaching assignment at the mission chapel, he confessed to Rosalind, "If the Lord does not work a miracle for me with this language, I fear I will be an utter failure as a missionary!" Picking up his Chinese Bible, he left worried but returned to the room bursting with joy two hours later.

"Oh Rose! It was just wonderful! When I began to speak, those phrases and idioms that would always elude me came readily, and I could make myself understood so well that the men actually asked me to go on, though Donald had risen to speak. I know the backbone of the language is broken! Praise the Lord!"[483]

Years later, a Chinese language specialist asked Jonathan, "Wherever did you get your style of speaking? Whatever you do, don't change it! You can be understood over a wider area in China than anyone I know!" God's miraculous answer to Goforth's prayer lasted for a lifetime!

Overcoming Attacks of Disease and Death

As we have seen with other missionary pioneers, the price of ministry in foreign lands was often at great personal cost. While building the mission house in Linching, the hired coolies, instead of walking for fresh water to make their mortar, had been filling their pails from an "indescribably filthy pool" nearby.

The Goforths didn't realize that this was happening. It's just a sad reminder that no matter where we go in ministry, we must take extra care to make certain that things are done right. Even though we trust people, we must still make the effort as leaders to closely supervise those whom we lead. In the Goforths' case, it was a painfully difficult lesson.

Dysentery broke out, first among the workmen; then McGillivray's Chinese teacher contracted it, dying within days. McGillivray himself became sick but recovered quickly. Tragically, a few days later, precious Gertrude became deathly ill. The Goforths rushed her to a medical missionary in the next village, and everything was done to save her, but her little body could not fight the disease. On July 24, 1889, the Goforths' firstborn child passed away. Heartbroken Jonathan wrote home to family, saying, "Gertrude Madeline is dead. Ours is an awful loss....None but those who have lost a precious treasure can understand our feelings."[484]

There was no cemetery for foreigners in Linching, so Jonathan and Donald took her small body to Pangchwang, fifty miles away, while Rosalind stayed home, recovering from a bout of dysentery, as well. Two years later, the men would return to Pangchwang once again to bury the Goforths' second child, Donald, who died from an accidental fall. The heartbroken parents fell on their knees before the Lord, surrendering all they had in their hearts and lives to spread the gospel to China's lost millions.

Stepping into the Promised Land

Although Jonathan still did not have permission to set up a mission station in Changte, in August 1891, he, Rosalind, and their five-month-old son, Paul, as well as McGillivray, moved to Chuwang, a small village of mud huts just inside the Honan border.

The Goforths had prayed that God would give them dedicated converts from the very beginning. They knew of missionaries in China, India, Burma, and elsewhere who had worked for many years without gaining converts, but the Goforths didn't think that was God's will for them.

Although the pioneer years in Chuwang were difficult, they were also filled with great blessings. The Goforths had prayed that God would give them dedicated converts from the very beginning. They knew of missionaries in China, India, Burma, and elsewhere who had worked for many years without gaining converts, but the Goforths didn't think that was God's will for them. Since it was God's purpose to save men and women through His human channels, why not do so from the beginning?[485] The Goforths and McGillvray went out believing for people to get saved. They prayed, worked, and believed for their converts, and God rewarded their faith.

The Demon Had to Go

On a cold winter day in 1892, Jonathan met a Chinese addict who was just thirty-eight years old but was bent over like an old man, reduced to nothing but skin and bones due to his opium use. In earlier years, Wang Fulin had made a living as a public storyteller, but now he was no longer fit for work.

Each day, Goforth would attempt to reach out to him with the gospel. "Wang Fulin, I tremble for you. The road you have chosen leads straight to hell....But there is hope in our Savior. He can save to the uttermost all who come unto God through Him."[486] Finally, Wang Fulin received the love of Christ into his life, but he didn't have the strength to fight the stranglehold of opium. Jonathan refused to give up and took Wang to the hospital in Changte for medical help.

On the fifth day of withdrawal, Wang came face-to-face with the enemy of his soul! Whether it was a dream or reality, he described what he saw:

> I had decided that it was senseless to fight against my cravings any longer. As I ran to escape the hospital, I was amazed to find a deep wide pit between me and the exit. If I failed to make the jump, I would certainly fall into the pit and break my neck.
>
> A fiendish-looking creature beckoned me from the pit to jump, knowing I couldn't make it. Then I heard a voice above me, urging, "Wang Fulin! Resist, resist!" It seemed to me that this was God's last warning![487]

Wang Fulin resisted Satan, and his craving, and opium's power over him was broken forever. He came out of the struggle a new man in Christ. In just a short time, God would use Wang Fulin to greatly bless Jonathan's ministry.

In 1894, the Goforths took their first furlough to Canada. The year before, Rosalind had given birth to a beautiful blonde girl, Florence Elizabeth. While in Canada, she gave birth to their fifth child, a baby girl they named Helen.

Just before they returned to Canada, they received the distressful news that the Chuwang region had been hit by great floods, and, as had been the case in Chefoo, all of their personal possessions were destroyed. But Rosalind's faith in God to meet their needs was growing deeper with each passing year.

Nonstop Preaching All Day

Finally, the Goforths received permission to move the mission to Changte, a city of more than 100,000 people. This was the same land Jonathan had walked and prayed for six years earlier. With gratitude for God's blessings, he and McGillivray began their new work.

From the first day, the Chinese people flocked to see the foreign missionaries. "I am delighted with the attitude of the people towards us," Jonathan recorded. "The Master is working in the hearts of men!"[488]

In fact, the Changte Chinese were so happy to have the Goforths there that they began to visit the mission compound by the thousands. McGillivray and a Chinese minister were traveling throughout the region as evangelists, so the mission work fell to Jonathan and Rosalind. While Jonathan preached to crowds of men that filled the chapel from morning to night, Rosalind, now fluent in Chinese, taught the female visitors.

"Even at mealtime, our windows were banked with curious faces!" Rosalind wrote. At times, she would send for Jonathan and say, "Please come and help me! There are crowds of women—I am so tired from preaching I can hardly speak!"[489] The Goforths desperately needed reinforcements.

One early morning, Jonathan approached Rosalind with his Bible open and read, "'*My God shall supply all your need according to his riches in glory by Christ Jesus*' [Philippians 4:19]. Surely we need an evangelist to help us! Rosalind," he asked, "do you believe God can supply all our need and fulfill this promise to us? I do. Let us unite in prayer that God will send a man who can relieve me in the chapel. Then I can help you, as well."[490]

They knelt together, and Jonathan prayed a fervent, believing prayer. Rosalind admitted later that she was not as certain to receive an answer as her husband. "It was as if we were praying for rain from a clear sky!"

The Unusual Answer

Yet, true to His promise, God fulfilled His Word: *"Before they call, I will answer; and while they are yet speaking, I will hear"* (Isaiah 65:24). Before the Goforths had even prayed, God was sending the answer—and what a surprising answer it was!

Two mornings later, a familiar face appeared at the mission door. It was Wang Fulin, who had traveled for three days to reach them. He was still free from opium, but no one looked less like an answer to prayer! Still emaciated from his earlier drug abuse, he was plagued with a hacking cough and was dressed like a beggar. But the Lord sees far past outward appearances into a man's heart. Since becoming a Christian, Wang had grown in his relationship with Jesus Christ.

Within two hours, he was clean, dressed in one of Jonathan's Chinese robes, and seated in the chapel. "Wang Fulin will be sharing his testimony in chapel today," Goforth announced.

From the first day of his ministry, Wang Fulin spoke with the power of the Holy Spirit. He had one call on his life now—winning souls for Jesus Christ. He preached in the chapel every day for the next three years. With his natural gift for storytelling, he shared Bible stories that sprang to life, especially the one of the prodigal son, a parable he could personally relate to because of his years of drug abuse. He always spoke as "a dying man to dying men—and every day, men came to Christ under his anointed ministry."[491]

"Days of Blessing"

"I am constrained to say Glory to God in the highest," Jonathan recorded on December 16, 1895, "for He is graciously manifesting His divine power these days….Such a number of men coming day by day that we have kept up constant preaching on an average of eight hours a day….Never in Canada or here have I before realized such power of the Holy Spirit."[492]

In just five months in Changte, more than 25,000 men and women had visited the mission and heard the gospel message.

In just five months in Changte, more than 25,000 men and women had visited the mission and heard the gospel message. Many believed on the Lord Jesus Christ and were saved; some became Chinese evangelists, traveling throughout Honan to bring the gospel to their Chinese brethren.

"The days of blessing continue," Jonathan wrote a few years later. "These days, the people bethrong us….It has been our privilege to see the manifest signs of Holy Ghost power among them. None but the Holy Spirit could open these hearts to receive the truth!"[493]

A Year of Happiness and Heartache

As the Changte mission grew, so did the Goforth family, doubling in four years with the addition of Gracie, Ruth, and baby Wallace. The home mission board sent the funds for a new house to be built with wooden floors, glass windows, a water pump, a stove with a chimney, and a cellar. Praying that the house would be a blessing and not a hindrance to the Chinese people, Jonathan immediately set up an "open house" policy.

He and Rosalind gave daily house tours to hundreds of curious Chinese men and women. But before the curious visitors could see a single room, they heard the message of Christ's salvation. "Some may think," Goforth wrote later, "that receiving visitors is not real mission work, but I think it is. I put myself out to make friends with the people, and I reap the results when I go to their villages to preach."[494]

During a pagan feast in the fall of 1899, more than 1,800 men and 500 women went through the house in a single day! The tours opened the hearts of the people to the gospel of Christ and helped the foreign missionaries to overcome Chinese distrust as nothing else could have done.[495]

Then, suddenly, after five years of great blessings in Changte, the Goforths entered into a time of agonizing trials. In the fall of 1899, their three-year-old daughter, Gracie, contracted cholera and passed away from the debilitating effects it had on her little body. Eight months later, seven-year-old Florence was stricken with a raging fever. She was diagnosed with spinal meningitis, and in just a few days, she also went home to the Lord.

It was the days of the Boxer Rebellion, when Chinese rebels rose up to kill all the "foreign devils" in inland China, most of whom were missionaries.

Rosalind held her remaining four children closer to her heart and prayed for God's comfort and strength as the dark clouds of persecution loomed on the horizon.

"Foreign Devils": The Boxer Rebellion Begins

Who delivered us from so great a death, and doth deliver: in whom we trust that he will yet deliver us. (2 Corinthians 1:10)

"Never can we forget the year 1900," Rosalind Goforth wrote. "The clouds of persecution had begun to gather, and the mutterings of the coming storm were heard on all sides of us. The first indication we had of coming danger was when our mail carriers to and from Tientsin were stopped and our mail returned to us. We were literally cut off from the outside world."[496]

Within days of the stopped mail, Jonathan received the urgent telegram from Chefoo, the event described in the opening of this chapter. "Flee south! Northern route cut off by Boxers!" It was the days of the Boxer Rebellion, when Chinese rebels rose up to kill all the "foreign devils" in inland China, most of whom were missionaries.

Without delay, the Goforths set out on ten heavily packed carts, along with their four remaining children—Paul, nine; Helen, six; Ruth, two; and baby Wallace, barely eight months—as well as other missionaries, helpers, and men who would drive the oxen-led carts. They left Changte at daybreak on June 28, 1900, never dreaming that many of their fellow missionaries and personal friends were already being put to death by the merciless Boxers.[497]

"Kill! Kill!"

The cry "Kill! Kill!" from the mouths of Chinese rebels resounded across China's hills, plains, villages, and cities. It was only by God's grace that Jonathan had chosen an alternate route—south from Changte, bypassing the killing fields of Kaifengfu.

Traveling by cart in north China.
(From *China and the Gospel: An Illustrated Report of the China Inland Mission*, 1906)

Nine days into their journey, on July 7, 1900, the Goforth party reached the small town of Hsintien and hurried into an inn for the night. Although they barricaded the gates with their carts, a mob began to gather outside the yard, throwing stones against the house and demanding the foreigners' possessions. It was a sleepless night.

The next morning, the missionaries quietly prepared to leave, no one expressing what they all felt—death was close at hand.

"Suddenly, without the slightest warning," Rosalind wrote, "I was seized with an overwhelming fear of what might be awaiting us. It was not the fear of *after* death but of torture that took such awful hold of me." As they gathered together for prayer, Jonathan withdrew *Clarke's Scripture Promises* from his pocket and read the first verses he saw:

> *The eternal God is thy refuge, and underneath are the everlasting arms: and he shall thrust out the enemy from before thee; and shall say, Destroy them.* (Deuteronomy 33:27)

> *Thou art my help and my deliverer; make no tarrying, O my God.* (Psalm 40:17)

> *I will strengthen thee; yea, I will help thee; yea, I will uphold thee with the right hand of my righteousness....The Lord thy God will hold thy right hand, saying unto thee, Fear not; I will help thee.* (Isaiah 41:10, 13)

> *We may boldly say, The Lord is my helper, and I will not fear what man shall do unto me.* (Hebrews 13:6)

The anointing of the Word of God brought comfort and boldness to each one of the travelers. "From almost the first verse," Rosalind recorded, "my whole soul seemed flooded with great peace. All trace of panic vanished, and we felt God's presence was with us. Indeed, His presence was so real it could scarcely have been more so had we seen a visible form."[498]

One of the Goforths' greatest strengths for ministry and life was that they had learned the value of always turning to the Scriptures.

One of the Goforths' greatest strengths for ministry and life was that they had learned the value of always turning to the Scriptures. Instead of talking to people about their difficulties, they turned to chapters and verses in the Word of God—our great encourager and comforter.

Saved from Beheading

Passing through the town gates as they left Hsintien, Jonathan said, in hushed tones, "There is trouble ahead." Two hundred angry Chinese men armed with guns, daggers, and swords were waiting for them. As soon as the carts had passed through the gate, the men rushed forward in a frenzy.

Jonathan jumped from his cart and cried, "Take everything, but don't kill." He was answered with a powerful blow from a Chinese sword. Screaming and confusion followed.[499]

Although a man struck Jonathan on the neck, wielding his sword with two hands, the wide, blunt edge of the sword hit him instead of the sharp blade. What was meant to behead Jonathan only left a wide bruise around his neck. But the furor was far from over.

"Fear Not, They Are Praying for You"

Rosalind Goforth described the violent assault on her husband's life that day:

> The thick pith helmet Jonathan was wearing was slashed almost to pieces....His left arm, which was raised to protect his head, was slashed to the bone in several places. A terrible blow from behind struck the back of his head, denting the skull so deeply that it was a miracle it was not cleft in two.
>
> As Jonathan fell, he seemed to distinctly hear a voice saying, "Fear not, they are praying for you." As he stood up in a daze, a man rushed up as if to strike, but whispered instead, "Get away from the carts!"[500]

By this time, the crowd was furiously ransacking the Goforths' possessions. One man struck out at baby Wallace with his sword, but Rosalind protected him from the blow with a pillow. Within minutes, the assailants dropped their weapons and returned to the carts.

Bleeding profusely, Jonathan grabbed his wife's arm and whispered to her, "Get down quickly. We must get away." As they stumbled with the children through a hailstorm of stones, one of the Chinese men shouted, "We've killed her husband—let her go," and they went back to their pilfering.[501]

A Plot to Kill Them All

Wounded and dazed, the entire Goforth party reached a nearby village where more sympathetic Chinese villagers provided food, water, and a gray medicinal powder that stopped Jonathan's bleeding and undoubtedly saved his life. As he lay on a cot looking white and ill, he comforted Rosalind with the words "Only *pray*. The Lord will give me strength, as long as He still has work for me to do."[502]

The party reached the city of Nang Yang Fu a few days later, where one of their cart drivers overheard a sinister plot being devised against them. The city's magistrate had commissioned a band of fifty soldiers to lay in ambush outside of the city. When the Goforth team continued their travels the next morning, they would all be murdered along the roadside. As part of the deception, the magistrate promised to send soldiers "to protect the missionaries on their way."

How would God deliver them this time? "God's hand was not too short that it could not save," Jonathan reminded them. They would put their trust in Him!

"A God of Deliverance"

Before dawn the next morning, the missionaries left, accompanied by the Chinese soldiers. Barely out of the city, they suddenly stopped the carts when one of the workers yelled, "Paul and Mr. Griffith are missing!" For over an hour, the Goforths anxiously searched on foot for their eldest child and the older missionary, and then an overwhelming peace enveloped them. The Lord was saying, "Peace. Be still." Jonathan left a wagon behind with a trusted servant to continue the search. He, Rosalind, and the rest of the party would continue on their journey with the soldiers.

When they made their way back to the other carts, the Goforths beheld an amazing sight! While they had been searching for Paul, the weary soldiers had climbed into the back of the carts and had fallen fast asleep! They were unaware as the cart drivers left the village on secondary roads leading far away from the site of the intended ambush. When the soldiers woke up miles later in the jungle, they were infuriated; but after shouts and threats, they left the missionaries and returned to the city. "Again, we saw that God was indeed a God of deliverance.... Never had the love of God seemed so wonderful as in that hour!"[503]

The Devil Loses

The horror was over! Within a day, Paul and Mr. Griffith were safely located, and the missionary party reached the city of Fancheng (modern-day Xiangfan) at midnight the next day. They were immediately placed on houseboats to travel the Han River to Hankow; the four Goforth children wept tears of joy at the sight of bread and milk on the boat. The entire party traveled the Yangtze River to the safety of Shanghai. By God's mercy, they had been saved from death! Since all of their possessions were gone once more, several Chinese seamstresses offered to sew clothes for the family's long voyage home to Canada.

On furlough, the Lord gave Jonathan hundreds of opportunities throughout Canada to share the story of how God had miraculously delivered them from the Boxer Rebellion. During the two years at home, Rosalind delivered their ninth child, a baby girl named Constance.

The Gospel Invasion

In January 1902, Jonathan returned "home" to Changte. Miraculously, none of Changte's Chinese Christians had been killed during the Boxer massacre, although they, like Jonathan, knew what it meant "to bear in their bodies the mark of Jesus Christ."[504] As soon as Rosalind received word that it was safe to join him, she sailed for China in the summer with their five children. She left the two oldest, Paul, eleven, and Helen, eight, at the Chefoo school for missionary children en route to Honan.

When Rosalind arrived, Jonathan could hardly wait to share his bold new vision for evangelizing Honan. "My plan," he said, "is to have one of my helpers rent a suitable place in each town in the outlying areas for us to live in. As a family, we will stay one month at each center and carry on aggressive evangelism.... Then, at the end of the month, we will leave an evangelist behind to teach the new believers while we go on to the next place to open it in the same way!"[505] Jonathan glowed with anticipation as he spoke, but Rosalind cringed in fear.

He was asking her to travel through Honan's poorest villages with Ruth, Wallace, and baby Constance? Exposing them to the diseases of smallpox, cholera, dysentery, and typhus? Rosalind thought of their four precious children already buried in Chinese soil and couldn't bear the thought of putting the others in danger. Jonathan was ready to commit his family to the life of a traveling evangelist; Rosalind was not.

She struggled long and hard with the decision. But when the two youngest children became ill at the mission house in Changte, Rosalind realized that sickness could find them anywhere and that she belonged in ministry beside her husband. Wallace recovered quickly, but Constance was too ill from dysentery to survive. She was the last of the Goforth children to die from China's tropical illnesses. During the following years, Rosalind gave birth to the last of their eleven children: Mary in 1903, and Frederick in 1906.

Jonathan Goforth

Revival Is Born

When Jonathan Goforth turned forty-five years old, a strange restlessness came over him. He could report that, during the three years he and his family had traveled throughout Honan, "without one exception, every place in which we stayed for a month and carried on this aggressive evangelism, we left behind what later became a growing church."[506] Still, his heart's prayer was, "I want to see more of God."

That summer of 1904, a small booklet on the Welsh Revival arrived from a supporter in England. The Holy Spirit was sweeping through Wales, bringing tens of thousands of people to Christ. Thrilled with what he read, Jonathan seriously considered the role the Holy Spirit played in Christian conversion. "*And when* [the Holy Spirit] *is come, he will reprove the world of sin, and of righteousness, and of judgment*" (John 16:8).

Not long after, a missionary friend in India sent him a book entitled *The Great Awakening,* which contains excerpts of Charles Finney's *Lectures on Revival.* After reading Finney's words over and over, Jonathan explained to Rosalind, "Revival simply means this: The spiritual laws governing a spiritual harvest are as real and tangible as the laws governing the natural harvest. If Finney is right, and I believe he is, I am going to find out what those laws are and obey them, no matter what the cost may be!"[507]

Immediately, Goforth began an in-depth study of the Holy Spirit in the Scriptures, taking notes in the margin of his Chinese Bible. He also wrote home requesting copies of Finney's autobiography and *Lectures on Revival.* He spent so many hours studying that Rosalind became concerned. Placing his hands on his wife's shoulders, Jonathan exclaimed, "Oh, Rose, even you do not understand! I feel like one who has tapped a mine of wealth! It is so wonderful! If only I could get others to see it!"[508] Jonathan Goforth was discovering the personal power of the Holy Spirit in the life of a believer in Jesus Christ.

Cooperating with the Holy Spirit

In early 1906, Jonathan left Changte to preach to the Chinese pilgrims attending a Buddhist festival in Hsunhsien. One evening, the Christian mission there was filled with men and women who did not know Christ.

As Goforth preached a message on 1 Peter 2:24, "*Who his own self bare our sins in his own body on the tree,*" he sensed the anointing of the Holy Spirit speaking through him in a powerful new way, opening the hearts of the people who listened. When he asked for decisions for Christ, nearly the whole congregation stood to its feet.

Goforth turned to the Chinese evangelists standing behind him and signaled to them to go out and pray among the people. Instead, they just stood looking at him in wonder. "Brother," one whispered, "the Holy Spirit for whom we have prayed so long was here in very deed tonight!"[509]

For the next year, every place where Jonathan preached, the Holy Spirit moved and people flocked to the altar to accept Christ. News of a Korean revival had reached China; Goforth, with the missionary director, Dr. R. McKay, made immediate plans to travel to Seoul. After his visit to Korea, Jonathan Goforth's life would never be the same.

The Korean Revival of 1907

The Korean Revival bloomed from the cornerstone of all great revivals—fervent prayer. In the summer of 1906, a group of Presbyterian and Methodist Christians in Pyongyang (present capital of North Korea) committed to praying together each day at four o'clock for the Holy Spirit to revive Korea. In January 1907, a Presbyterian and Methodist Bible conference was held in Pyongyang. During a missionary message on the importance of sharing the love of Christ among Christians, the Holy Spirit fell on the congregation.

"Instantly, it was realized," Goforth explained, "that the barriers had fallen, and that God, the Holy One, had come. Conviction of sin swept the audience. The service commenced at seven o'clock on Sunday evening and did not end until two o'clock Monday morning; yet during all that time, dozens were standing weeping, awaiting their turn to confess. Day after day, the people assembled, and always it was manifest that the Refiner was in His temple."[510]

Revival blazed through Korea, and 50,000 people came to Christ in that first year alone. The Holy Spirit was moving, and Korea was set on fire! The biggest prayer meeting in the world was being held in Seoul, Korea. For one year, the average weekly attendance at prayer meetings was 1,100. The revival was still going strong in 1910; in October of that year, 4,000 Koreans were baptized in one week.

"The Korean movement," Jonathan wrote in his book *By My Spirit*, "was of incalculable significance in my life because it showed me at firsthand the boundless possibilities of the revival method....Korea made me feel...that this was God's plan for setting the world aflame....Those missionaries seemed to carry us right up to the very Throne of God."[511]

"Is It Your Work or Mine?"

Goforth and McKay decided to travel back to Honan by way of Manchuria—a decision that would change the direction of Jonathan's ministry. As he preached at mission stations along the way, he shared testimonies of the Holy Spirit's anointing in Korea. Each of the missionary leaders begged him to return to Manchuria to conduct ten-day prayer meetings in his village.

In Changte, the Honan Presbytery willingly released Jonathan from his mission work to answer the call for Manchuria. His evangelistic travels would take him throughout the Manchurian province for a year, so Rosalind and the five children went home to Canada for an extended furlough. Paul was already there finishing his education.

With his family gone, Jonathan devoted himself wholly to the revival. In each village, he proclaimed, "The greatness of the work in Korea is '*not by might, nor by power, but by my spirit, saith the* LORD *of hosts*' [Zechariah 4:6]."

"The cross burns like a living fire in the heart of every address," he continued. The Korean people wept in repentance because they had taken Jesus Christ for granted, not living a life of gratitude and love toward the One who had redeemed them with His blood. "This is what has pricked them to the heart and caused multitudes to break out into a lamentable cry, 'God be merciful to me a sinner.'"[512]

In the beginning of the Manchurian revival, Jonathan was afraid he wouldn't know what to say as he addressed the Manchurian Christians. "I don't know how to conduct a revival," he protested in prayer. But the Lord told him, "Give them what I have given you."

When his first messages in Mukden seemed to fall on deaf ears, again he cried out to God in prayer. "What is the use of my coming here? These people are not seeking after the Holy Spirit. What can I do?" The Lord's voice seemed to come right back at him, "Is it your work or Mine? Can I not do a sovereign work? '*Call unto me, and I will answer thee, and show thee great and mighty things, which thou knowest not*' [Jeremiah 33:3]."[513]

Revival Sweeps Through Manchuria

From that day forward, the Holy Spirit moved. Before the week was over, the pastor and elders of the Mukden mission had repented of their hidden sins before God and the congregation, confessing their stealing, infighting, and adultery. Each church leader tearfully acknowledged, "I have disgraced the holy office. I herewith resign." There was weeping in prayer and confession as the Holy Spirit penetrated the hearts of the people.

When the tears finally ceased, the congregation unanimously reassured the pastor and agreed to appoint him to be their pastor once again. In the same forgiving way, they reinstated each of the elders, as well; their trust in the leadership had been restored. Revival swept through the congregation; hearts were rededicated to the Lord, and new believers were consecrated to Christ. The move of the Holy Spirit was flourishing in Manchuria!

As Jonathan traveled, the revival enveloped town after town. At first, skeptical missionaries greeted him with the warning, "Don't expect the same results here. We are hardheaded Presbyterians and we do not believe in any high emotionalism." But once the Spirit of God moved upon hearts, tears, prayers of repentance, and forgiveness would soon follow.

One of those "hardheaded" Canadian missionaries wrote a glowing letter home about the revival in Chinchow: "The church was crowded to the door with reverent attention on every face. The very singing was vibrant with new joy and vigor….The people knelt for prayer, silent at first, but soon, one here and another there began to pray aloud. The voices grew into a great wave of united supplication and died down into an undertone of weeping. The floor was wet with a pool of tears. The very air seemed electric!"[514]

In Shinminfu, where fifty-four Chinese Christians had been martyred during the Boxer Rebellion, many of the grieving family members still lived in the bondage of unforgiveness. As they confessed the anguish in their hearts, they were set free from their sins, such as acts of vengeance and even murder.

In each mission station, great waves of prayer would sweep the congregation, and lives were changed: Christians were cleansed, opium addicts were set free, and new believers were won to Christ. Canadian and British missionaries sent exciting letters home, celebrating the glorious revival; before long, the movement had gained worldwide attention.

Jonathan Goforth

"Jonathan Goforth went up to Manchuria an unknown missionary," Rosalind wrote in his biography. "He returned a few weeks later with the limelight of the Christian world upon him!"[515]

Revival Power in Changte

It was time for Goforth to return to his home base in Changte. His fellow missionaries, some skeptical of the reports from Manchuria, questioned whether the Holy Spirit would move with power in Honan, where "Goforth's faults and weaknesses were known." Seriously concerned, Jonathan opened the Word to Malachi 1:11: *"From the rising of the sun even unto the going down of the same my name shall be great among the Gentiles."*[516] The clear answer from the Lord restored Jonathan's faith. God would move mightily among the Gentiles; Jonathan needed to remain surrendered to the Holy Spirit.

From that point on, Goforth believed that "God had marked Changte for a special outpouring of divine blessing." By the seventh day of meetings, the presence of God became so powerful that Jonathan could not even preach a message. People crowded the altar to confess their sins, receive God's cleansing, and praise the Lord in His palpable presence. From all over China, Christians streamed into the city to experience the Changte revival and the anointing of God's Spirit in that place.

Casting Out Demons

In Kwangchow, Goforth and his evangelistic team came into contact with two demon-possessed people. The first was the wife of a well-known Chinese evangelist. When the evangelist began the first morning meeting, his wife disturbed everyone by crying out, "You're a pretty one to be leading a prayer meeting after the way that you have sinned." With a loud voice, she revealed every sin he had ever committed, even those he had committed before she met him. Recognizing an evil spirit was speaking, her husband answered, "While I was your slave, I did those things. But I am your slave no longer. The Lord Jesus has changed my heart." In the name of Jesus Christ, the woman was delivered from the evil spirit that very day.[517]

The second demon-possessed person was a non-Christian who came into a meeting and began to shout profanities in the middle of the service. When Jonathan spoke the name Jesus of Nazareth, the man began to writhe in his chair. As

Goforth prayed from the stage, an elder standing nearby placed his hand on the man's head and cried out, "Foul fiend, in the name of Jesus Christ of Nazareth, come out of him!" The man gagged and fell to the floor. When he stood a few minutes later, he was pale and trembling but in his right mind. He became a believer. Years later, both of these people were still walking with Christ, free from the enemy's power.518

Jesus told the disciples they would be sent out to heal and to cast out demons. Deliverance is still needed today in our modern world; the power to deliver did not end with the disciples. We are told to cast out demons wherever we encounter them, no matter where we are in the world. *"And these signs shall follow them that believe; in my name shall they cast out devils"* (Mark 16:17).

"What Is Revival?"

"What is revival," Goforth wrote in his book *By My Spirit*, "but simply the Spirit of God fully controlling in the surrendered life? It must always be possible then, as long as man yields. But are we ready to receive Him? Are we ready to pay the price of Holy Ghost revival?

"Finally, the call to revival must be a call to exalt Jesus Christ in our hearts as the King of Kings and Lord of Lords. He is like an Everest peak, rising from the level plain. There must be room only for Him, if we would have Him dwell with us at all."[519]

Speaking on behalf of Goforth and the Changte revival, Jonathan's close friend Dr. Murdock McKensie wrote to the home board:

> What has happened in Changte? Nothing more than what God has promised from the beginning. When the Holy Spirit is poured out He will convict the world of sin. The church in Changte has been baptized by the Holy Spirit and cleansed, and the cry of all of us here is, "Why did we so long despise His working, and trust in other ways to build up His kingdom?"
>
> What weighed most heavily on the conscience of all was that we had so long been grieving the Holy Spirit by not giving Him His rightful place in our hearts and in our work! While believing in Him, we had not trusted in Him to work in and through us....May we never forget that lesson!"[520]

For the next decade, Jonathan Goforth led revival meetings all over China. Often, he would preach for eight hours a day to crowds of up to 25,000 people. Wherever he preached, huge crowds of sinners experienced the saving grace of Jesus Christ, and an unknown multitude of Christians were brought into a closer relationship with God. Sick marriages were healed, opium addicts were powerfully delivered, and a new unity and love developed among Christian leaders throughout the country.

At times, his meetings looked like they were taken out of the book of Acts. He honored the move of the Holy Spirit within them and gave the Lord room to do what He wanted among the people.

For the next decade, Jonathan Goforth led revival meetings all over China. Often, he would preach for eight hours a day to crowds of up to 25,000 people.

Sharing the Vision in Great Britain

After the power of God fell in Manchuria and Changte, Goforth was excited to share the miraculous events with his fellow ministers in Canada. But his furlough in 1910 was one of the most disappointing times of his life.

From the first, many Canadian ministers accused him of using emotionalism to reach the unsaved in China. When Jonathan spoke to the Presbyterian General Assembly about the need for a Holy Spirit revival in Canada, as well, some pastors viewed him as a Spirit-filled man of vision, while others saw him as a fanatic to be shunned. Few Canadian churches opened their pulpits to him to deliver a revival message.[521]

The Goforths' furlough was salvaged by ministry opportunities that opened in the British Isles. Jonathan was invited to make an address at the famous World Missionary Conference of 1910 in Edinburgh, Scotland. With his family accompanying him, Goforth went on to conduct revival meetings in Edinburgh, Glasgow, and Wales. Most important, he had the opportunity to speak at Charles Spurgeon's Metropolitan Tabernacle for ten days, and then led a week of meetings in Keswick alongside British evangelist F. B. Meyer.

At the end of the successful Keswick meetings, Jonathan was pleasantly surprised when he received an invitation to serve as a missionary in the British Isles for a year. He was eager to accept the offer, but a cable from Canada ended those plans. "Return to China. Your field is there." Without protest, Jonathan received this as God's direction and returned to Changte with his family. A few years later, to show unanimous support of Goforth's revival ministry, his alma mater, Knox College, awarded him an honorary doctor of divinity.

"Intolerant!"

By the early twentieth century, "higher criticism," or "modernism," was being taught in many Bible schools and seminaries in the Western world. (It is still being taught in increasing amounts in mainline seminaries today.) Challenging the Bible as the inerrant Word of God, the "modernist" Bible scholars used human reasoning to interpret the Scriptures, searching for outside historical "proof" to determine which verses of the Bible were "true" and which were "human myths." Jonathon Goforth was incensed!

"It is a sorry state of affairs when professors, in the name of scholarship, think that their business is to undermine belief in the Word of God! We can't shut our eyes to the fact that this undermining has been done, and is being done, and the present condition of the church and the world shows the appalling outcome!"[522]

Goforth was never one to mince words when he believed the cause of Christ was being challenged. As a result, the Honan Presbytery and even the Home Board labeled him "intolerant."

"Intolerant!" he blazed back. "If you saw one undermining the foundation of a structure you, and others with you, had given the best of their lives to build, would it be intolerant to use every ounce of strength in combating the wrecker?"[523]

When the Canadian Home Board made a policy decision that missionaries on the field were free to make their own choice—they could either proclaim the inerrancy of the whole Bible or teach "the modernist" version of Scripture—Jonathan Goforth sent in his resignation.

Changes and Blessings

Not wanting to lose their most famous missionary on the field, the Home Board refused to accept his resignation. They asked Goforth to please remain on a small salary and continue his evangelism work in Honan province, giving up his Changte home. From that point on, he would be personally responsible for funding all his traveling and ministry expenses.

Jonathan agreed with the proposal; he did not want to desert the millions of unreached Chinese. With the board exercising less power over him, he could minister wherever the Holy Spirit led him, and the God of his deliverance would also be the God of provision. He reminded Rosalind, "All the resources of the Godhead are at our disposal!"

Although they had to leave their Changte home, the Goforths were soon given a missionary house in Kikungshan, a beautiful mountain plateau with a majestic view of a valley one thousand feet below. It was their home base, but every ten days, they preached in a new place, Jonathan eager to share the message of "the fullness of the Christ-life through the Holy Spirit's indwelling."[524] It was easier to travel now, because all of the children were currently living in Canada to finish their education or begin their adult lives.

At one session, General Feng broke down in front of his officers, crying for his beloved country and the Communist threat that was so close at hand. He pleaded with his men to join him in prayer for the future of their nation.

The Goforth Evangelistic Trust Fund that had been set up in Canada on their last furlough began to receive financial support from Christians around the world, even though financial appeals were never made. God's hand was on the ministry, and every need was met.

China's Christian General

In the summer of 1919, Jonathan received an unexpected invitation from General Feng Yu Hsiang of the Chinese Army to hold revival meetings for the thousands of officers and soldiers under his command. It led to one of the most fruitful ministries of his life.

The Goforths traveled south of the Yangtze River into the blazing heat of central China to meet with the general and his troops. Twice each day, Jonathan shared the message of Christ's salvation with more than one thousand Chinese officers, while Rosalind shared the love of Christ with their wives. At one session, General Feng broke down in front of his officers, crying for his beloved country and the Communist threat that was so close at hand. He pleaded with his men to join him in prayer for the future of their nation.[525] From this point on, General Feng was known as the "Christian General" throughout China.

"A few years ago," Jonathan wrote, "General Feng and all of his men were heathen. Now, for its size, the army under General Feng is the greatest Christian army on earth. We spent thirteen days in meetings with the army. On the last day, we baptized 960 men. That same day, 4,606 officers and soldiers partook of Communion." Within a short time, Goforth had baptized an additional 4,000 soldiers.[526]

In every part of his ministry, souls were being saved. "I am sixty-five today," Jonathan wrote. "Oh, how I covet, more than a miser does his gold, twenty more years of this soul-saving work."[527]

The Union Crisis

If ever a problem arose in Goforth's ministry, it was always related to church government, lukewarm Christians, or church committees. In 1925, a new situation emerged in Canada that required a great deal of prayer.

The Presbyterian Church of Canada was headed for a major denominational split. More than two-thirds of the Presbyterian congregations wanted to merge with the country's Methodist and Congregational churches to form a new denomination, the United Church of Canada. Goforth was uncertain what to do until he realized that those who wanted to break off tended to be more "modernist."

On January 5, 1926, Goforth voted to personally remain within the Canadian Presbyterian church. At sixty-eight years old, he was eager to continue his service in the mission field of China, and to stay out of church politics. His mission board agreed to send him back, as long as he appointed a younger missionary to travel as his assistant. Goforth chose Allan Reoch, who gratefully accepted his invitation and went to China with the Goforths, including their daughter Mary and her missionary husband, Robert Moynan.

By this time, the Goforths' six adult children were leading productive Christian lives. Ruth and Mary were married to Presbyterian missionaries, and Helen was married to a Christian surgeon, George Van Gorder, who spent several years teaching at a medical hospital in Peking. Paul and Fred were studying to serve as pastors, as well. But Wallace had chosen a different path, serving in the military instead of the ministry, rising to the rank of lieutenant colonel.

"Pack for Manchuria!"

Arriving back in China, Jonathan took Reoch to visit the growing churches in Changte, while Rosalind remained in Peking. The Goforths had to find a new place of ministry, since the North Honan province was now part of the Union Church. In January 1927, Goforth received a letter from the Irish Presbyterian Mission, inviting him to open a mission in Manchuria. With the enthusiasm of a young man offered his first missionary assignment, Jonathan sent a telegraph to Rosalind in Peking—"Pack for Manchuria!"[528]

God had chosen to send the lifelong missionaries to a province north of the Great Wall they had always called "the frozen land of snow and ice." Yet, God's plan was perfect. He had chosen the fiery sixty-eight-year-old revivalist for Manchuria because it was a land ripe for harvest—and, for the next eight years, the windows of heaven were opened!

What a time to minister in Manchuria! Thousands of refugees were flooding in from other provinces in north China because of political upheaval. When the Goforths arrived in Manchuria, "almost a million settlers from Honan, Chihli, and Shantung provinces poured in that same spring."[529] Towns were filled to capacity; new Chinese settlers were looking for stability.

During their first month of ministry in the city of Szepingkai, there were two hundred decisions to accept Christ. Excitedly, Jonathan wrote the mission board to send more recruits, but, lacking the necessary funds, they responded, "No recruits for an indefinite period." So he turned to prayer, asking God for more laborers.

In God's providential timing, a Bible school in Shantung, north China, had a graduating class of twenty missionary students with no place to minister. Dr. John Hayes, the headmaster, wrote a letter to Jonathan asking him if he could use a few of these young workers. Goforth's immediate reply was, "Send us all you can!" When Rosalind questioned warily, "But Jonathan, they can't live on air—where is the money to come for their support?" Jonathan gently chided her, "Where is your faith? If God sends us men, He will send money for their support."[530] And He did!

Seventy Years and Speeding Up

God's Word tell us that the days of the righteous get brighter and brighter: *"But the path of the righteous is like the light of dawn, that shines brighter and brighter until the full day*" (Proverbs 4:18 NASB). That was certainly true of the single-hearted Jonathan Goforth.

The following year, Goforth and his team opened a new mission field in the city of Taonan. Within the first two weeks, four hundred believers came to Christ. Eventually, they opened thirty mission outposts throughout Manchuria, having enough funds to place thirty team members on full salary. By now, Goforth had passed his seventieth birthday, but instead of slowing down, he seemed to speed up to get everything done while he still had the time.

The following year, Goforth and his team opened a new mission field in the city of Taonan. Within the first two weeks, four hundred believers came to Christ.

The Goforth's youngest son, Frederick, then twenty-three years old, was training for ministry in Canada. He visited his parents in Manchuria in 1929 and typed the manuscript for Jonathan's book *By My Spirit* as his father dictated stories of the Korean and Manchurian revivals.

In 1930, on their last furlough to Canada, the Goforths wrote the book *Miracle Lives of China*. Rosalind had successful cataract surgery that same year, but Jonathan suffered a severe retinal dislocation in his right eye. After several unsuccessful surgeries, he was resigned to losing his sight in that eye. In 1932, the Goforths returned once more to Manchuria, accompanied by their oldest son, Paul, who had been accepted by the Canadian Home Board as a missionary to China.

"If we will not do this work for Him, these millions shall perish," Jonathan wrote of his final return to China. "As long as the Lord of the Harvest gives me strength, I dare not stand still, but must extend the work."[531]

Canada Needs You

One night in late March 1933, Jonathan groped into the bedroom, where Rosalind had already fallen asleep. Jonathan woke her and whispered, "I fear the retina of my left eye has been dislodged."[532] The Goforths made the long trip to Peking, where Jonathan received painful eye injections for four months. In the end, nothing was successful. At seventy-four years old, Jonathan Goforth was completely blind but without complaint. He was determined to continue the Lord's work while he still had strength for the task.

Between the cutback in mission funds and the loss of his sight, Jonathan exclaimed, "The devil is trying his best to wreck our mission, but God is with us and He will bring us through!"[533]

Early in 1934, Jonathan started another full campaign of revival meetings in Manchuria, in spite of the "bitterest of winter blizzards." He had great success, even while fighting the symptoms of pneumonia. That same year, he received letters from two prominent Canadian pastors, asking him to consider returning home. "Have you ever thought that God may be demanding the greater sacrifice of coming home? That out of your ripe experience you might kindle the fires of missionary zeal that are on the decline in the home church?"[534]

Faithful Servant of Jesus Christ

Jonathan continued to preach Christ's salvation to eager men and women in China until November 1934, when Rosalind became seriously ill. He could no longer ignore the inevitable—it was time to go home. Paul was still on the mission field in China, so he was selected to accompany his parents to Canada. Jonathan's final missionary report for Manchuria was full of good news; in 1934, he listed 966 adult baptisms and $14,665 given by Chinese Christians to support the Manchurian missions. Jesus was building His church in the far northern lands of China.[535]

As the train carrying the Goforths pulled out of the Szepingkai station, a banner flew above them that read, "Faithful Servant of Jesus Christ!" Hundreds of Chinese Christians, saddened by their loss, crowded the platform for one last glimpse of their beloved pastor. The Goforths boarded the *Empress of Japan* and traveled one last time across the Pacific Ocean, celebrating Jonathan's seventy-sixth birthday while still aboard the ship.

Jonathan and Rosalind Goforth[536]

As soon as he reached Canada, Goforth was overwhelmed with requests to speak at churches and at meetings of mission organizations. His schedule included ten meetings a week. More doors opened throughout Canada and the United States than he could possibly enter. In the spring of 1936, at seventy-seven years old, Goforth spoke at revival meetings in Keswick, New Jersey, for ten days, and then traveled with Rosalind to Ben Lippen in Asheville, North Carolina, to enjoy a month-long Christian conference.

The Need for "Aggressive Evangelism"

Back in Toronto in September 1936, the seventy-seven-year-old Goforth gave twenty-two addresses in just seventeen days, never willing to pass up the opportunity to preach on "aggressive evangelism led by the Holy Spirit"—the most important part of mission work. "Oh," he had written earlier, "that God would give me an opportunity before I pass on to demonstrate to missionaries and to the home church what results would follow if we but gave God a chance by broadcasting this wonderful message of salvation by every possible means in our power!"[537]

In early October, the Goforths stayed at the home of their son Frederick, now an ordained Presbyterian minister. When Jonathan gave an address at Frederick's church on how the Spirit's fire swept Korea, the audience described his face as "radiant…aglow with the love of Christ." He was unusually quiet after the meeting, declining to eat supper because he was experiencing indigestion.

The seventy-seven-year-old Goforth gave twenty-two addresses in just seventeen days, never willing to pass up the opportunity to preach on "aggressive evangelism led by the Holy Spirit"—the most important part of mission work.

The following morning, October 8, 1936, Rosalind rose to get ready for the day. She saw that Jonathan was sleeping peacefully, his right cheek resting on his hand. After dressing and walking to his bedside, she realized he was no longer asleep but had quietly graduated to the eternal kingdom of God.

Just weeks earlier, at Ben Lippen, he had told her, "I rejoice to know that the next face I see will be my Savior's!" That morning, the seventy-seven-year-old missionary giant met his Savior face-to-face. *"I shall be satisfied when I awake with thy likeness"* (Psalm 17:15), the psalmist had written thousands of years earlier.

Jonathan Goforth's Coronation

On October 10, 1936, at Knox Church in Toronto, funeral services were held for the beloved missionary. "I think of today as being Jonathan Goforth's Coronation!" was the first line of his eulogy at the church service.

"Jonathan Goforth was a man like the apostle Paul....He had undaunted courage and perseverance; he had unflagging zeal and earnestness; and he had a heart which believed unto righteousness. He was a God-intoxicated man—fully surrendered and consecrated. Above all, he was humble.

"He was baptized with the Holy Ghost and with fire. He was filled with the Spirit, because he was empty of self....He knew what it was to pray the prayer of faith in the Holy Ghost."[539]

For almost fifty years, Rosalind Goforth had been a faithful partner to her pioneer husband. Following the call from God had cost the Goforths dearly; Rosalind had delivered eleven children in eighteen years, burying five of them in Chinese soil. She had devoted forty-seven years to serving beside her husband in China, and she devoted six years after his death to writing about their ministry together.

In 1937, Rosalind published Jonathan's biography, *Goforth of China,* a Christian classic about her husband's Spirit-filled ministry. Three years later, she wrote her own autobiography, *Climbing: Memories of a Missionary's Wife.* On May 31, 1942, at the age of seventy-eight, Rosalind died peacefully in Toronto. During her final moments, "her face lit up with expectation, and her last words rang with confidence: 'This is the summons from my King. I am ready to go!'"[540] She was buried in Mount Pleasant Cemetery, Toronto, beside her beloved husband.

"On and On Forever"

"We will never know how far-reaching Jonathan's ministry has gone," a friend wrote to Rosalind just after Jonathan's death. "I believe it will go on and on forever."[541]

It has been one hundred years since Jonathan Goforth rode on carts through the villages of China, sharing the gospel of Jesus Christ to thousands who eagerly embraced his message. It has been almost seventy years since the Chinese Communists attempted to slam the doors to the gospel of Jesus Christ forever. But the seed of salvation in Christ that was planted by Jonathan and Rosalind Goforth still flourishes. It cannot be weeded out by any human or supernatural force. The gospel goes *"on and on."*

At the time of Goforth's death, there were an estimated 200,000 Christians in China. By 1949, when the Communists expelled all Christian missionaries, that number had risen to 700,000. Today, although the official Chinese government estimate of Christians is only 14 million, independent organizations have estimated there are nearly 100 million Christians in mainland China—the majority of them in unofficial home churches. According to the 2007 International Religious Freedom Report, published by the U.S. Embassy in Beijing, since the mid-twentieth century, China has had the fastest growth in the number of Christians of any nation in the world, even under Communist persecution.

How many of these Christians were indirectly affected by Jonathan Goforth's ministry? There is no way to know for certain. However, the largest percentage of Christians in the nation resides in Henan Province in northern China, the field where Goforth served so faithfully for most of his ministry! Anointed by the Holy Spirit, that ministry goes *on and on* in China today.

In the later years of Goforth's life, when young missionaries would ask him for the secret of his success in winning converts, Jonathan's reply was always the same: "Because I just give God a chance to speak to souls through His own Word. My only secret in getting at the heart of big sinners is to show them their need and tell them of a Saviour abundantly able to save....And that [the sinner] can only attain unto the righteousness of God through faith in the Lord Jesus Christ, he readily yields."[542]

~

As we draw *God's Generals: The Missionaries* to a close, let us look at a text that best describes Jonathan Goforth's life—and the lives of other missionary generals, such as William Carey, Hudson Taylor, Amy Carmichael, and everyone who has obeyed the call to preach Christ to the lost souls of the world:

> *But one thing I do, forgetting those things which are behind and reaching forward to those things which are ahead, I press toward the goal for the prize of the upward call of God in Christ Jesus.* (Philippians 3:13–14 NKJV)

Will you press toward the high calling of God in Jesus Christ?

Will you be a witness for Him in your city, your country, or even to the far ends of the earth?

Will you go?

✯✯✯✯✯

ENDNOTES

Chapter 1: Zinzendorf

1. Paul Wemmer, *Count Zinzendorf and the Spirit of the Moravians* (Camarillo, CA: Xulon Press/Salem Communications, 2013), 36.
2. J. E. Hutton, *A History of the Moravian Church, 2nd ed.* (London: Moravian Publication Office, 1909), 175–176.
3. Ibid., 175.
4. Ibid., 177.
5. Janet Benge and Geoff Benge, *Count Zinzendorf: Firstfruit* (Seattle, WA: YWAM Publishing, 2005), 25.
6. Ibid., 26.
7. Hutton, *History of the Moravian Church*, 116.
8. Wemmer, *Count Zinzendorf and the Spirit of the Moravians*, 52.
9. Ibid., 53.
10. Ibid., 55.
11. Ibid.
12. August Gottlieb Spangenberg, *The Life of Nicholas Lewis, Count Zinzendorf*, trans. Samuel Jackson (London: Samuel Holdsworth, Amen-Corner, 1838), chapter 1.
13. Hutton, *History of the Moravian Church*, 120.
14. Ibid., 126.
15. For more information on John Hus, see *God's Generals: The Roaring Reformers* by Roberts Liardon (New Kensington, PA: Whitaker House, 2003).
16. Hutton, *History of the Moravian Church*, 245.
17. Wemmer, *Count Zinzendorf and the Spirit of the Moravians*, 77.
18. Hutton, *History of the Moravian Church*, 132.
19. Ibid., 131.
20. Ibid.
21. Spangenberg, *Life of Nicholas Lewis Count Zinzendorf*, chapter 3.
22. Wemmer, *Count Zinzendorf and the Spirit of the Moravians*, 98–99.
23. Ibid., 110.
24. Hutton, *History of the Moravian Church*, 148.
25. Ibid., 142.
26. Ibid., 149.
27. Ibid., 150.
28. Ibid., 156.
29. Spangenberg, *Life of Nicholas Lewis, Count Zinzendorf*, chapter 3.
30. Benge and Benge, *Count Zinzendorf: Firstfruit*, 107–108.

31. Spangenberg, *Life of Nicholas Lewis, Count Zinzendorf*, chapter 4.
32. Levin Theodore Reichel, *The Early History of the Church of the United Brethren, Commonly Called Moravians in North America, A.D. 1734–1748* (Nazareth, PA: 1888) 93.
33. Wemmer, *Count Zinzendorf and the Spirit of the Moravians*, 201.
34. Spangenberg, *Life of Nicholas Lewis, Count Zinzendorf*, chapter 5.
35. Benge and Benge, *Count Zinzendorf: Firstfruit*, 123.
36. *Gemeinreden (1748, Bibliographisches Handbuch zur Zinzendorf-Forschung A 181) in Hauptschriften [von] Nikolaus Ludwig von Zinzendorf*, volume 4, part 2, 311. (Translation by Dr. Peter Vogt.)
37. Ibid., part 1, 88–89.
38. Hutton, *History of the Moravian Church*, 182.
39. Ibid., 177.
40. Wemmer, *Count Zinzendorf and the Spirit of the Moravians*, 204.
41. Hutton, *History of the Moravian Church*, 246.
42. Ibid.
43. Ibid., 247.
44. www.moravian.org/the-moravian-church/board-of-world-mission/.
45. http://www.czherrnhut.de/gemeinde/werte/en/.
46. http://www.czherrnhut.de/jesus-haus/en/.
47. http://www.czherrnhut.de/gemeinde/hintergrund/en/.
48. Hutton, *History of the Moravian Church*, 151.
49. www.moravian.org.
50. Spangenberg, *Life of Nicholas Lewis, Count Zinzendorf*, introduction.
51. Hutton, *History of the Moravian Church*, 247.

Chapter 2: Brainerd

52. E. Myers Harrison, *Heroes of Faith on Pioneer Trails* (Chicago, IL: Moody Press, 1945), 15.
53. Ibid.
54. Ibid., 16.
55. Jonathan Edwards, *The Life and Diary of David Brainerd* (Grand Rapids, MI: Baker Publishing Group, 1989), 1.
56. Ibid., 2.
57. Ibid., 6.
58. Ibid., 8.
59. Ibid., 10.
60. Ibid., 11–12.
61. Ibid., 15.
62. Ibid., 18.
63. Ibid., 16.
64. Ibid., 119.
65. Ibid., 44.
66. Scanned from Jesse Page, *David Brainerd, the Apostle to the North American Indians* (London: S. W. Partridge & Co., 1891).
67. Edwards, *Life and Diary*, 46.
68. Ibid.
69. Vance Christie, *David Brainerd: A Flame for God* (London: Christian Focus Publications, 2009), 40.
70. Edwards, *Life and Diary*, 60.
71. Scanned from: Jesse Page, *David Brainerd, the Apostle to the North American Indians* (London: S. W. Partridge & Co., 1891).
72. Edwards, *Life and Diary*, 71.
73. Ibid., 81.
74. Ibid., 75.

75. Ibid., 102.
76. Scanned from: Jesse Page, *David Brainerd, the Apostle to the North American Indians* (London: S. W. Partridge & Co., 1891).
77. Edwards, *Life and Diary,* 166.
78. Ibid., 172.
79. Ibid., 220.
80. Ibid., 110.
81. Ibid., 127.
82. Ibid., 285.
83. Christie, *David Brainerd,* 296.
84. Edwards, *Life and Diary,* 159.
85. Ibid., 156.
86. Ibid., 119.

Chapter 3: Carey

87. George Smith, *The Life of William Carey: Shoemaker and Missionary* (Edinburgh: R. & R. Clark, 1885), 3.
88. Ibid., 5.
89. Ibid., 15.
90. Ibid., 17.
91. Janet Benge and Geoff Benge, *William Carey: Obliged to Go* (Seattle, WA: YWAM Publishing, 1998), 47–48.
92. E. Myers Harrison, *Heroes of Faith on Pioneer Trails* (Chicago: Moody Press, 1945), 43.
93. Ibid., 44.
94. William Carey, *An Enquiry into the Obligations of Christians to Use Means for the Conversion of the Heathen* (Moulton, England: William Carey, 1792).
95. Ibid.
96. Ibid.
97. Harrison, *Heroes of Faith on Pioneer Trails,* 44–45.
98. Smith, *Life of William Carey,* 57.
99. Ibid., 60.
100. Ibid.
101. Benge and Benge, *William Carey,* 86.
102. Ibid., 90.
103. Ibid., 92.
104. Ibid., 96.
105. Ibid., 122.
106. Ibid., 117.
107. Smith, *Life of William Carey,* 86.
108. Ibid., 88.
109. Ibid., 97.
110. Ibid., 61.
111. Ibid., 147.
112. Ibid., 121.
113. Ibid., 127.
114. Ibid.
115. Ibid., 131.
116. Ibid., 134.
117. Ibid., 137–138.
118. Ibid., 101.
119. William Carey, engraved by J. Jenkins, *The National Portrait Gallery, Volume III, published* © 1820 (litho), Home, Robert (1752–1834) (after) / Private Collection / Ken Welsh / Bridgeman Images.

120. Smith, *Life of William Carey*, 158.
121. Ibid., 108.
122. Ibid., 181.
123. Ibid., 184.
124. Ibid., 166.
125. Benge and Benge, *William Carey*, 184.
126. Ibid., 186.
127. Smith, *Life of William Carey*, 343.
128. Benge and Benge, *William Carey: Obliged to Go*, 189.
129. Smith, *Life of William Carey*, 357.
130. Ibid., 375.
131. Ibid., 384.
132. Ibid., 416.
133. Ibid., 426.
134. Ibid., 422.
135. Ibid., 431.
136. Ibid., 16.
137. Harrison, *Heroes of Faith on Pioneer Trails*, 36.

Chapter 4: Judson

138. Edward Judson, *The Life of Adoniram Judson* (New York, NY: Anson D. F. Randolph & Company, 1883), 26–29.
139. Courtney Anderson, *To the Golden Shore: The Life of Adoniram Judson* (Valley Forge, PA: Judson Press, 1987), 34.
140. Janet Benge and Geoff Benge, *Adoniram Judson: Bound for Burma* (Seattle, WA: YWAM Publishing, 2000), 30.
141. Anderson, *To the Golden Shore*, 38.
142. Judson, *Life of Adoniram Judson*, 12.
143. Anderson, *To the Golden Shore*, 52.
144. Ibid., 50.
145. Judson, *Life of Adoniram Judson*, 17.
146. Ibid., 19.
147. Ibid., 24.
148. Ibid., 33.
149. Ibid., 20.
150. Anderson, *To the Golden Shore*, 84.
151. Judson, *Life of Adoniram Judson*, 20.
152. Anderson, *To the Golden Shore*, 129.
153. Judson, *Life of Adoniram Judson*, 39.
154. Anderson, *To the Golden Shore*, 131.
155. Ibid., 133.
156. Benge and Benge, *Adoniram Judson*, 111.
157. Judson, *Life of Adoniram Judson*, 105.
158. Ibid., 54.
159. Ibid., 78.
160. Ibid., 76.
161. Ibid., 106.
162. Ibid., 127.
163. Ibid., 187.
164. Ibid., 144.
165. Ibid., 151.
166. Benge and Benge, *Adoniram Judson*, 157.
167. Judson, *Life of Adoniram Judson*, 154.

168. Ibid., 163.
169. Ibid., 194.
170. Ibid., 197.
171. Ibid., 210.
172. Ibid., 216.
173. Anderson, *To the Golden Shore*, 302.
174. Judson, *Life of Adoniram Judson*, 219.
175. Ibid., 221.
176. Ibid., 235.
177. Anderson, *To the Golden Shore*, 322.
178. Judson, *Life of Adoniram Judson*, 242–243.
179. Ibid., 246.
180. Ibid., 274.
181. Ibid., 262.
182. Ibid., 291–292.
183. Ibid., 291.
184. Ibid., 292.
185. Ibid., 298.
186. Ibid., 362.
187. Ibid., 377.
188. Ibid., 378.
189. Ibid., 393.
190. Ibid., 405.
191. Anderson, *To the Golden Shore*, 423.
192. Judson, *Life of Adoniram Judson*, 430.
193. Ibid., 422.
194. Ibid., 445.
195. Ibid., 450.
196. Ibid., 463.
197. Ibid., 485.
198. Anderson, *To the Golden Shore*, 465.
199. Ibid., 481.
200. Judson, *Life of Adoniram Judson*, 530.
201. Ibid., 532.
202. Anderson, *To the Golden Shore*, 496.
203. Ibid., 499.
204. Judson, *Life of Adoniram Judson*, 545.
205. Anderson, *To the Golden Shore*, 504.
206. Judson, *Life of Adoniram Judson*, 14–15.

Chapter 5: Hawaii

207. Hiram Bingham, *A Residence of Twenty-one Years in the Sandwich Islands* (Hartford, CT: S. Converse, 1848), chapter 11. Accessed at https://archive.org/details/aresidencetwent01bing-goog.
208. Char Miller, "The Making of a Missionary: Hiram Bingham's Odyssey," *Hawaiian Journal of History 13* (1979): 36–45, evols.library.manoa.hawaii.edu/bitstream/handle/10524/178/JL13C44.pdf?sequence=2.
209. Bingham, *A Residence of Twenty-one Years*, chapter 3.
210. Ibid.
211. Miller, "The Making of a Missionary," 43.
212. Bingham, *A Residence of Twenty-one Years*, chapter 3.
213. Ibid.
214. Ibid., chapter 2.

215. Ibid.
216. Ibid., chapter 3.
217. Lucy Goodale Thurston, *Life and Times of Mrs. Lucy G. Thurston* (Ann Arbor, MI: S. E. Andrews, 1882), 27.
218. Ibid.
219. Bingham, *A Residence of Twenty-one Years*, chapter 3.
220. Thurston, *Life and Times of Mrs. Lucy*, 40.
221. Ibid., chapter 1.
222. Ibid., chapter 4.
223. Ibid., chapter 7.
224. Ibid., chapter 4.
225. Ibid., chapter 7.
226. Ibid., chapter 5.
227. Ibid., chapter 6.
228. Ibid., chapter 8.
229. Ibid.
230. Ibid., chapter 9.
231. Ibid.
232. Ibid.
233. Ibid., chapter 10.
234. Ibid., chapter 9.
235. Thurston, *Life and Times of Mrs. Lucy*, 46.
236. Bingham, *A Residence of Twenty-one Years*, chapter 11.
237. Ibid, chapter 10.
238. Ibid.
239. Ibid.
240. Ibid., chapter 11.
241. Ibid., chapter 14.
242. Ibid., chapter 17.
243. Ibid.
244. Ibid., chapter 23.
245. Ibid., chapter 19.
246. Ibid., chapter 21.
247. Eileen Moffett, "Betsey Stockton: Pioneer American Missionary," Overseas Ministries Study Center, 1995, www.thefreelibrary.com/Betsey+Stockton%3A+pioneer+American+missionary.-a016921617, 2.), 2.
248. David W. Wills and Albert J. Raboteau, *African-American Religion: A Historical Interpretation with Representative Documents* (Chicago: University of Chicago Press, 2006), 2.
249. Ibid.
250. Wills and Raboteau, *African-American Religion*, 3.
251. Ibid.
252. "*Betsey Stockton's Journal—November 20, 1822–July 4, 1823*," The Trustees of Amherst College and African-American Religion: A Documentary History Project, 2006, 7–8. www.amherst.edu/~aardoc/Betsey_Stockton_Journal_l.html.
253. Ibid., 12.
254. Ibid., 16.
255. Ibid.
256. Moffett, "Betsey Stockton," 3.
257. Ibid.
258. Ibid.
259. Wills and Raboteau, *African-American Religion*, 4.
260. Ibid.
261. Moffett, "Betsey Stockton," 4.

End Notes

262. Titus Coan, *Life in Hawaii: Mission Life and Labors* (New York, NY: Anson D. F. Randolph & Company, 1882), 5.
263. Ibid., 7.
264. Ibid., 13.
265. Charles Finney, *Lectures on the Revival of Religion* (New York, NY: F. H. Revell, 1868), 13.
266. Coan, *Life in Hawaii*, 23.
267. Ibid., 43.
268. Bingham, *A Residence of Twenty-one Years*, chapter 21.
269. Coan, *Life in Hawaii*, 44.
270. Bingham, *A Residence of Twenty-one Years*, chapter 22.
271. Coan, *Life in Hawaii*, 55.
272. "Hawaii's Great Awakening," Gospel Truth Ministries, 2000, www.gospeltruth.net/hawaii_revival.htm.
273. Bingham, *A Residence of Twenty-one Years*, chapter 22.
274. Coan, *Life in Hawaii*, 45.
275. Ibid., 46.
276. Ibid., 49.
277. Ibid., 51.
278. Ibid., 52.
279. Ibid., 57.
280. "Hawaii's Great Awakening," 1.
281. Coan, *Life in Hawaii*, 67–68.
282. Ibid., 279.
283. Ibid., 82.
284. Ibid., 88.
285. Ibid., 89.
286. "Hawaii's Great Awakening," 1.
287. Coan, *Life in Hawaii*, 128.
288. Ibid., 130.
289. Ibid., 139.
290. Ibid., 90.
291. Ibid., 167.
292. Ibid., 119.
293. "Hawaii's Great Awakening," 2.
294. Coan, *Life in Hawaii*, 249.
295. Ibid., 236.
296. "Hawaii's Great Awakening," 2.

Chapter 6: Livingstone

297. Janet Benge and Geoff Benge, *David Livingstone: Africa's Trailblazer* (Seattle, WA: YWAM Publishing, 1999), 11–13.
298. Sam Wellman, *David Livingstone, Missionary and Explorer* (Uhrichsville, OH: Barbour Publishing, 1995), 29.
299. Ibid., 43.
300. Ibid., 44.
301. Benge and Benge, *David Livingstone: Africa's Trailblazer*, 75–77.
302. Ibid., 137.
303. Ibid., 43.
304. Ibid., 157.
305. Wellman, *David Livingstone: Missionary and Explorer*, 105.

306. Benge and Benge, *David Livingstone: Africa's Trailblazer*, 161.
307. Ibid., 161–163.
308. Wellman, *David Livingstone: Missionary and Explorer*, 116.
309. Ibid., 121.
310. Eugene Myers Harrison, *Giants of the Missionary Trail* (Wheaton, IL: Scripture Press, 1954), 145.
311. Benge and Benge, *David Livingstone: Africa's Trailblazer*, 73.
312. Ibid., 178.
313. Wellman, *David Livingstone: Missionary and Explorer*, 168.
314. Martin Dugard, *Into Africa: The Epic Adventures of Stanley & Livingstone* (New York: Broadway Books, 2004), 102.
315. Benge and Benge, *David Livingstone: Africa's Trailblazer*, 189.
316. Ibid., 196.
317. Wellman, *David Livingstone: Missionary and Explorer*, 183.
318. "MaryMoffatGravestone" by Soccerman321. Own work. Licensed under Creative Commons Attribution 3.0, http://commons.wikimedia.org/wiki/File:MaryMoffatGravestone.JPG#mediaviewer/File:MaryMoffatGravestone.JPG.
319. Wellman, *David Livingstone: Missionary and Explorer*, 184.
320. Benge and Benge, *David Livingstone: Africa's Trailblazer*, 199–200.
321. Ibid., 187.
322. Dugard, *Into Africa*, 210–211.
323. Harrison, *Giants*, 155.
324. Ibid., 228.
325. Ibid., 263.
326. Ibid., 280.
327. Ibid., 283.
328. Ibid., 156.
329. Ibid., 314.
330. W. G. Blaikie, *The Personal Life of David Livingstone* (New York: Harper & Brothers, 1881).
331. Harrison, *Giants*, 146.

Chapter 7: Taylor

332. Janet Benge and Geoff Benge, *Hudson Taylor: Deep in the Heart of China* (Seattle, WA: YWAM Publishing, 1998), 187.
333. Howard Taylor and Geraldine Taylor, *J. Hudson Taylor: God's Man in China* (Chicago: Moody Press, 1965), 311.
334. Ibid., 6.
335. Ibid., 7.
336. Ibid., 8.
337. Ibid., 11.
338. Ibid., 29.
339. Ibid.
340. Ibid., 31.
341. Ibid., 32.
342. Benge and Benge, *Hudson Taylor*, 58.
343. Ibid., 44–45.
344. Taylor and Taylor, *J. Hudson Taylor*, 17.
345. Benge and Benge, *Hudson Taylor*, 85.
346. Taylor and Taylor, *J. Hudson Taylor*, 59.
347. Ibid., 76.
348. Ibid., 99.

349. Ibid., 125.
350. Ibid., 129.
351. Benge and Benge, *Hudson Taylor,* 139.
352. Taylor and Taylor, *J. Hudson Taylor,* 143.
353. Ibid., 139.
354. Ibid., 151.
355. Ibid., 152.
356. Ibid., 162.
357. Ibid., 163.
358. Ibid., 165–166
359. Ibid., 171.
360. Ibid., 173.
361. Ibid., 187.
362. Benge and Benge, *Hudson Taylor, 183.*
363. Taylor and Taylor, *J. Hudson Taylor, 197.*
364. Ibid., 212.
365. Ibid., 208.
366. Ibid., 221.
367. Ibid., 219.
368. Ibid., 229.
369. Ibid., 233.
370. Ibid., 237.
371. Benge and Benge, *Hudson Taylor,* 199.
372. Taylor and Taylor, *J. Hudson Taylor,* 242.
373. Ibid., 247.
374. Ibid., 255.
375. Ibid., 277.
376. Ibid., 323.
377. Ibid., 324.
378. Ibid., 325.
379. Ibid., 312.
380. Ibid., 316.
381. Ibid., 350.
382. Benge and Benge, *Hudson Taylor,* 201.
383. Taylor and Taylor, *J. Hudson Taylor,* 353.
384. Ibid., 360.
385. Ibid.
386. Ibid., 240.
387. Overseas Missionary Fellowship International (OMF International), formerly China Inland Mission, www.omf.org.
388. Taylor and Taylor, 240.

Chapter 8: Carmichael

389. Amy Carmichael, *Gold Cord: The Story of a Fellowship* (Fort Washington, PA: Christian Literature Crusade, 1974), 33.
390. Ibid., 34.
391. Frank L. Houghton, *Amy Carmichael of Dohnavur* (Fort Washington, PA: Christian Literature Crusade, 1979), 38.
392. Ibid., 12.
393. Ibid., 22.
394. Elisabeth Elliot, *A Chance to Die: The Life and Legacy of Amy Carmichael* (Grand Rapids, MI: Fleming H. Revell, 1987), 19.
395. Houghton, *Amy Carmichael of Dohnavur,* 35.

396. Ibid., 36.
397. Ibid., 37.
398. Carmichael, *Gold Cord*, 15.
399. Houghton, *Amy Carmichael of Dohnavur*, 39.
400. Sam Wellman, *Amy Carmichael: Selfless Servant of India* (Uhrichsville, OH: Barbour Publishing, 1998), 26.
401. Elliot, *Chance to Die*, 37.
402. Ibid., 41.
403. Ibid.
404. Houghton, *Amy Carmichael of Dohnavur*, 14.
405. Ibid., 57.
406. Ibid., 59.
407. Ibid., 65.
408. Ibid., 67.
409. Wellman, *Amy Carmichael: Selfless Servant of India*, 53.
410. Houghton, *Amy Carmichael of Dohnavur*, 79.
411. Ibid., 87–88.
412. Ibid., 89.
413. Ibid., 91.
414. Ibid., 92.
415. Elliot, *Chance to Die*, 93.
416. Houghton, *Amy Carmichael of Dohnavur*, 97.
417. Elliot, *Chance to Die*, 100.
418. Wellman, *Amy Carmichael: Selfless Servant of India*, 78.
419. Elliot, *Chance to Die*, 117.
420. Ibid., 118.
421. Ibid., 122.
422. Houghton, *Amy Carmichael of Dohnavur*, 116.
423. Ibid., 122.
424. Wellman, *Amy Carmichael: Selfless Servant of India*, 98.
425. Carmichael, *Gold Cord*, 333.
426. Ibid.
427. Elliot, *Chance to Die*, 140.
428. Houghton, *Amy Carmichael of Dohnavur*, 127.
429. Ibid., 129.
430. Wellman, *Amy Carmichael: Selfless Servant of India*, 104–105.
431. Houghton, *Amy Carmichael of Dohnavur*, 52.
432. Carmichael, *Gold Cord*, 43.
433. Ibid., 44.
434. Ibid., 59.
435. Houghton, *Amy Carmichael of Dohnavur*, 161.
436. Carmichael, *Gold Cord*, 91.
437. Ibid., 95.
438. Ibid., 78.
439. Ibid., 117.
440. Houghton, *Amy Carmichael of Dohnavur*, 96.
441. Ibid., 200.
442. Carmichael, *Gold Cord*, 372.
443. Elliot, *Chance to Die*, 241.
444. Ibid., 253.
445. Carmichael, *Gold Cord*, 229.
446. Ibid.
447. Ibid., 287.

448. Ibid., 196.
449. Elliot, *Chance to Die*, 268.
450. Houghton, *Amy Carmichael of Dohnavur*, 287.
451. Ibid., 297.
452. Carmichael, *Gold Cord*, 314.
453. Katherine Makower, *Follow My Leader: Murray Webb-Peploe* (Eastbourne, England: Kingsway Publications, 1984), 83.
454. Ibid., 94.
455. Houghton, *Amy Carmichael of Dohnavur*, 310.
456. Amy Carmichael, *If* (Fort Washington, PA: Christian Literature Crusade), 16.
457. Houghton, *Amy Carmichael of Dohnavur*, 350.
458. Carmichael, *If*, 20.
459. Makower, *Follow My Leader*, 160.
460. Carmichael, *Gold Cord*, 372.
461. Makower, *Follow My Leader*, 164.
462. Elliot, *Chance to Die*, 369.
463. Ibid., 372.
464. Ibid.
465. Carmichael, *If*, 22.
466. Elliot, *Chance to Die*, 272.
467. Carmichael, *Gold Cord*, 203.

Chapter 9: Goforth

468. "Jonathan Goforth" by Greg Gordon. http://www.sermonindex.net/modules/myalbum/photo.php?lid=372. Licensed under Public domain.
469. Jonathan Goforth, *By My Spirit* (London and Edinburgh: Marshall, Morgan & Scott, LTD.), chapter 13.
470. Rosalind Goforth, *Goforth of China* (Grand Rapids, MI: Zondervan Publishing House, 1937), 162.
471. Ibid., 166.
472. Ibid., 22.
473. Ibid., 24
474. Ibid., 25.
475. Ibid., 29.
476. Ibid., 49.
477. Ibid.
478. Ibid., 56–57.
479. Ibid., 61–62.
480. Ibid., 70.
481. Goforth, *How I Know God Answers Prayer* (New Kensington, PA: Whitaker House, 2014), 11.
482. Goforth, *Goforth of China*, 58.
483. Goforth, *How I Know*, 88.
484. Ibid., 85.
485. Goforth, *How I Know*, 14.
486. Jonathan Goforth and Rosalind Goforth, *Miracle Lives of China* (Elkhart, IN: Bethel Publishing, 1988), 33.
487. Ibid., 35.
488. Goforth, *Goforth of China, 105*.
489. Ibid., 106.
490. Ibid., 107.
491. Goforth, *How I Know*, 19–20.
492. Goforth, *Goforth of China*, 110.
493. Ibid.

494. Ibid., 119.
495. Goforth, *How I Know,* 121.
496. Ibid., 25.
497. Ibid., 27.
498. Ibid., 27–29.
499. Goforth, *Goforth of China,* 135.
500. Ibid.
501. Ibid., 136.
502. Goforth, *How I Know,* 31.
503. Ibid., 33.
504. Goforth and Goforth, *Miracle Lives of China,* 63.
505. Goforth, *Goforth of China,* 156.
506. Ibid., 169.
507. Ibid., 179.
508. Ibid., 181.
509. Ibid.
510. Jonathan Goforth, *When the Spirit's Fire Swept Korea* (no publication information available), 5.
511. Goforth, *By My Spirit,* 29–30.
512. Goforth, *Goforth of China,* 187.
513. Goforth, *By My Spirit, chapter* 3.
514. Ibid., chapter 2.
515. Goforth, *Goforth of China,* 187.
516. Goforth, *By My Spirit,* chapter 4.
517. Ibid., chapter 8.
518. Ibid.
519. Ibid., chapter 13.
520. Goforth, *Goforth of China,* 194–196.
521. Ibid., 205.
522. Goforth and Goforth, *Miracle Lives of China,* 99.
523. Goforth, *Goforth of China,* 233.
524. Ibid., 239.
525. Ibid., 240.
526. Ibid., 252.
527. Ibid., 257.
528. Ibid., 270.
529. Ibid., 280.
530. Ibid., 282.
531. Ibid., 310.
532. Ibid., 315.
533. Ibid., 318.
534. Ibid., 330.
535. Ibid., 334.
536. "Jonathan Goforth and his wife" by Greg Gordon, http://www.sermonindex.net/modules/myalbum/photo.php?lid=371. Licensed under public domain.
537. Goforth, *Goforth of China,* 213.
538. Ibid., 348.
539. Ibid., 349.
540. Goforth, *When the Spirit's Fire Swept Korea,* 1.
541. Goforth, *Goforth of China,* 38.
542. Ibid., 54.